Abbreviations used to refer to statistical source publications

AAS	*Annual Abstract of Statistics*
BLS	*British Labour Statistics (Yearbooks)*
BLSHA	*British Labour Statistics Historical Abstract 1886–1968*
CBSS	*Compendium of Building Society Statistics*
DEG	*Department of Employment Gazette*
DSS	*Digest of Scottish Statistics*
DWS	*Digest of Welsh Statistics*
ET	*Economic Trends*
ETAS	*Economic Trends Annual Supplement*
FES	*Family Expenditure Survey*
FT	*Financial Times*
GHS	*General Household Survey*
HCS	*Housing and Construction Statistics*
LFS	*Labour Force Survey*
LHS	*Local Housing Statistics*
MDS	*Monthly Digest of Statistics*
MOLG	*Ministry of Labour Gazette*
MSBMC	*Monthly Statistics of Building Materials and Components*
NDHS	*National Dwelling and Housing Survey*
NIAAS	*Northern Ireland Annual Abstract of Statistics*
NIER	*National Institute Economic Review*
PINCCA	*Price Index Numbers for Current Cost Accounting*
SAS	*Scottish Abstract of Statistics*
SEB	*Scottish Economic Bulletin*
SHS	*Scottish Housing Statistics*
T & I	*Trade and Industry*
WET	*Welsh Economic Trends*
WHS	*Welsh Housing Statistics*
WST	*Welsh Social Trends*

(19)

SPON'S GUIDE TO
HOUSING, CONSTRUCTION AND PROPERTY MARKET STATISTICS

By the same author

Housing in Northern Ireland
(1974, Heinemann Educational Books)

Construction and the Related Professions
(1980, Pergamon Press)

Statistics Collected by the Ministry of Works 1941–56
(1980, Department of the Environment)

SPON'S GUIDE TO
HOUSING, CONSTRUCTION AND PROPERTY MARKET STATISTICS

M. C. Fleming, MA, PhD, FSS

Professor of Economics
Loughborough University of Technology

LONDON
E. & F.N. Spon

To the memory of my mother

First published in 1986 by
E. & F. N. Spon Ltd
11 New Fetter Lane, London EC4P 4EE

© *1986 M. C. Fleming*

Printed in Great Britain by
J. W. Arrowsmith Ltd, Bristol

ISBN 0 419 12670 8

British Library Cataloguing in Publication Data

Fleming, M. C.
Spon's guide to housing, construction
and property market statistics.
1. Construction industry – Great Britain
– Statistical services
I. Title
338.4'7624'0941   HD9715.G72

ISBN 0-419-12670-8

CONTENTS

TABLES

ABBREVIATIONS AND ACRONYMS

(Abbreviations used to refer to publications are listed inside the front cover)

A	Annually
ACAS	Advisory, Conciliation and Arbitration Service
ACE	Association of Consulting Engineers
ACOP	Annual Census of Production
APSAB	Average PSA Building (costs index)
APTC	Administrative, Professional, Technical and Clerical
ARCUK	Architects' Registration Council of the United Kingdom
B & CE	Building and civil engineering
BCIS	Building Cost Information Service (RICS)
BEC	Building Employers Confederation, also Business Education Council
BIA	British Insurance Association
BMCIS	Building Maintenance Cost Information Service (RICS)
BMF	Builders Merchants Federation
BMP	Building Material Producers (Common alternative to NCBMP – *q.v.*)
BS	British Standard or Building Society
BSA	Building Societies Association
BSO	Business Statistics Office
BTEC	Business and Technician Education Council
CBI	Confederation of British Industry
CCA	Current Cost Accounting
CEI	Council of Engineering Institutions
CIBS	Chartered Institution of Building Services
CIOB	Chartered Institute of Building
CIPFA	Chartered Institute of Public Finance and Accountancy
CITB	Construction Industry Training Board
Cmd	Command Paper
Cmnd	Command Paper
CNC	Cost of New Construction (index)

CODOT	Classification of Occupations and Directory of Occupational Titles
COI	Central Office of Information
COP	Census of Production
CSO	Central Statistical Office
Ctrs	Contractors
DE	Department of Employment
DES	Department of Education and Science
DHSS	Department of Health and Social Security
DIY	Do-it-yourself
DLO	Direct Labour Organisation
DoE	Department of the Environment
DoI	Department of Industry
DTI	Department of Trade and Industry
E & W	England and Wales
EC	European Community
EDC	Economic Development Committee (NEDC)
EEC	European Economic Community
EPR	Economic Planning Region
ESRC	Economic and Social Research Council
FCEC	Federation of Civil Engineering Contractors
FIS	Family Income Supplement
FOO	Former owner-occupier
FP	Firm Price (contract)
FTAT	Furniture, Timber and Allied Trades (Union)
FTB	First-time buyer
GB	Great Britain
GCE	General Certificate of Education
GDFCF	Gross Domestic Fixed Capital Formation
GDP	Gross Domestic Product
GIA	General Improvement Area
GLC	Greater London Council
GMBATU	General, Municipal, Boilermakers and Allied Trades Union
GP	General Practitioner
GRO	General Register Office
GRO(S)	General Register Office (Scotland)
HAA	Housing Action Area
HBF	House-Builders Federation
HIP	Housing Investment Programme

HMFI	Her (His) Majesty's Factory Inspectorate
HMSO	Her (His) Majesty's Stationery Office
HRA	Housing Revenue Account
HSE	Health and Safety Executive
HSIU	Housing Statistics and Intelligence Unit (SDD)
HVCA	Heating and Ventilating Contractors' Association
ICE	Institution of Civil Engineers
IHVE	Institution of Heating and Ventilating Engineers
IOB	Institute of Building
IQS	Institute of Quantity Surveyors
ISVA	Incorporated Society of Valuers and Auctioneers
KOS	Key Occupations for Statistical Purposes
LA	Local authority
LACSAB	Local Authorities' Conditions of Service Advisory Board
LBS	London Business School
LOSC	Labour-only sub-contract(or)
M & E	Mechanical and Electrical
MOHLG	Ministry of Housing and Local Government
MOL	Ministry of Labour
MOW	Ministry of Works
MSC	Manpower Services Commission
NADO(R)	Notification of Accidents and Dangerous Occurrences (Regulations)
NBPI	National Board for Prices and Incomes
NCBMP	National Council of Building Material Producers
NEDO	National Economic Development Office
NES	New Earnings Survey
NFBTE	National Federation of Building Trades Employers
NFHA	National Federation of Housing Associations
NHBC	National House-Building Council
NHS	National Health Service
NI	Northern Ireland or National Insurance
NIESR	National Institute of Economic and Social Research
NIHE	Northern Ireland Housing Executive
NIHT	Northern Ireland Housing Trust
NJCBI	National Joint Council for the Building Industry
OND	Ordinary National Diploma
OPCS	Office of Population Censuses and Surveys
PAYE	Pay-as-you-earn

PBR	Payment by Results
PER	Professional and Executive Recruitment
PILAH	Price Index of Local Authority Housebuilding
PIPSH	Price Index of Public Sector Housebuilding
PSA	Property Services Agency (DoE)
PSI	Policy Studies Institute
Pte	Private
Pub.	Public
QSSD	Quantity Surveying Services Division (PSA)
QSEs	Qualified Scientists and Engineers
R & D	Research and Development
R & M	Repairs and Maintenance
RIBA	Royal Institute of British Architects
RICS	Royal Institution of Chartered Surveyors
RPI	Retail Prices Index
RTB	Right-to-buy (legislation)
RV	Rateable value
s.a.	Seasonally adjusted
SAS	Small Area Statistics
SCD	Statistics Construction Division (DoE)
SCOTEC	Scottish Technical Education Council
SDD	Scottish Development Department
SEG	Socio-economic group
SI	Statutory Instrument
SIC	Standard Industrial Classification
SOEC	Statistical Office of the European Communities
SSHA	Scottish Special Housing Association
TEC	Technician Education Council
TGWU	Transport and General Workers' Union
TOPS	Training Opportunities Scheme
TUC	Trades Union Congress
UB	Unemployment Benefit
UCATT	Union of Construction, Allied Trades and Technicians
UGC	University Grants Committee
UK	United Kingdom
VAT	Value Added Tax
VOP	Variation of Price (contract)
WC	Water closet
WP	Working Principal or Working Proprietor
YOPS	Youth Opportunities Programme Scheme
YTS	Youth Training Scheme

ACKNOWLEDGEMENTS

The preparation of this book has made a number of demands on the time of other people and I am pleased to acknowledge their help. I am especially grateful to Dr Peter Stone, who kindly agreed to read and comment on the entire manuscript, and Harold Stott, Chief Statistician for housing at the Department of the Environment, who kindly found time to read the first draft of Part 1 of the book on housing and to comment at length, as well as responding to my numerous requests for information. I also owe a special word of thanks to Joe Nellis for the trouble he took in reading through many of the chapters in draft. In addition, I should like to thank the large number of people, including in particular official statisticians and the staff of private organizations, who have responded to my requests for detailed information and advice about the surveys and statistical data for which they are responsible. The staff of the inter-library loan service at Loughborough University have also provided invaluable help.

The typescript was produced by Mrs Su Spencer with customary excellence. No one could have greater good fortune than to be able to call upon her unsurpassed skills, helpfulness and reliability.

Finally I must thank my wife and family for bearing once again the author's burden of frequent absences of mind, body and good temper.

INTRODUCTION: GUIDE TO THE BOOK AND HOW TO USE IT

This book is meant to provide a quick, easy-to-use and up-to-date guide to the sources and nature of statistics about housing, construction, the property market and the related professions in Britain. An effort has been made to ensure that the information is up to date as of the autumn of 1985. It is meant as a manual for the use of all who have a regular need to use statistical data about housing, construction and the property market as part of their work, as a quick source of reference for others who need data in this area from time to time and as a text for students taking professional examinations related to housing, property, the construction industry and the architectural, surveying, engineering and other related professions.

The need for a book of this kind arises out of the author's experience that considerable time and effort are often needed to discover whether or not statistical data on a particular subject exist and then what limitations confront their use and interpretation. As far as housing, construction and the property markets are concerned, the need is reinforced by the fact that the scope of the subject matter is very wide and is matched by a corresponding diversity of sources. Statistical data are collected by means of a variety of regular and *ad hoc* enquiries conducted by various government departments and several private organizations. As a consequence, the data are scattered among a similar diversity of publications – there is no single publication which brings them all together. Likewise, there is no up-to-date and comprehensive guide to the sources and nature of the data available.

At an official level, significant improvements have been made to the presentation of information over recent years. Many of the official statistical *series* (as opposed to the results of irregular surveys or surveys covering housing and construction only as part of a wider subject area) are brought together in quarterly and annual volumes of *Housing and Construction Statistics* and the explanatory notes included in the annual volume have been improved. But it is inevitably limited in its scope to official sources and in the amount of independent appraisal that it can contain. The CSO's *Guide to Official Statistics* initiated in 1976 as a biennial publication has also gone a long way to satisfying a long-felt want but it suffers in providing no appraisal of the sources to which it refers and concentrates on the most recent sources. Further, its generalized approach naturally means that housing and construction receive no comprehensive and coherent treatment in their own right and the professions and the property market receive little or no attention at all. Unfortunately, the biennial frequency has been broken with the failure to publish the edition for 1984. The latest edition at the time of writing, refers to 1982 and no new edition is planned until the end of 1985.

Housing and construction in Great Britain are served by a highly-developed statistical reporting system which has evolved over a long period of time. Housing, for long a special concern of social policy, has been treated separately with regard to the collection of statistical data since before the Second World War. The construction industry too has also been treated separately from other industries with regard to the collection of statistical data for a period which now extends to forty-five years. At the same time, however, the industry is also included in more general statistical enquiries covering a wide range of other industries. In this respect it is unusual and possibly unique. These facts reinforce the need for a separate guide to the sources in these two areas. The construction professions and the property market are not well documented in official statistics and most of the information about these sectors comes from unofficial sources.

We concentrate here mainly on the statistical reporting system as it now exists and the data that are *currently* collected but with two main exceptions. First, particular care is taken to ensure complete coverage of areas where long-run series are important, as with output, employment and prices. Secondly, *ad hoc* surveys, which are particularly important in the field of housing, are considered as comprehensively as possible rather than being limited to the latest surveys only. Many changes have taken place over the years. A comprehensive appraisal of these developments and of the sources and nature of the historical series for construction up to 1977 and for housing up to 1972 has been provided in separate volumes in the series of *Reviews of UK Statistical Sources:* Fleming (1980a) and Farthing and Fleming (1974) respectively. These volumes are large, definitive sources of reference. By contrast, as explained at the outset, this book is meant to provide a concise but comprehensive and up-to-date guide to current sources in both of these areas.

SCOPE

The scope of this guide covers not only the most obvious areas of housing, construction, the construction industry and property markets but also information relating to construction materials and plant, the construction stock and the various related professions. Much of the statistical data available relate to Great Britain rather than the United Kingdom and this book is confined to Great Britain. However, consideration is extended to Northern Ireland sources when these form a constituent part of a UK series. Within Great Britain there has been an increasing tendency for data relating to the constituent countries of England, Wales and Scotland to be collected in separate collection processes and we have taken care to identify the separate sources for these countries. We also devote attention to regional and local area analyses. With one or two exceptions, however, we do not attempt to identify surveys carried out by local authorities and other bodies which relate to individual towns and small local areas.

ARRANGEMENT

The book is arranged by subject rather than by source. Although information about different subjects, such as output and employment, is sometimes covered in a single enquiry, an arrangement by subject is best suited to treating the two major problems that confront the user of housing and construction data. One problem is that the data that will serve the user's needs are often available in more than one form and from more than one enquiry. There is a need, therefore, for a clear statement of what is available according to a number of well-defined subjects. A second major problem, which arises out of the fact that similar topics are often covered in more than one enquiry, is the reconciliation of differences between one source and another. We treat these problems by devoting separate chapters to each subject and adopting the same format in each chapter. Each commences with an overview of the subject area showing the full range of information available followed by more detailed notes and commentary on each source. This serves to highlight the salient features of particular sources and to define the differences between similar sets of data. The objective is to make the volume quick and easy to use by conveying the range of information available as succinctly as possible and keeping the commentary brief by confining it to essentials but coupling this with signposts to more detailed information for those who have need of it.

HOW TO USE THE BOOK

There are two ways of using the book as a reference tool. First, each broad subject area is treated in a separate chapter and therefore best located by reference to the list of contents. This also lists the main sections into which each chapter is divided. Each section is then further divided by topic and each of these sub-sections is given a title and numbered using a decimal numbering system. Thus, for example, Chapter 3, which deals with the housing market, is divided into seven sections numbered 3.1–3.7. Section 3.1 is then sub-divided into five sub-sections numbered 3.1.1–3.1.5 etc. The scope and arrangement of each chapter is explained in an overview section at the beginning of each chapter. In turn, each main section of a chapter also defines at the outset the arrangement of topics within it. Thus each chapter has been expressly designed to facilitate the rapid location of specific topics within broad subject areas.

The second way of locating material is through the use of the detailed subject index at the end of the book. This naturally lists all the main topics listed as the titles of each section and sub-section etc. But it goes much deeper and thus the more well-defined a particular subject of interest is then the better it is to use the subject index.

PUBLICATION REFERENCES. Two separate lists of publications are included: the List of statistical sources and References. Publications containing statistical data are listed alphabetically by title in the List of statistical sources at the end of the book (p. 333). These are referred to in the text by *title*. Those referred to frequently are given an abbreviation, thus *Housing and Construction Statistics* is referred to as *HCS*. For ease of reference these publication abbreviations are listed inside the front cover. All other publications are listed alphabetically by author in the References (p. 375). These are referred to in the text by author and date of publication thus: Allen (1982).

PART 1
HOUSING

1
HOUSEBUILDING

This chapter covers all information about the construction of new houses. The material is arranged in five sections as follows:

1.1 Total new building: physical data
1.2 Total new building: value data
1.3 Local authorities and new towns – supplementary analyses of tender-stage data
1.4 Characteristics of new houses
1.5 Forward indicators and forecasts of housebuilding.

Information about the housebuilding *industry* is considered separately in Chapter 4.

1.1 TOTAL NEW BUILDING – PHYSICAL DATA

Physical data on total new housebuilding are collected officially by government departments. The National House-Building Council (NHBC) also compiles statistics relating to the dwellings registered with the Council. We deal with these two sources in turn.

1.1.1 Official statistics

(a) *Available data*

Information on housebuilding activity is obtained in returns submitted by local authorities and new towns to the DoE for England (monthly), to the Welsh Office for Wales (monthly) and to the Scottish Development Department for Scotland (quarterly). The topics covered are:

1. Stages of construction (starts and completions during the period and numbers under construction at the end of the

period) analysed by sector (public/private) and by sub-divisions of the public sector (local authority, new towns, housing associations and government departments).
2. Dwelling characteristics: for each of the categories above, houses are distinguished from flats in England and in Wales. In addition the following information is collected:
(a) Flats in Wales according to number of storeys (collection in England ceased in mid-1980)
(b) Number of bedrooms in England and Wales, and apartments in Scotland, in completed houses and flats for each type of owner
(c) Information for each individual building scheme for local authorities in Wales and in Scotland (collection in England ceased in mid-1980)
(d) Specialized or 'special needs' dwellings provided by local authorities, new towns and housing associations. Current tabulations cover dwellings for the elderly and for the chronically sick and disabled in England, for the elderly in Wales and for the elderly and disabled in Scotland.

In addition, analyses are made of local authority dwellings at the tender stage – these are considered in Section 1.3. See too Section 1.4 regarding the characteristics of new houses.

(b) *Publication sources*
The statistics obtained in these returns are summarized in greater or lesser detail in a number of official publications. A summary to indicate the range of information provided in each source is given in Table 1.1. The primary publication sources, in the sense of providing the most detailed analyses, are the quarterly and annual volumes of *HCS*, the quarterly *LHS* (which provides details for each local authority area in England and Wales) and for Wales and Scotland the respective national housing publications: *WHS*, *SHS* and SDD *Statistical Bulletins* (HSIU series). The earliest publication sources are a monthly DoE press notice entitled *Housebuilding* and the *MDS* (listed as the first and second items in Table 1.1). Analyses by owner (sectoral sub-divisions) differ from one source to another in the amount of detail provided. Again, the most detailed sources are those listed as primary sources above.

(c) *Interpretation*

Detailed notes about the basis of the figures will be found in the *HCS* (annual), in the *Notes and Definitions Supplement* to the *MDS* (CSO, annually) and in the Welsh and Scottish housing volumes. We draw attention here to the most important points only.

DWELLINGS AND DWELLING TYPE – SCOPE AND DEFINITIONS. It is important to note that the scope of the series is confined to permanent dwellings only – 'that is dwellings which may be expected to maintain their stability indefinitely (60 years or more)'; temporary houses and mobile homes are excluded. A *dwelling* is defined as a building or any part of a building which forms a separate and self-contained set of premises designed to be occupied by a single family. A *flat* is a dwelling forming part of a building from some other part of which it is divided horizontally. It includes maisonettes, which are flats containing more than one storey. A *house* is a dwelling which is not a flat and includes single-storey bungalows. For more detailed notes on definitions see *HCS* (annual).

STAGES OF CONSTRUCTION. The definitions are as follows:

Starts. A house or flat is counted as started on the date work begins on the laying of the foundation, including 'slabbing' for houses that require it, but not including site preparation. Thus when foundation work commences on a pair of semi-detached houses two houses are started, and when work begins on a block of flats all the dwellings which that block will contain are 'started'.

Completions. A dwelling is regarded as 'completed' when it becomes ready for occupation, whether it is in fact occupied or not.

Under construction. Dwellings are under construction during the period between start and completion as defined above. They are included in the 'under construction' figures immediately they are started and remain there even if work is temporarily suspended.

Table 1.1 Housebuilding statistics – summary guide to official sources
Part (a) Analyses by sector (public/private) and sub-divisions of public sector

Publication and frequency	UK	GB	England	Wales	Scotland	NI*	Regions	L.A. area	Other analyses and remarks
DoE Press Notice: Housebuilding (M)			S.C						Sectoral subdivision figures appear quarterly, others monthly. Monthly figures are given on seasonally unadjusted bases for latest 6 months and recent quarters and years.
Monthly Digest of Statistics (M)			S.UC.C	S.UC.C	S.UC.C				
Housing and Construction Statistics (Q)† (see remarks)	S.UC.C	S.UC.C	S.UC.C	S.UC.C	S.UC.C	S.UC.C	S.C.		Regional analysis for England. This is the most detailed source; for details of the additional analyses included see footnotes.
Local Housing Statistics (Q)			S.UC.C	S.UC.C			S.UC.C	S.UC.C	Figures for latest quarter and latest year by region, county and l.a. or new town area in E & W. Figures also given for dwellings started and completed outside l.a.'s own areas. Dwellings for the elderly and for the chronically sick and disabled (England only) are given in supplementary tables – see also footnotes below.
Annual Abstract of Statistics (A)	C		C	C	C	C			Includes analysis by number of bedrooms in E & W.
Economic Trends (M) } see Part (b)									Economic Trends Annual Supplement contains annual series from 1946.
Regional Trends (A) } see Part (b)									Also includes completions per 1000 population and by number of bedrooms.
Social Trends (A)	S.C								
Scottish Housing Statistics (A)‡					S.UC.C		S.UC.C	S.UC.C	Analyses for each district and region in Scotland and for the SSHA. Also includes analysis of apartment size of new dwellings by sector and analysis of the characteristics of dwellings in tenders accepted in the public sector – see text (Section 1.1.3).
Statistical Bulletin, HSIU series (Q)					S.C				
Scottish Abstract of Statistics (A)					S.C		S.C		Analyses for each district and region in Scotland.

Publication and frequency	UK	GB	England	Wales	Scotland	NI*	Regions	L.A. area	Other analyses and remarks
Scottish Economic Bulletin (BA)	see Part (b)								
Welsh Housing Statistics (A)				S.UC.C				S.UC.C	Includes annual series for house/flats completed by number of bedrooms by sector. For local authorities and new towns also includes series of dwellings in tenders approved and not yet started, analyses of size of scheme, floor area and cost. For housing associations includes registered number and units approved and completed.
Digest of Welsh Statistics (A)	see Part (b)			S.C.					Also includes annual series for houses/flats completed by number of bedrooms by sector.
Welsh Economic Trends (A)				C					Includes average annual building rates by decade and per 1000 population.
Welsh Social Trends (BE)									

Key: A = annual; BA = biannual; BE = biennial; E & W = England and Wales; LA = local authority; M = monthly; NI = Northern Ireland; Q = quarterly. The series included in each source are indicated by the following abbreviations: S = starts; UC = under construction; C = completions.

* These statistics are collected by the Northern Ireland Department of the Environment.

† *Housing and Construction Statistics* (quarterly volumes) give the following additional series:
(a) Starts and completions for New Towns by Region of England
(b) Completions by number of bedrooms for houses and flats separately for local authorities and new towns and for private owners separately
(c) Permanent dwellings in tenders approved for local authorities and new towns in England, Wales, Scotland and in Great Britain
(d) Specialized dwellings built by local authorities and new towns; housing associations; and all authorities for: (i) elderly (with/without wardens) and (ii) chronically sick and disabled (specially designed; mobility; all).

Housing and Construction Statistics (annual volumes) give the following additional series on an annual basis:
(a) Figures (S. UC. C) by sector for metropolitan counties, Greater London and Central Clydeside Conurbation
(b) Completions per 1000 population by countries of Great Britain and regions of England
(c) Completions by number of bedrooms for houses, flats and all dwellings separately in E & W by type of owner by region
(d) Completions (percentage distribution) for houses and for flats in E & W by type of owner (excluding housing associations) by region including analyses of flats by number of storeys up to and including 1979
(e) Analysis of apartment size of new dwellings in Scotland in tenders accepted for public authorities and in completions for private owners
(f) Specialized dwellings – as in *HCS* (quarterly) – see above.

Further analyses are prepared of the characteristics of dwellings in tenders approved in the public sector – see text (sub-section 1.1.3).
‡ Annual from 1983 edition, formerly quarterly (quarterly housing trends data for Scotland now appear in *Statistical Bulletins*).

(continued overleaf)

Table 1.1 (continued)
Part (b) Analyses by sector (public/private) only

Publication and frequency	UK	GB	England	Wales	Scotland	NI*	Regions	L.A. area	Other analyses and remarks
DoE Press Notice: Housebuilding (M)		S.C	S.C						Sectoral subdivision figures appear quarterly, others monthly. Monthly figures are given on seasonally adjusted and unadjusted bases for latest 6 months and recent quarters and years.
Monthly Digest of Statistics (M)		see Part (a)							
Housing and Construction Statistics (Q)† (see remarks)		see Part (a)							Regional analysis for England. This is the most detailed source; for details of the additional analyses included see footnotes.
Local Housing Statistics (Q)								L.A. area	Figures for latest quarter and latest year by region, county and l.a. or new town area in E & W. Figures also given for dwellings started and completed outside l.a.'s own areas. Dwellings for the elderly and for the chronically sick and disabled (England only) are given in supplementary tables – see also footnotes below.
Annual Abstract of Statistics (A)									Includes analysis by number of bedrooms in E & W.
Economic Trends (M)		S.C							Economic Trends Annual Supplement contains annual series from 1946.
Regional Trends (A)	C			C	C	C	C		Also includes completions per 1000 population and by number of bedrooms.
Social Trends (A)		see Part (a)							
Scottish Housing Statistics (A)‡		see Part (a)							Analyses for each district and region in Scotland and for the SSHA. Also includes analysis of apartment size of new dwellings by sector and analyses of the characteristics of dwellings in tenders accepted in the public sector – see text (Section 1.1.3).
Statistical Bulletin, HSIU series (Q)									
Scottish Abstract of Statistics (A)							S.C		Analyses for each district and region in Scotland.

Publication and frequency	UK	GB	England	Wales	Scotland	NI*	Regions	L.A. area	Other analyses and remarks
Scottish Economic Bulletin (BA)					S				
Welsh Housing Statistics (A)	see Part (a)								Includes annual series for houses/flats completed by number of bedrooms by sector. For local authorities and new towns also includes series of dwellings in tenders approved and not yet started, analyses of size of scheme, floor area and cost. For housing associations includes registered number and units approved and completed.
Digest of Welsh Statistics (A)				UC					Also includes annual series for houses/flats completed by number of bedrooms by sector.
Welsh Economic Trends (A)				C					
Welsh Social Trends (BE)	see Part (a)								Includes average annual building rates by decade and per 1000 population.

Key: A=annual; BA=biannual; BE=biennial; E & W=England and Wales; LA=local authority; M=monthly; NI=Northern Ireland; Q=quarterly. The series included in each source are indicated by the following abbreviations: S=starts; UC=under construction; C=completions.

* These statistics are collected by the Northern Ireland Department of the Environment.

† *Housing and Construction Statistics* (quarterly volumes) give the following additional series:
(a) Starts and completions for New Towns by Region of England
(b) Completions by number of bedrooms for houses and flats separately for local authorities and new towns and for private owners separately
(c) Permanent dwellings in tenders approved for local authorities and new towns in England, Wales, Scotland and in Great Britain
(d) Specialized dwellings built by local authorities and new towns; housing associations; and all authorities for: (i) elderly (with/without wardens) and (ii) chronically sick and disabled (specially designed; mobility; all).

Housing and Construction Statistics (annual volumes) give the following additional series on an annual basis:
(a) Figures (S,UC,C) by sector for metropolitan counties, Greater London and Central Clydeside Conurbation
(b) Completions per 1000 population by countries of Great Britain and regions of England
(c) Completions by number of bedrooms for houses, flats and all dwellings separately in E & W by type of owner by region
(d) Completions (percentage distribution) for houses and for flats in E & W by type of owner (excluding housing associations) by region including analyses of flats by number of storeys up to and including 1979
(e) Analysis of apartment size of new dwellings in Scotland in tenders accepted for public authorities and in completions for private owners
(f) Specialized dwellings – as in *HCS* (quarterly) – see above.

Further analyses are prepared of the characteristics of dwellings in tenders approved in the public sector – see text (sub-section 1.1.3).

‡ Annual from 1983 edition, formerly quarterly (quarterly housing trends data for Scotland now appear in *Statistical Bulletins*).

TIMING. From January 1980 in England and Wales (earlier in Scotland) the figures relate to actual building for the period covered and are subject to revision for late returns; previously figures were based on returns received in the period. For Scotland, monthly figures are not available and for the purpose of monthly series for Great Britain and the United Kingdom, estimates are included.

ANALYSES BY SUB-DIVISIONS OF THE PUBLIC SECTOR. Coverage of the term 'local authority' requires explanation, particularly because it differs depending on whether a detailed breakdown by type of authority is given or a condensed summary into two categories: 'local authorities' and 'other authorities'. In detailed breakdowns, the term is restricted to authorities which are local housing authorities under the Housing Acts; new town authorities are not included. In summary analyses, the term sometimes does cover new towns as well. It should also be noted that new houses provided by local authorities other than under Housing Act powers (e.g. for parks, welfare, water undertakings) are excluded; these are classified to 'Government Departments' or 'other authorities'. On the other hand, dwellings built by local authorities (i.e. financed by them) for sale to private owners are included (separate series of sales are available – see sub-section 3.5.4). In Scotland, the SSHA is treated as a local authority and, in Northern Ireland, the NIHE (and former NIHT) are so treated. Dwellings provided by County Councils in England and Wales are included under the heading 'Government Departments'. This category also covers dwellings provided or authorized by government departments for the families of prison staff, the armed forces and certain other services.

REGIONAL ANALYSES. Regional figures for local authority housing relate to building by the *local authorities located* in each region. They include, especially in the case of Greater London (GLC), dwellings which are situated outside the authority's own region. Details of dwellings provided by local housing authorities in England and Wales outside their own area, and of the distribution of GLC housing, are published quarterly in *LHS*.

HOUSING ASSOCIATIONS. Housing associations are societies, bodies of trustees or companies established for the purpose of providing housing accommodation on a non-profit-making basis. Associations registered with the Housing Corporation are eligible to receive public funds. The Housing Corporation was established in 1964 to promote the work of such associations. Full details of its activities including statistical data on loan approvals, tenders, completions and sales by type of unit in England, Wales, Scotland and Great Britain are given in its *Annual Reports.*

1.1.2 NHBC statistics

Statistics compiled by the NHBC relate to dwellings registered with the Council to be covered by the Council's insurance scheme. Most private sector housebuilding is covered, but it is important to note that not all the output of builders who are registered with the NHBC is necessarily covered by the NHBC system. Further, not all the dwellings in the NHBC figures are in the private sector: some housing association dwellings are included and some local authority and new town houses are covered too because they may be sold at some future date. The series, published quarterly by the Council in *Private House-Building Statistics,* are listed below together with further comments on their interpretation.

(a) *NHBC applications for dwelling starts*
These are recorded from the date of application and are analysed to show: (i) numbers in each country of the UK, in each county in England and Wales and each region in Scotland, and (ii) percentage distribution by region in Great Britain. The potential value of these figures is that, because they reflect an intention to build, they may give an earlier warning of market trends than official statistics which, as noted above, refer to actual starts. For comparative purposes the official private starts statistics are published alongside the NHBC applications. But the fact that the NHBC may not be limited to the private sector makes comparison problematic.

Other questions that arise with regard to the interpretation of the data relate to the timing of registration and the problem of cancellations. Under the NHBC system a builder should register

a dwelling at least 21 days before building starts. The NHBC
state that an application is typically made more than 21 days in
advance but that as it is accompanied by a fee, 'prudent builders
would not normally make it more than a few weeks before the
anticipated start date'. Late applications are accepted but these
involve the payment of an additional fee. No information is
available about the difference between planned and actual start
dates. With regard to cancellations, an allowance is made in the
published series on the basis of past experience that about 3%
of registered dwellings are ultimately cancelled; thus the
published 'starts' are an assumed 97% of gross applications. The
NHBC also state that cancellations are recorded within five
years of registration and that after five years the starts are
revised if necessary. A final point to note concerns the breakdowns by county. These are based on postal addresses of sites
but it is known that complete accuracy in the classification is not
achieved.

(b) *NHBC dwelling completions*
Unlike the starts figures, completions are analysed only by
countries of the UK. They are published alongside the official
completions statistics. But again comparison is affected by the
same issue of NHBC coverage referred to above and there may
also be a timing difference. Both aim to record the house when
it is ready for occupation. In the NHBC case this is when the
NHBC inspector certifies that the dwelling has been satisfactorily
completed in accordance with NHBC's technical requirements.
In the official statistics, completion is when the dwelling is
certified by a Building Inspector as completed in accordance
with Building Regulations. The NHBC state that a house is
normally reported completed in the official statistics at a later
date than in the NHBC's. This is because the official statistics are
recorded via a third party, i.e. a local authority, whereas the
NHBC figures are reported direct. However, an additional
complication is that there is no hard and fast rule regarding
whether a dwelling is completed by Building Regulation
standards or NHBC standards first.

(c) *NHBC dwelling types*
Analyses of 'starts' figures are made to show the percentage

distribution of six types of dwellings as follows: detached houses, detached bungalows, semi-detached houses, terraced houses, attached bungalows, flats and maisonettes.

(d) *NHBC timber-frame houses – market share*

Analysis of timber-frame 'starts' as a percentage of total starts for each country of the UK.

The NHBC also collect information about house prices; this is considered in Chapter 4.

1.2 TOTAL NEW BUILDING – VALUE DATA

Statistics on the value of new housebuilding, as opposed to physical data on numbers considered above, are available but they are compiled as part of series dealing with construction work in general and are considered separately later. Summary details are given here for the sake of completeness and convenience. There are two relevant series:

1. Statistics of the value of work done by contractors and direct labour in the public and private sectors – considered in Chapter 6 (Section 6.1) and
2. Statistics of expenditure by owners compiled as part of series on gross domestic fixed capital formation which cover both expenditure on new houses and on improvements to existing houses. These are considered in Chapter 3 (Section 3.7).

Related series of the value of work in orders received by contractors and in commissions received by private architects are noted in Section 1.5.

1.3 LOCAL AUTHORITIES AND NEW TOWNS HOUSEBUILDING TENDERS

1.3.1 Main series – England, Wales and Scotland

In addition to the statistics about dwellings started, under construction and completed considered above, more detailed analyses are prepared at the earlier, tender, stage for local authority and new towns dwellings. These are published in *HCS* (annual) along with detailed background notes as listed below.

1. Tenders accepted by local authorities and new towns as follows:

   (a) By size of scheme and average number of dwellings per scheme in England and Wales and in Scotland

   (b) By type of contract: firm price, direct labour estimates, contracts with fluctuation clauses in England and Wales

   (c) By type of dwelling: bungalows, houses, flats separately in England and Wales and houses and flats separately in Scotland

   (d) Density of persons per hectare (frequency distribution) and average number of persons per hectare in England and Wales

   (e) Average construction cost (substructure, superstructure) of dwellings in England and Wales to 1976 and England from 1977

   (f) Average floor area of dwellings in England and Wales until 1980 and England from 1981

2. Floor area and cost of construction by type of dwelling: bungalows and two-storey houses (each analysed separately according to number of bedspaces), old persons' dwellings and flats (analysed by number of storeys) in tenders approved for local authorities in England and Wales

3. Floor area and cost of construction by size of dwelling (apartments) in tenders approved for local authorities in Scotland

4. Dwellings (houses and flats separately) in tenders accepted by public authorities in Scotland analysed by storey height

5. Building density distributions: density of dwellings per hectare and density of persons (designed bedspaces) per hectare in tenders accepted by local authorities and new towns in England and Wales

6. Building densities by region in England and Wales – as in (5) above – and average number of persons per dwelling

7. Housing schemes by size in tenders accepted by local authorities and new towns: number of dwellings and number of schemes analysed by number of dwellings per scheme in England and Wales and in Scotland separately

8. Construction tender costs by region for local authorities in England based on a one-in-four sample of schemes showing:

percentage breakdown into substructure, superstructure, site works, covered car accommodation and total

9. Floor area and construction tender cost by region for local authorities in England and Wales showing percentage breakdown into cost of land, construction tender cost and fees; average total cost; average area per dwelling and average construction cost per square metre (excluding land and fees)

10. Type of heating in tenders accepted by local authorities, new towns and (from 1981) housing associations in England and Wales.

1.3.2 Supplementary series – Scotland and Wales

In addition to the series for Scotland included above, separate series are published in *SHS* as follows:

1. Floor area and construction costs in tenders accepted by local authorities, new towns and by the SSHA separately by number of apartments

2. Local authority dwellings: tenders accepted by size of scheme and average size of scheme

3. Local authority dwellings in tenders accepted by storey height for houses and flats separately.

For Wales, separate analyses of tender stage data are published in *WHS* – see Table 1.1.

1.4 CHARACTERISTICS OF NEW HOUSES

Most of the information available about the characteristics of new houses has been considered above. For convenience we bring the references together here and also refer to an additional source, making four potential sources altogether.

1. *New building – returns from housing authorities*. This source was considered in Section 1.1. To summarize, it provides analyses of: dwelling size by bedrooms in England and Wales and by apartments in Scotland, numbers of houses and of flats, number of storeys in Wales and formerly in England and specialized dwellings (as defined earlier).

2. *Dwellings in tenders accepted by local authorities and new towns.*

This source was considered in Section 1.3. To summarize, the topics covered are size in terms of floor area and bedspaces and type of dwelling.

3. *NHBC statistics.* This source was considered in sub-section 1.1.2.
4. *Private sector dwellings – surveys of building society mortgages.* The DoE, in conjunction with the BSA, has conducted a 5% sample survey of building society mortgages in the UK since 1968. Full details of the information obtained are considered in Chapter 3 (Section 3.4). In the present context, the information of relevance is analyses by type of dwellings, size (habitable rooms) and garage provision. In addition, individual building societies make analyses of the dwellings on which they themselves have made loans from time to time (see Section 3.4.2).

1.5 FORWARD INDICATORS AND FORECASTS OF NEW HOUSEBUILDING

Most of the sources which provide information of relevance for judging the level of future new building, and actual forecasts themselves, are considered elsewhere in this book because they are not confined to housing alone. For convenience we summarize the sources in Section 1.5.1 below but provide no further discussion. In Section 1.5.2 we note two supplementary sets of relevant data.

1.5.1 Summary of major sources

At one time, returns were obtained by the DoE from builders and property developers who undertake speculative house-building to obtain data about current and future levels of private sector building. These enquiries were ended in 1980. Currently, the relevant forward indicators are as follows:

1. Official statistics about starts and dwellings under construction – considered in Section 1.1
2. NHBC statistics about applications for starts by registered housebuilders – also considered in Section 1.1
3. Official statistics of dwellings in tenders approved or accepted by local authorities and new towns – considered in Section 1.3

4. Value of new orders obtained by contractors (including work started on speculative developments – considered in Chapter 7 (Section 7.1)
5. Series of the value of new commissions obtained for housing work by private architects and of the value of work entering the production drawings stage – considered in Chapter 15 (Section 15.3)
6. Statistics of planned public expenditure – considered in Chapter 3 (Section 3.6)
7. HBF state of trade enquiries – considered in Chapter 7 (Section 7.3)
8. Forecasts of future housebuilding activity – also considered in Chapter 7 (Section 7.4).

1.5.2 Supplementary sources

(a) *Building time lags*

Estimates of the time lags incurred between building starts and completions which may be useful in judging the future rate of completions on the basis of starts are made by the DoE and published in *HCS* (quarterly). It is important to note that the data are not based on observation but are statistical estimates based on the assumption that dwellings were started in the same order in which they were completed.

(b) *NHBC first-time buyers' ability to buy index*

This index, published quarterly in *Private House-Building Statistics,* is based upon the movement of average mortgage advances and deposits and average income of first-time buyers obtaining mortgage loans from the Nationwide Building Society. An account of the methodology is given by Hall and Richardson (1979). It is claimed that the movement of the index has generally been a leading indicator of housing starts of around two quarters.

2
HOUSING AND HOUSEHOLDS: THE STOCK AND ITS OCCUPANCY

Information about the housing stock is considered in two parts. We consider here series relating to its size, tenure and age distribution and statistics about changes to the stock. The latter consists of two elements: (a) changes in its size through gains and losses and related changes in its tenure and age distribution and, (b) changes in its characteristics as a result of renovation and related improvements and alterations work. We consider each in turn. In addition to the sources considered here, information about tenure and age distribution is available from a number of housing and household surveys which also provide data on other housing characteristics (including condition) and about its occupancy. These surveys are considered separately in Section 2.2.

2.1 THE HOUSING STOCK: SIZE, TENURE, AGE AND CHANGE

The arrangement of this section is as follows:

2.1.1 Size, tenure and age of the housing stock
2.1.2 The constituents of stock changes
2.1.3 Renovation and related statistics.

2.1.1 Size, tenure and age of the housing stock

Two kinds of information are available about the size of the housing stock: data in value terms and data in physical terms. The former are compiled as a component of estimates of the total capital stock of all fixed assets which are considered in Chapter 16 and no further discussion is offered here. We confine our attention to the physical data.

(a) *National and regional series*

Estimates of the size, tenure and age distribution of the stock in Great Britain are prepared annually by the DoE and published in *HCS* as follows:

1. Total stock by region, metropolitan county and conurbation
2. Analysis by tenure by country and region
3. Estimated age distribution by region
4. Stock of dwellings of Housing Associations (annual series from 1981), and
5. Estimated annual gains and losses.

WALES. In addition to the series above, analyses of the stock in Wales by tenure and estimated date of construction are given in the *DWS* and *WHS*, the latter including analyses by tenure for each county and district.

SCOTLAND. In Scotland an annual return is obtained from local authorities showing stock by tenure, vacancies, amenities (i.e. lacking inside WC or bathroom), dwelling type, size (apartments), age (construction period). Full analyses are not published. *SHS* gives figures on the estimated age distribution and the *SAS* includes series of the total stock split between the public and private sectors.

The DoE estimates of the size and tenure of the stock are based upon data collected in the decennial censuses of population with adjustments for enumeration errors, definitional changes and for changes taking place in the years between censuses. The estimates of the age distribution of the stock are made using data from the census reports back to 1851 together with assumed rates of new construction and demolition for periods before these were recorded, and further assumptions about the ages of dwellings lost from the stock. Thus the statistics collected in the censuses of population represent the primary, benchmark, data and we consider them below together with the definitional problems that arise. The censuses also provide information about the number of rooms, amenities and the occupation of the stock (see Section 2.2).

(b) *Housing stock statistics from the censuses of population*
Any count of the number of dwellings must face the question of
definition and, in particular, how to treat buildings which are
occupied by more than one household or which contain more
than one 'household space' – 'multi-occupied' buildings.
Difficulties in covering the latter satisfactorily have led to
changes in practice in successive censuses, culminating in the
1981 Census in which no direct count of dwellings, as such, was
made.

For the vast majority of dwellings, enumeration presents no
problems because the dwelling is a house, a bungalow, a
purpose-built flat etc. occupied by one household. Difficulties
are encountered, however, in adequately defining and identifying dwellings in multi-occupied buildings. The classification
of dwellings other than in multi-occupied buildings has varied
little in the censuses taken since the end of the Second World
War. But the treatment of multi-occupied buildings has varied
from census to census. A valuable summary of the methods
used in all of the censuses from 1951 to 1981 has been provided
by Roberts (1980) and our account here draws upon his work.

The concepts of 'dwelling' and 'household space' are fundamental to an understanding of the data. A dwelling is defined as
a building or any part of a building that forms a separate and
self-contained set of premises designed to be occupied by a
single family or household. The term 'household space' is used
to describe the accommodation occupied by a household for
living purposes or vacant accommodation intended for occupation by one household. A household is either one person living
alone or a group of people (who may or may not be related)
living, or staying temporarily, at the same address and sharing
common housekeeping.* Thus a dwelling is defined in terms of
'bricks and mortar': to change the number of dwellings in a

---

* The definition of a household was changed in 1981. Previously 'sharing
common housekeeping' was defined in relation to regularly eating at least one
meal a day together. In 1981 this condition was changed so that people sharing
a common living or sitting room, although not regularly eating together, counted
as a household. It will be appreciated that this change merged into one household, some that would have been separate under the old definition. The
previous definition had remained unchanged between 1961 and 1971. The
difference between the 1951 and 1961 census definitions is explained in GRO
(1968) Part II Ch. V.

building requires structural alteration. In contrast, the number of household spaces in a building can be changed at the whim of the occupants: a single family house can change from one household space to two simply by letting one room to a non-member of the household as, say, a bed-sitting room. As Roberts (1980) points out, each of these concepts has its value in describing the state of housing circumstances. The number of dwellings, number of rooms and amenities inform us about the size and the physical state of the housing stock. The number of household spaces and the characteristics of the occupants tell us how the stock is occupied and by whom.

The term 'multi-occupied building' is used to describe any building other than a block of purpose-built flats or maisonettes that contains more than one household space. Such buildings cover a wide range of circumstances. The number of dwellings counted in such buildings depends upon the structural separateness of the living accommodation of each household (or household space). Some buildings may be converted into self-contained flats providing the same degree of privacy and self-containment as in purpose-built flats. Others, however, may have undergone little or no structural change with, for instance, rooms let as bed-sitting rooms but with bathroom, WC and kitchen facilities shared by a number of households, or an unconverted house may be occupied by two households, one living upstairs and the other downstairs.

With regard to the classification of dwellings *other than in multi-occupied buildings,* houses occupied by one household (and which had not been altered for occupation by more than one household), bungalows, purpose-built flats and maisonettes, and flats attached to premises otherwise used for non-residential purposes (shops, offices etc.) have been counted as separate dwellings in all censuses. Private residences in the grounds of non-private establishments such as hotels and hospitals have also been counted as dwellings in all censuses other than in 1951: this group includes married quarters in defence establishments which meet the condition of being structurally separate. In 1961 and in the mid-term sample census in 1966, households occupying flats or suites of rooms within the main building of an establishment were also identified as occupying separate accommodation, but this procedure was discontinued in 1971. Non-permanent buildings (e.g. caravans, chalets, houseboats) have been counted as separate dwellings if they were occupied on census night or were someone's usual residence, in all censuses.

The treatment of multi-occupied buildings has varied from census to census. We give brief details here to convey the essence of the distinctions made; fuller details will be found in the reports of the censuses cited below and fuller summary details in Roberts (1980). In censuses before 1971, a dwelling was defined in terms of structurally separate living accommodation (not necessarily with a bathroom and WC) contained behind its own front door, with independent access to the street so that occupants could get out without passing through anyone else's living quarters. However, difficulties were experienced by enumerators in applying the definitions in practice and a quality check on the 1966 Sample Census (Gray and Gee, 1972) found that 12% of multi-occupied buildings had been incorrectly sub-divided into dwellings although, because of compensating errors, the overall impact on the estimate of dwelling stock was minimal. As a result a new procedure was tried in 1971.

For the 1971 Census, the approach was based on whether households shared either any rooms, or any corridors or other circulation areas. The accommodation occupied by households which shared access space in order to move between their rooms or which shared rooms, was grouped together and defined as a dwelling; a household which did not share in either of these ways was enumerated as occupying a single unshared dwelling. However, the 1971 classification had several shortcomings: in particular, some bed-sitting rooms whose occupants had to share a bathroom and WC with other households were counted as separate dwellings whereas bed-sitters had been specifically excluded in 1961 and 1966. Consequently, in preparing its dwelling stock estimates the DoE had to adjust the census figures – details are given by Roberts (1980).

The latest, 1981, Census used a simplified method of classi-fying household spaces and one which did not include a direct count of 'dwellings' at all. Enumerators were required to cate-gorize the household's accommodation as one of the following: (a) a caravan; (b) other mobile or temporary structure; (c) a flat or maisonette in a purpose-built block; or (d) other permanent building. In the latter case, the enumerator recorded whether the entrance from *outside* the building was shared with another household; and, if it was shared, the householder recorded whether the rooms occupied by the household were enclosed behind their own front door *inside* the building.* Each household space was assigned an access code, taking the values of 0, 1 or 2, determined solely by whether the household shared the entrance to the building from the outside with another household (code 1), or did not share (code 0), and regardless of the structural separateness of household spaces within the building. Code 2 was used to distinguish purpose-built flats or maisonettes. Households who shared the entrance to the building with other households were asked the question 'Are your rooms (not counting a bathroom or WC) enclosed behind your own front door inside the building?'.

In analyses of the 1981 Census data, household spaces (and answers to the questions on sharing, number of rooms and use of a bath and WC) were classified on the basis of their access code. For permanent buildings, the following seven categories are identified:

1. Purpose-built flats or maisonette (i.e. all access code 2 cases)
2. Accommodation with a separate entrance from outside the building (i.e. all access code 0 cases)
3. Self-contained accommodation with exclusive use of bath and inside WC and two or more rooms, with a shared entrance from outside the building
4. Self-contained accommodation with exclusive use of bath and inside WC and one room with a shared entrance from outside the building (flatlet)
5. Other self-contained accommodation, with a shared entrance from outside the building
6. Not self-contained accommodation with one room but without exclusive use of bath and inside WC, with a shared entrance from outside the building (bed-sitting room)
7. Other not self-contained accommodation with a shared

* In Scotland, additional information was collected about permanent housing: houses were divided into three categories (detached, semi- detached, terraced) and flats were categorized by the number of storeys in the building. In addition, information on the level of the household's accommodation was recorded (e.g. 'all of the first or higher floor, entry on first floor') and the means of access ('lift', 'external stair' or 'internal stair').

entrance from outside the building.

When no household was present on census night, enumerators were asked to record the access code, an estimate of the number of rooms in the accommodation and, where appropriate, the answer to the sharing question. It follows that in the absence of information on amenities for such household spaces in multi-occupied buildings, it is not possible to distinguish between some of the categories listed above.

As a consequence of this change in procedures for the 1981 Census, the DoE series of the total dwelling stock for 1981 had to be estimated. The estimates are based on the information on access recorded for each household space. In brief, the method used was to take the number of self-contained household spaces in permanent buildings and then to add an allowance for shared dwellings based on the assumption that on average 100 'not self-contained' household spaces were equivalent to 30 separate dwellings (20 in some areas of London where sharing is prevalent). All household spaces which were not in permanent buildings were assumed to be self-contained dwellings. Since only a very small proportion of dwellings are shared, the dwelling stock estimate is not very sensitive to the number of household spaces assumed per shared dwelling: the maximum possible error on this account represents less than 0.5% of total dwelling stock nationally (and only about 1% for London, the area most affected). Full details of the basis of the estimates are given by Roberts (1980).

CENSUS PUBLICATION SOURCES. Full bibliographic references are given in the List of Statistical Sources at the end of this book. For convenience the titles of the relevant national volumes are listed below. In addition, key statistics are also included in individual *County Reports** (reports for *Regions* in Scotland in 1981) and for every town, city and smaller urban area in 1981 in *Key Statistics for Urban Areas*.

1951:	E & W	*Housing Report*
	Scotland	*General Volume*
1961:	E & W	*Housing National Summary Tables*

* These are not listed in the List of statistical sources.

	E & W	*Housing Tables*
	Scotland	*Housing and Households*
	Scotland	*Housing National Summary Tables*
1966:	E & W	*Housing Tables*
	Scotland	*Housing*
1971:	E & W	*Housing Tables*
	Scotland	*Housing Report*
	GB	*Housing Summary Tables*
1981:	E & W	*Housing and Households*
	Scotland	*Housing and Households.*

Fuller details of published, unpublished and related tables on housing and households available from the 1981 Census are given in OPCS *User Guide 130/5* (revised June 1985).

2.1.2 The constituents of stock changes

(a) *Summary gains and losses*

Changes in the size of the stock are the net result of additions and losses that occur during a particular period. Additions may arise as a result of new building, the change of use of a building from non-residential to residential purposes or the conversion of an existing dwelling into a greater number of separate dwellings. Losses may occur as a result of demolition, fire etc., change of use or conversion (e.g. two terraced houses being combined into a single dwelling). Estimates of such gains and losses are made annually on the basis of returns made by local authorities, and published in *HCS* (annual). These estimates distinguish: new construction, 'other gains' (mainly net gains from conversions), slum clearance (estimates of the number of separate dwellings in buildings demolished or closed) and 'other losses' (covering the removal of post-war prefabricated bungalows and of former camps in temporary use for housing, loss through fire, flood or other damage, obsolescence, change to other use and removal to make way for new development of any kind).

Estimates of changes in the tenure and age distribution of the stock are more difficult. For this purpose broad assumptions have to be made about the impact of these factors coupled with such information as is available about transfers between tenures (e.g. sales of council houses) and age.

Some of the information used in the compilation of the summary statistics of gains and losses is published separately in more detail. In the main this relates to new building and dwellings demolished, closed or made fit. The former were considered in Chapter 1, the latter are considered below.

(b) *Dwellings demolished, closed or made fit*

For England and Wales data are published for unfit houses demolished as a result of statutory slum clearance action (according to whether or not they are in or adjoining a clearance area), dwellings closed and unfit dwellings made fit. Separate statistics for demolitions other than under slum clearance powers and for other losses (e.g. destroyed by fire) are collected but not separately published (note, however, the series for 'other losses' in the summary statistics referred to above). For Scotland separate series are published for houses demolished under both slum clearance and 'other action', and in each case according to whether dwellings were above or below 'tolerable standard'. Series for dwellings closed are also given but not for dwellings made fit.

The series are published for England and for Wales in *HCS* and *LHS* (data by region, county and local authority area); for Wales alone in *WHS* (data by district), *DWS* and *WST;* and for Scotland in *HCS, SHS* and *SAS.*

With regard to the interpretation of the data, reference should be made to the detailed notes and definitions given in *HCS* (annual). It is important to note that for slum clearance statistics purposes, a 'house' generally refers to a building and not to the separate dwellings contained within it. Demolition following closure is included in the demolition figures for the appropriate period and deducted from the net total of dwellings demolished or closed. No adjustments are made, however, for dwellings closed and subsequently made fit.

2.1.3 Renovation and related statistics

(a) *General series*

The most general statistics available are those relating to the value of 'repairs and maintenance work' (defined to include extensions, alterations and conversions work) done by contractors and direct labour organizations on housing in the public and private sectors. However, the data do not distinguish the nature of the work done. Further, it needs to be appreciated that work done on a DIY basis is not covered. The data are considered in Chapter 6.

Information is also collected in the annual *FES* about (a) payments to contractors for work done and (b) payments for building and decorating materials purchased, but again without any indication of the kind of work done. From 1971 to 1976 more specific information was collected in the *GHS* about (a) the installation/replacement of a bath or WC and (b) cost of improvements made to accommodation.

(b) *Grant-aided work*

Statistics derived from the administration of official grants for house renovation and improvement distinguish the payment of different sorts of grant but do not distinguish the types of work carried out. The grants are given to encourage owners and tenants to put resources into providing modern services and amenities in sound older houses or, alternatively, to increase the stock of satisfactory dwellings by converting outmoded houses and other buildings into modern housing units. The basic scheme was introduced in 1949 but the provisions under which assistance is made available have been changed from time to time. A brief account of each type of grant currently available for houses in private ownership is given in the following paragraphs. Much more detailed information will be found in the 'notes and definitions' section of *HCS* (annual). The grants normally referred to as 'renovation grants' are those described in paragraphs (i)–(iv). For local authority housing, government subsidies are available in appropriate circumstances.

(i) *Improvement grants.* These were first introduced in 1949 and are available at the discretion of the local authority, either for the improvement of existing dwellings or for the provision of dwellings by conversion of existing homes or other dwellings. The dwelling should be brought up to a prescribed standard.

(ii) *Intermediate grants.* These took the place of former 'standard grants' introduced in 1959. They are available as of right for the provision of any of the standard amenities that have been lacking for at least one year and the execution of associated repairs.

(iii) *Repairs grants.* These are payable at the discretion of local authorities for substantial and structural repairs to pre-1919 dwellings.

(iv) *Special grants.* These are available, at the discretion of local authorities, to the owner of a house in multiple occupation for the provision of standard amenities and for the provision of means of escape from fire and associated eligible repairs.

(v) *Energy conservation.* The Government introduced measures to improve the standard of insulation in the housing stock as part of the energy conservation programme in 1978. A programme of insulation work in the public sector was undertaken with a view to providing basic insulation in all public sector dwellings by 1988. In April 1980 the separate allocations to local authorities for insulation work were discontinued: authorities now decide how much of their block capital allocations to devote to such work. It should be noted that in addition to the work carried out under the public sector programme, insulation of public sector dwellings occurs as part of renovation work. In addition, a Homes Insulation Scheme (introduced in September 1978) made provision for grant assistance towards the cost of installing insulation in private sector dwellings and from 1 November 1979 was extended to cover public sector tenants.

(c) *General improvement areas (GIAs) and housing action areas (HAAs)*
Since 1969 local authorities in England and Wales have had power to declare GIAs for the improvement of areas of older housing to prolong their useful life and, since 1974, the power to declare HAAs. The latter are areas containing housing in a poorer state than might be expected in general improvement areas and where adverse living conditions are overlaid with social stress. Appropriate powers have been conferred upon authorities, not available elsewhere, to allow them to pursue their improvement programmes within these areas.

   Statistics derived from the administration of the various grant schemes and work done in GIAs and HAAs are published in *HCS* as follows:

1.   Number of dwellings and grant paid by type of scheme and sector for England and in the private sector (alone) for Wales
2.   Summary analyses of work completed by sector by region

3. Renovation of dwellings for disabled persons or for persons with special needs in England and Wales (partial data)
4. Renovations of dwellings in HAAs and GIAs
5. Energy conservation: number of dwellings and expenditure in England and in Great Britain and number of dwellings analysed by region, by sector and by whom work done (direct labour/contractors).

Data for each local authority area are given in *LHS*. Separate data for Wales by district are given in *WHS* and summary series in the *DWS*. For Scotland, series are published in *SHS*. Expenditure on grants is also included in separate financial accounts – see Chapter 3 (Sections 3.5 and 3.6).

2.2 HOUSING AND HOUSEHOLD SURVEYS

Housing and household surveys provide information about the attributes and occupancy of the housing stock and about households' characteristics. It is important to draw a distinction between the housing stock and the population of households because there is not a one-to-one correspondence between the two. Some dwellings may be unoccupied, others may contain more than one household and occasionally a household occupies more than one dwelling. Information may be obtained, therefore, by sampling either dwellings or households. As noted earlier (Section 2.1) the definition of what constitutes a separate dwelling also presents some difficulty.

The information available comes from a variety of regular, irregular and *ad hoc* surveys. As a consequence, it is not sensible to limit attention to current sources alone. But space precludes a detailed consideration of each source because the number is very large (there are over 30 sources, counting an annual series as a single source and twice as many if the latter series are counted as individual reports) and this, coupled with differences in scope and definitions, would demand an extended treatment. Our attention is also confined to national surveys, covering the UK and constituent countries of the UK, and conurbation surveys. Individual town and local authority surveys are not covered. Full details of each survey are given in the reports themselves. We limit our attention here to identifying the range of topics covered and to comment on the nature of the data, particularly that obtained in regular surveys.

Most of the surveys collect information about households and their circumstances rather than about houses as such. The most important exceptions are house condition surveys. The main topics covered in the surveys include the following: house size (number of rooms); amenities; type of building; age; fitness and condition; tenure; density of occupation (including measures of overcrowding and undercrowding), and household character-istics such as: size and composition; age of head of household; income etc. For convenience, we group the surveys together in six sub-sections as follows:

2.2.1 General surveys
2.2.2 Sectoral surveys
2.2.3 House condition surveys
2.2.4 Movers surveys
2.2.5 Homeless households
2.2.6 Miscellaneous housing and household surveys.

2.2.1 General surveys

A summary guide to the general surveys is set out in Table 2.1. There are four regular surveys: the decennial Censuses of Popula-tion, the annual General Household Survey *(GHS)*, the Labour Force Survey (now annual) and the annual Family Expenditure Survey *(FES)*. In addition, annual returns of the dwelling stock position and of households in need are made by each local housing authority in England to the DoE under the HIP system – these are considered in Chapter 3 (sub-section 3.5.3). The most important sources in the present context are the Censuses of Population and the *GHS*. Other surveys are one-off surveys designed to provide analyses of the housing situation at particular points of time. A useful review of the evidence relating to tenure and its association with household characteristics obtained from the surveys numbered 7–11 in Table 2.1 and from Donnison (1961) – sub-section 2.2.4 refers – has been provided by Murie (1974).

(a) *Censuses of Population*

As a census, the Census of Population naturally provides the most comprehensive coverage of the housing stock (all other surveys are based on samples) but, as may be seen from Table 2.1, the range of information collected is very limited and it is conducted only once in every ten years (with the sole exception of the mid-term census of 1966). The main importance of the census, therefore, is in providing benchmark figures, albeit for only two house characteristics: rooms and amenities. It is important to note, however, that definitions have not remained constant but have been developed and changed to some extent from census to census. We comment on each in turn.

ROOMS. The word 'rooms' is, of course, open to differences of interpretation, but the census authorities have always preferred to avoid undue complexity in definition and rely on common sense despite the inherent errors of response – see the discussion by Benjamin (1970) pp.43–6. The latest, 1981, census in asking for the number of rooms said:

> Please count the number of rooms in your household's accommodation. Do *not* count: small kitchens, that is those under 2 metres (6 ft 6 ins) wide, bathrooms, WCs. *Note.* Rooms divided by curtains or portable screens count as one; those divided by a fixed or sliding partition count as two. Rooms used solely for business, professional or trade purposes should be excluded.

The scope of the 1971 question was similar but was more specific in excluding 'small kitchens less than 6 ft wide, bathrooms, toilets, sculleries not used for cooking, pantries and storerooms, landings, halls, lobbies or recesses, offices or shops used solely for business purposes'. It also referred to 'large' rooms divided by sliding or fixed partitions rather than merely 'rooms' as in 1981. The 1971 count covered the same types as in 1966 with the exclusion only of small kitchens. In 1961, however, kitchens were counted only if they were used regularly for meals or as living rooms or bedrooms. In 1951 and in 1961, unlike later censuses, the rooms available for each household were determined by the enumerator. Any room in which the household lived, ate or slept was to be counted, including the kitchen if so used. A kitchenette where meals were eaten was also to be included. In 1961 an additional note was given that rooms available for living, eating or sleeping, but not actually in use,

Table 2.1 Housing stock characteristics and occupancy – summary guide to general surveys

Source*	Survey date(s) (frequency)	Areas covered	Data House characteristics			
			Size (rooms)	Ameni-ties	Type of building	Age
1. *Censuses of Population*	1951–81 (Decennial) + 1966	GB (see remarks)	x	x		
2. *General Household Survey (GHS)* (see remarks)	1971 (A)	GB	x	x	x	x
3. *Labour Force Survey (LFS)*	1973–83(BE) 1984 (A)	UK			x	
4. *Family Expenditure Survey (FES)*	1957 (A)	UK (by region)				
5. *National Dwelling and Housing Survey (NDHS)*	1977–8 and 1978–9	E (see remarks	x	x	x	x
6. *Welsh Housing and Dwelling Survey*	1978–9	W	x	x	x	
7. Conurbation surveys:						
(a) *Housing Survey Report No.6*	1966	W. Midlands	x	x	x	x
(b) *Housing Survey Report No.7*	1969	W. Yorkshire	x	x	x	x
(c) *Housing in Clydeside 1970*	1970	Central Clydeside	x	x	x	x

Fitness and condition†	Tenure or owner	Occupancy and household character-istics	Other (see remarks)	Remarks
	x	x		Analyses by country, region, county, local-government district, town, city and other areas. Special small area statistics (SAS) produced on request.
	x	x	x	Regular core topics are shown here; see Table 2.2 for full details of range of housing and household topics covered.
		x	x	Topics covered vary (core topics are shown here) – see table 2.3 for fuller details.
	x	x	x	Currently, in addition to household income and expenditure data, includes data on following characteristics: household size and composition; number of workers; households with married women; employment status, occupational grouping and age of head of household; central heating and other durable goods.
	x	x	x	Wide range of data collected (see text). Many cross-tabulations at national and regional level, London boroughs and larger areas of housing stress in 1977 (Phase I) and remaining inner city programme areas and a selection of others in 1978–9 (Phases II and III).
	x	x	x	Additional data on: RV; FH/LH; household characteristics (type, size, employment status, socio-economic group and age of head); sharing and concealed households; length of residence; council house waiting lists membership; vacant and second/holiday homes; off-street parking. Many cross-tabulations. Analyses of county and district level.
	x	x	x	Sub-regional studies following national 1964 survey (item 7).
x	x	x	x	Additional data on: rents; household characteristics (size, type, income,
x	x	x	x	socio-economic status etc.); density of occupation; satisfaction; household movement (see Table 1.4). Many cross-classifications. Report No.7 also gives data on: RV; kitchens; bedrooms; central heating; repair costs; second dwellings and journey to work. See also Table 1.4 (item 12).

(continued overleaf)

Table 2.1 (*continued*)

Source*	Survey date(s) (frequency)	Areas covered	House characteristics			Data
			Size (rooms)	Ameni- ties	Type of building	Age
8. *Scottish Housing in 1965*	1965	S	x	x	x	x
9. *Housing Survey in England and Wales 1964*	1964	E & W	x	x	x	x
10. *English Housing Trends*	1962	E	x	x	x	
11. *Housing Situation in 1960*	1960	E & W	x	x	x	x

Key: A=Annual; BE=Biennial; E=England; FH=freehold; GB=Great Britain; LH=leasehold; RV=rateable value (gross value for rating purposes); S=Scotland; W=Wales.

Fitness and condition†	Tenure or owner	Occupancy and household characteristics	Other (see remarks)	Remarks
x	x	x	x	First national housing survey in Scotland. Additional data on: bedrooms; RV; household characteristics (age, size, type, income); density of occupation; rents; household movement (length of residence, distance moved, reasons for movement and accommodation choice, preferences, characteristics of movers); recent buyers (characteristics, cost of house, deposit, repayment); intending and potential movers; mortgages; rent control; cars and garaging; satisfaction.
x	x	x	x	Data on household characteristics, household movement, finance and rent control also obtained.
	x	x	x	Additional data on: RV; household size and other characteristics (type, earners, occupation, income, age of housewife); satisfaction; length of residence; rents; rent control; household movement (tenure, distance of move, reasons for, choice of house, method of obtaining house, characteristics of movers, cost of property, loan finance); potential movement and attitudes. Numerous cross-tabulations.
x	x	x	x	Additional data on: floor area; RV; density of occupation (overcrowding, underoccupation); availability, use and sharing of rooms; type of landlord and tenancy arrangements; freehold, leasehold; inheritance; rents; income; employment; old persons; car use and garaging; journey to work (method and time); recent movers (purchase price and source of finance); potential movement

* Full publication references are given in the List of Statistical Sources at the end of this book.
† Special house condition surveys are listed in Table 2.5

should also be counted. More detailed notes on the comparability of the census data from 1951 to 1971 inclusive will be found in OPCS (1979), Part I, pp.48–52.

It will have been noted that a major difference has been in the treatment of kitchens. A post-enumeration survey carried out after the 1961 census (reported in GRO, 1968) indicated an over-statement of numbers of rooms of just over one half per cent mainly due to the treatment of kitchens. A quality check on the 1966 census (Gray and Gee, 1972) and the 1981 census post-enumeration survey (Britton and Birch, 1985) also indicated considerable errors in the recording of rooms.

AMENITIES. The amenities available to households provide an important index of housing quality and information has been collected in each post-war census as follows:

Amenity	1951	1961	1966	1971	1981
Cold water supply	x	x			
Hot water supply		x	x	x	
Cooking stove	x	x*	x*	x	
Kitchen sink	x	x*	x*	x	
Water closet	x	x	x	x	x
Fixed bath	x	x	x ⎱	x	x
Fixed shower			x† ⎰		

* Question restricted to households in shared dwellings and ascertained by the enumerator.
† Information not published.

With regard to interpretation, it is important to note that the questions asked have not remained the same in each census and this therefore affects their comparability over time. A useful official commentary for the censuses from 1951 to 1971 inclusive is given in OPCS (1979), Part I, pp.48–52. With regard to reliability reference should be made to the quality and post-enumeration checks referred to above.

(b) *General Household Surveys (GHS)*

Since 1971, the most important source for tracking developments between censuses has been the GHS which is an annual multi-purpose household survey. Its purpose is not only to bridge the gap between the decennial censuses of population but also to provide the means for studying the interrelationships between different subjects. Various 'core' subjects are included regularly, supplemented with special topics from time to time – a summary is included as Appendix A. The core housing topics are included in Table 2.1 but a more detailed summary of all the housing, household (and also migration) topics included in each survey from 1971 to 1985 is given in Table 2.2. As far as housing is concerned, it should be noted that these surveys have also been supplemented by two other surveys in the period since 1971: the regular LFS and the NDHS of 1977–79 both of which are considered below.

Much of the data collected in the GHS are published in reports under the same title along with a commentary on each major topic. Unpublished tabulations and the micro-data are also made available (see Chapter 8, Section 8.6).

(c) *Labour Force Surveys (LFS)*

The LFS are household surveys (like the GHS) primarily designed to collect information about the labour force (see Chapter 8, Section 8.5) but they have also been utilized to obtain information on housing and other topics for the use of govern-ment departments. They were conducted biennially from 1973 to 1983 and annually since then.

With regard to housing, the most extensive coverage has been in surveys since 1979, especially those for 1981 and 1984. A detailed summary of the housing topics covered from 1979 is given in Table 2.3. It will be seen that the 1979 questions were mainly concerned with various aspects of owning and renting (identifying in particular owners who had previously rented their dwellings), and that the 1981 and 1984 surveys extended these questions to the availability of rooms, amenities and sharing with other households. Of the pre-1979 surveys those for 1973 and 1975 are notable for their coverage of second homes (details are given as a footnote to Table 2.3). The only topics covered in all or most surveys are type of accommodation (all surveys) and tenure (all surveys from 1979).

Details of the published reports are given in Chapter 8 (Section 8.5) but it is important to note that very little of the housing data has been published. However, some unpublished tabulations are available and the full range of housing data, together with selected items from the main survey, are held at a computer

Table 2.2 Detailed summary of housing, household and migration topics included in the General Household Surveys 1971–1985

HOUSING (see also MIGRATION)

Present accommodation: amenities
Length of residence at present address*
Age of building
Type of accommodation

Number of rooms and number of bedrooms — 1971–85
Whether have separate kitchen
Bath/WC: sole use, shared, none
WC: inside or outside the accommodation
} 1971–85

Installation/replacement of bath or WC
Cost of improvements made to the accommodation } 1971–76

Floor level of main accommodation
Whether there is a lift } 1973–85

Tenure
Whether present home is owned or rented — 1971–85
Whether in co-ownership housing association scheme — 1981–85

Owner occupiers:
In whose name the property is owned — 1978–85
How outright owners originally acquired their home and source of any mortgage or loan — 1978–80, 1982–85
Whether currently using present home as security for a (second) mortgage or loan of any kind — 1980–82, 1985
Whether recent owner occupiers had previously rented this accommodation and, if so, from whom — 1981–82, 1985
and for how long — 1981–82
When first became owner-occupiers and previous accommodation history — 1985

HOUSING SATISFACTION — 1978
Overall level of satisfaction with present accommodation
Reasons for dissatisfaction
Satisfaction with specified aspects of accommodation
Troublesome features
Housing preferences

HOUSEHOLD COMPOSITION
Age*, sex*, marital status of household members
Relationship to head of household* } 1971–85
Family unit(s)
Housewife — 1971–80

MIGRATION

Past movement
Length of residence at previous address* — 1971–77

Previous accommodation:
Tenure — 1971–73, 1978–80
Household composition
Number of rooms — 1971–73
Bath/WC: sole use, shared, none
WC: inside or outside accommodation }

Reasons for moving from previous address* — 1971–77
Number of moves in last five years* — 1971–77, 1979–83

Potential movement
Identification of households containing persons who are currently thinking of moving* — 1971–78, 1980–81, 1983
Whether will be moving as whole household or splitting up* }

Renters:

From whom the accommodation is rented	1971–85
Whether landlord lives in the same building	1971–72, 1975–76, 1979–85
Whether have considered buying present home and, if not, why not	1980–85
Local authority tenants (how long and previous accommodation history)	1985

Housing costs

Gross value	1971–85
Net rateable value	}
Yearly rate poundage	1972–85

Type of mortgage, and current mortgage payments	1972–77, 1979, 1981, 1984–85
Current rent	1972–77, 1979, 1981
Rent rebate/allowance and/or rate rebate:	
Amount	1972–77, 1979, 1981
Whether received	1972–77, 1979, 1981, 1985
Purchase price	1985
Amount of mortgage or loan	1985

Central heating and fuel use

Whether have central heating	1971–85
Type of fuel used for central heating	1978–85
Type of fuel mainly used for room heating in winter	1978–83, 1985

Consumer durables

Possession of selected consumer durables	1972–76, 1978–85
Possession of a telephone	1972–76, 1979–85

Size of future household*	1971–76, 1980–81, 1983
Reasons for moving	1971–76, 1978, 1980–81
Proposed future tenure	1980–81, 1983
Actions taken to find somewhere to live	1971–76, 1980–81
Whether had experienced difficulties: In finding somewhere else to live	
In raising a mortgage/loan or in finding a deposit	} 1980–81

Frustrated potential movement

Identification of households containing persons who, though not currently thinking of moving, had seriously thought of doing so in the two years before interview*	} 1974–76
	1980
	1983
Whether would have moved as whole household or would have split up*	

Proposed tenure	1974–76, 1980
Reasons for deciding not to move	1974–76, 1980, 1983
Whether decision not to move was connected with rise in house prices	1974–76, 1980
Whether had experienced difficulties in raising a mortgage/loan or in finding a deposit	1980

* Including children

Source: *Report on the General Household Survey 1982* updated to 1985 by the author.

Table 2.3 Detailed summary of housing and household topics included in Labour Force Surveys, 1979–85*

Topic	Year				
	1979	1981	1983	1984	1985
Type of accommodation					
Type of dwelling†	x	x	x	x	x
With/without business premises	x		x	x	
Tenure	x	x	x	x	x
Rooms					
Number and type		x		x	
Bedrooms used for cooking		x		x	
Kitchen – use of and size		x			
Amenities					
Availability and type		x		x	
Sharing					
Rooms		x		x	
Access		x			
Amenities		x		x	
Owner-occupation					
With/without mortgage	x	x	x	x	x
Leasehold/freehold	x				
How acquired		x		x	
Source of mortgage or loan				x	
Whom bought from		x		x	
Previous renter of property?		x		x	
When started to buy				x	
Tenancy					
Rented/rent free	x	x	x	x	x
Furnished/partly furnished‡/unfurnished	x	x	x	x	x
Go with job	x	x		x	
Whom rented from	x	x	x	x	x
Landlord live in building?	x	x		x	
Action taken/considered re buying same or other property				x	
Rent registration		x			
Shorthold tenancies (length of term)		x			
Waiting list (on and how long?)				x	
Previous tenure of head of household		x**			
Length of residence				x	
Tenure one year ago				x	

* The 1973 and 1975 surveys focused on the possession of second homes. In 1973 for second homes other than caravans questions were asked on tenure, rent, rates, services included in rent and rooms. The 1975 survey covered type of accommodation and questions on the occupation and situation of caravans and houseboats.

† House or bungalow, flat or maisonette (purpose-built/non purpose-built), caravan etc. – but varying in detail: size of purpose-built blocks of flats was covered from 1981 to 1985 and number of storeys and availability of lifts in 1983.

‡ Not in 1979.

** If moved in past year.

bureau which provides a tabulation service (details are available from the DoE). The micro-data themselves are also available through the ESRC Data Archive at Essex University. The fullest set of published results for housing is for 1981 in *Labour Force Survey 1981* which gives analyses of households by tenure cross-classified by region, type of household, SEG and length of residence of household.

(d) *Family Expenditure Surveys (FES)*

Family expenditure surveys provide the only other regular source. As their name implies they are mainly concerned with the collection of data on family expenditure, but they also provide information on housing and household characteristics which for some time periods are not available from other sources – details are given in Table 2.1.

(e) *National Dwelling and Housing Survey (NDHS)*

The *NDHS* was a large-scale survey carried out as a result of the cancellation of the planned mid-term Census of Population in 1976. It was conducted in three phases in the period 1977–79 and was designed to provide up-to-date information on housing circumstances at national and regional level in England (a parallel survey was carried out in Wales – see Table 2.1). Phase I of the study (reported separately) covered the London Boroughs and 16 areas with major housing problems. Phases II and III covered the remaining inner city programme areas and a selection of others: 15 metropolitan districts and 20 non-metropolitan districts.

A wide variety of topics was covered. Apart from those listed in Table 2.1, information on house characteristics included the following: vacant and second homes, shared dwellings, number of bedrooms and differences from bedroom standard, main form of room heating and type of central heating. Information about occupancy and household characteristics included: density of occupation, type and size of household, sharing and concealed households, age, employment status and socio-economic group of head of household, ethnic group of household, satisfaction with property, length of residence and number of cars and vans available. The results are cross-tabulated by topic in considerable detail for each of the districts covered and comparisons are made with 1971 Census of Population data.

(f) *Other surveys*

Earlier, *ad hoc*, surveys designed to provide up-to-date information on the housing situation were carried out in 1964 and 1960 in England and Wales and in 1965 in Scotland – see Table 2.1. Other studies relating to particular local authority areas and new towns are not covered here.

2.2.2 Sectoral surveys

Surveys of particular sectors have covered unoccupied dwellings in Scotland in 1981, empty housing in England in 1977, the privately-rented sector in England in 1978 and privately-rented accommodation in London in 1963/64. Details are given in Table 2.4.

2.2.3 House condition surveys

(a) *Physical surveys*

Surveys aimed specifically at assessing the structural condition and fitness of houses are listed in Table 2.5 together with summary details of the data collected. Reference should also be made, however, to the lists of general and sectoral surveys given in Tables 2.1 and 2.4 respectively, for some of these also obtained relevant information about 'fit' and 'unfit' housing. Note too that returns of fit and unfit housing are made by local authorities as part of the HIP system – see Chapter 3 (sub-section 3.5.3).

It will be seen from Table 2.5 that the first two national house condition surveys, covering England and Wales, were carried out in 1967 and 1971. Subsequent surveys were carried out separately for England and for Wales in 1976 and 1981. For Wales earlier parallel surveys on a large enough scale to provide separate data were carried out in 1968 and 1973. For Scotland, a survey was carried out in 1983 covering inter-war private sector housing in the four Scottish cities but the results had not been published by the end of 1984. Earlier information was obtained in a 1965 survey – see Table 2.1 (item 8). Other surveys have covered conurbations: five conurbations in England between 1967 and 1969 (Table 2.3, item 12 refers), Central Clydeside in 1970 (item 8) and Greater London in two surveys conducted by the GLC in conjunction with the London boroughs in 1967 and 1979. Before the first national survey of 1967 the only other national figures related to houses recorded as statutorily unfit by local authorities in England and Wales and in Scotland in 1955 and in 1965 (Table 2.3, items 13–16).

A valuable discussion of the development of the concept of unfitness and of other housing condition indicators, and a review of the sources up to 1976, will be found in DoE (1977, Part III, Chapter 10).

In addition to recording information about structural condition and the cost of repairs, the house condition surveys record information about house characteristics and tenure – again details will be found in Table 2.3. The English surveys for 1976 and 1981 were also coupled with surveys of households and local authorities – we comment on these below.

(b) *Related household and local authorities surveys.*

An important development in 1976, repeated in 1981, was the supplementation of the physical house condition survey in England by an interview survey of households and a postal survey of local authorities. The aim of the interview survey was 'to gauge the characteristics and resources of households in different parts of the stock, their perceptions and intentions in relation to defects observed by the physical surveyors, and their record of carrying out works to their home over the last five years. The postal survey of local authorities was designed to establish the extent to which the sample dwellings had been subject to statutory or other action in recent times, or whether such action was proposed for the future'. The results of these surveys were reported separately in each year as Part 2 of the survey reports (see the List of statistical sources at the end of the book). For Wales a social survey was incorporated in 1981.

2.2.4 Movers surveys

Movers surveys provide information about the number of house-holds entering different tenures and moving between them, the characteristics and circumstances of households (analysed according to the tenures they are entering and leaving), reasons

Table 2.4 Housing stock characteristics and occupancy – summary guide to sectoral surveys

Source*	Survey date(s)	Area covered	Size (rooms)	Amenities	Type of building	Age	Fitness and condition†	Tenure or owner	Occupancy and household characteristics	Other (see remarks)	Remarks
1. Unoccupied Dwellings in Scotland	1981	S (by LA)	x		x	x		x		x	Published in SDD *Statistical Bulletin HSIU No. 1*, September 1983. Additional data on status of dwelling (e.g. newly completed, under conversion, second homes, holiday lets etc.) Various cross-classifications. Second homes are further analysed by area of residence of owner.
2. Empty Housing in England	1977	E (by region)	x	x	x	x	x	x		x	Report on 1977 Vacant Property Survey. Additional data on: RV; duration of, and reasons for, vacancy. Numerous cross-tabulations.

| 3. | *Privately-Rented Sector in 1978* | 1978 | E (by region) | x | x | x | x | x | x | x | Follow-up to 1978 *NDHS*. Additional data on: sharing of rooms and amenities; type of landlord; letting type (furnished, un-furnished), sub-sector and length; bedroom standard; tenant characteristics and income; rent and rates; and special topics: succession tenancies, tied accommodation, how accommodation found, responsibility for repairs and decoration. |
| 4. | *Privately Rented Accommodation in London* | 1963 and 1964 | ‡ | x | x | x | x | x | x | x | Contains variety of data on: letting type; duration of tenancy; characteristics of households, heads of households and landlords; over-crowding and under-occupation; rents, landlord–tenant relations. |

Abbreviations: see Table 2.1

* Full publication references are given in the List of Statistical Sources at the end of this book.

† Special house condition surveys are listed in Table 2.5.

‡ Greater London.

Table 2.5 Housing stock characteristics and occupancy – summary guide to house condition surveys

Source*	Survey date(s)	Area covered	House characteristics					Tenure	Occupancy and household characteristics	Other (see remarks)	Remarks
			Size (rooms)	Amenities	Type of building	Age	Fitness and condition				
1. *English House Condition Survey 1981*	1981	E (see remarks)	×	×	×	×	×	×	×	×	Comparable to 1971 and 1976 Surveys. Additional data on recent repairs and improvements. Information also obtained from social survey and local authorities – see text. Analyses by region and type of area.
2. *Welsh House Condition Survey 1981*	1981	W	×	×	×	×	×	×	×	×	Additional data on: repair costs; RV; situation (as in 1976 – see below); multi-occupation; lowest floor; potential GIA or HAA; condition of electrical installation; construction of external walls; social characteristics (age, sex, employment status of head of household). Analyses at county level. Second and holiday homes excluded.

No.	Survey	Year	Coverage									Notes
3.	*Greater London House Condition Survey*	1979	Greater London	×	×	×	×		×	×	×	Additional data on: repair costs; potential for area and public health action; multi-occupation; vacant dwellings (condition). Analyses for boroughs.
4.	*English House Condition Survey 1976*	1976	E	×	×	×	×	×	×	×	×	Comparable to 1971 and 1981 surveys. Information also obtained from social survey and local authorities – see text.
5.	*Welsh House Condition Survey 1976*	1976	W	×	×	×	×		×		×	Additional data on: repair costs; RV; situation (isolated, hamlet, village, town or urban conurbation); type of unsatisfactory environment (noise, air pollution, outlook).
6.	*Welsh House Condition Survey 1973*	1973	W	×	×	×	×		×	×	×	Additional data on: repair costs; RV. Analyses by sub-region.
7.	*House Condition Survey 1971*	1971	E & W	×	×	×	×		×	×	×	Additional data on RV; repair costs; central heating. Analyses by type of area and region.
8.	*Housing in Clydeside 1970*	1970	+	×	×	×	×	×	×	×	×	Additional data on: RV; structural problems; external maintenance and repair standards. Coupled with separate household survey – see Table 2.1.

(continued overleaf)

Table 2.5 (continued)

Source*	Survey date(s)	Area covered	House characteristics					Tenure	Occupancy and household characteristics	Other (see remarks)	Remarks
			Size (rooms)	Amenities	Type of building	Age	Fitness and condition				
9. Welsh House Condition Survey 1968	1968	W		x		x	x	x			Additional data on: repair costs; RV. Analyses by sub-region.
10. The Condition of London's Housing – A Survey	1967	Greater London	x	x	x	x	x	x	x	x	Additional data on: useful life; demolition plans; suitability for, and costs of, improvement or conversion; parking spaces. Data on household characteristics obtained in separate survey: *Characteristics of London's Households*.
11. House Condition Survey 1967‡	1967	E & W	x	x	x	x	x	x		x	First large-scale survey of structural condition and need for repairs. Data also collected on RV; cost of repairs; multi-occupation and environment. Analyses by region and type of area.

No.	Title	Year	Area							Additional data on:
12.	*Housing Survey Reports Nos. 1–5* (Conurbation surveys)**	1967–9	**	x	x	x	x	x	x	repair costs; RV.
13.	*Our Older Homes*	1965	E & W			x		x		Returns of unfit houses and dwellings made by local authorities.
14.	*Scotland's Older Houses*	1965	S			x		x		See also Table 2.1, item 7.
15.	*Slum Clearance 1955*	1955	E & W			x		x		First comprehensive post-war record of 'unfitness' based on returns made by local authorities. Data for each housing authority. Include proposals for dealing with unfit housing.
16.	*Slum Clearance – Proposals in Scotland*	1955	S			x				

Abbreviations: see Table 2.1

* Full publication references are given in the List of Statistical Sources at the end of this book.

† Central Clydeside Conurbation.

‡ Results published in *Economic Trends* No. 175, May 1968, pp. xxiv–xxxvi and in *Housing Statistics* Nos. 9, 10 and 14. The first publication of results from this survey was in the White Paper *Older Houses into New Homes* (Cmnd 3602).

** West Midlands, S.E. Lancashire, Merseyside, Tyneside and W. Yorkshire conurbations.

for moving and distances moved, and characteristics of the accommodation. Information is also collected from owner-occupiers about the financing of house purchase.

Three national surveys have been carried out but only the third, carried out in 1978 in England, has been reported in full: *Recently Moving Households*. The first and second surveys were carried out in 1972 and 1974 respectively and covered England and Wales. Reports on these surveys were not published but material from them was drawn on extensively in DoE (1977) Chs 2,3,6–9 inclusive. At a national level, earlier (limited) information about recent movers was obtained in housing surveys carried out in England and Wales in 1960 and 1964 (Table 2.1 – items 9 and 11), in Scotland in 1965 (Table 2.1 – item 8) and in an unofficial survey in England in 1958 reported by Donnison (1961).

Other movers surveys have been confined to conurbations: West Midlands in 1966 *(Housing Survey Report No. 6)*, West Yorkshire in 1969 *(Housing Survey Reports Nos. 7 and 8)* and the Central Clydeside Conurbation in 1970 *(Housing in Clydeside 1970)*.

In addition to these surveys, information about household movement between one area and another has also been obtained in the decennial censuses of population from 1961 and in *GHS*. Data obtained in the censuses of population are published in *Migration* reports (see under 'Census' in the List of statistical sources). In 1961 the relevant questions related to movement in the year preceding the census date and about the number of years a person had lived at his usual residence. In 1966, the question was extended to movement over a period of five years, as well as one year, but the question about length of residence was dropped. In 1971 and 1981 the statistics reverted to the one-year migration period alone as in 1961. Information obtained in the *GHS* has covered not only past movement but also potential movement and frustrated potential movement. Details are set out in Table 2.2 under the heading 'Migration'.

2.2.5 Homeless households

Regular returns are made by local authorities to central government under the Housing (Homeless Persons) Act 1977. Financial information on the operation of the Act is compiled by CIPFA. An outline of the system established by the DoE to collect statistics has been provided by Morrison (1976); but between 1980 and 1982 the scope of the system was reduced and less detailed data collected. Currently a half-yearly DoE *Press Notice: Homeless Households* ... gives national and regional results for the number of homeless households accepted by local authorities in England and a breakdown by priority need category. Supplementary tables available from the DoE on request give figures for: homeless households resident in temporary accommodation, those treated as intentionally homeless, households according to area where accepted and area one year previously, reason for homelessness, and a breakdown of homeless households by individual local authorities. The latter is reproduced in *LHS*. Detailed statistics for Wales are given in *WHS* and for Scotland in *SHS*. The CIPFA publication *Homelessness Statistics*, which covers England and Wales, aims to identify the costs incurred in the operation of the Act, covering the costs and staffing of accommodation and administration for each authority. It also includes an analysis of the numbers of households claiming homelessness.

2.2.6 Miscellaneous housing and household surveys

We consider here a miscellaneous group of surveys, carried out in the period since 1970, relating to various aspects of housing or households, namely, second homes, first homes (housing circumstances of young married couples), attitudes to letting, and shared ownership and low-cost home owners. Studies concerned with demographic aspects of households and family formation are excluded.

(a) *Second homes*

A 'second home' may be defined as 'a property which is the occasional residence of a household that usually lives elsewhere and which is primarily used for recreation purposes' (Downing and Dower, 1973). A useful discussion of the question of definition and the issues raised by second-home ownership has been provided by Coppock (1977). There are no regular statistics and the only information available comes from occasional surveys. The first attempt at a national survey was carried out by Bielckus *et al.* (1972). This estimated the number of second homes and considered the characteristics of the homes and their users. Coupled with this study is an appraisal by Downing and Dower (1973) of the issues raised by second-home ownership. This includes a bibliography of earlier studies. Rogers (1977) provides a useful summary and discussion of the sources up to the early 1970s. We now turn to later sources.

The subject was covered in the official *LFS* in 1973 and 1975 – see Section 2.2.1(c) above – and the *NDHS* of 1977–9 obtained details of vacant and second homes in England. In Wales information was collected as part of the comparable *Welsh Housing and Dwelling Survey* of 1978–9. For Scotland a sample survey of *unoccupied* dwellings following the 1981 census of population obtained data on second homes, holiday lets etc. – see Table 2.4. An earlier study by Dartington Amenity Research Trust (1977) reviews existing surveys and gives the results of seven new local surveys including estimates of the total number of second homes and details of the characteristics of owners and their types of homes. Within England and Wales a study of the South West was carried out in 1973 (South West Economic Planning Council, 1975). This provides data on numbers, location, type and age of buildings, their use and profiles of their owners.

(b) *First homes*

This is a study, reported by Madge and Brown (1981), based on a survey of young couples (who married in 1975) during the first two and a half years of their married life. The sample was not designed to be nationally representative but was drawn from three areas chosen for their distinctive and varied demographic and housing characteristics. The purpose was to examine what happens to households entering the housing market, including the institutional and individual constraints they face, the options open to them, the types of property they are competing for and the personal resources at their disposal.

(c) *Attitudes to letting*

An official survey to investigate the attributes, attitudes and policies of private landlords, private tenants and owner-occupiers was carried out in 1976 in areas which in 1971 had been predominantly rented in the private sector. The results are reported in *Attitudes to Letting in 1976* and include data on: the characteristics of the accommodation, occupants and landlords; rents; repairs and improvements; tenure history and tenant mobility.

(d) *Shared ownership*

'Shared ownership' schemes are aimed at promoting low-cost home ownership for first-time buyers. Under such schemes participants can part-own and part-rent their homes with the option to purchase outright when personal circumstances allow. A survey of eleven local authorities' schemes was conducted in 1981 to discover the extent to which the early shared ownership schemes had achieved the objectives of extending access to home ownership and providing a stepping-stone to full owner-occupation, and also to gain the consumers' views on shared ownership and ways in which it could be improved. The results, reported by Allen (1982), include analyses of: the characteristics of shared owners and property (dwelling type and size), previous accommodation, progression to full ownership, costs and finance, and residents' views on shared ownership.

(e) *Low cost home owners*

An official sample survey of purchasers of dwellings under special low cost home ownership initiatives in England to show which people had been helped by the initiatives and to compare the success of the different schemes, conducted in 1983, is reported by Littlewood and Mason (1984). Information is given about the characteristics of the purchasers and their previous housing history, the purchase process, the types of property and the purchasers' housing costs, the characteristics of shared owners and an assessment of purchasers' satisfaction.

3
THE HOUSING MARKET: FINANCE, EXPENDITURE AND TRANSACTIONS

This chapter is concerned essentially with financial statistics relating to the acquisition and consumption of housing. Personal expenditure is considered first. Attention is then devoted to the finance of house purchase and the operation of the private housing market, followed by the activities of public authorities. A final section places housing in a national economic context. The precise arrangement of topics is as follows:

3.1 Personal expenditure and related statistics
3.2 House purchase finance
3.3 Building societies: size, finance and structure
3.4 The housing market: houses and buyers
3.5 Local authority housing finance
3.6 Public expenditure
3.7 Housing in the UK national and regional accounts.

3.1 PERSONAL EXPENDITURE AND RELATED STATISTICS

This section covers sources of information on personal current expenditure on housing and the purchase of housing services, including related statistics about rent regulation and control and housing assistance. It is sub-divided as follows:

3.1.1 Personal expenditure
3.1.2 Local authority rents
3.1.3 Housing assistance
3.1.4 Rent regulation and control statistics

3.1.5 Expenditure on repairs, maintenance, decoration and improvement.

3.1.1 Personal expenditure

Certain difficulties confront the measurement of personal expenditure on housing because of its diverse nature, depending on housing tenure, the purpose of the expenditure and the problems introduced by subsidization and controls. Thus one might be interested in rents paid by tenants or in the amounts paid by owner-occupiers either for house purchase or in annual mortgage payments. Both of these relate to the purchase of housing services but may be affected by rent regulation and control and the provision of financial assistance including, in the owner-occupied sector, the provision of tax relief on mortgage interest payments. Indeed, these subjects themselves may form the focus of interest, rather than expenditure as such and demand their own statistical expression. Another subject of interest is expenditure on the upkeep and improvement of the physical fabric of the dwelling rather than the purchase of housing services. Further, in each of these cases interest may focus either on average expenditure per household or on total expenditure by all households in the aggregate. Our treatment here is determined by the variety of topics to be covered and by the nature of the available sources.

The primary source of information about incomes, rents and mortgage payments is the annual *FES*. Relevant information is also obtained in the *GHS* and in *ad hoc* surveys from time to time. We deal with each of these in turn.

(a) *Family Expenditure Surveys (FES)*
The survey has been conducted annually since 1957 on the basis of returns made by a sample of households. A detailed account of methodology has been provided by Kemsley *et al.* (1980). These surveys are particularly valuable because they not only provide information about the level of housing expenditure but also allow comparisons to be made of housing against other household expenditure and against income. In addition to the results included in the annual report on the survey, the DoE itself produces more detailed analyses. We consider each in turn

and then comment on the interpretation of the data. It may be noted too at this stage that the survey returns themselves are deposited at the ESRC Survey Archive at Essex University and are thus available for further analysis.

In the *FES* reports, analyses are made of income and expenditure (categorized below) according to tenure group as follows:

1. Rented unfurnished – local authority/other
2. Rented furnished
3. Rent free
4. Owner-occupied – in process of purchase/owned outright.

Income is analysed according to total household income and income of the head of household. Expenditure on housing is analysed, depending on tenure, according to two basic categories:

1. Payment such as rent, rates and water charges
2. Payment for repairs, maintenance and decoration.

For tenants living rent free and for owner-occupiers, it is important to note that an amount representing the 'weekly equivalent of rateable value' is substituted in place of rent. Mortgage payments and payments for outright purchase and for structural alterations are *not* included as part of housing expenditure but they are recorded under 'other payments recorded'. An Annex to the tables gives a breakdown of this item and also of the repairs, maintenance and decoration expenditure included under housing expenditure.

Analyses of the detailed expenditure data are made by income of head of household, administrative area and region. Total housing expenditure is analysed in addition by type of household, and by sex, age, occupation and employment status of heads of households.

DoE ANALYSES OF FES DATA. The DoE makes more extensive analyses of the *FES* data covering England and Wales and these are reported in *HCS* (annual) currently as follows:

1. Households by income and tenure group
2. Households in each tenure group by income and number of earners
3. Incomes by tenure and age of head of household

4. Income of owner-occupier by source of mortgage
5. Rent and mortgage payments by size and tenure
6. Rent and mortgage payments by tenure and age of head of household
7. Mortgage payments by source of mortgage
8. Households by income and rents as a percentage of income
9. Households by income and mortgage payments as a percentage of income.

INTERPRETATION. Detailed notes about the interpretation of the data are included in the reports themselves. With regard to the DoE analyses it is most important to consult the notes included in the annual *HCS*. The most important general points to note are first, that the estimates relate to a relatively small sample of households and some of the figures, therefore, are subject to substantial sampling error. Secondly, the tables include selected tenures and are not a complete coverage of all households. Important exclusions are accommodation rented furnished from private landlords, tenancies held by virtue of employment and accommodation which is rent-free or where the unrebated rent is less than 10% of the gross value for rating purposes. It should also be noted that in the DoE analyses some special definitions apply to the coverage of, and amounts analysed in, the tables on households with a mortgage and that the definitions of income differ from those used in the *FES* reports themselves.

(b) *General Household Surveys (GHS)*

The *GHS* is a multi-purpose social survey of households which has been conducted annually since 1971 covering a range of core topics and a variable set of additional topics from time to time. A summary is given in Appendix A and a more detailed list of those relating to housing is given in Table 2.2. It will be seen, with regard to housing costs, that information has been obtained in most years about rates, mortgage payments, rents and rent and rate rebates. Analyses are not always published but unpublished tables can generally be made available on request and, like the *FES* data referred to above, the primary data are available for further analysis through the ESRC Survey Archive at Essex University.

(c) *Ad hoc surveys*

Information on rents and mortgage payments has also been covered in a number of *ad hoc* surveys. These are noted in Table 2.1 (items 6–9) and Table 2.2 (items 2 and 3). It may also be noted that social surveys conducted in parallel with the English House Condition Surveys of 1976 and 1981 (Table 2.5, items 1 and 4) collected information on rents but no analyses were published.

3.1.2 Local authority rents

Information about the rents charged for houses owned by local housing authorities is published by the DoE and by the Chartered Institute of Public Finance and Accountancy (CIPFA) for England and Wales and by the SDD for Scotland.

(a) *DoE series – England and Wales*

The DoE series, published in *HCS,* give the average weekly rents (both rebated and unrebated) for England and Wales and for Greater London separately, for each year (generally in April). The figures exclude rates and service charges. Coverage extends to all local housing authorities but excludes county council tied accommodation and new town dwellings. More detailed information is provided by CIPFA (see below). Separate data for Wales, derived from CIPFA returns, are published in *WHS* to show average rents by type of dwelling cross-classified by date of construction.

(b) *CIPFA series – England and Wales*

Information is collected annually in April from virtually every housing authority (complete coverage is not always obtained) and the results published in *Housing Rents Statistics.* These provide in respect of *each* housing authority analyses of average weekly net unrebated rents according to size of dwelling (number of bedrooms) and type of dwelling and summary analyses according to type of authority and region. The volumes also provide information on the size and composition of each authority's dwelling stock according to age (until 1983), type and size of dwelling and statistics on rent rebates and allowances – considered below. Information on the aggregate amounts obtained from rents is available from each authority's Housing Revenue

Account – considered in sub-section 3.5.1.

(c) *SDD series – Scotland*

Information for each local authority in Scotland, somewhat similar in scope to that now published by CIPFA for England and Wales was published annually in *Rents of Houses Owned by Public Authorities in Scotland* until 1976. The data are now published in SDD *Statistical Bulletins* (HSIU series) with summaries in *SHS*. The *SAS* reproduces the average annual rent series.

(d) *Interpretation*

A number of factors need to be borne in mind in the interpretation of the average rents data. First, it needs to be appreciated that they do not permit comparisons to be made over time on a like-for-like basis because of changes in the underlying mix of properties on which the averages are based: changes in quality and the mix of dwellings by type etc. take place as a result of new building, demolition, improvement and loss from the stock through sales etc. Secondly, the level of rents actually paid by local authority tenants may be influenced by rent rebates (considered below). Likewise payments for rates may be reduced by rate rebates.

3.1.3 Housing assistance

The term 'housing assistance' is used to refer to financial assistance with housing costs. Until the introduction of Housing Benefit from November 1982 (in part) and fully from April 1983, assistance was given by means of rent rebates and allowances and rate rebates. The reform in 1982 involved a switch in administrative responsibility from the DoE to the DHSS although the new scheme is operated by local authorities. We consider the housing benefit and earlier scheme in turn below. In addition it should be noted that owner-occupiers continue to receive assistance in the form of mortgage interest tax relief (considered in sub-section 3.2.3) and are eligible for home improvement and repair grants (see sub-section 2.1.3). Tenants are also eligible for improvement grants.

(a) *Housing benefit*

The housing costs eligible for assistance through Housing Benefit are rent and rates, with varying practices in respect of water charges, heating allowances and amenity charges. Households on supplementary benefit can receive assistance on mortgage interest payments. Three separate forms of housing benefit need to be distinguished. First, households who qualify for supplementary benefit automatically qualify for housing benefit – the DHSS local office sends a certificate of entitlement to the local authority and these households are known as 'certificated' for administrative purposes. Secondly, households who qualify for housing benefit but are not eligible for supplementary benefit are known as 'standard' cases and the local authority applies a separate test of income to establish entitlement. Thirdly, households whose incomes are reduced below the appropriate supplementary benefit levels once they have paid rent and rates may apply for housing benefit supplement (paid by the local authority).

Although the scheme was meant to provide a simplified system, its application has been accompanied by considerable confusion for both claimants and administrators and the system is again under review – see Cmnd 9520 (1985) and Cmnd 9518 (1985), Chapter 3.

The available statistical information is limited. Figures of the number of households receiving housing benefit in the certificated and standard categories by type of rebate were given in *Social Trends 15* (1985), Table 8.24. Figures of the caseload and expenditure for both categories by type of rebate in 1984/85 were included in Cmnd 9518 (1985), p.33.

(b) *Rent rebates and allowances and rate rebates*

Rent rebates are designed to give specific assistance to tenants of local authorities. A national mandatory scheme was established in October 1972; previously rebate schemes had been operated by individual local authorities. A national scheme of rent allowances was designed to achieve the same purpose for tenants of private landlords and housing associations and was introduced in January and April 1973 for tenants in unfurnished and furnished accommodation respectively. A national rate rebate scheme designed to help householders in all tenures, was introduced in 1966. It should be noted, however, that there are presentational complications in the statistics of this area arising from the technicalities of how housing assistance is paid, and accounted for, to householders on supplementary benefit. For details, reference should be made to the detailed notes included in *HCS* (annual). Statistics about the operation of these schemes are available from the DoE, DHSS and CIPFA and are considered below. In addition, information has been collected in the *GHS* from time to time on whether or not assistance is received and on the amount – details are given in Table 2.2.

DoE AND DHSS SERIES. The DoE series, covering England and Wales, are published in *HCS* (annual) as follows:

1. Cost of rent rebate, rent allowance and rate rebate schemes
2. Rent rebates, rent allowances and rate rebates – number, average weekly amount and estimated percentage take up and
3. Households receiving supplementary benefit – tenants (distinguishing local authority and private tenants) and owner-occupiers.

For Wales separate data for the number of recipients of rent rebates, rent allowances and rate rebates and the amounts paid in each case are given in *WHS* and the *DWS*. Data on rent rebates and allowances in Scotland are included in *SHS*.

Analyses of the 'housing requirement' included in Supplementary Benefit (average amount and distribution) are made by the DHSS and published in *Social Security Statistics*.

CIPFA SERIES. CIPFA provide information in *Housing Rents Statistics* for each housing authority in England and Wales about the number of tenants in receipt of rent rebates, rent allowances and housing benefit supplement and the average weekly amount in each case.

3.1.4 Rent regulation and control statistics

Rent regulation or control has existed in some form since 1915. The current system of regulation derives from the Rent Act 1977 as amended by the Housing Act 1980 (and equivalent legislation for Scotland), and governs the rents and security of tenure of tenants of private landlords and housing associations. Under the legislation, four main categories of tenancy may be distinguished: regulated tenancies, controlled tenancies, restricted contracts and a miscellaneous group. We describe each category briefly before turning to the available statistics.

(a) *Tenancy categories*

REGULATED TENANCIES. These form the largest group. In these cases either the landlord or the tenant (or both jointly) or, since 1972, the local authority may apply to the Rent Officer for the registration of a fair rent or subsequently, if there is a disagreement, to a Rent Assessment Committee. Unless and until cancelled by the Rent Officer, the fair rent remains the maximum chargeable for the accommodation whether the tenant changes or not.

CONTROLLED TENANCIES. These were a legal category until 27 November 1980. Where the same tenancy had continued since July 1957 and the property had a low rateable value, the tenancy might still be controlled with the rent pegged at a level fixed in 1957. From 1969, it became possible to convert a controlled tenancy to the regulated category and from 1972 to 1975 a phased programme of decontrol was put into effect for properties in certain rateable value bands. From 28 November 1980 all remaining controlled tenancies became regulated tenancies.

RESTRICTED CONTRACTS. The great majority of lettings in this category are lettings by resident landlords (except for unfurnished tenancies granted before 1974 when the distinction between furnished and unfurnished ceased to have legal significance). The rent is almost always privately agreed but the landlord or tenant may apply to the Rent Tribunal for the registration of a reasonable rent.

OTHER CATEGORIES. Some households may be outside the categories listed above (e.g. rent-free or low-rent lettings, property with high rateable values and accommodation provided with a job). Agricultural tied cottages, however, received Rent Act protection from 1976. Under the Housing Act 1980 certain bodies may let dwellings built after November 1980 at market rents outside the provisions of the Rent Acts at 'Assured' tenancies.

(b) *Available statistics*

Statistics relating to the operation of the legislation are prepared by the DoE. Some are published in *HCS* and other, more detailed, figures are made available in 'Rent Officer Notes'. We consider each in turn.

Series are published in *HCS* (annual) and in abbreviated form (category 1 (b) below) for the most recent half years in *HCS* (quarterly) as follows:

1. Rent registration statistics:
   (a) Applications and determinations for England and Wales, Greater London, rest of England and Wales, Scotland
   (b) Average registered rents and change on previous rents for various categories of tenancy for England and Wales, Greater London, rest of England and Wales, Scotland
   (c) Rent re-registrations by rent registration areas
   (d) Analysis by type of case
   (e) References to rent assessment committees for England and Wales
2. Rent Tribunals: Restricted contracts, Rent Act 1977: England and Wales
3. County Court actions for recovery of possession of residential premises: England and Wales.

WALES AND SCOTLAND. In addition to the data for Wales and Scotland referred to above, categories 1 (a) and (b) are included in *SHS*. The *SAS* includes the series of average registered rents for Scotland and *WHS* gives series of mean registered rents and the number of cases analysed by county for Wales.

The 'Rent Officer Notes' are produced twice a year and contain more detailed information on rent registrations than that published in *HCS*. They are not published but are made available to outsiders by the DoE. One note gives the mean registered rents and the numbers of cases for each of the main categories of registration (regulated unfurnished, regulated furnished, housing association tenancies, and decontrolled cases) within each registration area. Further detail is also given about regulated unfurnished tenancies in London. A second note shows the movement of regulated unfurnished rents at re-registration for 'comparable' cases (those with no significant changes to the property or to the terms of the tenancy), within two years and nine months of the previous registration – new registered rents can be changed two years after the previous registration. In addition to those two series of notes, Rent Officers provide information about rents for four specific typical private rented property types, at the beginning and mid-point of each year. This is known as the 'beacons' exercise. Two tables are produced, one listing the latest rents information and showing the percentage increase over the rents reported for the previous period, and the other table giving estimated capital values for beacon properties in a number of 'key towns' and expressing the rent as a percentage of capital value.

3.1.5 Expenditure on repairs, maintenance, decoration and improvement

Two kinds of information are available: data collected from owners about expenditure and data from contractors about the value of work done. The main regular sources of data from owners are the *FES* and the *GHS*. Details of the data available from the *FES* are given in sub-section 3.1.1. The *GHS* obtained information on the cost of improvements made to accommodation each year over the period 1971–6.

Aggregate data are collected from contractors by the DoE about the value of repairs and maintenance work done on housing, distinguishing between the public and private sectors. The scope of this sector, however, is wider than the personal sector embracing all dwellings in private ownership. The data are considered in Chapter 6. It is important to note the problems that arise in attempting to cover such work comprehensively in returns from contractors, given the fact that much of the work is undertaken by small firms or by individuals acting in a private capacity. Work is also undertaken by householders themselves on a DIY basis. Some indication of the latter may be obtained from the series of expenditure on building and decorating materials etc. given in the *FES* reports.

3.2 HOUSE PURCHASE FINANCE

This section is concerned solely with the finance of house

purchase: in particular, the supply and sources of funds, interest rates, mortgage interest tax relief, transactions costs and mortgage possessions and arrears. Related statistics about building societies and the housing market are considered in Sections 3.3 and 3.4 and information about personal expenditure on mortgage repayments is covered in Section 3.1. Information about house prices and building costs is referred to here but is dealt with more fully in Chapter 4.

3.2.1 Supply and sources of funds

(a) *General considerations*

Comprehensive information about the supply and sources of funds for house purchase is not collected: the only regular information relates to the funds supplied by *institutional* sources in the UK. Apart from these sources, finance is also obtained from private loans and ready money. The only information available about these sources comes from movers surveys – considered in Chapter 2 (sub-section 2.2.4). The most important institutional source is building societies. The other main sources are banks, insurance companies and local authorities. The primary source of information for all institutional sources of funds is *Financial Statistics*. This brings together in a summary table (No. 9.4 from January 1985, formerly S5) statistics for loans on house purchase as follows: (a) amounts outstanding and net advances by building societies, local authorities, insurance companies and pension funds, the monetary sector (i.e. institutions recognized as banks or licensed to take deposits) and other public sector bodies (e.g. public corporations); and (b) gross advances and repayments of principal for building societies, local authorities and insurance companies and pension funds. Detailed notes about the statistics are given in *Financial Statistics Explanatory Handbook* (CSO, annually). Annual and quarterly series of gross and net advances by each main source are reproduced in the annual and quarterly editions of *HCS*. Further data for each institutional source are considered below.

(b) *Building societies*

For building societies, financial statistics are collected in considerable detail and are considered fully in Section 3.3. Here we merely note the relevant series in the general context of institutional sources of funds for house purchase. *Financial Statistics* includes monthly series of the number and value of commitments and advances, with the values split between new and existing dwellings, in both unadjusted and seasonally adjusted (s.a.) form. *HCS* includes the unadjusted series annually and quarterly. Other sources are *ET* which gives the adjusted series on new dwellings and *ETAS* which gives both actual and s.a. series. The detailed sources for building societies, considered more fully in Section 3.3, are the annual *Report of the Chief Registrar* (of Friendly Societies) and publications issued by the BSA: the quarterly *BSA Bulletin* coupled with a monthly press release *Building Society Monthly Statistics* which gives the latest figures. Long runs of figures and detailed explanatory notes are included in a *Compendium of Building Society Statistics (CBSS)*.

(c) *Banks*

In addition to the data noted above, supplementary statistics for banks are published in *HCS* to show the number of loans and average advances *approved* in the UK by type of dwelling (new/second-hand/all) and type of purchaser (first-time buyer/former owner-occupier), and the distributions of advances and dwelling prices.

(d) *Insurance companies*

For insurance companies, additional data are obtained from a sample survey and reported in *HCS* showing the number of primary loans *completed* in the UK and the average prices of dwellings by type (new/other/all).

(e) *Local authorities*

Estimated series are published in *HCS* for loans made by local authorities in England and Wales showing the number of dwellings and the amounts advanced to: (i) private persons for house purchase (excluding advances for sale of local authority dwellings) and for conversions, alterations or improvements and (ii) to housing associations for 'new build', acquisition of existing dwellings and for conversions, alterations or improvements.

3.2.2 Interest rates

Series to show the *average* rate of interest charged by building societies on mortgage loans are calculated by the Chief Registrar of Friendly Societies and published in his annual *Reports*. They are reproduced in *Financial Statistics, BSA Bulletin* and *CBSS*, the latter giving figures back to 1938. Rates 'recommended' or, from October 1983, 'advised' by the BSA and details of interest rates *paid* by building societies are also given in all of these publications except the Chief Registrar's *Reports*.

3.2.3 Mortgage interest tax relief

Owner-occupiers with a mortgage receive tax relief on their interest payments at their highest tax rate up to a mortgage loan ceiling which is reviewed annually (currently £30 000). Since April 1983 interest payments have been made net of tax under the Mortgage Interest Relief at Source (MIRAS) scheme. Mortgagors not liable for income tax make repayments effectively net of 'relief' at the basic rate of tax. The total value of relief is given annually in *The Government's Expenditure Plans* in which it appears as 'qualifying interest on loans for purchase or improvement of owner-occupied etc. property', in a set of 'additional analyses' showing direct tax allowances and reliefs. *Ad hoc* analyses are published from time to time in *Hansard* in response to parliamentary questions – most recently on 8 July 1985 (Cols 357–8) giving annual series from 1979–80 to 1984–85 and on 25 July 1985 (Cols 725–6) giving a breakdown of the value of relief and number of taxpayers receiving relief by income range for 1985–86. Complete annual series for the period from 1963/64 to 1984/85 and estimates according to income bands in 1983/84 were reproduced in NFHA (1985). For background information see DoE (1977) Part I, Chapter 4.

3.2.4 Owner-occupiers' transaction costs

Statistics recording the transaction costs involved in house-purchase are not collected but an interesting set of aggregate annual estimates for the period 1967–75 were published by DoE (1977) Part I, Appendix C. These covered legal fees for conveyancing and mortgages, commissions paid to estate agents, survey fees paid to building societies, stamp duty on conveyances paid by house purchasers, fees paid to the Land Registry for house purchase transactions, advertising and the premium on single premium indemnity policies taken out where mortgages are large relative to valuation.

3.2.5 Mortgage possessions and arrears

Two types of data are relevant: information about properties taken into possession and about loans for which repayments are in arrears. For the former, statistics relating to County Court actions for possessions in England and Wales have been published in *Judicial Statistics* since 1980. These show the number of possession actions entered, orders granted and warrants issued according to type (mortgage possessions, private and public – 'social type' – landlords etc.). Statistics for *building society* arrears and possessions have been collected from samples of building societies by the BSA since 1969. The data for the period 1969–1984 were published in *BSA Bulletin* July 1985, pp.18–20. This also provides a useful appraisal and discussion of the BSA and official data.

3.3 BUILDING SOCIETIES: SIZE, FINANCE AND STRUCTURE

Building societies are savings and loan institutions specializing in providing funds for house purchase and, as indicated above, they have come to constitute the most important source of housing finance. A useful recent study is by Boleat (1982). Their activities are well documented statistically on the basis of returns made to the Chief Registrar of Friendly Societies, whose job it is to exercise prudential supervision over their affairs, and to the BSA and government departments. We deal with each of these in turn.

3.3.1 Registry of Friendly Societies statistics

Annual *Reports of the Chief Registrar* provide statistical data derived from annual returns and accounts submitted by building societies back to 1890. They provide the main source of information on the size, finance, structure and development of the industry particularly before the initiation of more frequent and more detailed sample returns considered in Section 3.3.2. The main categories of information are:

1. Registration statistics: number on the register and an analysis of changes during the year (including mergers – 'transfers of engagements') for Great Britain, England and Wales and for Scotland
2. Number of societies, branch offices and distribution of staff by size of society (asset size group)
3. Numbers of: share investors, depositors and borrowers by size of society; share and deposit accounts by size of account and society, and new mortgages by size of advance
4. Financial statistics analysed by size of society as follows: assets and liabilities; financial ratios; share, deposit and mortgage transactions; investments made and realized; management expenses
5. Financial statistics not broken down by size of society cover analyses of income and expenditure, and advances by size of advance and purpose (owner-occupation, letting etc.).

Long-run series for the principal categories of information (numbers of societies, investors, borrowers and advances; the value of assets, liabilities, advances and management expenses) have been conveniently brought together by the BSA for the whole period from 1890 in the *CBSS*. This also includes important notes regarding their interpretation. Long runs are also published in the *Building Societies' Year Book*. An abbreviated summary is included in the *BSA Bulletin*. The BSA also publish an annual report on the activities of building societies, currently entitled *Building Society Fact Book*, which includes, *inter alia,* estimates of the Chief Registrar's figures for the latest year and separate data for each society that is a member of the BSA. Further details are given below.

3.3.2 Building society sample returns

(a) *Background*

In 1955 a new system of monthly, quarterly and annual returns from building societies was initiated in order to obtain more detailed and regular information than that available from the Chief Registrar. An account of the system is provided by the BSA in the *CBSS*. The returns, which are made to and processed by, variously, the BSA, the Bank of England and the DoE, are obtained only from a group of the largest societies (holding the bulk of the total assets of the movement) but the results are grossed up to represent all societies. These figures are adjusted, as necessary, retrospectively when the figures from the aggregation of the annual returns of *all* societies become available (generally in about July following the relevant year). The DoE return (BS4) provides a breakdown of the number and value of net new commitments and advances between new and existing houses. In addition, the statistics obtained in this return, and in a separate sample survey of mortgages, are both used to compile average house price series – these are considered in Chapter 4.

(b) *The available series and publication sources*

The returns referred to above provide analyses of balance sheet data and flows of funds in considerable detail. The most comprehensive results are published in *Financial Statistics* as follows:

1. Shares and deposits (receipts, withdrawals, interest credited and paid out, balances outstanding), mortgage lending (new commitments, advances, repayments), net investments and the liquidity ratio – monthly, quarterly and annual series (actual and s.a.)
2. Assets and liabilities at book value, net acquisition of assets and liabilities at cash value and a more detailed analysis of holdings and net acquisitions of investments – end year figures
3. New commitments and advances (number and values, with values split between new and existing dwellings and 'other') – monthly, quarterly and annual figures (actual and s.a.).

BSA publications also include most of the series together with certain additional analyses. The *CBSS* reproduces most of the annual and quarterly (not monthly) series in long runs and includes in addition: (a) a sources and uses of funds statement (based upon the other tabulations); (b) percentage analyses of the principal data (shares, deposits and lending figures as percentages of balances outstanding, and assets, liabilities, investments and sources and uses of funds figures as percentages of totals), and (c) figures of the number of advances and commitments (as well as their value) split between new and existing houses and 'other'. The quarterly *BSA Bulletin* also reproduces most of the figures (including monthly series). The annual *Building Society Fact Book* includes summary figures. The series for advances and commitments in particular are also reproduced in a number of other sources; these were noted in Section 3.2.1.

(c) *Supplementary analyses*

In addition to the major financial series referred to above, supplementary analyses are made for building society activity in Scotland from 1965 and for the activities of British-based societies in Northern Ireland. These are included in the *CBSS*. The BSA also make analyses of the structure of the industry which supplement those made by the Chief Registrar (e.g. analyses by size of society and the degree of concentration) and studies of its operations within the context of the savings market and the financial and economic environment. These are included in the *Building Society Fact Book* and the *BSA Bulletin*. The latter also includes special articles from time to time examining particular subjects in greater depth – convenient collections of the articles that appeared in various periods from 1974 to 1983 have been published separately (BSA, 1980, 1982, 1984).

Further information about the mortgage activities of building societies, the borrowers and the characteristics of the houses on which mortgage advances are made is collected in surveys made by the DoE in conjunction with the BSA – these are considered in Section 3.4.

3.4 THE HOUSING MARKET: ANALYSES OF HOUSES AND BUYERS

The only regular information about the characteristics of the houses being bought and sold and of house buyers comes from analyses of building society mortgages. The fact that analyses are based on building society transactions alone, is an important limitation in principle because they are not necessarily representative of all transactions. Other institutions tend to cater for different sectors of the market: local authorities tend to concentrate their lending 'down-market' while banks and insurance companies tend to concentrate 'up-market' (for details of the limited information available see sub-section 3.2.1). Likewise transactions which do not depend upon institutional sources of finance are likely to have different characteristics (some information is available from movers surveys – see Chapter 2, sub-section 2.2.4). Bearing this limitation in mind, analyses of building society mortgages provide information about the housing market not available from any other source. For this reason, and because building societies provide the main institutional source of finance, the data are obviously of great value. The most comprehensive source is a 5% sample survey of building societies in the United Kingdom conducted by the DoE in cooperation with the BSA. Individual societies also publish analyses of their own transactions from time to time (many publish regular analyses confined to house prices). We consider each of these sources in turn.

3.4.1 The DoE 5% sample survey of building society mortgages

(a) *Background*

This survey was started at the end of 1965 but, following revisions to the questionnaire, the present method of analysis was introduced in the second quarter of 1968 and most of the detailed series start in this period: only the main national series go back to the first quarter of 1966. Background details about the survey methodology etc. will be found in Evans (1975) and further notes and sample sizes are given in the 'Notes and Definitions' in *HCS* (annual). It is emphasized that the figures are subject to sampling error (approximate coefficients of variation of average dwelling price, advances and incomes are given in *HCS*).

The current questionnaire seeks information about the mortgage advance, the dwelling and the main applicant as follows:

1. *The mortgage advance:* the amount advanced; whether the advance is to be used wholly for the purchase of the property; the period over which the advance is due to be repaid; the

gross interest rate charged initially; the initial monthly repayment; the method of repayment

2. *The dwelling:* purchase price; location (region); period of construction; type of dwelling; freehold or leasehold; number of habitable rooms; whether there is a garage; net rateable value

3. *The main applicant:* sex; age; basic income; any other income on which the mortgage is based; previous tenure.

Some 150 computer tabulations are now produced from the survey data for each quarter. They are not published in full but are made available to research workers.

(b) *Publication sources*

The primary publication sources are *HCS* and BSA publications. Currently, *HCS* (annual) gives the following analyses over a run of eleven years:

1. Averages of: dwelling price, advance, and recorded income of borrower (each by region, by new and existing dwellings and by first-time buyer (FTB) and former owner-occupiers (FOO) and average price by type of dwelling.

2. Distributions of: dwelling prices, types of dwellings and ages of borrowers (each by new and existing dwellings and by FTB and FOO), mortgage advances, recorded income of borrower, ages of dwellings, and mortgage periods.

The quarterly *HCS* (Part 1) gives quarterly data for category 1 above, except for the analysis of average prices by type of dwelling, over a period of 2–3 years.

Until 1979 the most detailed published statistics appeared in supplementary tables in various issues of *HCS*. A complete index to these tables will be found in *HCS* No. 32, 1979, pp.iv–v.

The *BSA Bulletin* gives quarterly analyses of:

1. Percentage of mortgages going to FTBs and FOOs respectively and the averages of dwelling price, advance and income in each case

2. Distribution of mortgages by age of borrowers, previous tenure (FTB/FOO), type of mortgage, house prices, income of borrowers, age of dwelling, type of dwelling, mortgage amounts and deposits of borrowers

3. Distribution of loans by region, together with the major average figures for each region
4. Average regional house prices at the mortgage completion stage.

Longer runs of these figures except category 2 above are included in the *CBSS*. The *Building Society Fact Book* also includes distribution data for the latest year for each of the main categories of data. In addition, it should be noted that each April edition of the *BSA Bulletin* includes a survey of building society mortgage data which draws heavily on the sample survey results. The results are also used to analyse particular aspects of the market in special articles from time to time. Collections of the articles from 1974 to 1983 have been published separately (BSA, 1980, 1982, 1984).

(c) *Interpretation*

Apart from the question of sampling error, referred to above, the main *general* point to note about the survey is its coverage. The figures relate to mortgages advanced for the purchase of single dwellings which are to be used wholly or partly for owner occupation. Unlike the lending data covered in Section 3.2, it does not include mortgages for purposes such as the purchase of dwellings for letting, the purchase of more than one dwelling at a time and further advances. It should be noted too that the tables will cover cases where the sale may take place at less than 'market prices', for instance sales to sitting tenants including, for recent years, purchases of local authority houses at a discount (a separate analysis of the latter for 1983 appeared in *HCS 1973–83*, Table 10.16). With regard to particular categories of data, the main points to note relate to income and prices. The income of borrowers is the total recorded income but it should be noted that there is considerable variation in the details recorded by different societies, e.g. societies sometimes record the basic income of the first applicant, sometimes the total income from all sources including that of spouse or other joint applicant(s). The interpretation of the average price data, particularly when used for comparative purposes as between regions or over time etc., needs to take account of the fact that the underlying mix of dwellings according to type, age, size etc. varies. The question of measuring price trends over time on a comparable basis is dealt with in Chapter 4 (sub-section 4.1.2).

3.4.2 Individual building society surveys

Many building societies publish regular analyses of the prices of the houses on which they themselves have made loans – see Chapter 4 (sub-section 4.1.2). In addition, supplementary surveys of special topics are made by some societies from time to time providing data on house and buyer characteristics for particular categories of buyer or particular regions. Major societies in this respect are the Nationwide Building Society (surveys since 1980 have covered lending in the major conurbations and local areas, lending to women, FTBs, council tenants who buy, and house-buyers moving); the Halifax Building Society (loans for council house purchase in 1984 in *Regional Bulletin No. 4*); the Abbey National Building Society and the Anglia Building Society. The main point to bear in mind in the interpretation of these data is that the transactions of one building society may not be representative of all housing transactions nor even of building societies as a whole though, as large societies, all have access to large data bases.

3.5 LOCAL AUTHORITY HOUSING FINANCE

Local authorities carry out many housing functions. They are of central importance as providers of 'council housing' and this section is mainly concerned with this aspect of their activities. We also consider statistics relating to the rates levied by local authorities on the occupiers of houses and other property in their areas. Other aspects of local authority housing and housing functions are considered as appropriate in other chapters: new building in Chapter 1, the housing stock in Chapter 2 and building costs in Chapter 4. Rent information is covered in Section 3.1. The arrangement of this section is as follows:

3.5.1 Housing revenue accounts
3.5.2 Capital and other expenditure
3.5.3 Housing management and maintenance

3.5.4 Sales of local authority dwellings

3.5.5 Rating statistics

3.5.1 Housing revenue accounts

(a) *England and Wales*

Each local authority is required by statute to keep a Housing Revenue Account (HRA) in which are recorded the annual revenue income and expenditure in respect of dwellings and other property provided under Part V of the Housing Act 1957. The main items of expenditure are: loan charges in respect of moneys borrowed for the provision or improvement of local authority housing accommodation, supervision and management expenses, and housing repairs. The main items of income are: rents (excluding rates and water charges), Exchequer housing subsidies, rate fund contributions, and interest income from the sale of dwellings. A summary table for local authorities in England and Wales is included in *HCS* and for all authorities in the UK in the *UK National Accounts* (Blue Book) in a Local Authority 'Housing Operating Account' (Table 8.5 in 1983 edition).

More detailed information, including details for each individual authority in England and Wales is compiled by CIPFA in *Housing Revenue Accounts Statistics* (2 volumes: *Estimates* and *Actuals*). In addition to the items indicated above, these volumes also give details of: (a) capital expenditure met from revenue; (b) stock of dwellings and gross value; (c) sale of council houses (number, selling price, amounts received); (d) rents, arrears, reductions, refunds (and, in the *Estimates* volume, proposed rent increases); (e) management and maintenance costs per dwelling; and (f) rates of loan interest.

More detailed information is published separately for capital expenditure (considered below) and for rents and rent rebates (considered in Section 3.1).

(b) *Wales and Scotland*

For Wales data are published in *Welsh Local Government Financial Statistics* and *WHS*. For Scotland the primary sources are *Scottish Local Government Financial Statistics and Rating Review* (prepared by CIPFA, Scottish Branch). Summary data are given in *SHS*.

3.5.2 Capital and other expenditure

(a) *England and Wales*

The HRA, referred to above, is limited to recording a certain range of current expenditure only: certain items of current expenditure are not covered and no capital expenditure is covered other than that met from the revenue account. A summary of expenditure covering these items is published annually in *Local Government Financial Statistics* for England and Wales covering transactions in both revenue and capital accounts relating to: (a) housing and land to which the HRA relate, (b) improvement grants, (c) other housing, (d) slum clearance, (e) advances under the Housing Acts.

Data on capital expenditure and debt financing for each local authority throughout the UK is published annually by CIPFA in *Capital Expenditure and Debt Financing*. This covers all services, but housing is distinguished as a separate category. Summary series for capital expenditure on housing by local authorities is also separately distinguished in the *UK National Accounts* – see Section 3.7.

(b) *Wales and Scotland*

Separate data for Wales are given in *Welsh Local Government Financial Statistics* and a summary in *WHS*. For Scotland, similar data appear in *Scottish Local Government Financial Statistics*.

3.5.3 Capital expenditure controls – the housing investment programme (HIP) returns

Capital expenditure on housing and other purposes by local authorities is controlled by central government. A critical appraisal of the operation of the current system will be found in Audit Commission (1985). Each local authority receives, in late December or early January every year, a capital expenditure allocation for the year beginning in the following April in separate blocks, e.g. for education, housing, transport etc. Summary details are set out in the annual *Public Expenditure* White Paper including a separate analysis of the construction component – see Section 3.6.

As far as housing is concerned, control is exercised through the HIP system under which each authority is required to submit a bid for the capital spending they would like to make in the following year to the DoE. It should be noted, however, that in addition to their HIP allocation, authorities may also spend a specified proportion of the capital receipts from the sale of council houses and land, although the expenditure of this money is not restricted to housing purposes.

The HIP system involves the return of four forms. Form HIP1 is a numerical statement of the dwelling stock position and of households in need under various headings: (a) dwelling stock (specialized, unfit, fit but lacking basic amenities, non-substandard dwellings in need of renovation, difficult to let dwellings, total vacant); (b) households in need (overcrowded, specialized needs, concealed, sharing); (c) HRA stock available for letting and relets; (d) applications for loans for purchase of dwellings in private sector. The other three forms are: HIP2 which is a request for capital allocation under a number of different headings giving details of past, estimated and proposed payments and use of capital receipts; HIP3 covering low-cost home ownership schemes and HIP4 which relates to expenditure on long-term vacant dwellings. A useful history of the system from its introduction in 1977 to 1983 has been provided by Leather (1983). Less information is now collected than before (the details above refer to the returns for 1985–86.

In principle, the HIP returns provide a very valuable source of information on the housing situation and its development over time at the local level. However, certain reservations must be expressed about the reliability and comparability of the returns, partly because of differences in the interpretation of the questions and partly because of a lack of information on which to base the answers. In particular, local authorities are likely to have more reliable information about their own stock of dwellings than for those in the private sector. The DoE itself stressed in a memorandum to the House of Commons Environment Committee that the returns were subject to gaps in provision and considerable local variability and, further, were essentially subjective giving only the 'local authorities' own views on the housing situation in their areas (House of Commons Environment Committee, 1980, p.62). It has been suggested too that the use made of the information has discouraged many authorities from investing in the submission in recent years (Leather, 1983). With regard to the availability of the statistical data obtained in the HIP returns, little of the information is in fact published, but copies of all the returns are deposited in the House of Commons Library so that the information is available in a limited way. Interesting analyses of the returns made in 1979, 1980 and 1981, using this source, were published in *Roof* (Crine and Wintour, 1980; Matthews and Shaw, 1981; Matthews and Leather, 1982) and an official summary of those made in 1979 was included in the House of Commons Environment Committee Report (1980). In addition, the DoE produce a printout, local authority by local authority, within each block of questions from HIP1 which makes it easier to extract information on particular topics. This too is deposited in the House of Commons Library. The information in HIP2 on capital expenditure and receipts is used in arriving at final estimates for England as a whole for the latest financial year, while figures for future spend are used in projecting expenditure and receipts (see *Public Expenditure* White Paper referred to above). Other than those uses, regional and national estimates of local authorities' lettings in 1983–84 and dwellings vacant in 1984 for England and Wales were included in new tables (9.7 and 9.8) in *HCS 1974–1984*. Lettings data were also included in the 1984 and 1985 editions of *Social Trends* (time series from 1978–79 and earlier figures from a former Relets Enquiry which was discontinued after 1977) and in the 1985 edition of *Regional Trends* (regional breakdown for 1982–83).

3.5.4 Housing management and maintenance

Detailed analyses of expenditure on housing maintenance, and supervision and management, with appropriate unit costs per dwelling, are compiled by CIPFA for each housing authority in England and Wales and published in *Housing Management and Maintenance Statistics*. Maintenance expenditure is broken down into six categories and supplemented with information on decorating cycles and the percentage of work undertaken by direct labour. In addition, information is given on the number of dwellings (by number of storeys), number of staff employed on supervision and management by function and rent collection procedures.

3.5.5 Sales of local authority dwellings

(a) *England and Wales*

Series are compiled by the DoE and by CIPFA. The DoE publish national and local analyses separately. National data, covering England and Wales, are given in *HCS* (quarterly). For local authorities these show: (a) the numbers of 'full-ownership' and 'shared ownership' sales (separately) distinguishing in each case dwellings built for sale, 'right-to-buy' (RTB) and other sales to sitting tenants, and other sales of existing dwellings; (b) the capital value of sales (net of discount); (c) initial payments received and (d) percentage discount (English authorities only). For new towns separate series show numbers sold (a) to sitting tenants and (b) as vacant dwellings. Details are also given for local authorities and new towns of the progress of RTB applications. The annual *HCS* includes a less detailed national summary of numbers sold only.

At the local level, analyses of the numbers sold and of the progress of applications are published by the DoE for each local authority in *LHS*. CIPFA publish financial data for individual local authorities in *Housing Revenue Account Statistics* showing selling prices (total and average), and amounts received as initial payment as well as the numbers sold.

Further analyses are available from 1983 of those sales to former local authority sitting tenants which are financed by a building society mortgage and recorded in the DoE 5% sample survey (considered in sub-section 3.4.1) to show the average price by region, by type of dwelling and by age (first published in *HCS 1973–83*, Table 10.16). Analyses of council tenants buying with a mortgage from the Nationwide and Halifax building societies were published by the societies in 1982 and 1984 respectively – see sub-section 3.4.2.

(b) *Scotland and Wales*

Data for Scotland are published in considerable detail in SDD *Statistical Bulletins* (HSIU series) showing number of sales by district and analyses of total figures by agency (local authority, new town etc.), by dwelling type, size and age, and analyses of valuations and selling prices (by type and size) and of the distribution of percentage discounts. Summary annual data by district are given in *SHS* of numbers by type, average selling prices and average percentage discount. Separate data for Wales are published in *WHS* showing the progress of applications under RTB legislation and average prices for all sales, each by district.

3.5.6 Rating statistics

Rates are levied by local authorities on all property, not just housing. The housing component, however, is an important source of revenue and an important cost for tenants and owner-occupiers. The rating records also provide an important source of information about the housing and construction stock and constitute a sampling frame for many housing surveys. Details are compiled annually by CIPFA in *Rate Collection Statistics* to show for each local authority in England and Wales information on: rateable value by type of property, rebates and other constraints on the collection of rate income (empty properties etc.), arrears, speed and costs of collection. Use of the rateable value records to compile data on total floor space in different sorts of property is considered in Chapter 16. Further information on rate rebates is considered in sub-section 3.1.3.

3.6 PUBLIC EXPENDITURE

3.6.1 United Kingdom

The most important sources for total public expenditure on housing in the UK are an annual White Paper on *The Government's Expenditure Plans,* which gives future planned expenditure and past outturn figures for a run of years, and the *UK National Accounts* Blue Book which gives a run of past figures. The White Paper provides analyses in considerable detail of current and capital expenditure by spending authority and by function. The Blue Book contains a less detailed summary in a table entitled 'Analysis of Total Expenditure' in a section on 'General Government' broken down as follows:

Current expenditure on goods and services
   of which: Wages, salaries etc.

Gross domestic fixed capital formation: local authorities
Subsidies
Current grants to personal sector
Capital grants to private sector
Capital transfers to public corporations
Net lending to private sector
Net lending to public corporations

Current housing expenditure is also distinguished in separate sectoral accounts in the Blue Book for Central Government (subsidies) and for Local Authorities (receipts and expenditure on housing, subsidies, rent rebates and allowances). Capital expenditure tables (expenditure on gross domestic fixed capital formation) distinguish investment in dwellings by: public corporations, central government, local authorities. Public corporations cover a large number of bodies including The Housing Corporation, New Town Development Corporations and Commission and the Northern Ireland Housing Executive which is responsible for all public-sector housing in Northern Ireland. These data are considered further in Chapter 6. Brief summaries of the accounts for the UK appear in the *AAS* and *Social Trends*.

3.6.2 Wales and Scotland

The White Paper, referred to above, identifies separate categories for expenditure in Wales and in Scotland (and also in N. Ireland). A detailed breakdown for Wales appears in *WHS* and the *DWS;* summary data appear in *WST* and *WET*. For Scotland, analyses appear in *SAS* and *SHS*.

3.7 HOUSING IN THE UK NATIONAL AND REGIONAL ACCOUNTS

3.7.1 National accounts

The *UK National Accounts* (the Blue Book) are referred to at several places elsewhere in this chapter in a piecemeal fashion. Our intention here is to give more systematic consideration to the way in which housing is treated in the accounts. We first consider the principles employed in their compilation and then the reliability grading system used before turning to the individual published series and their reliability.

(a) *Principles*

The basic purpose of the accounts is to give an overall view of the economy by providing a measure of total economic activity – the total value of goods and services supplied – and to reveal the interrelationships among different sectors of the economy through an internally consistent set of accounts. Total economic activity – gross domestic product (GDP) – may be measured in three alternative, but identical ways: as a set of production activities, as a set of factor incomes generated from these activities or as a flow of expenditures on production outputs. Each is employed in the Blue Book.

Housing contributes to GDP in two basic ways: as a direct production activity in the supply of new houses but also in the supply of services contributed by the existing housing stock. With regard to the first, new building is included as part of the construction industry in the production and income accounts and not separately distinguished. It is distinguished in the expenditure accounts, however, for these make a distinction between current and capital expenditure and new housing (unlike other consumer durables) is treated as a capital item and shown separately in gross domestic fixed capital formation (GDFCF).

With regard to the valuation of the services rendered by the housing stock, practical difficulties arise because so much of the stock is owner-occupied and, therefore, no payment, which could be regarded as equivalent to rent in the rented sector, is directly made for its services. Mortgage payments are not equivalent because these are merely related to the loan obtained for purchase and some houses are in any case owned outright. Even in the case of the tenanted sector, rental payments may not reflect market values because of subsidies. Allowances have to be made, therefore, for these factors in both sectors.

In the case of owner-occupied housing, the value of the services it provides is regarded as equivalent to the net income which could be obtained by letting the dwelling commercially. This value is imputed by reference to the rateable value of the accommodation, adjusted for changes since the date of valuation for rating purposes in line with the rent component of the index of retail prices (considered in Chapter 4, sub-section 4.1.4). For the rented sector, rents are adjusted to include the estimated value of housing subsidies. The estimates are based on the figures of aggregate rateable values of domestic properties compiled by the Inland Revenue (considered in Chapter 16, sub-section 16.1.2) and information on rents and corresponding rateable values according to tenure collected in the *FES* (considered in sub-section 3.1.1). For further details of the statistical sources and methods used in the compilation of the series, see CSO (1985) pp.77–8 and 247–8. Details of the published series and the reliability gradings assigned to the figures by the CSO are given below.

In addition to actual and imputed expenditure on the purchase of housing services, expenditure is also incurred on the repair, maintenance and improvement of existing houses. Here, however, a distinction has to be made between current and capital expenditure. Improvement work, such as the installation of central heating or the building of an extension, represents new capital formation. Repair and maintenance expenditure, on the other hand, is simply devoted to the upkeep of the physical condition of the existing stock and, therefore, does not represent capital investment. But in practice the distinction is not clear cut because repair and maintenance work may often involve an element of improvement. There are also difficulties in collecting sufficiently reliable statistics about such work and not until the 1984 Blue Book was the attempt made to cover all improvement work as part of capital formation along with expenditure on the acquisition of new dwellings. Before 1984 the practice was to include only that part of such work that could be readily identified, namely work in the public sector and *grant-aided* work in the private sector.

The estimates introduced in the 1984 Blue Book were carried back retrospectively to 1973. They are derived from information collected in the annual *FES* and in the 1981 *House Condition Survey* but it is important to appreciate that they remain subject to large margins of error because of small sample sizes and the difficulty of defining improvements work adequately. The *FES* figures relate to expenditure on structural additions, enlargements and other improvements, including the installation of central heating. Rough estimates are included for expenditure by private landlords and developers. The value of improvements incorporated in the capital formation series is not shown separately.

With regard to investment in new dwellings, unlike investment in other new construction, statistics of expenditure are not collected directly because of the difficulty of distinguishing how much of the expenditure relates to the dwellings themselves excluding land. Instead the figures are derived from statistics of the value of output collected from builders by the DoE (see Chapter 6). These figures have to be adjusted to match the conceptual basis of GDFCF statistics and the UK coverage of the national accounts by allowing for (a) work in Northern Ireland, (b) the inclusion of professional fees, (c) changes in work in progress by builders on uncompleted dwellings (included in output but not capital formation) and (d) changes in builders' stocks of completed but unsold dwellings. Directly collected information on the stocks of completed and uncompleted dwellings is not available and estimates have to be made. These estimates were reviewed retrospectively and revised figures incorporated in the 1984 Blue Book along with the other revisions referred to above. The capital formation tables are considered more fully in the context of construction work generally in Chapter 6.

A detailed account of the national accounting concepts and methodology is given in CSO (1985). This updates an earlier guide by Maurice (1968). These works must be supplemented by reference to the notes included in each Blue Book. We next turn to the question of reliability and then outline the published series.

(b) *Reliability gradings*

The reliability of the series included in the Blue Book varies because they are not all based on directly recorded facts. In some cases sample data are used, in which case the series are subject to measurable sampling error. But in other cases estimates of varying degrees of reliability have to be made which can only be judged subjectively. The CSO do not find it possible to attach gradings to every individual series. The gradings used are explained in the official guide (CSO, 1985, pp.21 and 84) and are defined as follows:

Grading	Margin of error
A ('Good')	+ or − less than 3%
B ('Fair')	+ or − 3%–10%
C ('Poor')	+ or − more than 10%.

In some cases a D grading is given to margins of error exceeding 20%. These gradings may be taken to mean that, 'in the opinion of the statisticians and in their present state of knowledge, there is, say, a 90% probability that the true value of the figure referred to lies within the limits set by the grading' (CSO, 1985, p.21).

The gradings relate to the absolute values of the various components. The error in the *change* from year to year is generally regarded to be less than might seem to be implied by the errors attached to the individual values (CSO, 1985, paragraph 3.41). In some cases constant price series are less reliable than those at current prices. It should also be appreciated that figures for the most recent years are often preliminary estimates and thus more uncertain than the figures for earlier years. For a fuller discussion of these matters see CSO (1985) pp.21–2.

(c) *The published housing series and their reliability*

For the purpose of presentation in the Blue Book, the value of housing services is treated as a separate 'industry' in the production account recording GDP by industry and in tables of 'index numbers of output at constant factor cost' under the heading 'Ownership of Dwellings'. The index numbers are intended to measure *changes* in the level of net output of each industry over time. No separate reliability grading is given to the former series (but see below for the separate expenditure data). The index series is graded 'fair for periods up to five years and poor for longer comparisons' (CSO, 1985, pp.44–5).

The expenditure accounts make a distinction, as noted above, between current and capital expenditure, and are more detailed.

(i) CURRENT EXPENDITURE. Expenditure by consumers is classified under the personal sector accounts and sub-divided and graded as follows:

Reliability grading

Rents, rates and water charges:
  Imputed rent of owner-occupied dwellings   C
  Other rents   B
  Rates, sewerage and water charges   A
Maintenance, repairs and improvements by occupiers:
  Do-it-yourself goods   C
  Contractors' charges and insurance   D

Total   B

(ii) CAPITAL EXPENDITURE. The capital expenditure series are incorporated in the tables of gross domestic fixed capital formation. Current price series are sub-classified by sector as follows: private sector (personal sector, industrial and commercial companies), public corporations, central government, local authorities (trading, non-trading). Constant price series are not sub-classified by sector. Deflation to constant prices is carried out using DoE output price indices. These are considered in Chapter 13. The reliability gradings accorded to the current price series are B for the private sector and A for the public sector (CSO, 1985, p.198). These gradings are said to refer to 'the later years, except for the most recent'. The constant price series are not graded.

3.7.2 Regional accounts

Details of the regional accounts are given in Chapter 12 (sub-section 12.1.2). With regard to housing, they provide annual series from 1971 of (a) the contribution to regional GDP from 'Ownership of Dwellings' and (b) gross domestic fixed capital formation in dwellings in England, Wales, Scotland, N. Ireland and in each region of England. They are published in *Regional Trends* and in *Economic Trends* from time to time (most recently in November 1984). For Scotland, the series also appear in *SEB* and *SAS* and for Wales in *WET*.

4
HOUSING COSTS AND PRICES AND THE HOUSEBUILDING INDUSTRY

This chapter falls into two parts. The first, and major, part is concerned with all sources of information about the costs of housebuilding, the prices at which houses and housing land are sold and the price indices for housing incorporated in the retail price index. The second part relates to the housebuilding industry.

4.1 COSTS AND PRICES: HOUSEBUILDING, HOUSES AND HOUSING LAND

The arrangement of this section is as follows:

4.1.1 Housebuilding cost and price indices
4.1.2 House prices
4.1.3 Housing land prices
4.1.4 Housing in the Retail Price Index.

4.1.1 Housebuilding cost and price indices

The distinction made here between 'costs' and 'prices' is the distinction between the costs incurred by the builder, excluding profits, whereas 'prices' refers to the price paid by the purchaser. House price series, based on the sale of both new and existing houses, are considered separately in the next sub-section. In this first sub-section we are concerned with indices which attempt to measure housebuilding prices less directly. Seven series are available – four relating to prices and three relating to costs. The methodology employed in deriving these indices is also used in the calculation of indices for building costs and prices in general. Therefore, consideration of the methodology and details of the indices themselves are given in the chapter dealing with construction costs and prices (Chapter 13). Table 13.1 in that chapter provides a summary guide to all the available indices. It will be seen that each series is given a reference number and grouped together under three main headings. The relevant housing series are as follows:

A. *DoE output price indices*
   New housing – public/private (ref. nos. 1(a) and 1(b))
B. *Tender price indices*
   DoE price index of public sector housebuilding (PIPSH) (ref. no. 5)
   SDD housing tender price index for Scotland (ref. no. 6)
C. *Cost indices*
   Building housing cost index (ref. no. 10)
   SDD housing costs index – Scotland (ref. no. 11)
   BIA/BCIS house rebuilding costs index (ref. no. 12)

4.1.2 House prices

(a) *The available data and publication sources*

Information about house prices, for both new and non-new houses, is available from a large number of sources. Much of it is derived from the transactions financed by building societies. Two general surveys of building societies are conducted officially by the DoE in conjunction with the BSA, but over recent years many individual societies have begun to publish analyses based on their own transactions. Official surveys have also been instituted to cover insurance companies' and banks' mortgage lending. In addition, professional bodies such as the RICS and ISVA make qualitative assessments of changes in prices on the basis of reports from their members working in the housing market. Altogether there are currently fifteen regular sources.

The data are presented either as average prices or as price

indices measuring changes over time. In many cases the data are broken down to provide analyses for sub-categories such as regions, or by type of buyer (first-time buyer or former owner-occupier) or by house characteristics (type, age etc.). Table 4.1 lists all the available series and publication sources together with other details about each series: the type of data (average prices or price indices), periods covered, frequency and whether regional and other breakdowns are made etc.

(b) *Interpretation*

The existence of so many different sources of data, much of it conflicting in the evidence it provides, naturally raises a problem with regard to the choice of series for different purposes. An up-to-date critical review and comparison of these sources has been provided elsewhere (Fleming and Nellis, 1985a and 1981). Our consideration here, therefore, is limited to a brief discussion of the main matters which are important for the interpretation and use of the data.

We first consider the most general differences in the nature of the different sources. Apart from a basic distinction between those which are based on actual transactions and those which are not, there are a number of matters that should be noted. First, the data based on actual transactions differ in the stage of the mortgage process – approvals, completions or valuation – at which the price is recorded. The time-lag between approval and completion means that approvals are more up to date as indicators of price movements; on the other hand, some approvals do not proceed to completion. Valuation-stage data are more up to date still. A second point to note is that geographical coverage varies. Thirdly, some data are confined to new dwellings. Fourthly, data derived from the transactions of individual building societies may not necessarily be representative of all building society transactions nationally. Fifthly, it is important to recognize that building society transactions, which provide the main source for most of the data, are not likely to be representative of all housing transactions because other institutions cater for different segments of the market.

Turning next to the use of the data, a fundamental distinction to be drawn is between their use for measuring price levels as such, and their use for making comparisons of price movements over time or of price differences among regions. Given the great heterogeneity of housing according to type, age, size etc. the comparison of simple average prices does not allow the comparison of like with like if the underlying mix of dwellings changes over time or differs among regions.

With regard to price *levels,* the most comprehensive source (in the sense of not being limited to any particular sector of the market) is the Inland Revenue Survey of Conveyances (Table 4.1, ref. no. 3) but it possesses a number of disadvantages by virtue of time-lags before publication, limitation to one week each year and its indiscriminate coverage of sales at both market and non-market prices (e.g. council house sales and other sales to sitting tenants, sales between relatives etc.) The NHBC series of average sales prices (ref. no. 13) is potentially useful inasmuch as it also is not restricted in coverage to sales financed by any one institutional source of loans. But it is limited in covering *new* dwellings only and appraisal of the series is hindered by the lack of information about house characteristics. Of the remaining sources based on actual transactions, the majority are limited to building societies. The part of the market not financed by building societies is not well documented. The only information about *average* prices in the non-building-society sector comes from a sample of insurance companies (ref. no. 11), banks only providing price-distribution data (ref. no. 12).

With regard to building societies, there are two official surveys both conducted by the DoE. One, the DoE/BSA survey (ref. no. 1) has the advantage of covering a longer time span than the other, of being more frequent (monthly) and covering *all* transactions financed by the main societies (currently those with 80–85% of the total assets of the movement). But only since 1975 has any sub-categorization been made between the timing of transactions (approvals/completions – previously societies reported a mix of the two) and between new and non-new dwellings, and only since 1981 has a distinction been drawn between transactions likely to have taken place at market and non-market prices. It permits no analysis of the influence of changes in the mix of dwellings on price levels. An account of the historical development of this survey will be found in the *CBSS* (fifth edition, 1984) pp.87–8.

The other official survey is the DoE 5% sample survey of *all*

Table 4.1 Sources of UK house price statistics

Source* and form of data Ref. no.	Mortgage stage†	Period covered and frequency		Coverage
A. DATA BASED ON ACTUAL TRANSACTIONS				
1. DoE/BSA BS4 survey:				
Index and average prices	Hybrid	1956–1975	Q	GB
Index	Approved	1970–	Q	UK
Average prices	Approved/ completed	1975–	M	UK
2. DoE 5% sample:				
Average prices	Completed	1968–	Q	UK
Weighted index	Completed	1968(Q$_2$)–	Q	UK
3. Inland Revenue:				
(a) Average prices	Completed	1973–	A	E & W
(b) Price ranges	Completed	1983–	BA	GB
(c) Price increases	Completed	1983–	BA	E & W
4. Halifax B.S.:				
Standardized index	Approved	1983–	M&Q	} UK
Average prices	Approved	1983–	M&Q	
5. Abbey National B.S.:				
Average prices	Completed	1976–78(Q$_2$)	Q	
	Approved	1978(Q$_3$)– 1981(Q$_3$)	Q	} UK
Weighted average prices	Approved	1981(Q$_4$)–	Q	
6. Nationwide B.S.:				
Weighted index	Approved	1946–	BA	} UK
Weighted average prices	Approved		then Q	
7. Leeds Permanent B.S.:				
Average prices	Approved	1978(Q$_2$)–	Q	} UK
Weighted average prices	Approved	1983(Q$_4$)–	Q	

Information based on mortgages with building societies covering currently 80–85% of total assets of building society movement. New dwellings only until 1975 then new, non-new, all.

Average prices and weighted indices based on 5% sample of building society mortgages. Present analyses run from second quarter 1968. Weighted indices cross-classified and weighted by 4 characteristics – see text.
Breakdowns: new, non-new, all; regions and, for average prices, dwelling type and FTB, FOO. Regional indices are published annually in *HCS*.

Based on all conveyances in one week only each year. Average prices may be derived from total numbers and value of sales. Breakdowns: region; FH, LH.

Based on reports by District Valuers on activity in their areas. Price ranges are quoted for four types of new property (semi-detached house-estate type, detached house-estate type, detached house individually designed and flat in 3 or more storey block) and five types of second-hand property (pre 1919 terraced house, inter-war semi-detached houses and bungalows, post 1960 semi-detached houses and bungalows, post 1965 detached house and post 1960 flat in 3 or more storey block) in selected locations (over 170) in England (by region), Wales and Scotland.
Estimated average price increases for new and secondhand dwellings by region based on the data referred to above.

Standardized indices (monthly for UK, quarterly for regions) based on estimates of characteristics-prices for 13 characteristics – see text. Average prices and standardized indices based on all mortgages approved by the society.
Breakdowns: new, non-new, all; region; FTB/FOO (UK) and, for average prices, dwelling type and age (quarterly).

Data cross-classified and weighted by three characteristics (type, age, region). Breakdowns: new, non-new, all; region; type; age; FTB, FOO.

Data cross-classified and weighted by four characteristics (type, size, age, region). Breakdowns: new, non-new, all and, for average prices, region, type, age (weighted averages) and FTB and FOO (simple averages).

From 1983, data cross-classified and weighted by two characteristics (type, region). Breakdowns: region, type.

(*continued overleaf*)

Table 4.1 (*continued*)

Source* and form of data Ref. no.	Mortgage stage†	Period covered and frequency		Coverage
A. DATA BASED ON ACTUAL TRANSACTIONS (*cont.*)				
8. Woolwich Equitable B.S.: Average prices	Approved	1979–	Irreg	UK
9. National & Provincial B.S.: Average prices	Approved	1979–	A	UK
10. Anglia B.S.: Index	Valuation	1974–	BA	UK
11. Insurance company mortgages: Average prices	Completed	1968–	Q	UK
12. Survey of banks' mortgages: Distribution of prices	Completed	1982(Q$_4$)	Q	UK
13. NHBC: Average prices	Completed	1981(Q$_4$)	Q	E&W
14. Kenneth Ryden & Ptners:	Approved	1983–	BA	Scottish cities
B. DATA *NOT* BASED ON ACTUAL TRANSACTIONS				
(8) Woolwich Equitable B.S.: Average prices	n/a	1980–	BA	UK
15. ISVA/FW: Housing index and average prices	n/a	April 1978–	Q	E
16. RICS: Price trends	n/a	1977–	M	E & W
(13). NHBC: Average prices	n/a	1981(Q$_4$)	Q	GB

Key: A=annual; BA=biannual; B.S.=building society; E=England; E & W=England and Wales; FH=freehold; FOO=former owner-occupier; FTB=first-time buyer; LH=leasehold; M=monthly; n/a=not applicable; Q=quarterly.

* Publication sources are listed below.

† Mortgage stage refers to the time at which information is recorded (i.e. at the approved, completion or house valuation stage).

Publication sources:

Nos 1 and 2: *Housing and Construction Statistics.* Average prices also given in *Compendium of Building Society Statistics* and *BSA Bulletin*

No. 3(a): *Economic Trends* May 1974, Sept. 1976, Feb. 1978, Mar. 1979, Mar. 1980, May 1983)

No. 3(b): *Valuation Office Property Market Report*

Comments

Based on actual mortgage offers but only covers selected periods of one month and is published irregularly. Breakdowns: new, non-new, all.

Based on mortgages approved broken down by occupation only. Breakdowns: FTB.

Based on prices adjusted by surveyors to allow for factors affecting comparability. Breakdowns: new, non-new, all; region; age.

Based on advances made by a sample of insurance companies. Breakdowns: new, non-new, all.

Average prices not available. No breakdowns.

Based on returns by purchasers' solicitors giving the purchase price of *new* dwellings registered with the NHBC. Prices recorded to nearest £'000. Breakdown: region.

Average prices for various categories of property in Aberdeen, Dundee, Edinburgh and Glasgow for which the Halifax Building Society gave a mortgage.

Based on surveyors' assessments for individual towns.

Based on valuations of 'typical' houses by ISVA members in England only. Breakdowns: region; type.

Based on reports on price movements within % bands by estate agent members of RICS. Breakdowns: new, non-new; type, age.

Based upon *estimates* of selling prices provided by builders when applying to register a dwelling with the NHBC *before* starting construction. Prices recorded to nearest £'000. Breakdowns: region; type.

No. 4:	*National Bulletin* (monthly) and *Regional Bulletin* (quarterly)
No. 5:	*Homes – People, Prices and Places*
No. 6:	*Nationwide Building Society Bulletin*
No. 7:	*Housing Finance*
No. 8:	*Woolwich Review*
No. 9:	*Occupational Lending Survey* (not published)
No. 10:	*Housing Market*
Nos. 11 and 12:	*Housing and Construction Statistics*
No. 13:	*Private Housebuilding Statistics*
No. 14:	*Scottish Residential Property Review*
No. 15:	*The Valuer* and *Financial Weekly*
No. 16:	*Press Notice. RICS News*

Source: Adapted from Fleming and Nellis (1985a) with amendments.

building societies (ref. no. 2) considered earlier in Chapter 3 (sub-section 3.4.1). This is limited to transactions at the completions stage but permits an analysis according to new/non-new and also according to type, size and age-band of dwelling (although only dwelling type analyses are published).

Individual building societies may offer the advantage of providing more timely data and breakdowns not available elsewhere, but may suffer from under-representation in some areas of the country and possibly bias from time to time arising from differential lending policies. In contrast to the DoE 5% sample data it should also be noted that most societies base their analyses on transactions at the approvals rather than completions stage. Another factor to note is the practice used by some societies since the adoption of mix-adjustment processes (see below), of publishing average prices (at least for *all* properties) in mix-adjusted form only (e.g. Abbey National, Nationwide and Leeds Permanent building societies).

We turn next to the problem of comparing price movements over time in the face of changes in the underlying mix of dwellings from one time period to the next. Until recently only the Nationwide Building Society and Anglia Building Society made any attempt to allow for this problem and thus to produce reasonably comparable measures. Currently, the DoE and three other societies also produce 'standardized' or 'mix-adjusted' series – the Halifax, Abbey National and Leeds Permanent building societies.

All of the series based on actual transactions except two (Halifax and Anglia), have approached the problem by the use of weighting systems in which house prices for particular subcategories of houses, e.g. houses classified by size, type, region, etc. are calculated and then weighted together to produce an overall mean for each period, the weights – representing the proportions of houses with defined characteristics in a base-period – being held constant. In this way the element of non-comparability introduced by a varying mix of properties is eliminated, or at least reduced, depending on the number of characteristics for which it is possible to allow. At the most, only four characteristics are allowed for in these systems: region, house type, size (rooms) and age group (see Table 4.1). In 1983, the Halifax Building Society introduced a more sophisticated standardization method in which the influence of some thirteen characteristics on prices is allowed for simultaneously through the use of multivariate regression techniques. The methodology was developed for the Society by Fleming and Nellis who have provided full details elsewhere: a brief technical statement (1984a), a short simplified account (1984b) and a fuller technical account (1985b). The methodology used by the Anglia Building Society relies on assessments made by surveyors at the time of valuation which allow for the influence of various factors on the comparability of prices between one house and the next.

With regard to the choice of series to use, the main considerations are the scope of the standardization process, the representativeness of the data base and the time span of the series. The Halifax series possess the advantage of standardizing on the basis of more characteristics than the DoE and other societies, use a more refined way of allowing for their influence on prices, are based on a larger data base and are compiled monthly. Their limitation to one society is a disadvantage but it is the largest society and is known to have reasonably representative national coverage. However, these series run only from January 1983. The main alternative choices, especially for historical series, are the DoE weighted index which has been calculated retrospectively back to 1968 and the Nationwide series which are available back to 1946. Both standardize on the basis of fewer characteristics than the Halifax Building Society but the DoE has the advantage of covering all societies. For further comment on the choice of series, and on the series not based on actual transactions, see Fleming and Nellis (1985a).

4.1.3 Housing land prices

Information on transactions in England and Wales for land intended to be used for housing is obtained from returns from Inland Revenue District Valuers and analyses are published by the DoE and by the Inland Revenue itself.

The DoE analyses, published in *HCS,* are, broadly, restricted to private sector purchases of sites with planning permission for a known number of plots (or dwellings in the case of flats) and to sites of four plots or more because they are regarded as forming a different market to that for smaller sites. The current series are as follows:

1. Number of transactions, plots, hectares
2. Simple average and median prices per plot and per hectare
3. Index of weighted average prices per plot or hectare
4. Regional analyses of the number of transactions by sector of purchaser (public, private, other/not known) and, for the private sector, analyses of area sold and quartile prices per hectare.

These statistics replaced earlier series covering periods from 1963 also published in *HCS;* these were described in *ET* February 1971.

The measurement of land prices, particularly for use in comparing changes over time and differences between regions, raises problems of a similar nature but much more extreme than those involved in measuring house prices on a comparable basis. A discussion of the problems in the case of land prices and the methodology adopted by the DoE has been provided by Evans (1974). It is pointed out that 'a perfect index for housing land prices cannot be calculated because any piece of land is usually sold only once for development and no two pieces of land are identical, so one cannot compare the prices of exactly similar collections of land at different times'. The solution adopted is to calculate weighted average prices and indices all estimated on the basis of constant average density. Further details will be found in Evans (1974).

The Inland Revenue analyses are published twice a year in *Valuation Office Property Market Report* together with regional market commentaries. They show simply average values by region throughout England and Wales of three categories of site: small sites, bulk land and sites for flats and maisonettes.

4.1.4 Housing in the Retail Price Index

Monthly price indices to measure the movement of each of the main constituents of consumers' housing expenditure are incorporated as part of the retail price index (RPI). The current categories are:

Rent
Owner-occupiers' mortgage interest payments

Rates and water charges, and
Materials and charges for repairs and maintenance.

The primary source of publication is the *Employment Gazette*. A convenient source for the whole series from 1956 (housing as a single category until 1974) is *Retail Prices Indices 1914–1984*. A general description of the RPI methodology and sources of information is given in CSO (1967) and updating articles in *Employment Gazette* (issues for October 1975, pp.971–8 and February 1978, pp.148–50). It is important to note that mortgage interest payments were not included as part of the RPI until 1974. The methodology employed for this item is described in a report by the RPI Advisory Committee (Cmnd. 5905, 1975). Currently, certain issues relating to the way in which housing costs are reflected in the RPI, in particular, whether rent should be measured net of housing benefits and whether the present indicator of owner-occupiers' housing costs should be continued or changed, are under review by the RPI Advisory Committee.

4.2 THE HOUSEBUILDING INDUSTRY

It is not possible to define a housebuilding industry as such because although many builders do specialize in housing work, many also carry out a range of other construction work as well. It is not possible to distinguish it, therefore, separately from the rest of the construction industry, except in so far as contractors are required to distinguish their housing activities separately in statistical returns. The most important source of information in this respect is the censuses and large-scale surveys of private contractors conducted by the DoE. These provide analyses of the value of work done on housing and the number of operatives employed, analysed according to size and trade of firm. For details see Chapter 11. Information about the housing activities of direct labour forces is also discussed in that chapter.

PART 2
CONSTRUCTION

–

5
CONSTRUCTION: DEFINITIONS AND THE STATISTICAL REPORTING SYSTEM

Having considered housing in Part 1, the rest of this book is devoted to construction and the property market more generally. As a preliminary, it is important to consider how construction work is defined and how the statistics are collected, for this determines the scope of the available series and has an important bearing on their interpretation. This chapter, therefore, is meant to provide this essential background information. Subsequent chapters then treat each main subject area in turn.

5.1 CONSTRUCTION ACTIVITY AND THE CONSTRUCTION INDUSTRY

In the first place, it is necessary to explain what is meant by 'construction' and to draw a distinction between construction activity and the construction 'industry'. The scope of construction activity is very wide, covering the erection, adaptation, repair, maintenance and demolition of buildings of all kinds, including their internal finishes and services, and also the wide variety of other types of structure embraced by the term 'civil engineering works', e.g. roads, bridges, dams etc. The collection of statistics about such activities presents a problem for, unlike many manufacturing activities, where the work is carried out by easily recognizable firms operating at a fixed location, construction work is carried out by a variety of bodies including not only construction contractors as such, but also by firms whose main activity is not construction (carrying out work for themselves as well as acting as contractors), by public bodies such as local authorities and public corporations, by building workers and other individuals acting in a private capacity in their spare time as well as by individuals on their own account (DIY work). Further, the work is carried out at a continually changing set of locations since a construction site is a necessarily temporary place of work.

In practice it is impossible to cover all construction activities comprehensively in statistical enquiries. For this reason it is important to draw a distinction between construction 'activity' and the construction 'industry'. Collection of the data for the latter is a much easier task than trying to cover all construction activity inasmuch as it involves collecting information simply from production enterprises whose industrial classification can be predetermined on the basis of a well-defined set of principles. Unless the definition of the industry is drawn so wide as to embrace all construction activities and the collection procedures are so reliable as to ensure complete and accurate coverage, the two concepts of construction 'industry' and construction 'activity' will not coincide. It is in fact the case that the construction industry is narrower in scope than construction activity. This distinction is, therefore, an important one from the point of view of data interpretation.

For statistical purposes, the construction industry is defined, along with all other industries, in the *Standard Industrial Classification* (SIC). This was first introduced in the United Kingdom in 1948 and has been revised subsequently on three occasions. The latest (1980) revision (CSO, 1979), designed to bring the United Kingdom classification into line with that employed by the Statistical Office of the European Communities (SOEC), defines the industry as follows:

Division 5   Construction

Class	Group	Activity	
50			Construction
	500	5000	General construction and demolition work

500   5000   **General construction and demolition work**

Establishments engaged in building and civil engineering work, not sufficiently specialised to be classified elsewhere in Division 5, and demolition work. Direct labour establishments of local authorities and government departments are included.

501   5010   **Construction and repair of buildings**

Establishments engaged in the construction, improvement and repair of both residential and non-residential buildings, including specialists engaged in sections of construction and repair work such as bricklaying, building maintenance and restoration, carpentry, roofing, scaffolding and the erection of steel and concrete structures for buildings.

502   5020   **Civil Engineering**

Construction of roads, car parks, railways, airport runways, bridges and tunnels. Hydraulic engineering e.g. dams, reservoirs, harbours, rivers and canals. Irrigation and land drainage systems. Laying of pipe-lines, sewers, gas and water mains and electricity cables. Construction of overhead lines, line supports and aerial towers. Construction of fixed concrete oil production platforms. Construction work at oil refineries, steelworks, electricity and gas installations and other large sites. Shaft drilling and mine sinking. Laying out of parks and sports grounds. Contractors responsible for the design, construction and commissioning of complete plants are classified to heading 3246. Manufacture of construction steelwork is classified to heading 3204. The treatment of installation work is described in the introduction to the SIC*.

* The description is as follows: 'The installation of items which can be regarded as forming an integral part of a building, e.g. an electrical wiring system, heating and ventilating apparatus, is classified to Construction.'

503   5030   **Installation of fixtures and fittings**
Establishments engaged in the installation of fixtures and fittings, including gas fittings, plumbing, heating and ventilation plant, sound and heat insulation, electrical fixtures and fittings.

504   5040   **Building completion work**
Establishments specialising in building completion work such as painting and decorating, glazing, plastering, tiling, on-site joinery and carpentry, flooring (including parquet floor laying), installation of fireplaces, etc. Builders' joinery and carpentry manufacture is classified to heading 4630; shop and office fitting to heading 4672.

It will be seen that the SIC is drawn up not on the basis of economic activities but on the basis of industrial 'establishments', and that these are classified to an industry ('Divisions' and 'Classes' of the SIC) according to their principal activity. An establishment is defined as *normally* the whole of premises (such as a farm, a factory or a shop) at a particular address. Thus if a firm carries out its activities at several different addresses, for each of which separate information is available, each will be treated as a separate establishment and classified accordingly. Further, if at a single address a firm operates separate departments, for which separate accounts are available, each may be treated as a separate establishment and again classified accordingly. Where a single establishment is responsible for different economic activities it is classified to an industry in accordance with its major activity.

In applying the principles to construction it is not the practice to treat each site as a separate establishment. The establishment will normally be the office address from which the firm operates and a single return will be sought from this address in respect of all of its site activities. It will be appreciated, however, that construction *work*, as such, is only embraced by the definition for the industry if it is carried out by an establishment whose major activity is construction. Thus the building labour directly employed by firms classified to other industries, and its activities, are excluded unless it is employed as part of a distinct building or works department for which separate statistics can be provided. Conversely the non- construction activities of firms which are classified to construction, such as the off-site manufacture of components, are counted as part of construction unless they are carried on by a department for which separate accounts are kept and which, therefore, can be separately classified to an appropriate branch of manufacturing. The direct labour forces of government departments, local authorities, new towns and transport authorities are covered (currently) but not those of other public bodies. Other notable features about the scope of the definition are that activities which require the use of contractors' plant and equipment are included, although they do not necessarily serve to provide or maintain a structure of any kind, for example open-cast coalmining was included until 1980. On the other hand some construction-type activities are expressly excluded.

It will be appreciated, therefore, that as a consequence of the basis on which the SIC is drawn up and the way in which particular activities are classified, certain activities of a construction nature are not covered by the official statistics for the industry while other, non-construction activities are included. In addition, of course, a substantial amount of repair, maintenance and alterations work to dwellings, and possibly also to buildings such as small shops, offices and workshops, is carried out by their owners or occupiers themselves and this too is not covered by the official statistics for the industry.

Since 1948, when the SIC was introduced, the general principles have remained unchanged, but certain changes of detail have been made to the scope of the definition for construction from time to time. For details see Fleming (1980a, pp.98–9).

5.2 THE REGISTER OF CONSTRUCTION ESTABLISHMENTS

The collection of statistics from establishments falling within the scope of the definition of the industry given above, naturally rests upon a register of such establishments. Unfortunately, from the point of view of data collection, there is no compulsory registration requirement and thus those responsible for the collection of statistics must rely on other devices for compiling and maintaining a register. This presents severe difficulties in the case of construction because the number of establishments involved is very large, most of them are very small and the population of firms is continually changing because of high rates of entry to, and exit from, the industry. The problem is intensified by the fact that the work is undertaken at particular sites and not at a fixed location, as in a factory, which means that there is not necessarily an identifiable 'establishment' from which to collect information: many builders do not operate from a recognizable business address and construction sites are necessarily temporary locations.

The large number of small firms in the industry is partly due to the widespread practice of sub-contracting parts of the work both on normal 'supply-and-fix' and 'labour-only' bases, and this in itself adds to the difficulties of reliable data collection both on account of compiling a comprehensive register and in actually obtaining reliable returns. This aspect of the problem has itself been intensified in recent years through the growth in the practice of labour-only sub-contracting (LOSC) to 'self-employed' gangs or individuals.

These problems became particularly important following the ending of compulsory registration with the then MOW in November 1953 and as a result of the growth in LOSC in the 1960s and early 1970s. It is misleading, however, to think in terms of a single register. It is important to appreciate that enquiries are conducted by different government departments on the basis of different registers depending on the field of responsibility of the department and the focus of the enquiry. As far as the primary source of data on construction activity is concerned – the enquiries conducted by the DoE – the register problem has been largely overcome with the matching of its register with the more comprehensive register of traders registered for VAT purposes which was carried out in 1982. The problem remains, however, of covering the majority of self-employed workers who are not recorded on the register. These issues are discussed further later when considering the nature of the data available from each source.

5.3 THE STATISTICAL REPORTING SYSTEM:
    AN OVERVIEW

Construction in the United Kingdom is served by a particularly well-developed reporting system: one which has evolved over a long period of time but in its essentials has now existed for over forty years, having been established during the Second World War. Full details of the early history are given in Fleming (1980a). Most of the statistics are collected, of course, by government departments. We do not confine our attention, however, to official statistics: we also cover data provided by semi-official and private agencies.

As far as the official statistics are concerned, the primary source of data is the DoE which is the 'sponsoring' department for the industry and is also responsible for all housing matters. Prior to November 1970, however, housing and construction responsibilities were divided between separate departments: the Ministry of Housing and Local Government and the Ministry of Public Building and Works. At this time these departments were merged into the newly-formed DoE.

The main statistical information required about any industry is information about its production and labour force. It is important to note, however, that the enquiries conducted by the DoE provide the *primary* source of official statistics about output and employment: they do not provide the only source. Information on these subjects is also provided by other departments as part of their responsibilities for collecting statistical data for industry more generally. In this respect the construction industry is unlike most other industries in being served by more than one department. Thus for some subjects there is more than one source of information, while for others, although there may be only one source, the responsibility may or may not be that of the DoE.

5.4 RELIABILITY

In considering the statistics available and their interpretation we devote attention wherever possible to the question of their reliability. But the sources of error to which a set of data may be subject are numerous and it is not always possible to provide more than qualitative guidance.

Errors may occur for a variety of reasons. For inquiries based on random samples the data are naturally subject to sampling error which may be quantified. Other errors may arise because of an incomplete sampling frame, incomplete response, errors in the completion of returns and errors in processing and in these cases it is not possible to quantify the margins of error statistically. These other errors may introduce both inaccuracy and bias. An incomplete sampling frame and response may mean that the sample data are not representative and may be biased in a particular direction. For example, deficiencies in a register of firms may mainly involve small firms whose characteristics differ from those of other firms. Likewise deficiencies in response may be unevenly distributed across the sample set. Deficiencies in the sampling frame may also lead to error in the grossing-up of the results. Errors in the returns themselves and in processing may be randomly distributed and offsetting, on the other hand, it is possible that some types of firm in particular may be more likely to make inaccurate returns.

It will be appreciated that, provided the magnitude of errors and the incidence of bias remain constant, the importance of errors may be much less in the measurement of trends over time than in the measurement of absolute levels at any one point in time. On the other hand, to the extent to which the measurement of trends requires the use of series measured in monetary, as opposed to physical, units which have to be converted from current to constant prices, the scope for error may be enlarged depending on the reliability with which price trends themselves may be measured.

With regard to the reliability of official statistics in general, an important development in recent years following reviews of government statistical services (Rayner reviews) carried out in 1979–80, has been a loss of quality as a result of reductions in sample sizes and in the frequency of inquiries and the ending of other inquiries altogether – see Hoinville and Smith (1982) and Mayes (1984).

As far as the construction industry itself is concerned, the problems discussed above confront the official statistician with severe difficulties for the reasons outlined earlier in this chapter: the fact that much construction activity is carried out by non-construction establishments, the difficulties that have been experienced in maintaining a complete register of firms and the statistical problems associated with the growth of self-employment in the industry and of transactions designed to evade tax (the 'hidden economy'). There is no doubt that construction work constitutes an important part of the hidden economy. The reliable measurement of trends in output and new orders is also hindered by difficulties in the reliable measurement of price trends.

It is important to be aware, therefore, not only of the inherent limitations of the available data but also of the difficulties that confront their quantification. We comment on these matters wherever appropriate and also report the official reliability assessments assigned to particular series wherever these are available. The main systematic attempt to grade the reliability of series is made by the CSO in relation to series published in *Financial Statistics* (using qualitative gradings) and in *United Kingdom National Accounts* (using a quantitative grading system in which quantified margins of error are assigned to at least some of the series).

6
OUTPUT AND
EXPENDITURE

Most industrial production statistics in Britain are collected from producers classified to industries in accordance with the Standard Industrial Classification outlined in Chapter 5. For construction there are two such sources:

1.   Enquiries conducted by the DoE
2.   Enquiries conducted by the BSO.

The primary collection responsibility has rested with the DoE and its predecessor departments (the Ministry of Public Building and Works between July 1962 and November 1970 and the Ministry of Works before July 1962) since 1941. The BSO has covered construction in annual censuses of production (ACOP) since 1974. These sources both provide output data which are in turn used as inputs for other series such as the index of industrial production and input–output tables. In addition a valuable source of information about construction work is available from the clients' 'expenditure' side of transactions as a consequence of the fact that all *new* construction work represents capital formation and is thus recorded separately in the *UK National Accounts* and in various surveys of capital expenditure. Statistics are also collected about new contracts obtained by contractors and the capital investment intentions of potential clients. These and other forward-looking statistics are considered separately in the next chapter. This chapter is concerned solely with actual output and expenditure data and is arranged as follows:

6.1 DoE output statistics
6.2 BSO Census of Production for construction
6.3 Construction in the indices of production and construction

6.4 Input–output tables
6.5 Capital expenditure statistics
6.6 Output data for specific types of building
6.7 Construction overseas by British contractors.

6.1 DoE OUTPUT STATISTICS

6.1.1 The available series

Construction output is measured by obtaining returns from contractors and direct labour organizations (DLOs) and is defined as the value of work done during a specified period. It does not refer to contracts completed. The current series has been compiled on a regular quarterly basis since 1955. With effect from the fourth quarter of 1979, however, an important development in collection method was introduced in which returns are sought for individual projects rather than for work done in the aggregate. This has allowed a breakdown by type of work to be made in much greater detail than hitherto and also permits an analysis by regional location of the work. Details of the series available back to 1955 are given in Table 6.1. It should be noted that this table gives details of time series only. Analyses of output by size of firm, trade of firm etc. which are prepared for one quarter only each year are considered separately in Chapter 11. A detailed history of the inquiries to 1977, including a full account of the series produced before 1955, will be found in Fleming (1980a).

6.1.2 Interpretation

The most important matters that need to be considered from the point of view of interpretation are as follows:

1. Scope and coverage of the collection procedures
2. The measurement of output, and
3. Problems of adjustment to constant prices.

(a) *Scope and coverage of collection procedures*
With regard to the scope of the data, we would draw attention again to the principles underlying industrial production statistics

discussed in Chapter 5. The essential point is that the statistics measure the output of the construction industry defined in accordance with the SIC and not total construction activity. This is particularly important in construction where much work, especially of a repairs and maintenance nature, may be carried out as DIY work.

With regard to the coverage of the collection procedures, it is important to draw a distinction between the data compiled under the new project-based system introduced in 1981 (with retrospective revision of series back to the fourth quarter of 1979) and the 'firm-based' system which went before. Under both systems the maintenance of a comprehensive register of firms is essential but problems arising from an incomplete register were more acute under the firm-based system because of the way the output returns were required to be made (for further discussion of this point see the sub-section headed '(b) The measurement of output' below).

The steps taken to maintain and improve the register of firms are considered in Chapter 5 (Section 5.2). Deficiencies in the recording of output due to deficiencies in the register grew particularly bad during the 1960s and early 1970s. Eventually, in 1973, very substantial revisions were made to the output series retrospectively back to 1963 (DoE, 1973). After 1973, improvements were made to the range of information sought in the returns from contractors on the register which enabled better estimates of total output to be made than before. This information related to the value of work done and payments made for work done, under sub-contract (see Table 6.1). As the deficiencies in the register relate to the small firms, many of which carry out work under sub-contract, and to work done by self-employed workers under labour-only sub-contract, this information was helpful in enabling estimates to be made of the 'unrecorded output' of firms and labour-only workers not on the statistical register. Finally, in 1981, the project-based system was introduced, the basic aim being to overcome the problems inherent in the previous system and thus to improve the reliability of the output estimates. The firm-based enquiry remained, for reasons given below, but the sub-contracting questions, introduced in 1974, were dropped in 1982.

(b) *The measurement of output*

The principle adopted for the measurement of output is to define it as the value of work done in a specified period as opposed to the value of contracts completed. Contractors are actually asked to return the amount chargeable to customers for work done together with the value of work done on their own initiative, such as the building of dwellings or offices for eventual sale or lease, and work done by their own operatives on the construction and maintenance of their own premises. Until the introduction of the project-based system, firms and DLOs on the register were required to make aggregate returns of all their contracts subdivided only into five broad type-of-work categories for new work and three categories for repair and maintenance work – as shown in Table 6.1. As noted earlier, this system, referred to as the 'firm-based' system, possessed certain disadvantages. The new system operates by directing enquiries at firms on the register, as before, but instead of requiring returns in the aggregate, focuses on individual projects and is able to overcome to some extent the problems associated with the previous system. We now turn to consider the methodology employed under the old and new systems in more detail.

As construction jobs generally extend over long periods of time, sometimes several years, the practice of requiring a return of the value of work done each quarter requires the partial valuation of jobs still under construction. In principle, this should present no difficulty, especially because in most cases in Great Britain (certainly for most *new* building and civil engineering works other than private speculative building and work on their own premises) contractors receive regular (generally monthly) progress payments during the course of a contract based upon valuation certificates. Valuations are based on measuring the work completed to date and a certificate is issued showing the amounts due when agreement is reached between the client's consulting architect or engineer and the contractor. Actual payments to the contractor are based on the valuation less a retention which becomes payable only after the completion of the contract.

Despite the existence of progress valuations for most work, there remain a number of potential sources of error. In brief,

Table 6.1 DoE output time series for Great Britain

Series	Frequency	Breakdowns	Publication sources Primary	Publication sources Secondary	Remarks
1. Contractors and DLOs: (a) Values at current prices (b) Values at constant prices, s.a. (c) Indices at constant prices, s.a.	Q	8 types of work*	DoE *Press Notice: Output and Employment in the Construction Industry* and HCS	MDS; ETAS; AAS (ann. ser.) ETAS MDS; ET; ETAS.	Estimates for Wales and Scotland appear in DWS and SAS respectively.
2. Contractors:† (a) All work – values at current prices (b) All work – values at constant prices	A	8 types of work*	HCS		
(c) All work – values at current prices	Q	8 types of work* x region.	HCS	*Regional Trends* (annual)	Series from 1979 (Q4) only.
(d) New work – values at current prices	Q	23 types of work*	HCS		
3. DLOs: (a) All work – values at current prices (b) All work – values at constant prices	A	4 types of work*	HCS		Series from 1969; earlier series back to 1963 are available on request from DoE, SCD. Series for the period back to 1955 but not broken down by type of work were published in HCS and former *Monthly Bulletin of Construction Statistics*.

* The types of work distinguished are as follows:

8 types: New housing (public/private), other new work (public/private industrial, private commercial), repairs and maintenance (housing/public non-housing/private non-housing).

23 types (for a full description of these categories see the notes and definitions section of *HCS*, annual volumes):

Public sector		*Private sector*	
Housing	Offices, garages, shops	Housing	Commercial:
Gas, electricity, coal mining	Roads	Industrial:	Offices
Railways, air transport	Harbours	Factories	Shops
Education	Water	Warehouses	Entertainment
Health	Sewerage	Other	Garages
Factories, oil, steel, warehouses	Other		Schools and colleges
			Agriculture
			Other

4 types: New housing, other new work, repairs and maintenance (housing/other work).

† From 1974/5 to 1982 the DoE also collected data on sub-contract work from contractors on the register as follows: Work done as sub-contractor, Work done as labour-only sub-contractor (to 1980), Work done for firms by other sub-contractors, Payments made to labour-only sub-contractors (1980) broken down by type of work (new housing/new non-housing/repairs and maintenance). Annual sries were published according to size of firm in *HCS* (annual).

they relate to the methods actually used by contractors for making their return and the fact that valuations may not necessarily correspond exactly with the value of work actually done during a particular period. First, until the introduction of the project-based enquiry, contractors were required to exclude from their return the value of work done for them by other contractors under sub-contract in order to avoid double counting. Such sub-contract work should be picked up in the returns from the sub-contractors involved provided that they were included on the register. The value of sub-contract work *is* included on the main contractor's valuation certificate *but not separately specified*. Overstatement can arise, therefore, when the main contractor fails to deduct such sub-contract work as is picked up separately on a sub-contractor's return. Understatement can arise when it is deducted by the main contractor but not picked up on a sub-contractor's return. The problems posed by the division of work between main and sub-contractor and a deficient register were tackled in 1974 by the inclusion of separate questions on the value of work done *for* them by sub-contractors and *by* them as a sub-contractor.

A further source of error may arise where, despite their existence, valuation certificates are not used for making the returns. Very little information is available about contractors' practices in this respect but two investigations in the late 1960s showed that only about half based their estimates on valuation certificates; the rest based their estimates either on costing systems, or on the number of operatives employed multiplied by a typical output per head figure, or the reporting of some fraction of turnover for the last accounting year. Even where valuation certificates were used, some firms based their return not on the value certified but on the cash payments received (i.e. the value less retention).

Finally, it is worth noting that valuation certificates themselves can be a source of error with regard to recording the timing of the work during the contract period. One reason is that valuations are based on the prices for the various elements of the work included in bills of quantity. These rates, however, may not accurately reflect costs of the work to which they relate. For instance, the rate for work required in the early stages of a contract may be pitched high in order to inflate income during the early part of the contract period and vice versa; apart from this factor, each rate may or may not include appropriate allowances for overheads and profits and 'preliminaries'.* Further, payments for variations to the original contract specification ordered during the progress of the work may or may not be paid for at the time they are carried out – some may be left for settlement at the end. For these reasons it is possible for there to be a lack of correspondence between the value of work actually done in a period and the valuation certificate.

On the basis of the discussion above it will be appreciated that the collection of accurate output statistics is faced with important practical and conceptual problems. A much fuller discussion of these matters will be found in Fleming (1980a, section 2.3). The project-based system of enquiries is able to meet some of these problems and we now turn to consider this system more closely.

THE PROJECT-BASED ENQUIRY SYSTEM. A full description of the project-based enquiry has been given by Wheatcroft (1981). In brief, the enquiry differs from the previous system in that information is collected about progress on individual contracts rather than the value of work done in the aggregate. Information about new contracts is initially obtained in a separate enquiry into new orders (considered in Chapter 7). A sample of these contracts is drawn each month and their progress is followed through to completion. The contractor awarded the contract is required to provide an estimate of the cumulative value of the work done on the contract to the end of each quarter *including, it should be noted, the value of sub-contracted work.* Thus the previous problem of underrecording output due to a failure to cover all sub-contract work, either through an incomplete register or other reasons, is effectively removed by this new system.

As the information about individual contracts includes specific details of the type of work involved and its location, detailed analyses by type and region, as indicated in Table 6.1, can be readily made. Previously, regional analyses could only be made by classifying all of a firm's output to the same region as its

---

* 'Preliminaries' are essential expenses which are incidental to the execution of particular contracts, e.g. insurances, fencing, the provision of temporary road-ways, site sheds, offices, canteen facilities, water supply, etc.

registered office address. Wheatcroft (1981) provides a comparison to show how misleading the old classification was – a bias towards Greater London being especially marked.

Certain problems, however, are not removed by the new enquiry. Repair and maintenance work – a major part of total output – still has to be based on the old firm-based enquiry system because it is not covered in the new orders enquiry and thus information about the repair and maintenance jobs coming forward is not available. As small firms are particularly important in this field, deficiencies in the register are likely to mean that this sector is open to greater margins of error. Also it is particularly important to note that *total* new output has still to be estimated from the firm-based enquiry because some new work is not carried out under a specific contract and may not be separately identified in the new orders enquiry. It is essential to appreciate, therefore, that in the aggregate the output series is still dependent on estimation to allow for unrecorded output by small firms and labour-only sub-contract workers.

(c) *Constant price series*

The great variety of different types of work covered by construction, and the lack of a standard product even within any one type of work category, makes the representative measurement of price changes over time especially difficult and introduces yet another source of potential error in the measurement of real (i.e. constant price) output movements over time. Over recent years improvements have been made in the measurement of price changes and new 'output price indices' were introduced for the purpose of deflating output values from current to constant prices in 1978 (retrospective revisions being carried back to 1970). It is inevitable, however, that the measurement of price changes should remain open to error and thus caution is still required in evaluating small apparent movements in the direction and rate of change of output in real terms as these may well lie within the range of potential error. The index used up to 1978 was subject to potentially more serious sources of error. For further discussion of the problems of price measurement, the price indices available and the measurement methodologies used, see Chapter 13.

6.2 BSO CENSUS OF PRODUCTION FOR CONSTRUCTION

6.2.1 Background

The purpose of the Census of Production (COP) is to collect information on a consistent basis for all industrial production industries (including construction) for a range of topics including not only production (or sales) but also purchases, capital expenditure, stocks, employment and payments for wages and salaries. The first COP was taken in respect of 1907. This system of enquiries therefore predates that established by the DoE and its predecessors for the construction industry (which dates, as noted earlier, from 1941) and covers subjects that are not included in the DoE enquiries which are restricted to output and employment. The latter are covered by the DoE, however, in more detail than in the COP and so the two enquiries may be regarded as complementary.

In 1970 the pattern set in earlier censuses was changed and a new system devised, though construction was not covered in the new system until 1974. We confine our attention here to the current system; a full account of the post-war censuses for construction taken before 1974 will be found in Fleming (1980a, section 5.3).* The main change between the old and new systems was the removal of questions about detailed product sales and purchases and the establishment of the new COP on an annual basis following a standard pattern. The most important development since then has been the introduction of 'slimline' censuses in 1980 designed to reduce the form-filling burden on industry. These involve fewer questions and an extended use of sampling. The sampling scheme used for construction differs from that used for other industries and from 1979 all firms employing less than 20 persons have been excluded altogether. It is proposed to hold more substantial 'benchmark' censuses every five years with the first such census being held for 1984.

The construction census is taken on the basis of the DoE register (see Section 5.2) and covers both private contractors and

---

* A summary of the statistics obtained from 1907 to 1970 has been published as *Historical Record of the Census of Production 1907–1970*.

DLOs. Reference should be made to the introductory notes in each volume which define the precise scope of direct labour coverage.

6.2.2 The published analyses

The results of the census for construction are published annually as *Business Monitor PA 500* covering the United Kingdom. A separate census is taken in Northern Ireland and the results incorporated with those for Great Britain. Until 1979 separate results were given for Great Britain as well as the UK. For the period 1974–80 a summary time series of the principal results was included in *HCS 1972–1982*. We now turn to the information collected and the analyses published. For this purpose we focus on the latest results available at the time of writing (those for 1982, published in 1984), and then comment on planned developments and differences from previous censuses.

(a) *Subjects covered*

The subjects covered were as follows:

1. Number of undertakings
2. Employment – Total
               – Employees
3. Gross output – Total
                 – Per head
4. Costs:
    (a) Purchases of construction and other materials, fuel and electricity and goods for merchanting or factoring
    (b) Wages, salaries and employers' National Insurance contributions etc. (separately distinguished to 1980)
    (c) Cost of industrial and non-industrial services received.
5. Gross value added at factor cost – Total
                                      – Per head
6. Capital expenditure:
    (a) New building work
    (b) Acquisitions and disposals of land and existing buildings; vehicles; plant and machinery
    (c) Total net capital expenditure.

(b) *Breakdowns*

Two types of breakdown are made covering each of the subjects listed above, apart from the exceptions noted below, as follows:

1. By industrial sub-divisions.
   Analyses made for all subjects except employees. Currently the sub-divisions are the five 'Groups' (Groups 500–504) defined under the SIC (1980); for details see Chapter 5, Section 5.1.*
2. By size of undertaking (in terms of total employment). Analyses made for all of the main subjects except items 4(a), 4(c), 6(a) and 6(b).

(c) *Operating ratios*

Ratios are presented according to industrial sub-division as follows:

1. Gross value added per head
2. Gross value added as a percentage of gross output
3. Gross output per head
4. Wages and salaries as a percentage of gross value added
5. Average wages and salaries of employees
6. Net capital expenditure per head
7. Net capital expenditure as a proportion of gross value added.

(d) *Periods covered by returns*

A percentage analysis of the twelve-month periods covered by the returns.

As noted earlier, the information collected in the censuses was reduced with the introduction of slimline enquiries from 1980. In construction, the number of questions asked was reduced from 32 or 19, depending on sample stratum, to 12. It will be appreciated, therefore, that more detailed information is available from the censuses up to 1980 than now. In the main this information provided more detailed breakdowns of costs. The planned 'benchmark' census of 1984 will again provide more information about costs and also employment and the

---

* Before the introduction of the SIC (1980) twenty-three trades of firm were distinguished.

composition of turnover.

6.2.3 Interpretation

Each census report contains notes and definitions which are important for purposes of interpretation. In addition a separate volume, published as *Business Monitor PA 1001* for each census, sets out in greater detail the notes for guidance and explanations. Apart from the guidance given in the official publications, the following matters are worthy of note especially in comparison with the corresponding DoE output data.

(a) *Gross output*

Unlike the firm-based returns made to the DoE (Section 6.1 refers), 'gross output' includes not only a firm's own output but also any work carried out for that firm by sub-contractors. These returns, therefore, overcome one of the problems faced by the DoE in firm-based enquiries in covering work carried out under sub-contract when the firms involved in doing that work are not included on the register. A further implication worth noting is that although the returns are now restricted to firms above a certain size, the effective coverage of output (but not employment) is wider because the coverage of sub-contract work in the main contractors' returns means that any such work carried out by sub-contractors below the size limit is covered.

(b) *Net output*

It is important to appreciate that the figure for net output included in pre-1974 censuses does *not* represent the net contribution of the construction industry to national output because it remains gross of inputs of 'non-industrial services'. The figure of 'gross value added at factor cost', which is calculated by deducting from net output the cost of non-industrial services received, approaches more closely the definition of net output, or value added, used in the national accounts statistics.

(c) *Coverage*

It is important to bear in mind the changes in the coverage by size of firm and in the use of sampling from time to time. Between 1974 and 1978 all firms on the register with 20 or more employees, a sample of smaller firms and all public authority DLOs within the scope of the SIC were covered. From 1979 the coverage was reduced to exclude all firms employing less than 20 and half of the firms employing between 20 and 49.

(d) *Timing*

Finally, it is important to recall that, unlike DoE data, the returns do not all relate to a calendar year as respondents may provide information on a financial year basis.

6.3 CONSTRUCTION IN THE INDICES OF PRODUCTION AND CONSTRUCTION

6.3.1 The available series

An index of construction output was a constituent index of the 'index of industrial production' until the introduction of the SIC (1980). The term 'production industries' is now reserved for those falling within Divisions 1–4 of the SIC and the combined index for these industries with construction (Division 5) is now referred to as the 'Index of Output of Production and Construction Industries'. The purpose of the index is to measure changes in the volume of output. Construction accounts for around one seventh of the new combined group and is therefore a particularly important constituent of the index. The principal index covers the UK as a whole but subsidiary indices are prepared for each country of the UK. The construction index is quarterly although the 'all industry' index itself is prepared monthly – the monthly construction constituent being estimated (as the output data are not collected monthly) and not published. The publication sources for each index are listed below. Methodological matters and questions relating to interpretation are considered in the next sub-section.

PUBLICATION SOURCES. For the UK the primary publication source is *British Business* but the index is first released in a CSO *Press Notice: Index of Output of the Production Industries*. Secondary sources are: *MDS, ET, ETAS* (long runs) and, for annual series only *AAS* and *UK National Accounts* (table of 'index numbers of output at constant factor cost'). Separate output indices for

Great Britain are noted in Table 6.1.

For Scotland and Wales the primary publication source is *British Business* but the Welsh index is first released in a Welsh Office *Press Notice: Index of Production and Construction for Wales.* The index for Scotland is also given in *SAS* and *SEB,* the latter including sub-indices (see below) and for Wales in *DWS* and *WET.* For Northern Ireland see the *NIAAS.*

6.3.2 Methodology and interpretation

It is important to note that the purpose of the indices is to measure changes in the net contribution of each industry to total industrial production. They ought to be based, therefore, on changes in net output (i.e. gross output less inputs of materials and services from other industries). However, such information is not obtainable frequently enough and a measure of gross output is taken instead. The measurement of gross output itself presents certain problems, particularly in ensuring comprehensive coverage of the industry, and a number of steps have been taken over time to maintain and improve the reliability of the series. These are discussed in Section 6.1. As we indicate there, the conversion of current price output series to constant prices in order to obtain a measure of real volume changes, is also beset by special problems. The indices are open, therefore, to important potential sources of error. In the past these have led on occasion to substantial retrospective revisions (DoE, 1973; Beckett and Glass, 1984). Despite recent improvements potential sources of error must unavoidably remain and the indices need to be interpreted in this light.

(a) *The UK index*

The index for the UK is a weighted average of the index for Great Britain and that for Northern Ireland. An official description of the method of compilation is given in CSO (1976b).

(b) *Indices for Great Britain and Northern Ireland*

A discussion of the output statistics for Great Britain and the indices based upon them is given in Section 6.1. The Northern Ireland constituent index included in the UK index was at one time estimated by the CSO on the basis of employment data and not published. It is now based on local output data. Recently, however, doubts about the reliability of the series for Northern Ireland have led to a major review with retrospective revisions being carried back to 1971 (Beckett and Glass, 1984). See also Fleming (1980a, chapter 9) for discussion of Northern Ireland output data.

(c) *Indices for Scotland and Wales*

The indices for Scotland and Wales are based on the data collected by the DoE (Section 6.1 refers). For Scotland six sub-indices are also published currently in *SEB* as follows: new housing (public/private), other new work (public/private), repairs and maintenance (housing/other). Descriptive articles will be found in *SEB* No. 10, 1976 and Welsh Office (1976). Until the introduction of the DoE project-based enquiry (with effect from the fourth quarter of 1979) a major problem was in obtaining reliable information about the actual regional location of work done by local or English contractors. The new enquiry provided a better method of estimating regional output. Previously, special steps were taken to provide estimates for Scotland and Wales: before 1971 by obtaining direct returns from contractors of actual output in Scotland and Wales and then by the estimation of forward-workload on the basis of new orders statistics. For further details see Fleming (1980a, sections 4.4.5 and 5.2.1.2). The price indices used for deflation purposes are the same as those used for Great Britain and involve the assumption, therefore, that price movements in each country are the same.

6.4 INPUT–OUTPUT TABLES

6.4.1 United Kingdom

Input–output tables are designed to show the flow of economic activity between industries. They show, therefore, the outputs of each industry and the inputs obtained by each industry from every other industry. The tables are published irregularly in the *Business Monitor PA 1004* series, the latest edition relating to the year 1979 (earlier tables in the series relate to the years 1970, 1971, 1972 and 1974).

Accounts of the methods of devising the tables are given in

the published source. As far as construction is concerned it needs to be appreciated that its inputs of materials etc. are drawn from a wide variety of other industries and that the amount of detailed information available about these inputs is limited. Before 1970 some information about inputs was obtained in the COP, but even at this time as much as 60–70% of the value of materials purchased by the construction industry remained unclassified (CSO, 1970, p.16 and CSO, 1973, p.6). Since then the information available has been reduced. For other industries the COP has been supplemented by a Purchases Inquiry but this does not cover the construction industry. As a consequence, the incorporation of construction into the input–output framework does require a good deal of estimation and the results must be interpreted accordingly.

6.4.2 Scotland

Tables for Scotland in 1979 were published as *Scottish Input–Output Tables for 1979* along with a full account of sources and methods. As far as the construction industry is concerned it should be noted that no independent information on inputs exists and that the tables therefore rely on the equivalent UK tables for estimation purposes. These tables succeed unofficial estimates prepared for 1973 in *Input–Output Tables for Scotland.*

6.5 CAPITAL EXPENDITURE STATISTICS

All expenditure on *new* construction work represents capital investment. Statistics about investment, broken down by type of asset, therefore provide an important additional source of information about construction activity. First, they provide a largely independent source of information about the volume of activity which may be contrasted with the production data obtained in the census of production and DoE enquiries. Secondly, they provide analyses by industry and sector not available from other sources. The most important statistics are those incorporated in the official *United Kingdom National Accounts;* these are considered in the following sub-section. The primary sources on which these are based are considered in sub-section 6.5.2. Investment in stocks and work in progress is considered in sub-section 6.5.3.

6.5.1 Gross domestic fixed capital formation (GDFCF) series

(a) *The series and sources*

There are two basic series, one for 'gross' and one for 'net' domestic capital formation (these terms are defined below) and each of these in turn differentiates between dwellings and 'other buildings and works' (as well as other assets). Both series are produced at current and constant prices. The gross series are available annually from 1946 (except that no breakdown between dwellings and other work was made for 1946), together with a retrospective estimate for 1938; and quarterly from 1954. The net series are available for 1938 and annually from 1948. For more recent years analyses have been made of the gross series by sector (public/private and institutional sector, i.e. companies, public corporations etc.), and by industry (or industry group). The net series differentiate dwellings only by sector.

The primary source of publication of the annual series is *United Kingdom National Accounts* (the 'Blue Book') and for the quarterly series *Economic Trends*. Convenient secondary sources (although these do not all reproduce the full detail) are the *MDS* and *ETAS*. Annual series only are also included in the *AAS* and in *HCS* (annual volume).

(b) *Interpretation*

We confine our attention here to the essential principles on which the accounts are based and other matters which are important for purposes of interpretation. Full details of the sources and methods used for compiling the accounts were set out in an official guide in 1968 (Maurice, 1968) and in a revised edition published in 1985 (CSO, 1985). Reference may also be made to a short guide by Copeman (1981) as well as to updating notes included in the annual Blue Book itself.

RELIABILITY. Current reliability gradings are given in CSO (1985) but for four relevant categories only as follows:

		Reliability grade
Dwellings	– private	B (3–10%)
	– public	A (less than 3%)

Construction industry   C (10–20%)
Transfer costs of land and buildings   C (10–20%)

These estimates refer to the series at current prices. Constant price series are less reliable but are not graded. No reliability gradings are given to asset groups other than dwellings, so there is no assessment for other buildings and works. For further details of the reliability grading system itself see Chapter 3, sub-section 3.7.1 (b).

PRINCIPLES. The term 'fixed capital formation' is defined as investment in physical productive assets that yield a continuous service beyond the period of account in which they are purchased. The term 'gross' signifies that no deduction is made for wear and tear, obsolescence and accidental damage (as regards 'net' statistics see below). The term 'domestic' denotes that the statistics are confined to assets located in the UK.

Capital formation also takes place in the acquisition of stocks and work in progress, that is goods awaiting sale or use in future production and partly finished goods awaiting completion. This does not represent investment in fixed assets and thus does not constitute part of GDFCF. In the case of the construction industry, of course, the goods it produces are primarily fixed assets (the exception is repair and maintenance works on existing buildings). But there is a timing difference between the execution of the work and expenditure on it; this is particularly important in the case of completed but unsold dwellings. Consequently, separate estimates are made for construction along with other industries. These are considered in sub-section 6.5.3.

Within the bounds defined by these definitions there are two important points of principle to note at the outset regarding the scope and nature of the series. The first is that investment in buildings and works is measured at the purchasing end of the transaction in terms of the cost to the purchaser – largely independently from the output statistics (the main exception is housing) which are measured from the opposite, 'supply', side of the transaction on the basis of returns provided by producers (contractors) of the value of work done. The capital formation series thereby form part of an integrated set of accounts dividing expenditure between consumption and investment. Henceforth, for convenience, we refer to the fixed capital formation statistics as the 'expenditure series' to distinguish them from output data. The second point of principle concerns the question of how far all expenditure on construction work ought to be included in the series, for it can be argued that not all construction work represents an addition to the nation's stock of productive assets. In particular, work of repairs and maintenance may be regarded as merely maintaining the existing stock of buildings and works intact and thus does not represent a net addition to the stock. In practice, however, maintenance work often involves an element of improvement which *can* be regarded as enhancing the stock. To accept the distinction between ordinary 'maintenance' and 'improvement', however, involves the difficulty of distinguishing one from the other in practice and renders the definition of capital expenditure somewhat imprecise. Despite this problem, the convention followed *in principle* in the UK accounts is to include the expenditure on improvements (including extensions and structural alterations etc.) as well as all new building, but to exclude all expenditure on routine repairs and maintenance.

In practice the part of repairs and maintenance expenditure included is determined partly by the accounting conventions adopted by clients in the industrial and commercial field for allocating expenditure between capital and current accounts. For privately-owned dwellings all such expenditure was excluded, except for that which was grant aided, because of the lack of sufficiently reliable information, until 1984 when a new series of estimates to cover all such work were introduced – see Chapter 3 (Section 3.7).

A further important point to note about the scope of the series is that it extends not only to the costs of the buildings and works themselves but also to expenditure incurred in the course of their acquisition, e.g. the professional fees of architects, surveyors, consulting engineers, solicitors etc. and items such as the cost of a clerk of works on large projects etc. They also include the capitalized value of interest charges incurred during long periods of construction. The cost of land, which is merely a transfer payment, is not included but the costs incurred in the transfer of the land *are* included.

CLASSIFICATION BY INDUSTRY AND SECTOR. The classification is based on ownership not use. Thus, for example, office building by property developers will be classified to the services sector regardless of the sector or industry to which the user belongs. With regard to capital expenditure *by* the construction industry itself, it should be noted that this extends to private firms in the industry only; expenditure by public sector DLOs is excluded.

DIFFERENCES BETWEEN EXPENDITURE AND OUTPUT STATISTICS. Differences between the expenditure and output series arise partly because of differences in geographical coverage (UK for expenditure data and the BSO census series, Great Britain for DoE data), or differences in the coverage of the industry (exclusion of some firms in the BSO census). There are also differences in timing between the two types of data – actual expenditure may not be coincident in timing, of course, with the actual execution of the work. Apart from these reasons there are a number of factors that help to account for differences between the expenditure and output series. We list the main factors here briefly; a much fuller discussion has been given by the author elsewhere (Fleming, 1980a, Section 5.4.3).

1.   Certain expenditure is counted as part of capital formation but not output, e.g. professional fees, transfer costs of land and buildings (separate series for the latter are given in the Blue Book).
2.   The expenditure series may include work carried out by firms which are not included within the SIC definition for the industry either because of deficiencies in the construction register or because construction work is not their principal activity. On the other hand, some work may be classified as construction output but not counted as capital formation, e.g. construction work for military purposes (which is conventionally treated as current, rather than capital, expenditure) and other work by contractors which is not related to buildings or works, e.g. open cast coal production,* the painting of plant etc.
3.   Next there is a group of what one might call 'allocational' differences. Firstly, the principle on which expenditure is

* Excluded from the scope of the SIC definition in the 1980 edition.

allocated between capital and current accounts will not be the same for all building owners. There may also be some incentive to classify work as current rather than capital or vice versa in order to offset expenditure against tax. Secondly, in the firm-based DoE output returns the contractor is required to distinguish between new work and repair and maintenance, counting as part of the latter 'improvements, conversions, extensions, alterations and redecorations' in the case of housing but in the case of non-housing work counting extensions and 'major alterations and improvements' as *new* work. It is notable, therefore, that housing and non-housing are treated differently and that it is up to individual contractors to decide what constitutes 'improvements'. Thirdly, work on demolition and site clearance is classed as construction output but the expenditure may be classed as expenditure on land rather than buildings.

4. On the expenditure side, the client may have difficulty in making an appropriate distinction between 'buildings' and 'plant'. For instance, some construction work such as the foundations for heavy plant is so closely associated with the plant that the work may be suitably classified as either one or the other, even though it may be carried out by a construction contractor. Again, tax considerations may also bias the allocation of expenditure between plant or building inasmuch as tax allowances or investment grants etc. may be available for one but not the other, or be available at a higher rate for one. In fact discrimination in this way has generally favoured plant over building (see Mellis and Richardson, 1976 for a useful account of the development of investment incentives).

5. In some contracts materials may be supplied to contractors by the clients and in such cases output returns will not cover the value of these materials but capital expenditure returns will.

6. Generally most expenditure on construction will flow to domestic contractors. However, the vast expansion of expenditure in the 1970s in prospecting for, and exploiting, oil and natural gas in the North Sea, in which contractors were involved in building drilling platforms and pipelines, led to a substantial expenditure by the petroleum and natural gas industry going to foreign, rather than domestic contractors.

6.5.2 Other capital expenditure series

The other sources of capital expenditure data available are, in the main, the primary sources on which the capital formation series considered above are based. They are notable, however, in providing data by industry at a lower level of aggregation. We consider the sources in two parts: surveys of industry and then public sector sources.

(a) *Industry surveys*

Information is obtained from two sources: the annual census of production (ACOP) and a set of other surveys. The ACOP covers all establishments in the UK engaged in industrial production (i.e. mining and quarrying, manufacturing, construction and gas, electricity and water supply industries). The results are published in a large number of separate industry reports in the *Business Monitor PA* series. The other surveys are carried out either quarterly, annually or biennially, depending on sector, to obtain quarterly capital expenditure data and also to obtain data for sectors not covered in ACOP, in particular, for distribution and services sectors. The results of these surveys are released initially as a *Press Notice: Capital Expenditure in...*[date] and then in more detail in *British Business;* the analyses of type of asset are given in constant price, seasonally adjusted form only.

(b) *Public sector sources*

The annual public expenditure White Paper: *Public Expenditure to ...*[year] includes series of past 'outturn' as well as future planned expenditure on construction in the public sector. For further details see Chapter 7 (sub-section 7.2.1). For local authorities, analyses of capital expenditure by asset are published in *Local Government Financial Statistics, England and Wales; Welsh Local Government Financial Statistics* and *Scottish Local Government Financial Statistics.*

6.5.3. Capital formation in stocks and works in progress

Estimates of the value of stocks and work in progress for construction and other industries are published by CSO in *United Kingdom National Accounts.* In principle these should cover stocks of materials and fuel and any work in progress not included in the estimates of GDFCF considered above (as we noted earlier, the fact that progress payments are made during the course of construction means that some work in progress is included in the GDFCF figures even though the assets are not yet in productive use). For the construction industry, therefore, the figures cover the value of work in progress that has not been paid for including stocks of uncompleted dwellings and also stocks of unsold completed dwellings. However, no estimate is included for the value of contractors' stocks of materials and fuel.

Three series are published: increases in book value by industry (i.e. physical increase and stock appreciation) and values of physical increases at both current and constant prices. The methods of estimation used are described in CSO (1985), p.212. Reliability gradings are assigned to the book value series only, that for construction being graded C (i.e. a margin of error exceeding 10%).

6.6 OUTPUT DATA FOR SPECIFIC TYPES OF BUILDING

Data for housing are considered in Chapter 1. Apart from that, the only data available relate to various types of building in the public sector.

(a) *Educational building*

Quarterly series are published in *Statistics of Education* for England and Wales, *Scottish Educational Statistics* for Scotland (to 1974) and *Education Statistics for the United Kingdom* showing value of projects by type, at different stages of progress, and the number of new places provided. Some of the data are also included in the *MDS,* indeed historically this was the primary source. Detailed notes about the series, important for purposes of interpretation, are set out in footnotes to the tables and in the annual *MDS Supplement.* It is important to note in particular that there are significant differences in the basis of the figures for Scotland as distinct from England and Wales.

(b) *University building*

Capital expenditure figures are given in *University Statistics, Volume 3 Finance.*

(c) *Health service building*

Capital expenditure on hospital and some other health service buildings is given in annual *Accounts* under the *National Health Service Acts* for England and Wales and for Scotland separately. The data cover not only construction work strictly defined but also related fees and equipment.

(d) *Road building*

Statistics relating to the value and mileage of new road building are published in *Transport Statistics, Great Britain.* Annual reports for each country of Great Britain are issued as *Policy for Roads: England, Roads in Wales* and *Roads in Scotland.*

6.7 CONSTRUCTION OVERSEAS BY BRITISH CONTRACTORS

A census of British contractors undertaking construction work overseas has been taken annually each April by the DoE and its predecessors since 1955. Data are obtained for each country to show:

1. Total value of contracts obtained
2. Estimated value of work done
3. Value of work outstanding at 31st March each year.

The results are analysed by geographical area and are published, along with a commentary on some of the outstanding contracts obtained and the firms involved, in *British Business* generally in October or November each year. The series are also published in *HCS* (annual volume). An estimate of overseas earnings appears annually in *United Kingdom Balance of Payments.* This was based upon the information collected in the DoE returns until 1982–83. Since then it has been based on the DTI 'Overseas Transactions Inquiry' – see Chapter 12 (sub-section 12.2.3).

7
FUTURE OUTPUT AND EXPENDITURE: FORWARD INDICATORS AND FORECASTS

In this chapter we consider the information available to indicate the forward load on the construction industry and the output forecasts compiled by various organisations. The chapter is divided into four sections as follows:

7.1 Value of contractors' new orders
7.2 Investment intentions surveys
7.3 State of trade enquiries
7.4 Output forecasts.

In addition to the data considered in this chapter, there are two other sets of data that record information about projects at various stages of the pre-construction process. These are: (a) the value of private architects' design work (considered in Chapter 15) and (b) forward indicators for specific types of building, in particular: housing (considered in Chapter 1) and educational building and roads (considered in Chapter 6).

7.1 CONTRACTORS' NEW ORDERS

7.1.1 Background and the series available

The contractors' new orders series is the most important immediate indicator of future levels of output. It provides a fairly short-term indicator, however, because it represents contracts already awarded and work on site on most contracts can generally be expected to start within a few months of the contract being signed. One limitation of the data as an indicator of total future output levels, however, is that they cover new work only and work to be carried out by contractors only: the work to be done by DLOs is not covered and, likewise, the substantial element of total output represented by repairs and maintenance work is not covered. Nonetheless it covers the major part of construction activity and is thus a valuable series.

The statistics are collected by the DoE from a sample of contractors on its statistical register. The results, grossed up, are available quarterly from 1956 (4th quarter) to 1963 and then monthly from January 1964. Until 1964 the data were collected under broad type-of-work categories, as for output (see Chapter 6). From 1964 the contractors have been required to provide details of individual contracts and this has enabled more detailed analyses by type of work to be made and also analyses by regional location. Indeed until the introduction of the 'project-based' enquiry for the collection of output statistics in 1981 (Chapter 6 refers), the new orders data provided the only reliable indicator of the regional distribution of construction work. A detailed history of the enquiry and a specimen form will be found in Fleming (1980a, Appendix VII).

The new system of new orders returns introduced in 1964 also allows analyses to be made of the number and value of orders received according to size and also of their estimated duration, although information about the latter has been published only since 1979. Full details of the series published are set out in Table 7.1.

7.1.2 Interpretation

We comment here on the most important factors affecting interpretation of the series under three main headings:

(a) Scope and reliability of the data
(b) Valuation of orders
(c) Deflation to constant prices.

Table 7.1 Contractors' new orders statistics for Great Britain

Series	Frequency	Publication sources		Remarks
		Primary	Secondary	
1. Values at current prices:				
1.1 National series				
(a) By 20 types of work and sector*	M	Press Notice: Orders for New Construction	MDS (to 1983 Q2); AAS (ann)	MDS included separate series for 'work not covered by orders' until 1983 (Q1).
(b) By 5 types of work and sector*	Q	HCS	MDS; ETAS (total only)	
1.2 Regional series†				
By 5 types of work and sector*	Q	HCS		
2. Values at constant prices:				
By 5 types of work and sector,* s.a.	M	Press Notice: Orders for New Construction	ET and ETAS (see remarks)	Series for housing and private industrial work in ET and ETAS plus total orders in ETAS.
	Q	HCS		
3. Index numbers:				
By 5 types of work and sector,* s.a.	M	Press Notice: Orders for New Construction	ET and ETAS (see remarks)	Total orders only in ET and ETAS.
	Q	HCS		
4. Number and value of orders by size: Percentage distribution of number and value of orders by value range by 5 types of work and sector.*	A	HCS Annual		
5. Number and value of orders by duration: Percentage distribution of number and value of orders by expected duration by 5 types of work and sector.*	A	HCS Annual		

* The classification by type of work and sector are the same as for output statistics – see Table 6.1.
† Regional series by 15 types of work and sub-regional series (66 in Great Britain) for all work are available on request from the DoE, Statistics Construction Division. For Scotland, series are included in the SAS and SEB as follows: annual series of 20 types of work at current prices and by 5 types of work at constant prices and by 5 types of work at constant prices in SAS and quarterly series at current prices for five types of work in SEB. For Wales annual series by 5 types of work at current prices are included in WET.

(a) *Scope and reliability of the data*

We suggested above that the new orders series is particularly valuable as an indicator of changes in the level of demand on the industry. The reasons for this are twofold and relate to the nature of the data themselves and the method of collection. First, unlike the value of construction output, a new order can be precisely defined at a point of time whilst the value of output, which inevitably has to be carried out over a period of time, will normally need to be based, at least in part, on estimates. In addition, until the introduction of the 'project-based' enquiry for the collection of output statistics in 1981, the method of collection of data on new orders meant that it was more reliable than output because of the problem of covering all the work done under sub-contract in the output enquiries. In the new orders enquiry, information has always been collected for the order as a whole, and not separately for such parts of it as are let under sub-contract. Thus the problem of ensuring full coverage by collecting information from sub-contractors as well as from main contractors, as in the 'firm-based' output enquiries, does not arise. Even now, it should be appreciated that despite the intro-duction of the 'project-based' output collection system, the figures for total output still depend on the 'firm-based' system (see Chapter 6). By their very nature, therefore, statistics of new orders are likely to be more reliable than statistics of output. At the same time, however, it is well to recognize that the new orders series has not escaped altogether from the difficulties of maintaining comprehensive coverage of the industry due to the problem of maintaining a comprehensive register of firms (see Chapter 5, Section 5.2).

Further scope for error arises, as in other enquiries, if the returns are not completed correctly. In particular, it is believed that some contractors, particularly specialist firms, fail to exclude all repair and maintenance work and sub-contract work from their returns. As a consequence, the value of new orders tends to be overstated and an adjustment is made to compensate for this (for further discussion see Fleming (1980a) p.136). On the other hand, the exclusion of all sub-contracts may lead to under-counting. Sub-contracts obtained from other construction con-tractors need to be excluded in order to avoid double counting. But those obtained from contractors who are not regarded as part of the construction industry should be included, otherwise the work is not covered at all. Express instructions to make such a distinction have been regularly given on the questionnaires since July 1967 but it leaves the contractor with the problem of making such a distinction in practice.

With regard to coverage of the data, it is important to remember that they cover orders received by contractors only (excluding DLOs) and for *new work* to be carried out in Great Britain. Work to be carried out overseas is covered in a separate enquiry (see Chapter 6, Section 6.7). The term 'new work' is defined, as in the case of output, to include such work as extensions, 'major alterations (i.e. improvements)', site preparation and demolition *except for housing*, for which extensions, alterations, and conversions work is excluded. Also as in the case of output, the value of building sites and the costs of architects' and consultants' fees are meant to be excluded from the returns. Included, however, is work to be carried out by the builder on his own initiative. This would be work either on premises for the builder's own use or work on buildings destined for eventual sale or lease; a large component of it is speculative housebuilding but it may also cover such buildings as shops, offices, storage premises etc. Cases where it is the builder's practice to sell plots of land and obtain a contract to build from the purchasers are also included in this category. It is worth noting perhaps, that such work is in a different category from other work inasmuch as it represents work *started* (currently)* as opposed to orders *received* in the case of clients. A quarterly series of the value of this work, referred to as 'work not covered by orders' was published in the *MDS* until 1983 (see Table 7.1).

(b) *Valuation of orders*

The value of a new order will normally be explicit, being the price accepted by the client, but there are certain instances where this is not the case or where the value has to be estimated. Work undertaken on a contractor's own initiative is one such case. Others are serial contracts (that is 'continuation' or 'run-on' contracts) in which the total value may not be known; in this

* Until 1964 it represented an estimate of work 'expected to be started' in the quarter following the enquiry.

case the actual value of work *done* in the period covered by the return is supposed to be included. In the case of 'package deals', that is work for which the builder is responsible for design as well as construction, the estimated value of the building, civil engineering and associated work should be included.

There is another aspect of valuation which it is important to note when using the statistics for forecasting purposes. New orders will be transformed into output over a period of time but the value of a particular job on completion (the price paid by the client) will not necessarily be the same as the original contract sum (the value which will have been recorded as a new order). There are two reasons for this. One is the fact that variations are commonly made to a job as it proceeds which allow the contract sum to be amended. The other is that a contract may contain fluctuation clauses which allow the builder to claim for increases in the unit cost of labour or materials, or both, which take place in the contract period. Cost reimbursement and measurement contracts too will generally have a completion value different from the original estimate. Some contracts, normally those which are expected to have a short duration, may be quoted at a 'firm price' but these may still be affected, of course, by variations to the contract. All this means, therefore, that the aggregate value of orders over time represents a varying mix of orders priced on the basis of different pricing systems, particularly important being the difference between fixed and variable price quotations. In general, the value reported as new orders in the aggregate is regarded as being likely to understate the amount payable by the time the work has been completed. For this reason certain compensating adjustments are made to the published series in particular to those for private non-housing work (again see Fleming (1980a), p.136 for further details).

(c) *Deflation to constant prices*

As we mentioned earlier in discussing construction output statistics, severe practical and conceptual difficulties are involved in the satisfactory measurement of price changes for construction work. These are discussed in Chapter 13 along with a review of the available price indices. These difficulties are particularly acute in the case of new orders. It will be appreciated that the aggregate of new orders consists of a widely varying mix of essentially one-off projects, varying not only according to type and physical characteristics but also according to the basis on which price has been determined. The price of each project will be determined not only by current factor costs but also by antici- pated changes in these costs, depending on the planned construc- tion period and whether or not a firm or variable price is quoted, and also by changes in planned profit margins which in turn will be influenced by the tendering climate and perhaps by the nature of the work.

Ideally, therefore, in order to deflate new orders to constant prices, price indices are required to reflect these twin sources of diversity and change in them over time. It was not until 1973, however, that indices were developed which approached these requirements. Until 1973, the index used for deflation purposes was the same as that used for the deflation of output – the DoE 'CNC' index (an index which has itself been superseded). Quite apart from its suitability as an output deflator, this index was not a satisfactory deflator for new orders inasmuch as it attempted to measure changes in the price level for currently- executed work rather than tendering levels for work yet to be started. In 1973 indices directly based on tender price information, rather than merely unit factor costs, were introduced and retrospective revisions were made to the previously published series back to 1970.

Deflation is now performed separately for different types of work as follows:

Public sector	Private sector
Housing (England and Wales)	Housing
Housing (Scotland)	Industrial buildings
Public works – building	Commercial buildings
Public works – roads	
Public works – civil engineering excluding roads	

The deflators used for the types of work listed above are con- sidered in Chapter 13. For the public sector, the relevant indices are the tender price indices listed in Table 13.1 (Part B, series nos 2 and 4–6). For private non-housing work special indices are prepared by BCIS. For private housing, the housebuilding tender index is combined with an index of house prices adjusted for movements in land prices.

For purposes of publication, the constant price series are prepared only for five categories of work (the public sector categories listed above being combined into housing and non-housing categories). This contrasts with the 20 types distinguished in the current price series. It will be appreciated, of course, that to devise separate price deflators for each of these 20 types would demand a much more extensive data-capturing system, especially in the private sector, than is at present available.

(d) *Summary*

In summary, two points should be stressed with regard to interpretation. One is that even at current prices it is difficult to know what precise meaning may be attached to the 'value' of new orders in the aggregate due to the nature of pricing for work yet to be done and, in particular, the variations in the mix of work with different anticipated construction periods and, within this, further variations in the mix of FP and VOP contracts. It should also be borne in mind that in any one time period the figures, especially those for specific types of work, can be unduly affected by the placing of exceptionally large contracts. At constant prices the difficulty is compounded by the problem of devising satisfactory measures of price changes. As we indicated above, important improvements to the constant price series were introduced in 1973 but it is important to bear in mind the inevitable margins of error that must remain.

7.2 INVESTMENT INTENTIONS SURVEYS

There are three relevant surveys, two of which are quantitative and one qualitative.

7.2.1 Public expenditure plans

Plans for public expenditure are published by the Government in an annual White Paper entitled *Public Expenditure to...*[year]. The construction components of the plans were not separately distinguished in the White Papers themselves until January 1979 (Cmnd 7439) but analyses were published independently by the DoE in *HCS* from the time of the 1976 White Paper. Figures are given of planned capital expenditure on construction for some years ahead and actual outturn figures for some years past. Coverage was originally limited to Great Britain but now extends to the United Kingdom.

These statistics are particularly valuable in covering the public sector comprehensively but it should be noted that, as the data refer to capital expenditure, new construction work only is covered; repairs and maintenance expenditure is excluded. It should also be appreciated that the data will cover contracts already in progress as well as new contracts to be let. They are also inevitably subject to changes in government policy.

With regard to the planning of public expenditure, a recent critical appraisal of the criteria used by public bodies responsible for investment in renewal, improvement and maintenance of major parts of the nation's infrastructure, namely roads and bridges, water mains and sewers, housing, the NHS estate, school buildings and the central government's civil estate, has been prepared by NEDO (1985). Background papers on each sector bring together much useful data about the size and condition of the stock in each sector and expenditure.

7.2.2 DTI survey of investment intentions

This survey is undertaken twice a year (three times a year until 1980) and provides estimates for up to two years ahead. Separate results are given for manufacturing industry and for distributive and service industries. They are first published as a Press Notice by the DTI: *Industry's Investment Intentions for...*[years] and then in *British Business*. A summary is also included in *Economic Trends*. The data obtained relate only to investment as a whole: they do *not* distinguish construction from other assets. However, the survey is worthy of note because construction constitutes a major part of total investment. A full description of the survey is given by Lund *et al.* (1976); see too O'Connor (1978). A comparison of forward estimates of capital expenditure based on these surveys with actual outturn has been published in *British Business* each year since 1978 (27 October) updating an original study carried out by Lund *et al.* (1976). The latter, in contrast to the regularly published series, incorporated disaggregated analyses by type of asset.

7.2.3 CBI Industrial Trends Survey

This is a qualitative survey in which member firms of the CBI in *manufacturing* industry are asked, among other things, whether they *expect to authorize* more, the same or less capital expenditure in the following 12 months than in the previous 12 months. Building expenditure is distinguished separately. General results, which are weighted to take account of the industry and size of response, are published in a Press Release: *The CBI Industrial Trends Survey*. Summary details are later included in *ET* as part of a table of 'indicators of fixed investment...'. Separate results for Scotland are published in *SEB*.

7.3 STATE OF TRADE ENQUIRIES

7.3.1 Background and interpretation

A number of trade associations in the construction industry carry out state of trade enquiries amongst their members. Their aim is to provide a quick qualitative impression of the direction of trends in trading conditions in their respective sector of the industry. The basic question which is common to all enquiries, therefore, is whether the anticipated volume of work or the level of orders or enquiries etc. is more, the same or less than in a previous period. Beyond this the enquiries differ in asking various questions related to current and future activity levels and trading conditions.

With regard to the interpretation of these enquiries, perhaps the most important fact to bear in mind is that the enquiries depend upon the voluntary cooperation of the members of the trade association concerned and are not generally based upon formal sampling methods. The results too are frequently not 'weighted' or 'grossed-up' to allow for the relative importance of respondents (although it should be noted that the results are often sub-divided by size of respondent). It follows that the respondents and the results may not *necessarily* be representative of the membership of the association concerned. In turn the membership of an association may not be representative of an entire industry or sector of it. We give brief details of the surveys currently carried out below. The most important survey is that carried out by the Building Employers Confederation (BEC) formerly the National Federation of Building Trades Employers (NFBTE).

7.3.2 BEC state of trade enquiry

The BEC is the central organization of employers in all sections of the building industry in Great Britain. It has conducted quarterly state of trade enquiries since the early 1960s. Currently (1985) they are based on samples of around 500 member firms and cover the following questions: enquiries received by type of work compared with the previous quarter, anticipated volume of work this year compared with last and current capacity of operations. The results are issued as a *News Release* which is widely reported in the trade and national press. Unweighted results were published until 1985 when a weighting system was introduced based on size of firm (in terms of the number of employees). Previous results were then retrospectively weighted back to 1982.

7.3.3 HBF state of trade enquiry

The House Builders Federation (HBF) is affiliated to the BEC and began a separate quarterly state of trade enquiry amongst its members in England and Wales in the middle of 1976. Questions are asked about changes in: current purchaser interest, visitors on site and net reservations, margins, starts (planned percentage change), demand constraints ranked in order of importance, mortgage availability situation and demand for labour. The results are issued as a *News Release*.

7.3.4 FCEC civil engineering trends survey

The Federation of Civil Engineering Contractors (FCEC) has conducted a national quarterly survey amongst its members since 1977. A return is sought only from firms which have civil engineering work on their books at the time of the inquiry. Questions are asked about: the state of the order book, employment, the amount of plant idle, materials and labour supply position, the number of invitations to tender being received and the number of tenderers on lists, and the future outlook for their business (estimated future business and estimated employment trend). The results are made available on request.

7.3.5 HVCA state of trade enquiry

The Heating and Ventilating Contractors' Association (HVCA), representing heating, air conditioning, ventilating, refrigeration, piping and domestic engineering employers in the UK, initiated bi-annual state of trade enquiries in 1975. The subjects covered are: the trend in the real volume of orders, the level of capacity working currently and anticipated, the volume of output compared with one year before and one year ahead, the availability of craft labour and views about tender prices. Summary results are issued as a *News Release.*

7.3.6 BMF builders' merchants index and trade trends survey

The Builders Merchants Federation carry out two state of trade surveys. One is a monthly survey by class of trade (heavy, light and mixed) and by region throughout the UK. Members return their total turnover figures for the month in question and these are aggregated, according to the divisions referred to above, and the results shown both as a 'rolling annual index' (i.e. the value for the previous twelve months compared with the corresponding period one year earlier) and as a monthly comparison of the current month with the same month in the previous year. The index is produced in two forms: one using the current values as returned and one using the values deflated to constant prices, using for this purpose the official DoI construction materials price index (see Chapter 14). Currently, returns are obtained from around 2000 members (representing, the author is informed, around 15% of the membership). The results are published in the Federation magazine *Builders Merchant* and are circulated to participants and to certain subscribers who pay an annual fee (the Federation reserves to itself the right to accept or reject applications for subscriber status from outside organizations). A summary statement of the results is incorporated in *BMP Statistical Bulletin* which is a collection of construction statistics compiled by the NCBMP from official and other sources.

The BMF Trade Trends Forecast, carried out half yearly,

includes questions on future trends in the level of trade and feelings regarding trade for the next six months and twelve months. Results are published in the trade and national press.

7.4 OUTPUT FORECASTS

Forecasts of construction output are available from four sources: the National Economic Development Office (NEDO), the National Council of Building Materials and Producers (referred to as BMP), the National Institute of Economic and Social Research (NIESR) and London Business School (housing only).

7.4.1 NEDO construction forecasts

Forecasts of construction output in Great Britain for a period of two or three years ahead are prepared by the Joint Forecasting Committee of the Economic Development Committees (EDCs) for Building and Civil Engineering every six months and published in *Construction Forecasts*. Separate forecasts are made for new work and repairs and maintenance. Those for new work are sub-divided by sector (public/private) by type of work (housing or non-housing with private non-housing being further sub-divided between industrial and commercial work). Those for repairs and maintenance are sub-divided between housing, public non-housing and private non-housing.

We give a brief account here of the methodology used for arriving at the forecasts based upon the account given by the author elsewhere, Fleming (1980a, pp.188–9). The forecasts are not based upon a formal statistical model. They are determined by informal consensus amongst groups of forecasters in a two-stage process. In the first stage, three panels (referred to as sub-groups) of people, drawn in the main from construction companies, building materials producers and employers and trade associations but acting in a private capacity, prepare forecasts for three separate sectors: housing, private non-housing and public non-housing. This forecast is a 'consensus forecast' which is arrived at after discussion amongst the members of each panel at a formal meeting at which, after presenting his or her own initial forecast, each member is invited to change his or her forecast in the light of the discussion until a consensus emerges.

Each member makes his initial forecast independently although each is provided with relevant statistical data and a background paper on the macroeconomic outlook. The second stage of the process is for the reports from the three sub-groups to be considered by the Joint Forecasting Committee of the Building and Civil Engineering EDCs, which may alter the forecasts made by the sub-groups, particularly in the light of developments that may have taken place subsequent to the work of the sub-groups. It is this committee (its membership is listed in the published reports) which gives formal approval to the forecasts as published.

The reliability of the forecasts is naturally a matter of some interest but no evaluation is included in the published reports. For some discussion of the problems of evaluation see Fleming (1980a, p.189).

7.4.2 BMP forecasts

The BMP forecasts are prepared under the auspices of the National Council for Building Materials Producers. They are published in *BMP Information* and provide a breakdown into six categories of work (five for new work and one for repairs, maintenance and improvement) for two or three years ahead (the final year in qualitative terms). Like the NEDO forecasts, these are also prepared by a 'forecasting panel' but are of longer standing than the NEDO series. In the case of BMP, forecasting panels were started in 1956 and meet two or three times a year. They consist of a small panel of experts and industrialists from firms and trade associations in the construction industry, as well as the staff of BMP. Like the NEDO forecasts too, the methodology depends partly upon statistical evidence and partly upon subjective assessments. Analyses are made of trends in the DoE series for construction output and new orders and these, together with consideration of the general economic and political situation and probable future trends, trends being experienced in forward demand for the main product sectors, coupled with the experience and expertise of panel members, are 'distilled' into the final forecasts.

7.4.3 NIESR forecasts

Forecasts for various industries, including construction, are made by the NIESR twice a year for a period two years ahead and published along with the quarterly economic assessment in the *National Institute Economic Review*. The construction forecast is based mainly upon the macroeconomic forecasts for gross domestic fixed capital formation but the final predictions are often modified in the light of the evidence from the forward indicators for construction which we have considered in this chapter. A full description of the National Institute's macroeconomic model is given in Britton (1983).

7.4.4 LBS forecasts

The London Business School (LBS) Centre for Economic Forecasts publish quarterly forecasts for a number of macroeconomic variables, derived from an econometric model of the economy, in *Economic Outlook*. The only forecast of direct relevance to construction is one for fixed investment which includes a separate category for housing. Other investment expenditures are not sub-divided by type of asset.

A useful appraisal of the LBS, NIESR and other models will be found in Wallis *et al.* (1984).

8
EMPLOYMENT

This chapter covers all statistics relating to employment in the construction industry. All other labour statistics, with the exception of those relating to wage rates, earnings, and hours of work (which are dealt with in Chapter 11) are considered in Chapter 10. There are seven general sources of employment data and these are considered in turn as follows:

8.1 Department of the Environment (DoE)
8.2 Department of Employment (DE)
8.3 BSO, Censuses of Production
8.4 Construction Industry Training Board (CITB)
8.5 OPCS, Labour Force Surveys
8.6 OPCS, General Household Surveys
8.7 OPCS, Censuses of Population

Three further sections deal with sources on special employment topics as follows:

8.8 Public authority construction manpower
8.9 Qualified manpower
8.10 Employment on research and development.

The seven main sources differ in a number of ways. The main sources are the DoE and DE, both providing regular time series for intervals of less than one year. The other sources are less frequent: annual, biennial and decennial. They also differ in their coverage of different categories of labour, in their coverage of the industry, in the scope of the data collected and in the range of analyses (relating to the characteristics either of the labour force or of the employing firms) that the primary data permit. Methods of collection also differ – some enquiries being

directed at the individual worker and others at the employer –
and these naturally affect the kind of data it is possible to collect
and the kind of analyses that can be made. We now turn to
consider each source in turn.

8.1 DoE SERIES

8.1.1 The available series

As we indicated earlier, the DoE is the 'sponsoring' department
for the construction industry and provides the primary employment time series. We deal here only with the series available
from 1955 because this year marks an important dividing line
following the ending of war-time controls over the industry.
Details of the pre-1955 history and series will be found in
Fleming (1980a).

In essence, the system used to obtain the employment data
has remained unchanged since 1955. Basically two series of
returns have been maintained. First, regular returns from a
sample of contractors (monthly to 1977 and then quarterly)
supplemented with returns from DLOs (see below) for the
purpose of providing a regular employment time series through
the year. These enquiries were also used on a quarterly cycle to
obtain figures broken down by type of work for both employment and output until July 1979. Secondly, it has always been
the practice too to extend the scale of these enquiries once or
twice a year (currently once in October). At one time this larger-
scale enquiry was conducted as a census and, until 1976, was
used to obtain detailed information about the occupational composition of the labour force. Since 1976 the occupational data
have been collected by the CITB, but the extended 'Annual
Return' has remained and, like the foregoing censuses, is used
as the basis for making analyses of the structure of the industry
(considered in Chapter 11).

Details of the current series and historical details of the pre-
current series from 1955 are given in Table 8.1. The series labelled
(1) derive from the regular sample returns; the series labelled (2)
derive from the CITB, the DoE 'Annual Return' and former DoE
censuses.

Table 8.1 DoE employment statistics for Great Britain

Series	Current series dates and frequency	Historical details and remarks
1. Regular time series:		
1.1 Employees in Employment		
(a) Contractors – Operatives	1955–77(M), then (Q)	Broken down by type of work, quarterly, to July 1979.
APTC	From 1955(Q)	
(b) Pub. Auths – Operatives	1967–72(A), then (Q)	Quarterly series interpolated in half-yearly returns until 1982 when quarterly frequency introduced.
APTC	1967–72(A), then (Q)	Monthly (estimates) from 1971 to 1977 and monthly averages back to 1967.
(c) Total	1967–72(A), then (Q) (see remarks)	
1.2 Self-employed	From 1975 (biennial) (see remarks)	Quarterly series (introduced in *HCS* No. 25, 1978) of Working Principals and DoE *estimates* of total self-employed ran from 1973 to 1982 (April). Annual estimates may be carried back to 1967 (*HCS* No. 6, 1973 Supp. Table 1). Current figures rely on data obtained in the LFS.
1.3 All manpower	From 1975 (Biennial) (see remarks)	Historical series depends on availability of estimates for self-employed labour – see above.
2. Annual analyses (see remarks):		Available for particular months only each year – currently October.
2.1 Contractors:		
Operatives by craft	From 1957(A)	Collected by CITB since 1977 – see text. Details of sub-classifications of these data by trade of firm etc. and pre-current publication sources are given in Table 11.1
Apprentices (trainees) by craft	From 1957(A)	
APTC staff by type	From 1965(A)	
Working Principals (Proprietors)	From 1963(A)	
2.2 Local authorities' direct labour	See Table 11.2	

Current publication source: *Housing and Construction Statistics.*

8.1.2 Interpretation

(a) *Scope and coverage*

With regard to the interpretation and use of the data, the most important matters to note relate to the scope and coverage of the series. As with the output statistics (Section 6.1 refers), a major problem over time has been the difficulty in ensuring complete coverage of all construction labour because of an incomplete register of firms and incomplete coverage of labour working under labour-only sub-contract. Complete coverage is still not obtained in the returns but estimates are now made of unrecorded labour. These were introduced in 1978 (*HCS* No. 25) and carried back retrospectively to 1973. However, it should be noted that the series of operatives employed by contractors by type of work (now discontinued) – series 1.1(a) in Table 8.1 – incorporated no such estimates and neither do the annual analyses listed as series 2.1. More recently (particularly in 1981 and 1982), cross-matching of the DoE register with that maintained for VAT purposes has done much to remedy the register problem, though it needs to be appreciated that the register does not cover the majority of self-employed workers.

The current series for self-employed construction workers are estimates based on the statistics collected in the censuses of population (see Section 8.6) and Labour Force Surveys (see Section 8.5). The pre-current quarterly series was based, in addition, on information about the number of Working Proprietors and payments made to labour-only sub-contract workers which was obtained in the DoE firm-based returns. It is important to note that the series for Working Proprietors covers only those whose firms are on the DoE's statistical register.

(b) *Definitions*

Definitions of the main labour categories – operatives, trainees, APTC staff and Working Proprietors (formerly Working Principals) – are given in *HCS* (annual volume).

(c) *DLOs*

It is important to note that the coverage of DLOs has changed under successive revisions of the SIC. Under the current, 1980, version coverage extends to government departments, local authorities, new towns and nationalized industries in the transport sector ('where information is available'). Coverage within these authorities is meant to extend to all employees engaged mainly on construction work, whether or not they are employed in a separate building department of the authority. For details of changes in the scope of the SIC definition over time, see Chapter 5 (Section 5.1). The frequency of the DLO returns was increased from half yearly to quarterly in 1982.

8.2 DEPARTMENT OF EMPLOYMENT (DE) SERIES

8.2.1 The principal employment series

The Department of Employment is the department with the primary responsibility for the compilation of labour statistics for the whole economy. In this role it collects employment data for construction along with other industries on a consistent basis. Until the Second World War these statistics were the only regular source of employment data. As noted above, however, they were supplemented from 1941, as far as construction was concerned, by the statistics collected by the then Ministry of Works (now the DoE) which then became the primary source of statistics for the industry. The series compiled by the two bodies do not necessarily agree, largely because of differences in the methods of collection.

(a) *The series available and sources*

The current DE series run from June 1971 and relate solely to employees in employment (periodic estimates only are made for the self-employed – see below). They are as follows:

1. *National (GB and UK) series:* monthly – males*, females (all/part–time).
2. *Regional series:* quarterly – totals.

With the introduction of the 1980 SIC (*Employment Gazette,* December 1983) the series for construction have been subdivided into four sub-sectors.

---

* Annual/triennial census analyses also distinguish between full-time and part-time employment for males as well as females.

The series are based partly on 'censuses of employment', taken annually up to 1978 and then triennially, which provide benchmark figures. The monthly and quarterly series are obtained by extrapolation from, and interpolation between, the benchmark figures. In the case of construction, the DoE series (discussed above) are used for this purpose; since the ending of DoE monthly enquiries at the end of 1977 the monthly series have been determined by interpolation between the DoE quarterly estimates (*Employment Gazette*, 1978, p.511).

Before June 1971 three series were compiled on the basis of an annual count of national insurance cards, each on GB and UK bases, with estimates made for months between counts, as follows:

1. Numbers in employment = 'employees in employment' plus the self-employed (estimated since not all self-employed were covered by the national insurance scheme). This series was discontinued after November 1965.
2. Employees = employed persons (as distinct from the self-employed) for whom cards were exchanged *(including, the unemployed)* sub-classified by sex, region and two age groups (under/over 18 years).
3. Employees in employment = 'employees' minus *registered* unemployed, sub-classified by sex.

The last count of national insurance cards was held in June 1971 in parallel with the new census of employment in order to provide a link with the new series, but there is nonetheless an important discontinuity at this point (see below).

Estimated series for the self-employed and other subsidiary DE series are considered in sub-section 8.2.2.

PUBLICATION SOURCES. The primary publication source is the *Employment Gazette*. The series up to 1968 are conveniently brought together in the *British Labour Statistics Historical Abstract, 1886–1968* and continued in subsequent *BLS Yearbooks*. An *Historical Supplement* issued with the *Gazette* for August 1984 provides long-run series (part annual and part quarterly) for various periods, according to series, from June 1971 to March 1984 for national series and from June 1977 to March 1984 for regional series. The main secondary sources for the national series are the *MDS* and the *AAS* (annual series) and *Regional Trends* for the regional series.

(b) *Interpretation*

Our discussion here is confined to the current, census-of-employment, series from 1971. A full discussion of the previous, card-count, series from 1948 to 1971, and of the discontinuity in 1971, will be found in Fleming (1980a).

The census of employment is taken by means of a postal enquiry of employers. For this purpose the list of employers used is the list of 'pay points' from which employers send their PAYE payments to the Inland Revenue. Each pay point is asked to show on the return the numbers of *employees* for whom it holds pay records (not merely those for whom it pays tax – some employees, of course, may not come above tax thresholds). Thus the census may be said to measure jobs rather than people – a person with say two regular jobs with different employers in the census week would be counted twice. Coverage extends to employees who are temporarily absent due to sickness, holidays, short-time, stoppages or any other reason, whether or not they are being paid. Employers are also asked to include employees who did not work on the census day but whom they employ regularly and who would work for them on some other day in the census week. In addition to the unemployed, who are automatically excluded, the following categories (amongst others not relevant to construction) are specifically excluded from the returns: working proprietors; partners; the self-employed; directors not under a contract of service; wives working for husbands; husbands working for wives; and former employees still on the payroll as pensioners only.

Apart from any errors that may arise from double counting persons with two jobs in the census week, the series are open to other potential sources of error. One relates to the coverage of small firms. Even under the annual census system small pay-points (less than three employees) were covered only every third year, it being assumed that the aggregate number of employees involved did not vary significantly between full censuses. Small firms are, of course, particularly numerous in the construction industry and subject to change because of the ease of entry and exit. Further, the desire to evade tax payments that has contributed to the growth of self-employment in the construction industry may also mean that some employers do not appear on the list of pay-points and therefore their employees would not be counted in the census. Another source of error concerns census information supplied by non-construction firms which may not identify separately a construction department and the employees concerned will then be wrongly classified to a non-construction activity. This is certainly a problem in the case of direct labour employed by public authorities which tends to be classified to the sector appropriate to the authority (national or local government etc.) rather than construction. Finally, of course, the extrapolated and interpolated series will be open to the same sources of error, with regard to movement over time, that may have afflicted the DoE series from time to time – see Section 8.1.

REGIONAL CLASSIFICATION. With regard to regional classification, employers are asked to give the numbers of employees working at each of their business addresses (sites in construction), but the necessity for contractors to sub-divide their returns is an obvious source of potential error. However, it seems likely that the classification is more reliable than under the previous card-count system (Fleming, 1980a).

CONTINUOUS SERIES 1959–73. The DE has attempted to overcome the discontinuity in the series in 1971 by using the information provided by the parallel enquiries of June 1971 to adjust the earlier series so as to provide continuous series at both the national and regional level. Adjustments are also made to allow for earlier sources of discontinuity including revisions to the SIC. An account of the adjustments (together with the series for Great Britain) is given in the *Department of Employment Gazette,* March 1975; series for the UK and a regional series (covering the period 1965–75 only) were published in the *Gazette* in October 1975 and August 1976 respectively. However, the estimates provided in these series must be used with caution for they depend, as is stressed in the article itself, upon the assumption that the relationship between the old and the new series at the time of the discontinuity can be applied retrospectively to the whole of the earlier series. The regional series for construction are especially open to doubt for the reason given earlier.

8.2.2 Subsidiary DE employment series

(a) *Series for the self-employed from 1961*

Estimates of the number of self-employed persons (i.e. persons working on their own account with or without employees) for construction and other industries in Great Britain are prepared from time to time. The estimates are made, according to sex, by using data from the censuses of population as benchmark figures and information from the DoE (numbers of Working Principals) to 1974 and from the Labour Force Surveys from 1973 for interpolation and extrapolation purposes. The figures have been published in various issues of the *Employment Gazette* as follows:

Years and frequency	*Date of Gazette*
1961–74 (A)	December 1976
1971–75 (A)	
1977–81 (Biennial)	June 1983*
1981, 1983, 1984	March 1985

Reference should be made to the issues of the *Gazette* cited above for a description of the estimation methods used. It is important to recognize that the construction estimates are open to a substantial margin of error. It is notable that the estimate for 1981 obtained by updating from the 1971 base and also from the *LFS* are both much higher than the figure obtained from the 1981 census of population. However, it is suggested that under-counting may have occurred in the 1981 census and that this affected construction more than other industries.

(b) *Local authority manpower*

This series, initiated by the DE (and still published in the *Employment Gazette)* is discussed in sub-section 8.7.1 as it is no longer compiled by the Department.

(c) *Age analyses*

Annual analyses of the age distribution of employees by sex in

---

* *N.B.* Incorporates revised estimates and replaces series for the period 1971–79 published in January 1982.

Great Britain were made on the basis of 1% samples of national insurance records from 1950 to 1971 and published in the *Employment Gazette* (last appearing in 1972, p.535). More recent sources are the Censuses of Population (see Section 8.6) and Labour Force Surveys (see Section 8.5).

(d) *First employment of young people*

Regular series were compiled each year from 1951 to 1974, classified according to region, sex and class of employment, based on analyses of national insurance cards. The series were published in the *Employment Gazette* and *BLS Yearbooks*. Following the abolition of cards, a new annual survey of school leavers was initiated in 1978. The results, which are restricted to England and Wales, provide analyses for all entrants and for apprentices, separately, by sex and age according to industry and occupational group. No surveys were taken in 1981 and 1982. The results, together with details of the methodology have been published in the *Gazette* as follows: 1978: December 1980; 1979: March 1982; 1980: May 1984; 1983: October 1984. In 1984 the survey was replaced by a more comprehensive cohort study of school leavers run by the MSC.

8.3 BSO CENSUS OF PRODUCTION EMPLOYMENT DATA

The annual census of production (ACOP) was considered fully earlier in the context of output statistics (Chapter 6). Like the DoE and DE employment sources, the ACOP returns are obtained from employers (using the same register as the DoE). But unlike those sources, for which the data relate to employment at specific points of time, the ACOP returns relate to *average* employment over a period of twelve months (e.g. an average of the figures for the last pay-week for each calendar month). The period of twelve months, it should be noted, does not necessarily relate to a calendar year but may be taken as a business year at the discretion of the firm making the return. The returns are meant to cover all *persons* (including self-employed) other than casual employees.

Separate data were collected in each census from 1974 to 1980 for operatives, other employees and total employment (including Working Proprietors). Since 1980, 'slimline' censuses have required a return of total employment only. Breakdowns of employment, as before, are to be obtained in periodic 'benchmark' censuses (the first of which is to be held in respect of 1984). The census results for construction are published in *Business Monitor PA 500*. For further details of the analyses made and the scope and conduct of each census reference should be made to Chapter 6 (Section 6.2).

8.4 CONSTRUCTION INDUSTRY TRAINING BOARD (CITB) STATISTICS

8.4.1 Series and sources

The CITB was established in 1964 under the Industrial Training Act 1964. The statistics may be considered under two headings: manpower statistics and training statistics. The latter (including financial information about training levies and grants) are considered in Chapter 9 (Section 9.1). In addition, the Board carries out *ad hoc* labour surveys from time to time but these are not normally published and they are not considered here.

The manpower data are obtained from all firms on the CITB register in Levy Returns each April and October. These provide information about the number of employees (operatives and APTC staff), with trainees shown separately, and the number of self-employed labour-only workers employed, all broken down by occupation. Currently 44 occupations are distinguished – see Table 8.2 for details. The results are published in the *CITB Annual Report*. A summary of the occupational data is included in *HCS* (annual volumes) along with DoE data.

It is important to note that the data relate solely to firms registered with the CITB and must be interpreted, therefore, in the light of the scope and coverage of the register.

8.4.2 Interpretation – the CITB Register

The scope of the industry as defined for CITB purposes does not coincide exactly with the definition under the SIC. There are a number of notable differences. For instance, certain aspects of structural engineering that come within the scope of construction in the SIC come within the scope of the Engineering Industry

Table 8.2 Occupations defined in CITB statistics*

Managerial staff	Demountable partition erectors
Architects, surveyors and engineers	Terrazzo workers
Technical staff	Plumbers and gas fitters
Draughtsman and tracers	Heating and ventilating
Foremen	engineering workers
Clerical and sales staff	Other mechanical engineering
Bricklayers	services workers
Masons	Electricians
Carpenters and joiners	Crane drivers
Painters	Earth moving plant
Plasterers	operators
Roof slaters and tilers	Other mechanical plant
Paviours	operators
Miscellaneous craftsmen (excluding	Bar benders and steel fixers
mechanical engineering services)	Steel erectors
Scaffolders	Concretors
Roof sheeters	Gas distribution mainslayers
Roofing felt fixers	Plant mechanics
Floor and wall tilers	Other building and civil
Ceiling fixers	engineering skilled workers
Mastic asphalters	Unskilled workers
Floor coverers	Other occupations
Floorers	
Glaziers	
Fencers	
Demolishers	
Steeplejacks	
Cavity wall insulation operatives	

* The number of occupations was increased from 34 to the 44 categories listed here in the *CITB Annual Report* for 1981/82. This includes figures for earlier years back to October 1978 but it should be noted that these were converted using the same factors as for the October 1980 and April 1981 figures.

Training Board rather than the CITB. On the other hand, joinery manufacturers producing industrialized building components and prefabricated buildings or sections of buildings, and firms constructing shop and office fittings do come within the scope of the CITB but are not classified to construction in the SIC. Likewise, the activities of local authority and other DLOs, some of which are embraced by the SIC definition, are excluded from the scope of the CITB. For precise details of the scope of the definition of the industry for CITB purposes, reference should be made to the statutory authority.*

How far the CITB register succeeds in covering all firms within scope is naturally difficult to assess, but it would be surprising if the CITB achieved greater success than the DoE, whose construction register has suffered from admitted deficiencies in the past (see Chapter 5). Details of firms on the DoE register were passed to the CITB when the latter took over responsibility for collecting the occupational data in 1977. For firms which undertake training there is, of course, a financial incentive to register in order to obtain training grants. But for others there is the disincentive that registration entails an obligation (with the exception noted below) to pay the training levy. Certain firms, however, are expressly excluded, namely firms *without employees* (whereas the DoE endeavours to cover all firms). There is, further, less incentive to cover firms below a certain size in that the levy is payable only on payrolls above a defined sum. However, the incentive exists to the extent that small firms can grow during a year, and CITB grants are payable to all firms on the register whether or not they are excluded from levy. The manpower returns themselves cover all firms on the register including those not subject to the levy.

The CITB register was initially compiled in 1964 on the basis of one maintained by the then Ministry of Labour. This was confined almost entirely to employers with five or more employees – a total number of 37 000 which was eventually reduced to 34 200 upon registration (CITB first *Annual Report*). Comparison with the construction register maintained by the DoE and its predecessors is of interest although direct comparison is not

---

* Currently this is SI 1980 No. 1274 as amended by SI 1982 No. 922. It may be noted that the latter added the activities of the manufacture of bricks and the preparation of stone for building purposes to the scope of the definition.

appropriate because of the difference in scope. As at April 1964, the then MPBW register recorded 62 000 firms employing one or more *operatives* – a difference of 28 000 firms. A more recent comparison shows 50 371 on the CITB register in 1982 *(Annual Report 1982/83)* as against 88 897 employing two or more persons on the DoE register (i.e. excluding single-person firms) in October 1982 *(HCS 1973–83)* – a difference of 38 000 on a much enlarged register. Some of this difference will be accounted for by firms consisting of more than one person but without employees.

8.5 OPCS LABOUR FORCE SURVEYS (LFS)

8.5.1 Background

The *LFS* is a multi-purpose household survey initiated in 1973 to satisfy EEC statistical requirements. Its main purpose is to produce regional and national statistics of employment and unemployment in the UK for comparison with other EEC countries, but it has also covered a wider range of topics relating to the labour force and also housing. As information is sought from individuals, as opposed to employers, the survey offers the advantage of being able to provide data that cannot be obtained readily, if at all, from employer surveys. A summary of the topics covered in each survey from 1973 to 1985 is given in Appendix B. From 1973 to 1983 surveys were made biennially, but from 1984 an annual frequency has been adopted with a staged series of interviews to be carried on through the year to provide more regular information about trends.

As far as construction is concerned, the *LFS* is particularly important in providing data that are not available from other sources (e.g. on self-employment) and permits the cross-classification of the topics covered though substantial sampling error may be involved in such analyses because of small sample sizes. Many of the analyses that the data base permit are not published but may be made available – see below.

8.5.2 Analyses

The published results have regularly included analyses of

employment (distinguishing employees from the self-employed) analysed by industry and by occupational *group,* each sub-classified by age and sex. The reports for 1979 and 1981 also include analyses of employment by ethnic origin and sex. Industrial analyses for other topics including, for example, economic position, qualifications, professional activity and job mobility are available on request and details are given in the reports cited below. It may be noted too that from 1975 most of the raw data ('micro-data') have been deposited with the ESRC Survey Archive at Essex University (after the removal of information which would identify individuals and the aggregation of certain categories) and is thus available to research workers for further analysis.

8.5.3 Publication sources

For the first five enquiries from 1973 to 1981 three reports entitled *Labour Force Survey* were published; the first of these covered the three enquiries from 1973 to 1977 but gave results mainly for 1977. For 1983 and Spring 1984 preliminary results were published in the *Employment Gazette* for July 1984 (revised in March 1985) and May 1985 respectively. Early results are also issued as *OPCS Monitors (LFS* series).

8.6 OPCS GENERAL HOUSEHOLD SURVEYS (GHS)

The *GHS,* like the *LFS* considered above, is a multi-purpose sample survey of households. But, as its name implies, it is a more generalized survey, specially designed to serve the data needs of many government departments simultaneously. It covers a wide range of regular core topics every year, including employment, and a variety of supplementary topics from time to time. Major advantages of the *GHS* are the opportunity it affords to study the interrelationships among different subjects and the link it provides, for some subjects, between the more comprehensive, but less frequent, censuses of population considered below (Section 8.7).

A summary of the topics covered since the initiation of the survey in 1971 is given in Appendix A. As far as employment is concerned, the *GHS* provides less specific coverage than the *LFS* and the published results from the *GHS* do not generally contain analyses by industry. However, many unpublished tables are available and, since the late 1970s, the *GHS* micro-data (that is, the anonymous but detailed results for households and their members) have been deposited after a lapse of time at the ESRC Survey Archive at Essex University and are available for analysis by research workers.

The results of each survey, together with commentaries, are published in an annual volume entitled *General Household Survey.* Early results are published in a special *GHS* series of *OPCS Monitors.* Hakim (1982) considers the *GHS* in the context of other surveys and provides much useful background information and references.

8.7 OPCS CENSUS OF POPULATION EMPLOYMENT DATA

8.7.1 Background

Since the Second World War censuses of population have been taken every ten years from 1951 plus a mid-term census in 1966. Two aspects of the census make it an extremely important source of information. First, the means by which it is conducted – particulars being recorded in respect of each individual with completed schedules being collected by enumerators with a duty to ensure that they have been properly completed – makes it possible to collect particularly detailed information and, generally speaking, particularly reliable information. Secondly, the information collected provides statistics of a kind which are either not available from other sources or which, although duplicated elsewhere, provide a valuable check on the accuracy of other sources. However, it needs to be remembered that the census is not entirely free from error, either on account of the use of sampling within the census or inaccuracies in the returns (some information about this is available from post-enumeration checks). An important development in recent years has been the introduction of regular sample surveys of households in which information is also collected directly from individuals and these provide an important link between censuses. These are the General Household Survey from 1971 (considered in Section 8.6) and the Labour Force Survey from 1973 (considered in Section 8.5).

8.7.2 The available data

(a) *Occupation, industry and characteristics*

With regard to employment, two types of analysis are made: one according to the occupation of individuals and the other according to industry. The occupational classification follows a system in which certain occupations are grouped together including one group for 'construction occupations'. But as a consequence of the distinction between industry and occupation, it should be appreciated that persons in construction occupations may be occupied in a variety of non-construction industries and vice versa. Classification by industry in the post-war period has been in accordance with the SIC. Within these classifications, subsidiary analyses are made according to various characteristics of the labour force: age, sex, employment status (employed/self-employed and various sub-divisions of these categories), social class, socio-economic group, marital condition of female workers and nationality.

(b) *Regional and local data*

Many of the industrial and occupational analyses are broken down according to region and local administrative areas. These analyses, unlike some of those available from other sources, classify each individual, as far as possible, according to the actual place of work (including building sites in the case of construction) specified on the census forms. In some cases, however, the place of work is not specified, in which case the classification is made according to area of usual residence, if known, or to the area of enumeration. Generally, however, the census statistics provide the most comprehensive and accurate source of regional and local area employment data for construction. Since 1961 information has also been obtained about the migration of labour from one region to another over defined periods prior to the census.

(c) *Education and qualifications*

A major development in the range of information collected in the census has been the inclusion of questions about qualifications since 1961. The analyses according to industry provide data for the number of qualified persons analysed according to subject and type of qualification. We consider these data separately in Section 8.9. 'Education' tables provide information about the ages at which full-time education ceased.

8.7.3 Publications and unpublished sources

As we indicated above, analyses are generally made according to a variety of characteristics: sex, employment status, social class etc. We provide a guide here to the location of the principal analyses for each census. Full bibliographic details for each report are given in the List of statistical sources at the end of this book. Analyses of the data for regions and local areas are made in considerable detail. The reports cited below generally contain regional sub-divisions of the principal occupational and industrial data, but reference may also be made to separate reports for each county – these are *not* listed here. For the latest, 1981, Census a useful guide is the *Census 1981 User Guide Catalogue* (OPCS, 1985).

(a) *Industry and occupation analyses*

For 1951 and 1961, separate volumes of *Industry Tables* and *Occupation Tables* were published for England and Wales and a single, combined, volume for Scotland. From 1966 the data appear in *Economic Activity* volumes: one for Great Britain and one for Scotland.

(b) *Labour migration analyses by industry and occupation*

Reports are made from 1961 in separate *Migration Tables* for either England and Wales or Scotland or Great Britain (again, see the List of statistical sources for details).

(c) *Workplace and transport-to-work analyses by industry and occupation*

Analyses are available from 1961 for England and Wales or for Scotland in reports variously titled as *Workplace Tables* or *Workplace and Transport...* or *Occupation, Industry and Workplace Tables* (Scotland in 1961).

(d) *Education analyses (terminal education age) by occupation*

Data are available for 1951 and 1961 only and were published for England and Wales in *General Tables* and *Education Tables* respectively, and for Scotland in reports on *Occupations and Industries* and *Terminal Education Age* respectively.

(e) *Guides to the occupational classifications*
A separate guide is issued for each census under the title *Classification of Occupations* (GRO, 1956, 1960, 1966; OPCS, 1970, 1980).

(f) *General reports and guides*
A *General Report* is published for each census (except 1966) which gives background information about the conduct of each census, the processing of results and other explanatory material. At the time of writing (mid–1985) the general report on the 1981 census had not been published but in the meantime a separate *Definitions* volume is available. Useful general guides to the censuses are also available. The latest official guide is *Guide to Census Reports, Great Britain 1801–1966* (OPCS, 1977). Useful unofficial guides are: Benjamin (1970) and Rhind (1983).

(g) *Unpublished data*
Increasingly the formats for the release of census data have been diversified from book format to include magnetic tape, microfilm, computer printout and loose pages of printed tables, all of which are commonly referred to as the unpublished tables or data. Little more than 2% of the 1971 census output of tables were presented in the published volumes (Hakim, 1982, p.45). A series of OPCS *User Guides* are the main source of information on the availability of unpublished census data – see the *Census 1981 User Guide Catalogue* (OPCS, 1985). Micro-data from the census are not made available.

8.7.4 Interpretation

As a source of employment statistics, the principal merits of the census of population data follow from the fact that information is recorded, as we stressed earlier, separately for each individual in the population. This makes possible classifications of the labour force in greater detail and with a greater accuracy than is generally possible in other types of enquiry in which returns are made by employers in respect of whole groups of persons, rather than individuals, and which may be critically dependent upon the adequacy of sampling frames, sampling methods and levels of response etc. As we indicated earlier, however, the census statistics themselves are not without error. There are three principal sources of actual or potential error: sampling errors, bias and other inaccuracies.

With regard to sampling error, although the decennial censuses are censuses in the sense of being based on 100% enumerations of the population, much of the detailed information relating to occupation, industry and (from 1961) qualifications, is based on samples (generally 10%). In 1961, 10% of households received more detailed questionnaires; in 1971 and 1981, 10% of completed questionnaires were analysed in greater detail than the other 90%. The 1966 census was taken wholly on a sample basis. Details of the sampling methodology are given in the relevant reports. As regards bias, this was detected in the sample element of the 1961 census and 'bias correction factors' (printed in the census reports) need to be applied to the published results. The third source of error arises from inaccuracies in the completion of returns and errors of subsequent classification. Inaccuracies in the completion of the forms are, of course, difficult to detect but some information is available from coverage and quality checks (post-enumeration surveys) held following the censuses from 1961 – see GRO (1968), Gray and Gee (1972), OPCS (1983) and Britton and Birch (1985). In addition, comparisons were made after the 1951 and 1961 censuses of death registration records for a sample of those dying soon after the census in order to check the occupational classification. This showed a disturbingly low level of agreement. However, this evidence cannot be taken at its face value as evidence of mis-classification in the census, since death registration records may themselves not necessarily be valid: the fact that the informants in each case differ (the man himself at the census, a relative at death) tend to make discrepancies likely. Details of these checks are given in GRO (1958, 1968). It is felt that the accuracy of the occupational classification has improved over the years (Benjamin, 1970).

The classification by industry is made by matching information about the name, address and business of employer to an industrially classified register in the census office. The classification, therefore, is not solely dependent upon the information provided about industry on the census form. Nonetheless, it is not likely that absolute accuracy is achieved – the possibilities remain of inaccurate or incomplete information on the census form and deficiencies in the register. *A priori,* however, it would seem plausible to suggest that the twin sources of information in the census of population make it more, rather than less, likely that the industrial classification obtained in the census is superior to other sources. Certainly the 1961 post-enumeration survey found very little error of response, in general, for this category.

8.8 PUBLIC AUTHORITY CONSTRUCTION MANPOWER

References have been made above to sources of data about the construction labour directly employed by authorities in the public sector collected along with data for private contractors: these sources are the DoE (Section 8.1) and the BSO censuses of production (Section 8.3). Here we deal with two more specific sources. One of these is confined to local authority manpower, the other provides an industrial analysis of all labour employed in various parts of the public, as well as the private, sector.

8.8.1 Local authority manpower

From 1952 to 1974 annual series for the employment of construction workers by local authorities (classified by full-time/part-time and sex) in England, in Wales and in Scotland (three separate series) were compiled by the DE (and former MOL) on the basis of a special return from local authorities which was issued in order to allow construction labour to be appropriately classified to construction under the SIC and not under Local Government Service. For England and Wales, the series was replaced in 1975 with quarterly data obtained in Joint Manpower Watch surveys conducted by LACSAB. For Scotland, similar surveys have been conducted since 1976 by the National Joint Council for Local Authority Services in Scotland. The results of these surveys are first published in quarterly *Joint Manpower Watch* press releases issued by the DoE, Welsh Office and Scottish Office for England, Wales and Scotland respectively. Primary publication sources otherwise are the *Employment Gazette* for England and for Wales and the *MDS* for all three countries. Other sources are: *Local Government Financial Statistics, England and Wales, Welsh Local*

Government Financial Statistics for Wales alone and the *SAS* for Scotland. It should be noted that these data differ from those obtained in the censuses carried out by the DoE (Section 8.1) ostensibly because the DoE attempt to cover employment of all building and civil engineering workers in all departments of the authority whereas the statistics referred to here are narrower in scope, being confined to employment in separate direct works departments as such.

8.8.2 CSO series of employment in public and private sectors

Since 1959 annual series have been compiled by the CSO, showing employment of construction direct labour by each of three parts of the public sector – central government, local authorities and public corporations – together with a fourth series for the private sector. These are published in an article (currently annual) on 'Employment in the public and private sectors...' in *Economic Trends*. The series for local authorities and the private sector are based on DE sources (see Sections 8.2 and 8.8.1); the other series are CSO estimates (again they differ from the data collected by the DoE – see Section 8.1 – probably because of a more comprehensive classification of construction labour in the DoE enquiries).

8.9 QUALIFIED MANPOWER

8.9.1 Introduction

The term 'qualified manpower' may be used in more than one sense. When enquiries were initiated in this field, in the mid–1950s, it was narrowly defined in terms of persons possessing certain precisely defined scientific and technological qualifications. The term is now used more widely, however, to cover all persons with qualifications at a level above GCE A–level or equivalent. Useful general surveys of statistics in this field will be found in Wroe and Bishop (1971), Whybrew (1972) and Butler (1977). In construction the main demand for qualified manpower arises in connection with the design of buildings and other structures and related engineering and surveying services. This demand is partly filled by employment within construction firms and DLOs, but much of this labour is employed in independent architectural, engineering and surveying practices. Statistics about the latter are considered separately in Chapter 15. Our attention here is confined to the statistics relating to the construction industry in a narrow sense, i.e. contracting and DLOs. In the construction industry the Chartered Institute of Building (CIOB) – formerly the Institute of Building (IOB) – has evolved as an institution performing a professional role for persons con-cerned with building in various managerial, technical, adminis-trative and educational positions and setting its own examina-tions. However, the Institute is not a qualifying association in the same sense as other professional institutions are and for this reason it is not considered in Chapter 15 along with other profes-sional institutions relating to the construction industry. For the same reason statistics relating to CIOB membership are less comprehensive than the more general, official, enquiries relating to the employment of qualified manpower in the industry. We examine the latter sources first, therefore, then note CIOB statistics.

8.9.2 Employment of qualified manpower

(a) *Historical background*

Currently relevant information is obtained in the decennial censuses of population, in biannual CITB returns and in the *GHS* and *LFS*. Historically, a series of triennial sample surveys, covering construction and other industries, were conducted over the period from 1956 to 1968. An account of these surveys, in the context of construction, and publication references will be found in Fleming (1980a, pp.215–6). We may also note the National Training Survey commissioned by the MSC in 1975 and 1976 to 'provide a comprehensive picture of the stock of skills in the labour force, the education and training undertaken to acquire them and the uses to which they were put'. Information was also recorded on those sampled, enabling analyses by age, occupation, industry and geographical location to be made. A complete report on the survey was never published but a number of special analyses were made including one for construction used in a study by NEDO (1978). For further details of the survey see Claydon (1980).

(b) *Censuses of population as sources of qualified manpower data*
Statistics of qualified manpower have been collected in each of
the censuses of population since 1961. However, there are differences in the information obtained. In the 1961 census the question
referred to the possession of degrees or equivalent qualifications
in engineering, technology and science only (the same classification as in the triennial surveys referred to above); but this
excluded architecture and surveying. In the 1966 and subsequent
censuses the question was extended to cover all qualifications
obtained after reaching the age of 18 and entailing study at a
level *above* that required for GCE A–level or SCE. In 1971 and
1981 information was also sought about the possession of GCE
A–level or its equivalents, information which has enabled the
'non-qualified' population to be sub-classified by academic level
(as well as by industry etc.). Published reports provide analyses
according to industry and occupation and by type of qualification, subject and academic level as well as other characteristics.
But in addition much census information is also available in
various unpublished forms (as indicated above in Section 8.7).

PUBLICATION SOURCES. In 1961 the data were given in a report on
Scientific and Technological Qualifications and from 1966 to 1981 in
reports on *Qualified Manpower*. In addition retabulations of the
1966 and 1971 data were prepared to provide QSE tables on a
basis 'as nearly as practicable' comparable with those for 1961.
These were published for 1966 in *Scientific and Technological Qualifications* as part of the *Census 1966* series of reports and, for 1971,
in a DoI study: *Persons with Qualifications in Engineering, Technology
and Science.* Further, two CSO studies provide useful summaries
and commentaries on the data in the context of the population
as a whole: *Qualified Manpower in Great Britain – the 1966 Census of
Population* and *Qualified Manpower in Great Britain – the 1971 Census
of Population.* Full bibliographic details are given in the List of
statistical sources at the end of the book under 'Census'.

INTERPRETATION. Apart from the widening in the scope of the
enquiries from 1966, a number of factors are relevant for the
interpretation of the results, particularly those in the full reports
for 1966 and 1971, as opposed to the more limited QSE tables.
First, surveying is counted under 'technology' in the full reports

but not in the other volumes. Secondly, where people have more than one qualification they are classified according to the most recent highest attainment listed in the full reports, but in the other volumes they are classified according to the *first* science or technology qualification obtained at degree or equivalent level. Thirdly, the QSE tables do not include qualifications which are not accepted for membership of professional institutions. With regard to the accuracy of the returns themselves, it should be noted that evidence was obtained of under-recording in the quality check made after the 1966 census (Gray and Gee, 1972) and that there is evidence that qualifications recorded in 1966 were not recorded in 1971 *(Qualified Manpower Tables* for 1971, p.viii). Finally, it is important to note that all the results are subject to sampling error (the analyses in each case are based on 10% samples) and that bias was detected in the 1961 and 1966 results – see the reports themselves and especially the DTI report: *Persons with Qualifications in Engineering, Technology and Science 1959 to 1968* (pp.125–6). Detailed information about each particular census, relevant for purposes of interpretation are given in the *General Reports* and *Definitions* volumes and in the general guides referred to above.

(c) *DoE censuses and CITB levy returns*

Relevant information, inasmuch as it shows the employment of APTC staff broken down by type, were obtained in DoE censuses of contractors from 1965 to 1976 and in censuses of local authority DLOs from 1966 to 1980 (see Section 8.1). It is important to note, however, that the analyses are not based on any definition of qualifications. Equivalent enquiries are now conducted by the CITB for firms within its scope (see Section 8.4). We consider the data further in relation to the other sources below.

(d) *The GHS and LFS*

Analyses of the qualifications data obtained in these surveys are not systematically published and we therefore devote no further attention to them here. However, unpublished analyses may be supplied and the micro-data are available for analysis – for further details see Sections 8.5 and 8.6.

(e) *Comparability of the surveys*

Questions relating to the comparability, reliability and interpretation of the triennial manpower surveys in relation to the statistics from the censuses of population and the DoE censuses were discussed in Fleming (1980a, pp.217–8).

CENSUSES OF POPULATION AND DoE/CITB DATA. Comparison of the data from these censuses is hampered by the fact that they are not defined in the same way: the scope of the census of population data is defined precisely in terms of certain qualifications; the DoE census is more concerned with employment rather than qualifications and the breakdown by occupation is not defined in terms of qualification as such. In this respect the DoE data are best compared with the general occupational analyses of the censuses of population as opposed to the qualified manpower tables (see Section 8.7). The same is true with regard to the current CITB data considered in Section 8.4. But in this case it needs to be remembered too that the CITB register is not classified in accordance with the SIC.

8.9.3 New supply of qualified manpower

Information about new supply in terms of the numbers of people newly-obtaining certain qualifications in different subject areas is available from education statistics which are considered in Chapter 9. More specifically, statistics are compiled annually by the UGC in respect of university graduates showing first destination (where known) according to subject of qualification and sector of employment and published, currently in *University Statistics Volume 2*. Similar data for polytechnic first degree and higher diploma students are prepared annually by the Polytechnics Careers Advisers Statistics Working Party and published in *First Destination of Polytechnic Students*. Statistics for the numbers of university students according to subject of study are given in *Education Statistics Vol. 1*. For polytechnic students and information for students on vocational training courses, including CIOB surveys of students on building courses, see Chapter 9 (Section 9.1.3).

8.9.4 Chartered Institute of Building (CIOB) membership statistics

Membership statistics are given in an annual *Yearbook and Directory of Members*. More detailed information is available from periodic surveys of the membership. Particulars are given below.

1966: details of the functions performed, the field of employment and analyses by size of firm, published in the 1966 *Yearbook*

1975: information as above but reported in greater detail in *Institute of Building (1976)*. This survey also obtained information about the members who were also members of other professional institutions

1976: survey of fields of employment of members, reported in *Building Technology and Management,* January 1979, p.xv

1983: analyses of employment by type of employer and sector and by function reported in *Building Technology and Management,* November 1983, pp.20–21 and January 1984, p.37.

CIOB education statistics are considered in Chapter 9.

8.10 EMPLOYMENT ON RESEARCH AND DEVELOPMENT

Statistics about the labour (both 'qualified' and 'unqualified') employed on research and development have been collected as part of surveys of industrial research and development expenditure, carried out annually by the DoI and its predecessors from 1967 to 1972, and again in 1975, 1978, 1981 and 1983 covering private industry, public corporations and research associations (central government was included for the first time in 1975). The expenditure surveys, which were commenced earlier, are considered separately in Chapter 12. In 1972 and 1975 the results were sub-divided by product group (including construction); before 1972 the product group classification was confined to private industry and the published results did not distinguish construction as a separate category. The surveys for the private sector are based on the census of production register of enterprises employing over 100 employees and reporting expenditure on R & D in a preliminary enquiry. From 1972 the results provide, for construction, analyses of employment by: sector (as defined above) and by occupation (scientists and engineers; technicians, laboratory assistants and draftsmen; administrative and clerical staff and others). The results have been published as follows:

1972: *Trade and Industry*, 1975, pp.397–401
1975, 1978 and 1981: *Business Monitor MO 14*.

The results of the 1983 survey published in *British Business*, 18 January 1985, pp.130–2 do not include an employment breakdown for construction. For surveys up to 1972, the results of both the expenditure and the employment parts have been brought together, along with further background information, in a report by the CSO (1976a).

9
LABOUR STATISTICS OTHER THAN EMPLOYMENT

Employment statistics are covered in Chapter 8. This chapter covers all other labour statistics apart from those relating to labour costs (including wage rates, earnings and hours of work) which are considered in Chapter 10. The subjects covered in this chapter are as follows:

9.1 Labour training and education statistics
9.2 Unemployment, redundancies, vacancies, placings, turnover and mobility
9.3 Accidents
9.4 Industrial disputes
9.5 Trade unions and industrial relations practices.

9.1 LABOUR TRAINING AND EDUCATION STATISTICS

Training is carried out by employers, in training centres run by the MSC or the CITB and in educational establishments. We deal with sources for each of these categories in turn. Vocational training is also covered in the *LFS* and *GHS* – see Sections 8.5 and 8.6.

9.1.1 Apprentices/trainees in employment

Since 1977 statistics of the number of trainees analysed by occupation have been collected by the CITB from firms in scope (see Section 8.4) in April and October each year. The results, which cover persons in all occupations (manual and non-manual, apprentice and non-apprentice crafts) and of all ages, are published in *CITB Annual Reports.* Before 1977 similar statistics were collected by the DoE in Censuses of Contractors (see Section 8.1). However, it should be noted that before 1975 (back to 1949) the statistics in this area were confined to the employment of *apprentices.*

APPRENTICE REGISTRATION STATISTICS. Data on the number of registered apprentices are not published but are available from apprentice registration bodies: the National Joint Training Commission for England and Wales (a Standing Committee of the NJCBI) and the Scottish Building Apprenticeship and Training Council (a section of the Scottish Building Employers Federation) for Scotland. Interpretation of these registration statistics should take account of certain limitations in their scope. First, they refer only to those apprentices undergoing training under certain approved conditions and who are formally indentured, whereas the CITB and former DoE census statistics, referred to above, cover apprentices employed under unwritten, as well as written, agreements. Secondly, they refer to 'building' trades narrowly defined. For other trades (e.g. civil engineering, electrical, plumbing) apprenticeship schemes are administered by other bodies (a list of these bodies is available from the CITB, since to qualify for training grants from the CITB trainees must be registered with these bodies). Thirdly, even for 'building' trades as such certain apprentices *may* not be registered (e.g. those employed in the maintenance department of non- construction firms and public authorities). Finally, it should be noted that apprentices are not necessarily in their first year of training; thus series showing the number of registrations in a 12–month period do not provide an accurate indication of entry to the industry at this level.

9.1.2 CITB and MSC training statistics

Apart from on-the-job training provided by employers for their own trainees, referred to above, training in construction trades is also provided directly by the CITB (the primary training agency) in its training centres, in public educational establishments and under the auspices of the MSC. For the CITB, figures are given in *CITB Annual Reports* along with figures for those undergoing training in public educational establishments and within companies. CITB statistics in general are considered more fully in Chapter 8 (Section 8.4).

The MSC introduced a Training Opportunities Scheme (TOPS) in 1972, the intention of which was to provide unemployed adults (over the age of 19) with the opportunity to learn new skills or update existing ones. Training is carried out at Skill Centres (formerly Government Training Centres) run by the MSC, at colleges of further education, private colleges and at employers' establishments. Statistics of the *total* number of training completions in the construction trades are published in *MSC Annual Reports*. For young people the MSC introduced a Youth Training Scheme (YTS) in 1983 (progressively replacing former schemes including YOPS), the aim of which is to provide a bridge between school and work through a year-long period of training and work experience and to provide a foundation of skills for future development. For construction, the CITB became the primary managing agent, responsible for operating the scheme on a national basis. Data for the first year appear in the *Annual Report* for 1983–84.

9.1.3 Education statistics

(a) *Official statistics*

Statistics for university students throughout the UK according to subject of study are given in *University Statistics Vol. 1,* and analyses of the first destination of graduates by field of employment are given in *University Statistics Vol. 2*. Statistics for other 'major' educational establishments (i.e. polytechnics, other maintained and assisted establishments, grant-aided – direct grant and voluntary – establishments) and adult education centres in England are recorded in *Statistics of Education – Further Education*. This gives figures of student numbers or course enrolment on courses leading, *inter alia,* to recognised qualifications in building, and entries and successes in examinations as follows:

1. Numbers of part-time day and of block release students (separately) by age, sex and industry of employer
2. Course enrolments by mode of attendance, sex and subject of study (in the construction field these are building, civil

engineering, surveying and architecture) broken down according to advanced and non-advanced courses in (a) all establishments and (b) polytechnics.

Courses are regarded as advanced if the standard of instruction extends above that required for GCE A–level, the OND or the BTEC (formerly TEC or BEC) and SCOTEC certificates or diplomas. All other courses are regarded as non-advanced.

WALES AND SCOTLAND. Separate statistics for Wales, as under item 1 above, are published in *Statistics of Education in Wales*. Data for Scotland (formerly published in *Scottish Education Statistics*) are now available in *Statistical Bulletins* issued by the Scottish Education Department though these provide analyses at the level of broad subject groups only.

(b) *CIOB surveys*

In addition to the official statistics, referred to above, related data are also collected by the CIOB in surveys which it has conducted annually since 1966/7 on the basis of a questionnaire sent to universities, polytechnics and colleges of technology in the UK and, since 1971, the Republic of Ireland, that run building courses at technician level or above. The results were published in the Institute's journal *Building Technology and Management* up to the year 1980–81 (July/August 1981 issue) and since then have been issued annually by the Institute as a pamphlet entitled *The Chartered Institute of Building Survey of Student Numbers*. Currently (1983–84), analyses are given for the number of students by type of attendance (full-time, sandwich, part-time) and by year of attendance as follows:

1. Numbers on courses below degree level in England and Wales, in Scotland and in Ireland separately, plus a regional analysis for England and Wales, each broken down by course (BTEC and SCOTEC awards, College diplomas, courses for CIOB awards)
2. Numbers on degree courses in building, building surveying and quantity surveying in England and Wales (by region), in Scotland and in Ireland
3. Students on BTEC and SCOTEC courses analysed by technician function (i.e. building, architecture, quantity or building surveying).

9.2 UNEMPLOYMENT, REDUNDANCIES, VACANCIES, PLACINGS, TURNOVER AND LABOUR MOBILITY

9.2.1 Unemployment statistics by industry and occupation

Regular analyses of unemployed persons by previous industry and by occupation were made by the Department of Employment (DE) until May 1982. Since then the only information available is that collected in the *LFS* (considered in Chapter 8, Section 8.5) and in the decennial censuses of population (see below).

Until May 1982, statistics were compiled by the DE by counting people registered for work at a Jobcentre or Careers Office. Registration was a condition of entitlement to unemployment benefit, but with effect from October 1982 the registration was made voluntary (see *Employment Gazette*, September 1982, pp.389–93). The records of claimants to benefit now held at Unemployment Benefit Offices do not contain information about industry of last employment or occupation. Occupational analyses of voluntary registrants are not made as only a small proportion of the unemployed register and consequently such analyses would not be regarded as representative.

(a) *Former DE series*

The former DE industrial series were published in the *Employment Gazette*. The occupational analyses were published partly in the *Gazette* (the occupations in which persons were seeking work) and partly in *HCS* (analyses specially prepared for the DoE of the occupations of *craftsmen* whose last employment was in the construction industry). Further discussion of the series will be found in Fleming (1980a), pp.223–5.

(b) *Census of population data*

The decennial censuses of population (considered in relation to employment in Chapter 8, Section 8.7) also provide statistics about the members of the working population who were out of work at the time of the census, analysed according to occupation. They are published in the *Occupation* or *Economic Activity* volumes, references to which are given under 'Census' in the List of statistical sources at the end of the book. These statistics do not coincide with the DE statistics of registered unemployment for a number of reasons: a detailed discussion of the points of difference will be found in GRO (1966), pp.xxviii–xxix; see also Garside (1980), pp.130–8. It should also be noted that post- enumeration surveys conducted by the OPCS have also shown that the census figures are open to error, caused particularly by persons who were in employment but sick, wrongly returning themselves as unemployed.

For a detailed discussion of the nature of the unemployment statistics in general up to 1979, see Garside (1980).

9.2.2 Redundancy statistics

Statistics of redundancies in construction and other industries, based on administrative procedures arising from the employment protection and redundancy payments legislation are compiled by the Department of Employment. Three series are produced: (i) advance notifications; (ii) redundancies confirmed as 'due to occur' and (iii) statistics based on redundancy payments made after redundancies have taken place. An article describing the nature of these statistics is contained in the *Employment Gazette* for June 1981, pp.260–2; it is emphasized that the statistics do not provide comprehensive coverage of all redundancies. A subsequent article in June 1983 (pp.245–59) provides previously unpublished series for construction and other industries under categories (ii) and (iii) above for each year from 1977 to 1982; and series (iii) for 'confirmed redundancies' is now carried forward monthly in the *Employment Gazette* (the series are available on a consistent basis only from 1977). For Wales alone a category (i) series for construction and other industries from 1974 to 1979 was given in the *DWS* (1980 ed).

9.2.3 Vacancies and placings

(a) *Vacancies*

Analyses of vacancies in construction and other industries notified to Jobcentres are compiled quarterly (monthly analyses were made until June 1976) and published in *Employment Gazette*. Quarterly occupational analyses are also made but for broad occupational groups only. At one time much more detailed occupational analyses were specially prepared for construction and published elsewhere: crafts cross-classified by region in the *MBCS* until April 1972 and by craft and region (not cross-classified) for two months each year in the *ABCS* up to 1970. *HCS* reproduced national totals only.

With regard to interpretation, the salient point to note about the data is that they represent not a total count of vacancies but only those which have been notified to Local Employment Offices (Jobcentres) or Careers Offices and which remain unfilled at the date of the count. It should also be noted, that the series from these two types of office are open to duplication and, therefore, should not be added together. There are certain discontinuities in the series: (i) the opening of Jobcentres in 1973 led to a rise in the proportion of vacancies notified, (ii) the adoption from December 1972 of the CODOT occupational classification led to discontinuities in the occupational analyses (as in the case of unemployment analyses) and (iii) before January 1976 the craft analyses related only to males.

(b) *Placings*

Statistics on placings (i.e. persons placed in employment through the Employment or Careers Offices) are published in *Employment Gazette*. Analyses by industry were prepared monthly until January 1970. Since then data have been collected quarterly and on an occupational basis only, covering those placed by Employment Offices but not by Careers Offices.

9.2.4 Labour turnover and mobility

(a) *Turnover*

The term 'labour turnover' refers to the movement of workers into, and out of, employment with one particular employer. In contrast to manufacturing industry as a whole, no regular series are available for construction.

(b) *Mobility*

Two types of labour mobility may be defined: industrial and occupational mobility which involve respectively changes of industry and changes of occupation. Naturally the two may be related. Regular statistics were not obtained until the initiation of the *GHS* and *LFS* in the 1970s. Analyses on both occupational and industrial bases may be prepared from the results of these surveys but none are systematically published – see Chapter 8 (Sections 8.5 and 8.6 respectively) for further details of these surveys including the availability of unpublished data.

The only other information comes from occasional surveys. The most important recent survey is *Labour Mobility in the Construction Industry* carried out by the OPCS by means of interviews with just under 2000 construction workers in the period March–June 1979. The research aims were: (i) to measure the *rate* of past employment mobility among men currently employed as manual operatives, (ii) to describe the character of this mobility, particularly in terms of the *way* in which men leave one employer and join another, (iii) to examine some of the *hazards* of mobility with particular reference to involuntary mobility and men's entitlement to redundancy payments and (iv) to enquire into the *antecedents* of mobility as they may be found in men's personal characteristics, in the nature of their work, their employers, or in other aspects of their experiences over the five years preceding mid–1979, and to learn something of the relationship between men's attitudes towards mobility and work in construction and their actual behaviour.

Relevant information was also obtained in the 1975 National Training Survey (Claydon, 1980), covering construction and other workers, in which information was obtained about the work and training history of each person interviewed. Full results of the survey were not published but some of the results for two construction trades (carpenters and joiners and bricklayers) were given in NEDO (1978). Details of earlier surveys will be found in Fleming (1980a), p.227.

9.3 ACCIDENT STATISTICS

There are problems associated with the use and interpretation of accident statistics arising out of under-reporting, changes in scope and other causes of discontinuity in the series. At the time of writing (mid-1985) new reporting arrangements are being considered, following a legislative change introduced in 1983, which will inevitably involve a major discontinuity. The following discussion relates to the statistics collected up to the end of 1982. There are two sources: the Health and Safety Executive (HSE) and the Department of Health and Social Security (DHSS). The former covers accidents *reported* or *notified* under the Factories Acts and Health and Safety at Work legislation. The latter refers to accidents *compensated* under social security legislation relating to industrial injuries. We consider each source in turn and then consider questions of interpretation.

9.3.1 HSE – reported/notified accident – statistics

(a) *Background*

Until the end of 1980, accidents which occurred on 'building operations' or 'works of engineering construction' had to be reported to HM Factory Inspectorate (HMFI) – a component part of HSE – in accordance with the Factories Acts. The legal responsibility for reporting rested with the 'occupier' of such premises (the contractor in the case of construction sites) and covered accidents which caused the death of a person employed there or which prevented him, as a result of injury, from earning full wages at the work at which he was employed for a period of *more than 3 days.* In addition, notification extended to 'dangerous occurrences' (e.g. the collapse of a crane) and industrial diseases (not to be confused with 'prescribed industrial diseases' under the Social Security Acts).

On 1 January 1981 new reporting regulations* came into force which replaced the direct reporting requirement with one in which information was supplied by DHSS arising out of their administration of claims for industrial injuries benefit. However, in the case of fatal and 'major injury' accidents (a new category of definition in the NADO Regulations), notification had to continue to be given (by the quickest practicable means – by telephone in most cases) to HSE or appropriate enforcing authority, with written confirmation following within 7 days on a separate direct reporting form. For this reason and because the scope of the new regulation was wider (see below) there is an important discontinuity in the figures at this point. In summary, the effect of the new regulations was to increase the 'catch' of 'over 3 day injuries' partly because some injured non-employees

---

* The Notification of Accidents and Dangerous Occurrences (NADO) Regulations 1980. SI No. 804.

were now recorded but also because more comprehensive coverage was obtained of employees in sectors such as construction which suffered from severe under-reporting previously. A guide to the new regulations was published in HSE (1980).

The position changed substantially again in April 1983 following the implementation of the Social Security and Housing Act which affected the Industrial Injuries Benefit Scheme. The effect of this was to reduce the available information coming from DHSS (by, it was thought, a factor of about 5), though not that sent directly to HSE. It was for this reason that, as mentioned above, new reporting arrangements were proposed in a consultative document in 1983 (HSC, 1983). These proposals were still under review at the time of writing in 1985. The statistics for 1983–85 will be fragmentary.

(b) *The available analyses*

For statistical purposes, analyses of reported accidents are made in considerable detail: type of accident, nature of injury etc. and also incidence rates, including, from 1969, separate analyses of serious accidents based on a 5% sample. In 1978 a New Accident Classification was introduced permitting more detailed analyses by accident type, agency of accident, nature and site of injury and by task performed. Statistics are also published relating to the issue of enforcement notices and the number of prosecutions under construction regulations and the results in each case.

(c) *Publication sources*

Primary publication sources are *Health and Safety Statistics* from 1975 and also, from 1976, reports on *Construction – Health and Safety* (these reports contain more detailed analyses and review the accident record, problems encountered, actions taken etc.). Summary data are first issued as a *Press Release* by the HSE. Before 1975, the primary source was the *Annual Report of HM Chief Inspector of Factories.* These sources all provide annual data. Summary monthly and quarterly data are published in *Employment Gazette* for fatal accidents (monthly) and both fatal and non-fatal accidents (quarterly).

In addition there are a number of special reports on construction accidents. Three reports on fatal accidents have been prepared by the Health and Safety Executive (1978, 1979, 1981) and two more general reports on the accident record of the industry for the period 1954–58 (Cmnd 953, 1960) and in 1966 (Ministry of Labour, 1967).

The main secondary publication sources, all of which contain summary data only are: *HCS* (annual volumes) for fatal accidents and total reported accidents and, for fatal accidents only, the *AAS, MDS,* the *British Labour Statistics Historical Abstract* (which contains the series from 1896 to 1968) and the *BLS Yearbooks* until 1976.

9.3.2 DHSS – compensated industrial accident – statistics

The DHSS compile statistics of 'compensated' industrial accidents and diseases from claims submitted under the Industrial Injuries scheme. From April 1975 the provisions of the National Insurance (Industrial Injuries) Act 1946, as amended, were incorporated in the Social Security Act 1975. The Act provides benefit for incapacity for work, or disablement, or death, caused by injury due to an accident at work. Industrial death benefit is payable to the dependant of a person who dies from an industrial accident or disease. Injury benefit is paid for a maximum of 26 weeks to a person who is incapable of work as a result of any industrial accident or disease. Disablement benefit may follow a period of injury benefit, but the statistics refer to injury benefit only. The following points indicate the coverage of the statistics:

1. The Act applies to persons in 'insurable employment' which was redesignated as 'employed earner's employment' in the Social Security Act 1975
2. Some fatal industrial accidents and diseases do not result in a payment of industrial death benefit because there are no dependants
3. The industrial classification is determined by DHSS on the basis of information provided by the employer and may differ therefore, from that in DoE and HSE records.

It may also be noted that the fatal accident data cover *all* death benefit awards, while the series based on industrial injury benefits awards are derived from samples of claimants and are, therefore, subject to sampling error.

PUBLICATION SOURCES. The primary publication source is *Social Security Statistics* but series from 1970/1 are also reproduced in *Health and Safety Statistics*.

9.3.3 Interpretation

Interpretation of the data needs to take account of a number of factors – but broadly speaking these relate to questions of accuracy and the coverage of the data. With regard to the fatal accidents data, little doubt about accuracy arises: the only doubt about the HSE (HMFI) figures would be in marginal cases where there was some doubt about the cause of death. The DHSS statistics may under-record to the extent to which death benefits were not payable. The HMFI injury and dangerous occurrence statistics, however, are known to be seriously deficient, perhaps of the order of 50% (see *Health and Safety Statistics* 1975 edition, p.10). It is generally recognized that the DHSS statistics provide a more reliable measure of the number of accidents.

Turning to the scope of the data, there are two important matters to bear in mind, one relating to coverage in industrial terms and the other in terms of the labour within the scope of the legislation. With regard to industrial coverage, the HMFI data collected prior to the introduction of the NADO regulations in 1981 referred to construction *processes* rather than the construction *industry* as such. For instance, an accident on 'building operations' carried out by the maintenance staff of a factory would appear under construction in the process classification, whereas in an industrial classification it would be recorded under manufacturing industry. Conversely, accidents on joinery work, for example, carried out by a builder in his own workshops would be classified as a factory *process* but could be classified to construction in an industrial classification. From 1978 the HSE began to use an industrial classification basis. But for the purpose of maintaining a continuous series over time, it has continued to distinguish separately those accidents occurring in construction processes covered by the 1961 Factories Act definition of building operations and works of engineering construction. The relevant figures are given in *Construction – Health and Safety*.

The distinction made above between the data based on process and industrial classifications is of the greatest importance when examining trends over many years. In this context, however, another problem concerns the extent to which under-reporting in the HMFI figures remained constant. It appears that it has in fact varied: there was a sharp rise in reported accidents, for example, in the early 1960s and it is suggested that this was not entirely due to there being more accidents, but arose partly from improved reporting resulting from publicity and changes in the law – see the *Annual Report of the Chief Inspector of Factories* for 1961 (Cmnd 1816) and *Construction – Health and Safety 1976*. There have also been changes in the scope of the regulations relating to construction processes from time to time – details are given in *Construction – Health and Safety 1976* and in the *Annual Reports of the Chief Inspector of Factories*.

With regard to the coverage of the total labour force, the data are deficient in their coverage of the large numbers at risk in the industry who work as self-employed labour. Prior to the introduction of the NADO regulations in 1981, the legal accident reporting requirement did not extend to the self-employed, and even under the NADO Regulations such accidents continued not to be directly reportable unless they involved fatalities or major injuries, and then only if the person involved was working under the overall control of another person (i.e. a contractor). Self-employed persons working independently (e.g. a decorator working in a private house) would be exempt from the reporting requirement. However, some accidents are voluntarily reported or notified to HSE and these have been recorded and shown separately in the statistics since 1978. To the extent that such workers are not in 'employed earner's employment' they would also not appear in the DHSS industrial injury statistics. A further complication in the examination of trends is that the HSE began to use a new accident classification in 1978.

A final notable factor with regard to the scope of the data is that from 1981 under the NADO Regulations fatal and major injury accidents to members of the public arising out of, or in connection with, work activities became notifiable.

INCIDENCE RATES. The problems of interpretation are compounded further in the calculation of incidence rates by the fact that, under the process classification, the numbers at risk had to be estimated because the official employment statistics are industrially based and consequently cover persons who are not at work on construction *processes* and, therefore, not within the scope of the legislation. Even on an industrial basis the employment statistics are open to sources of error (see Chapter 8, Sections 8.1 and 8.2). The incidence rates will also have been affected by the marked changes in self-employment in the industry which, before the introduction of the NADO Regulations in 1981, meant that when self-employment was growing relative to direct employment, an increasing part of the labour force was not covered by the reporting requirement. Further, it is particularly important to note that from 1981 the incidence rates are calculated on a completely different basis from earlier years. From 1981 the rate has been based on all *employees* at risk whereas previously it was based on operatives at risk only – i.e. excluding APTC staff. In so far as the latter represent a safer group, the effect is to reduce the calculated rate.

9.4 INDUSTRIAL DISPUTES

9.4.1 Available data and sources

(a) *Principal series*
Statistics relating to stoppages of work due to disputes concerning terms and conditions of employment are compiled monthly by the Department of Employment and cover the United Kingdom. There are three basic series:

1. Number of stoppages beginning in a defined period
2. Number of workers involved (both directly and indirectly involved but at the establishment where the stoppage occurred only)
3. Number of working days lost.

The primary publication source is the *Employment Gazette.* Secondary sources are the *AAS* (annual series) and the *MDS* (monthly series for category 3 only).
   Supplementary series are as follows:
1. Annual industrial analyses of the three basic series in respect of the disputes known to have been official – series from 1960

introduced in *Employment Gazette 1972*

2. An annual summary article in *Employment Gazette* provides further information about 'prominent' stoppages in the period
3. Regional industrial analyses of the basic series from 1955
4. Industrial analyses by cause of the dispute from 1959 (earlier analyses by cause did not give an industrial breakdown). A description of the classification used for the analyses by cause is given in *Department of Employment Gazette* 1973, pp.117–20
5. Incidence rates showing the number of working days lost per 1000 employees annually from 1959.

(b) *Other data*

STRIKERS' OCCUPATIONS. Occupational analyses of the persons involved in strikes are not regularly compiled but an analysis for the period 1966–73 by broad CODOT groups is reported in *Employment Gazette,* March 1980, pp.237–9.

CONCILIATION AND ARBITRATION. Information about conciliation and arbitration is incomplete and not analysed by industry. Details of the number of cases dealt with by the Advisory, Conciliation and Arbitration Service (ACAS) are given in its *Annual Reports.*

9.4.2 Interpretation

With regard to the interpretation of the strike statistics, there are a number of matters relating to their scope and accuracy that are important. With regard to the scope of the statistics, it should be noted that they cover both strikes and lockouts (without distinction) but that they refer to 'stoppages' as distinct from 'disputes' (which may not lead to an actual stoppage of work). The scope of the data is also limited by excluding stoppages which do not arise primarily over terms and conditions of employment. This means that 'political' strikes are not included. They are also limited by a recording threshold: stoppages involving fewer than 10 workers or lasting less than one day are excluded unless the aggregate number of days lost exceeds 100.

Interpretation of the data also needs to take account of certain difficulties involved in compiling the data with precision. There is no statutory obligation to report stoppages and it is possible for some to occur which go unrecorded. This may be particularly important in construction, given the large number of scattered sites of widely varying sizes in operation at any one time and the constant flux in the situation as some sites close down and new ones open up. Further, the distinction between workers directly and indirectly involved must often be difficult to make for construction bearing in mind the fact that sub-contractors' labour may be prevented from working on a particular site by a dispute involving another contractor's employees – and thus (apparently) be indirectly involved in the dispute – but in fact they may not be put out of work since they may simply transfer to another site. For the same reason determination of the number of days lost may be difficult. Likewise, reliance on voluntary information from employers or trade unions with regard to the cause of disputes etc. may be a source of error.

With regard to the incidence rates, it should be noted that they are not entirely satisfactory as indicators of strike-proneness, as the total number of days lost (on which the calculations are based) includes days lost at the establishments concerned by workers who were both directly and *indirectly* involved. Also the employment series, constituting the denominator in the calculations, includes APTC workers, who are normally less involved in stoppages, and the proportion of these varies considerably from one industry to another.

With regard to inter-industry comparisons, it should be appreciated that accuracy of reporting is likely to be greater for some industries than others so that a comparison between one industry and another cannot always be taken at face value. The statistics are also limited as indicators of industrial disputes inasmuch as no account is taken of forms of pressure other than strikes, e.g. the 'work-to-rule', the 'go-slow' and the 'overtime ban'.

Further discussion of the data and useful studies of strike activity will be found in Durcan *et al.* (1983) covering the period 1946–73 and in Smith *et al.* (1978) covering the period 1966–73. Both of these studies refer to construction along with other industries. Creigh (1984) provides a useful up-to-date review of the literature on British strike activity in general and discusses the available statistical material and case studies.

9.5 TRADE UNION STATISTICS AND INDUSTRIAL RELATIONS PRACTICES

9.5.1 Trade union membership

Accurate analyses of trade union membership according to industry are not available because many trade unions have members in more than one industry and figures which would enable an allocation by industry to be made are not readily available.

Official classifications by industry are compiled by the Department of Employment and published annually in *Employment Gazette,* but it is most important to note that, apart from special *ad hoc* estimates made for 1964, they are made by assigning the *total* membership of each union to the industry with which the majority of its members are believed to be connected. But in cases of unions with widely dispersed membership (e.g. the TGWU) industrial assignation in this way is unrealistic and the figures are placed in an un-classified group. Many 'unskilled' and 'semi-skilled' labourers in the construction industry are included in the membership of such general unions. The publication of industrial breakdowns was stopped in 1968 (because of their unreliability) but resumed from 1979 in the *Employment Gazette,* February 1982, pp.54–6, giving data for a reduced number of industrial groups (construction remaiₙᵤ a separate category). Details of the industry or industrial group to which the membership of each union is allocated is not normally published but information for the period from 1892 up to 1974 can be found in Price and Bain (1980). The main unions currently for the construction industry are UCATT, TGWU, GMBATU and FTAT.

The problem of multi-industry membership has been tackled in unofficial studies. The most comprehensive analyses have been compiled by Bain and Price (1980). This work provides an annual series for construction and other industries of the level and density of union membership over the period 1892–1974; full details of the nature of the data and the way in which the series were built up are included.

The only other information available about trade union

membership on an industrial basis comes from *ad hoc* enquiries. The estimates for 1964, referred to above, were made by the Ministry of Labour and published in Royal Commission on Trade Unions and Employers' Associations (1968), p.23. Questions on trade union membership were also included in a survey reported in *Employment Gazette,* 1981, pp.265–71; in the 1975 National Training Survey (unpublished – see Claydon, 1980) and in a survey carried out for the Phelps-Brown Committee (Cmnd 3714, 1968).

Information about the membership of individual trade unions (above a certain size) is listed in the annual reports of the Certification Officer for Trade Unions and Employers' Associations from 1976 (formerly in those of the Chief Registrar of Friendly Societies) and details for those affiliated to the TUC are given in its annual reports but, as stressed above, it needs to be remembered that trade union membership cuts across industrial boundaries.

9.5.2 Trade union finance

Information about the finance of 'listed' trade unions is contained in the reports of the Certification Officer referred to above and prior to 1976 in those of the Chief Registrar of Friendly Societies. At one time the reports of the Chief Registrar provided an industrial grouping but this was subject to the same lack of precision as the membership statistics referred to above and was discontinued.

9.5.3 Industrial relations practices

Information here again depends on *ad hoc* surveys. Surveys designed to find out how industrial relations were actually conducted at 'workshop' level in construction and other industries and about the attitudes of, and part played by, trade union officers, management staff etc. were carried out in 1966 for the Royal Commission on Trade Unions and Employers' Associations and reported in Government Social Survey (1968). Updating surveys were carried out in 1972, 1973 and 1980 but only the latter, reported in Daniel and Millward (1983), covered construction. A survey on the extent of closed shop arrangements in construction and other industries was published in *Employment Gazette,* January 1980, pp.16–22 and a survey of construction and five other sectors of non-manufacturing industry (extending an earlier survey for manufacturing industry) was reported in *Employment Gazette,* June 1981, pp.265–71 covering the following topics: the pattern of trade union recognition, trade union membership, shop steward representation, closed shop arrangements, existence of joint consultative committees, consultation and the size of establishment, election and selection of committee members, views on the success of committees and the existence of health and safety committees.

10
WAGE RATES, EARNINGS, HOURS AND LABOUR COSTS

This chapter is arranged as follows:

10.1 Basic wage rates and normal hours of work
10.2 Actual earnings and hours of work
10.3 Total labour costs.

The first part covers information about the standard rates of pay and normal hours of work agreed between organizations of employers and workers. The second part, covering actual earnings and hours, reflects work in excess of the agreed normal hours and related overtime rates of pay, together with bonus payments etc. The third and final part is concerned with two subjects: first, information on the total unit costs incurred by employers in employing labour, covering both payments to labour and associated on-costs, and secondly, aggregate information on the total wage and salary bill.

10.1 BASIC WAGE RATES AND NORMAL HOURS OF WORK

10.1.1 Actual wage rates and normal hours

The primary source of information about basic rates of wages, normal basic hours and general conditions of employment of manual workers, determined nationally by collective agreements between employers and trade unions for various sectors of the construction and other industries was the annual publication *Time Rates of Wages and Hours of Work* until 1982 when it was replaced by a loose-leaf publication available on subscription from the Department of Employment. In addition to information on basic rates and hours, this gives details of minimum earnings levels, general supplements, provisions for pieceworkers, shift-workers etc. and also overtime rates, young workers' rates and holidays-with-pay arrangements. Developments with regard to pay and conditions are also monitored in *IDS Reports.*

Times series of the principal rates from 1947 to 1968 were included in *British Labour Statistics: Historical Abstract 1886 to 1968 (BLSHA)* and continued in *BLS Yearbooks* until 1976.

10.1.2 Index numbers

Series of official index numbers for basic weekly and hourly wage rates and normal hours were published for the first time in 1971 in the *BLSHA* providing monthly series for the period from June 1947 to December 1968. The series were carried forward in the *BLS Yearbooks* until December 1976 and in the *Employment Gazette* until December 1983 when the series were discontinued. The index of *weekly* wage rates was reproduced in *MDS* and *HCS* (annual series).

INTERPRETATION. Care is required in the use and interpretation of these data. The negotiated rates vary not only over time, but also between one area of the country and another and between different categories of labour, especially, in the construction industry, skilled and unskilled labour. Over time the differential paid for skill has been reduced and thus the rate for unskilled labour has shown a greater relative increase than skilled rates. Further, many of the differences between one area of the country and another have been eliminated by a gradual process of upgrading, so that the rates of increase for the same type of labour have been greater in some areas than others. A single index number is, therefore, an amalgam of all these factors and measures the relative rate of change for neither any particular category of labour nor for any particular area of the country. In practice, of course, the influence of these factors on the index number itself depends upon the way it is calculated. Unfortunately details of the weights applied to skilled and unskilled rates and different regions have not been published and it is, therefore, not possible to make any judgements about these matters.

10.2 ACTUAL EARNINGS AND HOURS OF WORK

As with the information on wage rates and normal hours considered above, the prime responsibility for the collection of actual earnings and hours worked data for construction and other industries rests with the Department of Employment (DE). The Department defines earnings as the total gross remuneration which employees receive from their employers in the form of money before the deduction of income tax or of the employees' contributions to national insurance and pension funds. Income in kind and employers' contributions to national insurance and pension funds are excluded (for data on these categories see Section 10.3). DE surveys designed to measure average earnings and hours have been carried out from 1946 in the case of manual workers and from 1959 to 1980 in the case of non-manual workers. Commencing in 1968 these enquiries were supplemented by 'New Earnings Surveys' (NES) which provide much more detailed information. We consider the information provided by the DE in five sub-sections as follows:

10.2.1 Earnings and hours of manual workers (UK) from 1946
10.2.2 Earnings of non-manual employees (UK) 1959 to 1980
10.2.3 New earnings surveys (GB) 1968 to date
10.2.4 Monthly index of average earnings
10.2.5 Subsidiary DE series.

A sixth sub-section refers to various supplementary sources.

10.2.1 Earnings and hours of manual workers (UK)

(a) *Average earnings and hours*
Until the introduction of the NES in 1968, surveys were conducted each April and October from 1946 to 1970 and then in October in each year, based upon a panel of firms willing to supply information. Similar data are available at intervals back to 1886 – see Dean (1980) and *BLSHA* – but we are concerned here only with the period from 1946. The number of workers regularly covered (manual *employees)* is very large – several

hundred thousand – and represents a large proportion – generally around half – of the total recorded labour force. Data are collected on an aggregate basis only, i.e. data for total amounts paid, total hours worked and the total number of workers covered, enabling averages to be calculated. In October 1960 information was also obtained about the distribution of earnings – see below. The available series show average weekly and hourly earnings and average hours sub-classified as follows:

1. Until 1979 – full-time men (21 and over), youths and boys (under 21), women (18 and over) and part-time women (18 and over); then continued as in item 2 below
2. From 1980 – workers on adult rates (distinguishing full-time males and females and part-time females), and workers on other rates (distinguishing full-time males and females)
3. Regional analyses for full-time men from 1960 to 1979 and then for 'males on adult rates' from 1980.

The change made in the enquiries from 1980 introduces a discontinuity but it was felt that the previous separation of workers by a rigid age criterion had become increasingly unrealistic (see *Employment Gazette*, March 1981, pp.110–1).

PUBLICATION SOURCES. The primary publication source is the *Employment Gazette* but the whole series for the principal categories is conveniently summarized up to 1968 in *BLSHA* and carried forward in the subsequent *BLS Yearbooks* until 1976. The national series of average *weekly* earnings for full-time males and females (separately) on adult rates are reproduced in the *MDS;* separate data for Scotland appear in *SAS* and for Wales in *DWS* and *WET*.

(b) *Distribution of earnings*

In the October 1960 enquiry an additional question was included to obtain details of the numbers of full-time manual men and women whose gross earnings in a particular week fell into certain ranges. Analyses of the results for construction and other industries were published in *Ministry of Labour Gazette* in 1961. Subsequent information about the distribution of earnings of both manual and non-manual employees is available from the NES – see sub-section 10.2.3.

10.2.2 Average earnings of non-manual employees (UK), 1959 to 1980

This enquiry was discontinued after the enquiry for October 1980. It was carried out in October of each year from 1959 (except for 1971 and 1972) covering the earnings of non-manual (APTC) employees in construction and other industries on similar lines to that for manual employees referred to above. From October 1973 its coverage was restricted to full-time employees only. The results, giving figures of average weekly earnings for males and females separately, were published in *Employment Gazette* (last appearing in March 1981). The series up to 1968 were brought together in *BLSHA* and continued in the *BLS Yearbooks* to 1976.

10.2.3 New earnings surveys (GB) 1968 to date

(a) *Background*

The salient point about the NES which distinguishes it from the other surveys referred to above, is that information is obtained from employers about *individuals* as opposed to aggregate data covering groups of employees. Consequently, it is possible to make analyses according to the characteristics of the individual and the nature of his or her employment. However, it should be noted that the surveys relate only to *employees* – the self-employed (of particular importance in construction) are not covered. Each survey covers a random 1% sample of all employees in construction and other industries. The first survey was carried out in September 1968; subsequent surveys have been carried out annually since 1970 each relating to an April pay-period.

The main purpose of the surveys is to obtain information about the levels, distribution and make-up of earnings of employees in the various occupations, industries and major wage negotiating groups. The general aim is to keep survey questions unchanged so as to obtain directly comparable results. But some questions are only repeated at intervals of several years. These have covered such topics as types of incentive payments, holiday entitlement, length of service, types of collective agreement, sick pay schemes, pension schemes and earnings of apprentices and other trainees.

Before 1984 the surveys related to men aged 21 and over or women aged 18 and over. From 1984 they relate to male or female employees on adult rates. There is, therefore, some discontinuity between 1983 and 1984, but some results of the 1983 survey were published on both bases to provide a link in the 1983 reports. A detailed description of each survey is published along with the results. These also include information on sample numbers and sampling errors.

(b) *The analyses*

The basic analyses provide data on average weekly and hourly earnings; average hours worked; the distribution of earnings; amounts received for (and percentage of workers receiving): overtime payments, PBR, and premium payments. Supplementary analyses provide more detail on hours worked (normal basic/overtime); PBR payments (regular/periodic); for those receiving overtime and premium payments; and for those affected/not affected by absence. Most of the analyses are made by agreement, by industry and by occupation (based on KOS) and in each case for manual and non-manual employees each by sex. A further, particularly valuable, feature of the NES from the point of view of measuring changes in earnings over time, is the practice of including 'matched samples' of persons covered in successive enquiries. Finally, it should be noted that unpublished tabulations may be made available on request.

(c) *Publication sources*

The results of the NES are reported in great detail in six separate volumes under the general title of *New Earnings Survey* currently arranged (1984 results) as follows:

Part A   Streamlined analyses and key results by agreement
Part B   Report, summary analyses and other analyses by agreement
Part C   Analyses by industry
Part D   Analyses by occupation
Part E   Analyses by region and age group
Part F   Hours, earnings of part-time women employees and earnings of trainees.

A useful secondary source for some of the key results for construction is *HCS* (annual volume) which provides annual series over eleven years of: (a) the basic data on the level, make-up and distribution of average earnings for male manual and non-manual workers, (b) average earnings of male manual workers by craft, and (c) comparison of earnings and hours for construction with other industries.

10.2.4 Monthly index of average earnings (GB) from 1963

All of the earnings enquiries referred to above provide the basis for indices of average earnings. From January 1963, however, they have been supplemented by a further enquiry, on a smaller scale, to obtain information on a *monthly* basis covering construction and other industries in Great Britain. Details of the methodology, including retrospective revisions, are given in *Ministry of Labour Gazette* March 1967, p.214. From January 1976 new series have been introduced which, for construction, include 'hitherto uncovered employees' in the national and local government fields (see *Department of Employment Gazette* April 1976). The monthly index covers all workers – manual and non-manual, full-time and part-time of both sexes without distinction. Until 1966, however, separate indices were published for weekly-paid and monthly-paid employees. The results are published currently in the *Employment Gazette* and reproduced in *MDS* and *HCS* (quarterly). The earlier series were brought together in the *BLSHA* up to 1968 and in the *BLS Yearbooks* to 1976.

10.2.5 Subsidiary DE series

(a) *Occupational earnings and hours of work (GB) 1964–70*

Enquiries to obtain occupational data for men in certain manual occupations in construction were initiated in June 1964 and repeated in each subsequent January and June until January 1970 (except in the case of the heating, ventilating and domestic engineering sector of the industry, for which a further special enquiry was held in June 1970). Since then, occupational data have been collected in the NES. The surveys covered all large firms and a sample of smaller firms on the then MOL register – further details are given with the results. The enquiry was conducted separately for constructional engineering firms and other construction firms.

The results provide data in respect of those receiving adult rates of pay for weekly and hourly earnings (including and excluding overtime premium payments), and for hours of work, according to occupation, differentiating between constructional engineering and other construction. The results for the latter are also broken down by region as far as possible and by size of firm (from January 1965). They were published in *Ministry of Labour Gazette* – those for the first 'pilot' enquiry being published in the issue for January 1965, pp.21–3 and those for the final enquiry in *Department of Employment and Productivity Gazette* for November 1970. A summary of the weekly earnings data for construction other than constructional engineering up to 1968 was included in the *BLSHA* and in subsequent *BLS Yearbooks* to 1970. As with the other earnings enquiries referred to above, it should be appreciated that these results do not cover the earnings of men working as self-employed.

(b) *Payment by results (PBR)*

Since 1968 the NES has provided statistics about PBR in construction and other industries (see sub-section 10.2.3). Earlier sources of information are reviewed in Fleming (1980a), p.96.

10.2.6 Supplementary sources of income and hours of work data

Our attention here is confined to the period from 1971. Earlier sources, including surveys conducted by, or for, the NBPI in the period 1968–71, are reviewed in Fleming (1980a), p.234. Regular surveys of relevance are the *GHS* (covering hours and income), the *LFS* (hours), the 1971 census of population (hours) and *Reward Regional Surveys* (salaries). *Ad hoc* surveys have covered income in 1972 (OPCS inquiry), earnings and hours in 1973 (NEDO survey), earnings and hours of local authority building workers in 1979, salaries in building contracting and surveying in 1979 and wages and conditions in the construction industry (GMBATU survey) in 1984. We consider each in turn.

(a) *GHS and LFS*

These surveys are considered in Chapter 8 (Sections 8.5 and

8.6). They both cover a range of topics (summarized in Appendices A and B) including hours and income in the case of the *GHS* and hours in the *LFS,* as well as industry of employment and occupation. Systematic analyses of these subjects are not in fact published but available tabulations may be supplied on request and, it should be noted that the microdata themselves are made available for analysis by research workers.

(b) *Census of population data*

The 1971 census analyses (reported in *Census 1971, Great Britain – Economic Activity, Part IV)* provide frequency distributions of hours worked classified by industry, occupation and sex for the whole labour force. They therefore provide, since they are not confined to employees alone, information not available from other sources. The topic was not included in the 1981 census. Earlier censuses covered hours worked in 1961 and 1966 only and for part-time workers only.

(c) *Reward Regional Surveys*

This is a private organization which conducts, *inter alia,* a twice-yearly survey of salaries of managerial, administrative and technical staff in various industries. The results, published in *Reward – Salary and Living Cost Report,* are analysed according to job categories, functions and rank. The categories relating to construction are few and need to be treated with caution because of small sample sizes in this sector. These surveys are the successor to analyses based on the salaries of persons *seeking* employment and registered with PER, the results of which were published in *Reward* (this included a special supplement on salaries in the construction industry in 1979).

(d) *OPCS voluntary income enquiry 1972*

This survey was linked to a 1% sample of the 1971 Census of Population but conducted separately on a voluntary basis. The level of response obtained was not high but the enquiry is of considerable importance because of its wide coverage of the labour force. It covered categories of the labour force not covered in other enquiries, or for which separate information is not available (e.g. the self-employed), and also allowed analyses to be made according to characteristics of the labour force not covered elsewhere (e.g. according to educational attainment and qualifications). A report on the survey (OPCS, 1978) does not include statistical data but gives a list of tables which are available on request.*

(e) *NEDO survey of operatives' earnings and hours 1973*
This survey was carried out by the Building EDC, in order to provide information for the negotiation within the National Joint Council for the Building Industry of a new wages structure, and provides information and analyses not available elsewhere. Information was collected in one payweek in May 1973 about the composition of earnings and hours, the pay of apprentices and adult trainees, the operation of pension schemes and length of service. In addition, information was collected for comparative purposes, about *annual* earnings in contrast to weekly earnings. The results were analysed according to size of site and type of contractor. A summary of the results and details of the survey itself, which was based on the register of firms held by the Building and Civil Engineering Holidays Scheme Management company, were published in NEDO (1974).

(f) *Surveys of local authority building workers 1979*
Separate surveys were carried out in England and Wales and in Scotland for the Standing Commission on Pay Comparability. The results, given in the Commission's report (Cmnd 8014, 1980), provide data on the make-up of earnings by craft and the numbers employed in each skill category.

(g) *Salary surveys of building contractors and surveyors 1979*
Two surveys were conducted by the Building Business Unit of salaries and other rewards in November 1979. The survey of building contractors was limited to seventy one companies and reported in *Salaries and Benefits in Building Contracting*. It provides data on salaries and benefits (bonuses, company cars, fringe benefits) for six key job functions among building managers (estimators, buyers, surveyors, contracts staff, site managers

---

* A similar type of enquiry was carried out after the 1966 Census of Population in England and Wales but confined in the main to qualified manpower. The results, published as *Statistics of Education Special Series No. 3,* give, *inter alia,* industrial analyses by age, subject of qualification and status.

and site agents). The other survey, based on a one in five random sample (30% response) of members of the RICS, Institute of Quantity Surveyors and Society of Surveying Technicians, was reported in *Quantity and Building Surveyors Survey of Salaries and Rewards in the United Kingdom.* The purpose of the survey was to obtain data on pay and other benefits received by ·building surveyors, quantity surveyors and surveying technicians. The returns on salaries are analysed by fields of employment, levels of responsibility, qualifications, region and age.

(h) *GMBATU survey 1984*

This survey, reported in *Survey of Wages and Conditions in the Construction Industry,* covered a total of 1507 people in 26 companies ranging from the very large to the very small and gives basic rates, bonuses, allowances etc. for labourers, craftsmen and occasionally other groups such as drivers. Results are given for individual companies.

(i) *Guides to surveys*

   Ad hoc surveys for construction and other sectors are regularly monitored by Incomes Data Services (IDS) and reported in *IDS Report* (IDS, fortnightly). Salary surveys are noted in *Directory of Salary Surveys* (IDS, annually).

10.3 TOTAL LABOUR COSTS

The term 'total labour costs' may be interpreted in two ways: first, all unit costs directly incurred by employers in connection with the employment of labour and, secondly, information about the total wage and salary bill in the aggregate. We cover sources on both of these subjects here.

10.3.1 Labour cost surveys (GB) from 1964

(a) *Published analyses*

Between 1964 and 1975 four surveys of total labour costs in construction and other industries were conducted by the DE and its predecessors. From 1975 to 1981 the surveys were held triennially, following the entry of the UK into the EEC, and co-ordinated with EEC statistical requirements. After 1981 frequency was reduced to four-yearly. The range of information covered has remained much the same and is best indicated in detail by reference to the latest (1981) results. Separate analyses are available for manual and non-manual employees. The published results, however, show total labour costs per hour for all employees broken down as follows:

1. Wages and salaries – distinguishing separately the amounts included for: holidays and other time off with pay; absence due to sickness, or injury or maternity; periodical bonuses
2. Wages and salaries of apprentices and full-time trainees
3. Percentages of total costs accounted for by:
    (a) Wages and salaries
    (b) Statutory National Insurance contributions
    (c) Provision for redundancy (net)
    (d) Voluntary social welfare payments
    (e) Training (excluding wage and salary element)
    (f) Training (including wage and salary element)
    (g) Employers' liability insurance, benefits in kind and subsidized services
    (h) Government subsidies (negative cost).

(b) *Unpublished analyses*

Apart from separate data for manual and non-manual employees referred to above, additional analyses are available for: labour costs additional to wages and salaries for hours worked (manual, non-manual, total); annual labour costs per employee by size of establishment or firm; annual hours worked per employee; annual labour costs per employee (manual, non-manual).

(c) *Publication sources*

The results of the surveys are published in the *Employment Gazette*. The survey dates and publication dates are as follows: 1964 (December 1966 and March 1967)*; 1968 (August and October 1970)†; 1973 (September and October 1975); 1975 (September, November and December 1977); 1978 (January 1981); 1981 (May 1983). The results of the 1984 survey are due to be published early in 1986. Details of the execution of the

* Reprinted in *Labour Costs in Great Britain in 1964*.
† Reprinted in *Labour Costs in Great Britain in 1968*.

surveys are included in the published reports.

(d) *Interpretation*

With regard to interpretation, it needs to be remembered that the surveys cover employees only and thus do not reflect the payments made for the services of self-employed labour working under LOSC arrangements. With regard to the comparability of results over time, it may be noted that the sampling thresholds used for construction have been changed on a number of occasions and that, to the extent that the composition of labour costs varies by size of firm, the direct comparability of results may have been affected. With regard to coverage, the author is informed that local authority DLOs were not approached for the 1978 and 1981 surveys but were included in earlier surveys and again in 1984. The construction industry sample has been based on the DE Census of Employment register (see Section 8.2) since 1978; earlier surveys were based on the records of firms involved in the regular DE wages inquiries (see Section 10.2).

10.3.2 Total wage and salary bill

The relevant sources of information about the total wage and salary bill have been considered elsewhere in this book and we merely draw together the appropriate references here. First in importance are the industrial analyses incorporated as an integral part of the national accounts prepared for the UK since 1946 and at a regional level, since 1971 – these are both considered in Chapter 12 (Section 12.1). These accounts are based upon data derived from the income taxation statistics considered in Section 12.7. Further aggregate information at the national level is available from the annual censuses of production for construction which provide figures of expenditure on wages and salaries (with breakdowns for operatives and other employees) and for sub-divisions of the industry for some years – see Chapter 6 (Section 6.2) for further details.

11
ORGANIZATION AND
STRUCTURE OF
THE INDUSTRY

11.1 INTRODUCTION

It is important to remember that the British construction industry consists of two parts – private contractors and public sector direct labour organizations – but that published statistics may relate to one part alone. In this chapter we focus attention on the statistics which provide information about the structure and organization of each sector, i.e. details of the number of firms or direct labour organizations, their output and their employment sub-classified by size, or by trade of firm, or by region etc. The sources of time series data about output and employment in the two parts of the industry are considered separately in Chapters 6 and 8 respectively. The major sources of structural analyses are the enquiries conducted by the DoE and censuses of production carried out by the BSO. Both of these sources were considered earlier in the context of output and employment. In the present context each is considered below in Sections 11.2–11.4. An important additional source of information about the numbers and trades of firms in the industry is provided by VAT registration statistics, considered in Section 11.5. This source also provides information about new entry to, and exit from, the industry. Statistics about company acquisitions and mergers are considered in Section 11.6. Statistics about company liquidations and bankruptcy are considered along with other financial data in Chapter 12.

11.2 DoE ANALYSES FOR PRIVATE CONTRACTORS

11.2.1 Background and the data available

The DoE provides the primary source of information about the organization and structure of the industry on the basis of detailed analyses of regular large-scale enquiries. These enquiries were conducted as censuses of all firms on the register until 1976. Since then, although the term 'census' was retained for some time, sampling methods have been increasingly used for the smaller firms and the enquiry is now referred to as the 'Annual Return' to distinguish it from the more frequent sample returns of output and employment. Those firms not included in the October enquiry receive, however, a 'Small Firms Return' providing basic information on size and trade (essentially for register-proving purposes). With effect from 1984 this simple inquiry is being spread throughout the year rather than being concentrated in one quarter.

We confine our attention to the current series of enquiries which have run on a reasonably comparable basis (apart from problems in maintaining a comprehensive register) since 1955. Details of the pre–1955 censuses back to 1941 and a more detailed account of all the censuses up to 1977 is given in Fleming (1980a).

The main change introduced in 1955 was reclassification of the industry in accordance with the SIC, former enquiries having been carried out under the terms of war-time Defence Regulations. Censuses were taken in September 1955 (unpublished) and April 1956 and then regularly in April and September each year from 1957 to 1970 when they were combined into a single annual census taken in October, commencing in 1971. This enquiry continues to the present day, obtaining data in respect of third quarter output and October employment. In the previous bi-annual censuses, the April census was used to obtain information about employment and output, and the September census was used to obtain detailed information about the composition of the labour force.

Details of the analyses published from 1956 to 1983 (the latest available at the time of writing) together with their publication sources are given in Table 11.1. It will be seen that the number of analyses was increased in 1963 and 1965 but was subsequently

Table 11.1 DoE analyses of industrial structure – private contractors in Great Britain from 1956 (starting dates of current series and periods covered by pre-current series)

Data	Two-way classifications					One-way classification		
	By size of firm		By trade of firm		By region			
	By trade	By region	By type of work*	By region	By type of work*	By size of firm	By trade of firm	By region
1. Number of firms:								
(a) Totals	1956 to date	1957 to date	–	1957–78	1957–78	1956 to date	1956 to date	1956 to date
(b) Employing APTC staff	1965–78	1965–78	–	1965–77	–	1965–78	1965–78	1965–78
2. Output (one quarter only)								
(a) Value of work done	1956 to date	1957–78	1956 to date	1957–78	1956–78	1956 to date	1956 to date	1957 to date
(b) Value of work done and sub-contracted work	1979–81	–	–	–	–	1979–81	1979–81	–
3. Employment:								
(a) Operatives	1956 to date	1957–78	1956–78	1957–78	1957–78	1956 to date	1956 to date	1956 to date
(b) Operatives' occupation	–	–	–	–	–	1957–76	1957–76	1957–76
(c) Trainees (apprentices) until 1974	1963–78	1963–78	–	1963–78	–	1963–78	1963–78	1963–78
(d) Trainees (apprentices) by craft	–	–	–	–	–	1957–76	1957–76	1957–76
(e) APTC staff	1965 to date	1965–78	–	1965–78	–	1965 to date	1965 to date	1965–76
(f) APTC staff by type	–	–	–	–	–	1965–76	1965–76	1965–76
(g) Working Proprietors (Working Principals until 1970)	–	–	–	–	–	1963 to date	1963 to date	1963 to date
(h) Total manpower	–	–	–	–	–	1963 to date	1963 to date	1963 to date

Publication sources
1956: *Statistics Collected by the Ministry of Works 1941–56, Vol.1*
1957–70: *Bulletin of (Construction) Statistics Supplements.*
1971–78: *Private Contractors' Construction Census*
1979 to date: *Housing and Construction Statistics* (annual volume).

* Since 1979 four types of work have been distinguished: all new work and three categories of repairs and maintenance work (housing, public non-housing, private non-housing). From 1966 to 1978 eight categories were distinguished as in the output time series – see footnote to Table 6.1. Before 1966 three categories were distinguished: new housing, new non-housing and total repairs and maintenance.

reduced in scope in 1976 and 1978. We now turn to matters relating to the interpretation of the data.

11.2.2 Interpretation

(a) *Number of firms*

The most important point to note with regard to the interpretation of the data on the number of firms is that the figures should not be regarded as being necessarily comprehensive. As we indicated earlier, in Chapter 5, there has been no compulsory registration requirement and important difficulties have been experienced in maintaining an up-to-date register. Consequently changes in the number of firms cannot be interpreted safely, if at all, as evidence of trends. The maintenance of the register is considered more fully in Chapter 5. It should be noted in particular, that major discontinuities occur in 1973/74 (when, as a result of special inquiries, 25 000 firms were added to the existing register of 70 000 for the first time), and again in 1982 when 45 000 firms were added as a result of matching the DoE and VAT-based registers (considered in Section 11.5). In the intervening period continuing difficulties had been experienced, although from 1977 firms newly-registered for VAT were systematically added to the register.

Another point to note with regard to the interpretation of the figures of the number of firms is that, strictly speaking, they refer to the number of 'reporting units' rather than firms as such – a point which is now made clear in the currently published sources. Firms under common ownership or control may or may not make separate returns and some firms may make more than one return in respect of its activities in different parts of the country. Finally, it is worth noting that the number of firms include those not trading at the time of the census. Hence in the analyses by size of firm it is possible for the figure for the smallest size group to exceed the figure for total employment in the group.

(b) *Number of firms employing APTC staff*

The definition of APTC staff was altered in 1971, resulting in the re-classification of around 10 000 persons as Working Proprietors rather than APTC. Analyses of the number of firms employing APTC staff will therefore have been affected from this date:

many firms run by a Working Proprietor and employing no other APTC staff would have been included before 1971 but not subsequently.

(c) *Value of work done and employment*

Reference should be made to Chapter 6 (Section 6.1.2) for matters relating to the interpretation of the value of work done figures and to Chapter 8 (Section 8.1.2) regarding employment.

(d) *Analyses by size of firm*

Firms have always been classified by size on the basis of employment, but in 1965 the change was made from classification according to the number of operatives employed to one based on total employment (including Working Principals and all other APTC staff as well as operatives). Comparative data on the new and the old bases is to be found in the *Bulletin of Construction Statistics Supplements* for 1965. Summary data for an extended range of size groups (again including comparative data for 1965) over the period 1959–70 were published in the *Annual Bulletin of Construction Statistics* for 1970.

(e) *Analyses by trade of firm*

Currently, 21 trades of firm are distinguished (plus a miscellaneous group), the list having been expanded at various times since 1957 when it consisted of 12 trades. The general principle of the classification is that each firm classifies itself on the basis of the one activity which forms the most significant part of its turnover. However, information about trade has been sought regularly in each census only since 1971. Before then periodic reviews were carried out notably in 1957, 1968 and 1970, each of which led to an expansion in the number of trades distinguished and also, in 1957 and 1968, to some reclassification.

In 1957 many of the firms which had been previously described as 'General Builders' were reclassified as specialist firms (notably as 'Painters') but the reclassification was not introduced in published results until 1958 so that there is a discontinuity between 1957 and 1958. Nearly all trades were affected by the 1968 reclassification, but the extent of the discontinuities may be observed from comparative figures prepared on the basis of the new and the old classifications. The information about trade regularly sought in each enquiry from 1971 has been used for the classification of published results with effect from 1974.

A further point to note arising from the periodic nature of the classification by trade before 1971 is that such switches as took place in the major activity of a firm from one trade to another (e.g. from 'Plumber' to 'Heating and Ventilating Engineer') will have gone undetected. At the same time, it must be remembered that deficiencies in the coverage of the register of firms will also affect comparisons of the trade composition, especially inasmuch as new entrants are an important source of change. Particular note should be taken of the effects of the inclusion of 25 000 previously unrecorded firms which were added to the register in 1973 followed by subsequent decline and then expansion again after 1977 and especially in 1982. It should also be noted that classification by trade is affected by changes to the SIC. Under the current (1980) SIC, specialist opencast coal contractors and plant hirers without operatives have been excluded from the industry. The latter are now classified to the services sector and are covered in BSO enquiries. The results of the first enquiry, in 1982, were reported in *British Business* 10 August 1984, p.591, giving figures for the number of businesses, total turnover, stocks and capital expenditure.

Interpretation of the analyses by trade of firm for employment and work done according to type of work, should have regard to certain problems that arise and the practices adopted. Certain trades only are affected, namely those of demolition, plant hire and scaffolding contractors. The employment work done by demolition contractors is attributed, in the analyses according to type of work, to that type of work which is to replace the structure being demolished but where this is not known the work (and employment on it) is assigned to the same type of work as that being demolished. Not all demolition work, of course, is carried out by demolition contractors. Plant hire firms are not generally able to specify the work on which plant has been used and the practice adopted is to distribute the figures of employment and work done over different types of work proportionately to the distribution of the figures for all other firms. Before 1968 the figures were distributed over new work only on the assumption that little plant was hired for repair and maintenance work; since then they have been spread over all work. Similarly in the case of scaffolding firms, employment and work-done figures are distributed proportionately over all work. These points are important when considering the work done by these trades analysed by type of work, but it will be appreciated that the effects on the analysis of type of work for all trades combined is small since the activity of these particular trades is a small part of the total.

Finally, a problem that arises in connection with the plant hire figures is that of double counting. Plant hire firms are not in the same category as other specialist firms since they do not normally carry out work on a contract themselves. Consequently, contractors will not exclude payments made to these firms, as they would in the case of other specialist firms working as sub-contractors. Hence total output will include the element of plant-hire costs incorporated in the return of output of firms using hired plant and again in the returns of 'output' by plant hire firms themselves. Analogous situations do not arise in the case of *goods* supplied by one contractor to another because contractors are instructed to exclude the value of goods made for sale from their returns.

(f) *Analyses by region*

As indicated earlier, regional analyses for building work present a major problem because of the fact that the production units do not occupy a fixed location but move about from site to site and many may work on more than one site at the same time. Before 1955 contractors were required to make a return of operatives employed according to the region in which they were working, but in the new system of censuses established after 1955 all regional analyses have been based upon the location of the reporting office. This represents a major limitation of the regional data. The current regional output *time series,* considered in Chapter 6 (Section 6.1) are not so limited because of the introduction of the project-based enquiry, but the analyses under consideration here remain unavoidably based on the regions of registration of the firms.

(g) *Analyses by type of work and sector*

Apart from the issues discussed above in relation to the classification by trade of firm, the following characteristics of the data are important to note. First, it may not be possible to classify certain operatives by type of work (e.g. transport workers, stores and warehouse staff, canteen workers and operatives employed on the manufacture of goods for sale) and they are therefore returned as a separate total; the figure is not published separately, however, but is allocated *pro rata* among the various categories of work. Secondly, the employment and output data differ in timing: the statistics of employment refer to employment on the pay-day in one week each year whereas the output statistics refer to the estimated value of work done in the quarter up to the end of the preceding month. Thirdly, there is a discrepancy in the treatment of goods manufactured for sale by the contractor: the value of such goods are meant to be excluded from the return but the number of operatives engaged on their manufacture are meant to be included. However, the value of goods both made and used by the contractor are included. Fourthly, it should be noted that the term 'repair and maintenance' is defined differ-ently in respect of housing and non-housing work. For housing it includes work of 'improvements, house/flat conversions, extensions, alterations and redecoration' whereas on non-housing work 'extensions, major alterations and improvements' are defined as new construction (the term 'major alterations' is left undefined).

Finally, it is worth noting that the boundaries between the public and private sectors may be altered from time to time by measures such as nationalization and privatization. These affect the classification of output and employment by sector and possibly also the division between contractors and DLOs if the organizations affected directly employ construction workers and are within the scope of the SIC definition of the industry.

11.3 DoE CENSUSES OF DIRECT LABOUR ORGANIZATIONS

11.3.1 Introduction

The DoE and its predecessor departments have taken regular censuses of the direct labour departments of local authorities (including new towns), public utilities and government departments in the period since 1955* following much the same pattern as that set for contractors from 1957 onwards; that is to say twice-yearly censuses in April and September, statistics about employment and output by type of work being obtained in April and more detailed statistics about employment being obtained in September. But unlike the contractors' censuses, for which the biannual enquiries were replaced by a single annual enquiry from 1971, this biannual pattern was retained until 1982 when it was placed on a quarterly footing. However, the only detailed analyses of the data providing information about the structure of the sector relates to local authorities and new towns alone. It may also be noted here that since 1981 local authorities have been required to prepare separate accounts and manpower statements relating to the operation of their DLOs and that summaries of the data are published by CIPFA – see Chapter 12, Section 12.3 for further details.

11.3.2 Local authorities and new towns direct labour

(a) *Data available*

Regular breakdowns of the DoE census data have been published only since 1961. Details are set out in Table 11.2. It will be seen that the scope of the published analyses was expanded during the period, notably in 1968. However, some of the information for the period before 1968 (in particular, data on the employment of operatives and apprentices by occupation back to 1957 and APTC staff back to 1966) is available on request from the DoE Statistics Construction Division. Since 1968 the scope of the analyses has been reduced as data collection has been reduced, as in the case of contractors. We now turn to questions of interpretation.

(b) *Interpretation*

COVERAGE OF AUTHORITIES. The coverage of the enquiry extends to all local government authorities throughout Great Britain including, currently, those for new towns. The latter were not covered, however, until September 1964 and not included in

---

* As in the case of contractors, information about censuses taken before 1955 will be found in Fleming (1980a).

Table 11.2 DoE census analyses of local authorities' and new towns' direct labour in Great Britain from 1961* (starting dates of current series and periods covered by pre-current series)

Data	One-way classifications				Two-way classifications		
					By type of work†		
	By size of authority	By type of authority	By region	By type of work†	By size of authority	By type of authority	By region
1. Number of authorities:							
(a) Employing direct labour	1968 to date	1961 to date	1961 to date‡	—	—	—	—
(b) Total	1968 to date	1968 to date	1968 to date‡	—	—	—	—
2. Output (value of work done)	1968 to date	1961 to date	1961 to date	1961 to date	1968 to date	1961 to date	1961 to date
3. Employment							
(a) Operatives	1968 to date	1961 to date	1961 to date	1961–81	1968–80	1961–80	1961–80
(b) Operatives by occupation	—	1968–80	—	—	—	—	—
(c) Trainees (apprentices) by occupation	—	1968–78	—	—	—	—	—
(d) APTC staff by type	—	1968–80	—	—	—	—	—

Publication sources
1961–70: *Monthly Bulletin of Construction Statistics*
1971 to date: *Housing and Construction Statistics*.

* This table covers the published analyses of results from 1961 to 1983 – the latest available at the time of writing. New towns were not included in the published results until April 1966. No census was taken in April 1974. The results of local authority censuses taken in the period from 1956 to 1960 were not published at the time but certain analyses of the April 1956 census results were published retrospectively in *Statistics Collected by the MOW 1941–56* as follows: Number of authorities employing direct labour, number of operatives employed by type of work, and value of work done by type of work (1st quarter 1956), each analysed by region, type of local authority and size of local authority.

† From 1968 four types of work are distinguished: new work and repair and maintenance work, each split between housing and non-housing. Previously the repair and maintenance figure was not split.

‡ Analyses were not published for 1974, 1977 and 1978.

published results until April 1966. The direct labour department of the Scottish Special Housing Association (SSHA), it should be noted, is treated as a contractor not as a direct labour organization (some data on its direct labour force are contained in its *Annual Reports).*

EMPLOYMENT OF OPERATIVES AND TRAINEES. The returns are meant to cover all operatives and trainees (male and female) 'wholly or mainly engaged on building and civil engineering work – i.e. work which otherwise would be undertaken by building and civil engineering firms' on a specific day.

EMPLOYMENT OF APTC STAFF. There is an important distinction to be made between the statistics of APTC staff employed by local authorities and those for contractors. Whereas the activities of the latter are naturally related solely to the work being undertaken by contractors, in the case of local authorities such staff may be engaged on design, management, control etc. of building and civil engineering work irrespective of whether the work is to be carried out by the local authority's own direct labour or by contractors.

OUTPUT DATA. Output is an estimate of the value of work done during a specified period of three months by the operatives defined above – i.e. a sum calculated to cover the cost of materials, wages and the establishment charges attributable to the work carried out. However, it was not until 1981 in England and Wales and 1982 in Scotland that local authorities were required by law to act on a quasi-commercial basis and follow a common code of accounting (see Chapter 12, Section 12.3). Thus there is an important change in the basis of the figures at these dates. Earlier figures will have included no profit element (a target rate of return is now imposed) and there may be some doubt about the appropriate allocation of overheads. The value excludes the cost of land, legal costs and professional fees.

CLASSIFICATION BY TYPE AND SIZE OF AUTHORITY. Before September 1968 only County Councils were distinguished from other types of authority in England and Wales and in Scotland. Since then analyses have been published for each type of local authority. The analysis by size of authority refers to the size of the direct labour force as determined by the number of *operatives* employed. This contrasts with the size analyses for contractors which have not used operatives as the basis since 1965.

CLASSIFICATION BY REGION. These are naturally based upon the regional location of the local authority. Information about work carried out for other authorities is not collected but it seems reasonable to assume that it would be a small or negligible proportion of the total.

CLASSIFICATION OF OPERATIVES, TRAINEES AND APTC STAFF BY OCCUPATION. The categories distinguished are the same as for contractors (see Section 11.2) except that the sub-division of *professional* staff according to occupation (architect, surveyor, engineer) – abandoned in the case of contractors after 1974 – was retained.

11.3.3 Government departments' and public utilities' direct labour

The DoE also conducts censuses of the direct labour employed by government departments, public utilities and other public bodies. Detailed analyses are not published but the Department may supply some of the data on request. The only published data have been occasional *ad hoc* analyses – see Fleming (1980a) pp.122–3 for details. Coverage of these bodies has never been complete and over time has gradually been reduced as some have been expressly excluded from the scope of the SIC definition – see Chapter 5.

11.4 BSO CENSUSES OF PRODUCTION FOR CONSTRUCTION

This census has been discussed in Section 6.2 in the context of output and expenditure statistics and reference should be made to that section for full details. We merely draw attention here to its relevant features from the point of view of structural analyses of the industry. There are two features, in particular, which made the data an important complement to those collected by the DoE. One is that separate analyses by size are made for *all* public sector undertakings within the scope of the SIC definition for the industry, as opposed to the analysis limited to local authorities and new towns published by the DoE. The other is that breakdowns by size (size of firm in the private sector and size of undertaking in the public sector) and by trade of firm in the private sector ('sub-divisions of industry') provide data not only for the value of work done and employment (as in the DoE censuses) but also for net output and value added, for the costs of inputs (wages, salaries, materials etc.) and for capital expenditure. The trades of firms distinguished in the analyses by 'sub-division of industry' (until 1979) paralleled those distinguished by the DoE but in addition included separate categories for opencast coalmining contractors and for plant-hiring contractors with, and without, operators.

11.5 VAT REGISTRATION STATISTICS

VAT registration statistics provide a further, particularly valuable, source of information about certain structural features of construction and other industries. They are particularly valuable because of their virtually comprehensive coverage and because of the analyses that administration of the register permits. Comprehensive coverage arises out of the fact that anyone carrying on a business with a turnover greater than a specified (fairly small) exemption limit is legally required to register and, moreover, has a financial incentive to do so owing to the administration of the tax.

Analyses of the number (stock) of businesses ('taxable persons') on the register, classified by trade and also by legal status (information not available from any other source), are published in annual *Reports of the Commissioners of HM Customs and Excise*. In addition to analyses of the stock of businesses, changes to the register are used to provide data on starts and stops (births and deaths) of businesses and on their lifespan. The results are published from time to time in *British Business;* details are as follows:

Analyses	*Publication date*
1. Stock (number) of businesses:	
(a) by turnover size – annually from 1978–79	First published 23 Jan. 1981, pp.183–5

(b) in assisted areas, 1982	11 Nov. 1983, pp.536–9
(c) by county, 1979 and 1983	18 Jan. 1985, pp.106–10
2. Starts and stops (births and deaths):	
(a) UK Analyses – annually from 1980	First published
	29 Jan. 1982, pp.204–7
(b) by turnover, 1980–83	18 May 1984, pp.10–13
(c) by region, 1980–83	2 Nov. 1984, pp.350–3
(d) in assisted areas, 1982	10 Feb. 1984, pp.240–3
(e) by county, 1980–83	18 Jan. 1985, pp.106–10
3. Lifespan of businesses, 1973–82	12 Aug. 1983, pp.838–45
	and 7 Oct. 1983, pp.306–10

THE VAT AND DoE REGISTERS. Reference was made earlier to the difficulties faced by the DoE in maintaining a comprehensive register of firms because of the lack of a compulsory registration requirement and the use it has made of the VAT register to bring its own register up to date (Chapter 5 and Section 11.2.2). The two registers were matched in 1982. However, it may be noted that differences in the size of the registers may remain because of the fact that it is possible for a single firm (reporting unit) on the DoE register to have more than one VAT registration number and consequently to be recorded as more than one unit on the VAT register. Discrepancies may also occur because persons may be registered for VAT purposes, and classified to construction, who only carry out construction work in their spare time and are not recorded on the DoE register.

11.6 COMPANY ACQUISITIONS AND MERGERS

11.6.1 Series available and sources

Statistics of the number of, and expenditure on, acquisitions and mergers by construction and other companies in the UK are compiled by the DTI. The data on this subject extend back to 1954 but series according to industry have been published only for the period from 1960 – annually up to 1967 and then quarterly. The primary source of publication currently is *Business Monitor MQ7.* This was introduced in 1971, but the third issue – November 1971 – contained the full annual series back to 1960. *British Business* contains summary information each quarter. Before 1971 the series were included in the *Board of Trade Journal* and its successor publication *Trade and Industry,* the issue for

26 August 1971 containing a descriptive article (pp.388–9). A summary and discussion of the earlier data from 1954 (up to 1961), including a summary by industry for the period, will be found in *Economic Trends,* April 1963.

11.6.2 Interpretation

The first point to note is that the analyses are restricted to acquisitions of *companies:* they do not cover the acquisition of unincorporated businesses which, of course, are particularly important, numerically, in the construction industry.

Secondly, it is important to appreciate that there is no statutory reporting requirement and that the series have had to be compiled, therefore, using incomplete sources of information. Up to 1969 the series were compiled on the basis of the accounts of *quoted* companies included by the Board of Trade in its analyses of company income and finance (see Chapter 12, Section 12.2). From 1969 coverage was widened on the basis of reports in the financial press to cover companies generally (the quarterly series introduced in 1968 to supplement the previous annual series had also been based on reports in the financial press). The change in 1969 showed that the previous figures for construction had been seriously understated. Comparative results on the basis of the old and new statistical populations showed that the effect of the change was to increase the construction series in 1969 by factors of well over two – in contrast to manufacturing industries for which the increases were very much less *(Board of Trade Journal,* 1970, p.526 refers). However, the series compiled since 1969 still remains incomplete, excluding in particular many small acquisitions. Given the large number of small firms in the construction industry it would seem reasonable to believe that the series for the industry is still particularly affected. Of the two types of data provided – numbers (companies acquiring and companies acquired) and expenditure – it is likely that the latter is less open to error proportionately than the former (in contrast to the earlier period) since it is the smaller mergers and acquisitions that are now more likely to be missed. Unfortunately, it is impossible to judge how large the errors may be.

Finally, it should be appreciated that the classification by industry is limited, in that it is made only on the basis of the *acquiring* company. Thus the classification for construction shows the number of acquiring companies classified to the industry, the number of companies acquired (not all of which may be construction companies), and expenditure on acquisitions. Information on the number of construction companies, as such, taken over either by other construction companies or by companies in other industries is not given.

12
FINANCIAL STATISTICS

This chapter covers all sources of statistics of a financial nature which are not considered elsewhere in this book. Data on housing finance and housing costs and prices are covered in Chapters 3 and 4 respectively; construction output and expenditure statistics are considered in Chapters 6 and 7; labour costs and materials prices are dealt with in Chapters 10 and 14 respectively while information on total construction costs and prices is dealt with in Chapter 13. Statistics of expenditure on acquisitions and mergers are considered in Chapter 11 (Section 11.6). This chapter covers the following topics:

12.1 Construction in the national accounts
12.2 Company income and finance
12.3 Local authority direct labour organizations
12.4 Bank loans and advances
12.5 R & D expenditure surveys
12.6 Company liquidation and bankruptcy
12.7 Taxation statistics

12.1 CONSTRUCTION IN THE NATIONAL ACCOUNTS

The purpose of the national accounts is to provide a measure of total economic activity – gross domestic product (GDP) – and to reveal something of the anatomy of the economy by providing analyses of: the contribution to total output made by each industry, the incomes generated and the flows of expenditure – each being an alternative way of looking at total economic activity but each being integrated into a single set of accounts. Construction, of course, forms an integral part of these accounts and indeed represents one of the country's major industries in terms of its relative contribution to GDP and especially, because of its pre-eminence as the producer of capital assets which regularly constitute around half of gross fixed capital formation every year. National (UK) accounts are available for the whole of the period since 1946, regional accounts have been developed more recently and are more limited in scope.

12.1.1 UK accounts

The accounts are prepared by the CSO and published annually as *United Kingdom National Accounts* – commonly referred to as the Blue Book. Quarterly accounts were introduced in the mid-1950s but these do not provide relevant information for construction except for capital formation data which were considered earlier in Chapter 6 Section 6.5. Construction is represented in the accounts under each of the three ways of looking at economic activity referred to above – output, income and expenditure – and we examine each of these in turn.

(a) *Output*

The contribution made by the industry to total national output (series available from 1948) is published in a table of 'Gross Domestic Product by Industry'. It is not the same as the value of its gross output – statistics about which were considered in Chapter 6 – because this value incorporates the contribution of goods and services supplied by other industries. Rather, it is a measure of net output – the value added by construction activity itself. But the figure included in the Blue Book is in fact not derived from output statistics at all but is based upon the aggregation of factor incomes generated in the industry. The statistics of 'net output' regularly published in the Census of Production reports (Section 6.4 refers) are also not the same; only since 1973 (1974 in the case of construction) has it been possible to define value-added in the census, following the addition of questions on payments for non-industrial services (see Mitchell, 1978, for fuller discussion). A further Blue-Book table gives 'index numbers of output at constant factor costs' showing the changes in output over time in real terms, i.e. the change in value added at constant costs and prices.

(b) *Income*

Separate figures are given in a table entitled 'Gross Domestic Product by Industry and Type of Income' as follows:

1. Income from employment
2. Gross profits of companies and income from self-employment.

It will be appreciated, that 'income from self-employment' includes, indistinguishably, the value of the labour of the self-employed person as well as his profits. All of the income figures are based on the statistics compiled by the Inland Revenue as a consequence of its taxation functions, after due allowance is made for the income of people who are not subject to tax. These statistics are considered in Section 12.7. It may be noted here, however, that the construction estimates are open to error because of the problem of tax evasion on the part of self-employed construction workers.

(c) *Expenditure*

Expenditure can be looked at from two points of view: expenditure by other industries and sectors of the economy *on* the work done by the construction industry and, secondly, expenditure *by* the construction industry itself. The products of the construction industry are primarily capital goods and are distinguished in accounts of 'gross domestic fixed capital formation'. These provide separate data for expenditure on 'buildings and works' broken down according to industry and sector for whom the work is carried out. These statistics are an important source of information about construction work and, therefore, they have been discussed in the chapter dealing with output (Chapter 6). As we note there, expenditure on repairs and maintenance to buildings and other construction works is not regarded as part of capital formation, but a separate figure for this item is shown as a footnote to the tables in the Blue Book (based, however, on output rather than expenditure returns and relating to Great Britain rather than the UK).

(d) *Expenditure by the construction industry*

Expenditure *by* the construction industry itself on capital formation (not on purchases for non-capital purposes) is given in tables of gross domestic fixed capital formation by industry at current and constant prices and by type of asset at current prices. It is important to note, however, that the construction industry here is not defined in accordance with the SIC, all public sector direct labour departments being excluded. For information about non-capital expenditure, reference should be made to the BSO censuses of production (Section 6.2) and input-output tables (Section 6.4).

(e) *Capital stock*
In addition to the annual series of expenditure on capital formation, the national accounts also include estimates of: the accumulated capital stock of buildings and works and other assets, the capital stock of the construction industry itself and related figures of 'capital consumption'; these are considered in Chapter 16.

The compilation of the national income and expenditure accounts naturally follows certain conventions and draws upon the wide variety of statistical sources considered elsewhere in this book. A detailed account of the conventions and of the sources and methods used was set out in an official guide in 1968 (Maurice, 1968) and in a revised edition published in 1985 (CSO, 1985).

12.1.2 Regional accounts

The only official regional figures at an industrial level available show the estimated contribution to GDP in England, Wales, Scotland, Northern Ireland and in each region of England each year. The official regional accounts run from 1971. They were published for the first time in *Economic Trends* No. 277, 1976, and are now continued in *Regional Trends*. Detals of the methodology are given in CSO (1978b). It is important to note that the estimates are made using the income approach to measurement and are open to error. One problem is in drawing a distinction between the income-earner's region of residence and region of work – a problem which may affect construction more than most other sectors perhaps. Regional analyses of gross domestic fixed capital formation are also made but, apart from a separate category for dwellings, do not distinguish buildings and works from other types of assets. Apart from the official series a number of unofficial estimates, particularly for Scotland and Wales, have been prepared. These provide longer historical series and more detailed analyses. They also use different methods of estimation. But, as with the official series, they are subject to important margins of error which it is difficult to quantify, particularly for construction, because of the nature of the underlying statistical sources (discussed elsewhere in this book) and the approximate methods of estimation involved. For references to studies before 1971, see Fleming (1980a, p.246). For subsequent studies, see Lythe and Majmudar (1981) for Scotland (providing series for 1961–71) and Wanhill (1980) for Wales (providing estimates for various years from 1948 to 1970 – with annual series available on request – including a breakdown of GDFCF by industry and for buildings and works).

12.2 COMPANY INCOME AND FINANCE

12.2.1 Statistics from company accounts

(a) *Summary analyses*

As far as the construction industry is concerned, it needs to be appreciated that the analyses of company accounts, particularly those of public quoted companies, provide only very limited coverage of the industry because it is dominated by private companies, partnerships and sole traders. The proportion of public companies is extremely small and the proportion quoted or 'listed' on the Stock Exchanges is infinitesimal.

Summary analyses of company accounts for construction and other sectors have been prepared since 1949 but their bases have been changed on a number of occasions. The current analyses run from 1977 and are published in *Business Monitor MA3*. They are based on a representative sample of all sizes of industrial and commercial companies and provide three separate summaries of the accounts: an income appropriation account, a balance sheet and a statement of sources and uses of funds. Summaries are also given of information which companies have been required to include in their annual reports since the passage of the 1967 Companies Act, viz: turnover, exports, political contributions, charitable contributions, contracts for capital expenditure placed but not provided for, aggregate remuneration paid to UK employees per year and the average number of employees per week in the UK.

Before 1977 the analyses were based on a panel of companies (as opposed to a representative sample). Two distinct periods need to be distinguished: (i) 1949–60 and (ii) 1960–77. It also needs to be noted that although separate analyses for construction are available they were not always included in the regular published sources. We consider each of these periods in turn.

(i) 1949–60. Analyses were confined to companies quoted on UK stock exchanges. Construction was *not* distinguished in the published analyses (NIESR, 1956 and *ET* periodically) but separate tabulations of the whole period for construction are available in Board of Trade (1962). An analysis and discussion of the data for quoted construction companies in the period 1949–53 (less than 50 companies) will be found in Tew and Henderson (1959).

(ii) 1960–77. In 1967 the analyses were extended in scope to cover both quoted and non-quoted companies and carried back to 1960. However, coverage was limited according to certain size criteria (changed from time to time to try to maintain roughly equal coverage from one period to the next – for details see the published reports). The results were published in *Statistics on Incomes, Prices, Employment and Production* from 1960 to 1968 and then in *Business Monitor M3* (the first issue containing the results back to 1964). These publications do contain a separate category for construction *but* confined to 'listed' (i.e. quoted) companies only. The results for unlisted construction companies were consolidated into a larger grouping but they are available separately on request from the DTI (Economics and Statistics Division).

OVERSEAS-OWNED CONSTRUCTION COMPANIES. Since 1969 separate official analyses have been prepared for those companies operating in the UK which are owned by a company overseas. A comparison and general commentary on the accounts of such companies, analysed according to whether they were overseas controlled or UK controlled, was published in *Economic Trends* No. 238, 1973. Subsequent figures are available on request from the DTI (Economics and Statistics Division). The number of construction companies concerned is very small indeed.

UNOFFICIAL SURVEYS OF COMPANY ACCOUNTS. Regular analyses are published by the *Financial Times (FT)* and *The Economist* (on subscription). They are generally available more frequently than the official summaries, but it should be realized that they represent simple summaries of the accounts received up to a short time before publication. Consequently, they are not comprehensive and comparisons over time may be affected by changes in the composition of the group covered from one period to the next. Further details of the *FT* analyses are given in Bell and Greenhorn (1984). In addition to regular summaries, useful data also come from *ad hoc* studies. Two large enough to provide breakdowns by industry (including construction) are Bannock (1975), which covered over 900 private construction companies from the late 1960s to early 1970s, and Hay and Morris (1984) which covered over 100 unquoted construction companies and includes comparisons with quoted companies for various periods in the 1970s (value added, rates of return and growth rates).

(b) *Individual company accounts*

Since the passage of the 1967 Companies Act every limited company, public or private, has been required to file copies of its accounts with the Registrar of Companies and these are open to inspection by the public. Before the 1967 Act some private companies had been exempt from this requirement. Lists of large companies classified by industry, ranked by size together with key figures from their accounts are compiled by private commercial organizations. Examples are *The Times 1000*, Inter-Company Comparisons Ltd (ICC), which publishes a variety of financial surveys and business ratio reports for various sectors of construction and other industries, and Jordan Dataquest which publishes annual surveys of large public and private companies. A wide variety of company accounting information and other financial data is also available on a computerized data base system with on-line access run by Datastream International Ltd, based in London. Organizations such as Extel Statistical Services also provide a service on subscription of regular up-to-date company information on filing cards for the use of stockbrokers and other subscribers.

(c) *Interpretation of company accounts*

There are a number of matters which are important from the point of view of the interpretation of the summary analyses of construction company accounts and that in individual company accounts. First it is important to appreciate the scope of the data. We have already stressed its marked limitations from an industrial point of view because of the importance of private companies, partnerships and sole traders in the construction industry. On the other hand, it is important to recognize that the accounts reflect *all* the economic activities of the companies: many large companies carry out construction work overseas and some have interests in other fields of economic activity (a company is classified to construction if that represents its major field of activity). There is a contrast, therefore, with most of the other official statistics for the industry considered elsewhere in this book, which are confined to domestic activity and in which the collection of statistics from constituent 'establishments' of the company permits a more accurate classification.

Next it is important to recognize that the accounts are beset by problems of comparability, first because of the differences in the application of standard accounting practices and secondly, because of differences in the extent to which (if any), and the way in which, accounts are adjusted from the traditional historic cost basis to one reflecting the variable effects of inflation on the values of the constituent items in the accounts. Therefore, interpretation needs to be based partly on a consideration of the particular accounting practices employed. These problems are intensified in trying to aggregate the accounts of different companies and it is for this reason that steps have had to be taken to standardize the accounts as far as possible in the preparation of the official summary analyses referred to above. Valuable discussions of the nature and limitations of the official standardized accounts in general terms have been provided by Singh and Whittington (1968) Appendix A for the period up to 1960 and by Meeks and Whittington (1976) Appendix B for the period from 1960 to 1971. See too Erritt and Stibbard (1978). For a full discussion of the nature and limitations of historic cost accounting reference should be made to the report of the Sandilands

Committee (Cmnd 6225, 1975), Ch. 7.

With regard to construction companies in particular, a number of specific factors are relevant to the interpretation and comparison of accounts. For instance, differences in the amount and value of land held for speculative building or investment purposes may introduce marked divergences between accounts which may otherwise be similar. Differences in the classification of this item in the accounts – it may apparently be included under stocks or fixed assets for instance – may also be important and will certainly influence measures of return on capital employed, depending on how capital is defined. Also important is the fact that companies may vary considerably in the proportion of plant which they hire in undertaking their contracts; this too will alter apparent return on capital employed and make comparisons between companies difficult to interpret. Further, different practices adopted by construction companies in taking profits – i.e. during contracts or at the end of contracts – introduce an additional hazard when making comparisons. Differences in the degree to which contracts are sub-let will also influence apparent rates of return and the pattern of the accounts. Still further scope for divergence is introduced by differences in the treatment of retention monies and the value of work in progress.

12.2.2 Quoted securities

Details of the securities of all companies listed on the Stock Exchange are given in the *Stock Exchange Official Yearbook*. Statistics of their nominal and market values, interest and dividends of the total of listed securities grouped according to industry, including separate categories for 'contracting and construction' and 'building materials' (divided in several sub-categories) are published quarterly in *The Stock Exchange Fact Book*. Information about share prices and related information (dividends, dividend yields and price/earnings ratios etc.) are published in the daily press, principally the *Financial Times* and *The Times*. An index of the share prices of quoted construction companies is compiled jointly by the *Financial Times*, the Institute of Actuaries and the Faculty of Actuaries and published daily in the *Financial Times* as one of the series of FT-Actuaries Share Indices which cover various industrial sectors. Currently the 'contracting, construction' sector covers 29 companies. Background information and details of the method of calculation are given in Bell and Greenhorn (1984). Since 1972 the journal *Building* has also published its own Building Share Index. In contrast to th FT-Actuaries index, however, this index covers not only contractors but also companies which supply building materials or services to the construction industry (covering initially 30 companies and then 50 companies). The indices were introduced in the issues of *Building* for 4 February, 1972, pp.60–1 and 5 May, 1972, p.67 but details of the method of calculation were not given.

12.2.3 Overseas investment, earnings and assets

Surveys are conducted annually to obtain information about overseas earnings and investment by construction and other companies. The results are given in *Business Monitor MA4*. This shows in respect of inward and outward investment, statistics of net earnings and net investment according to area and country. Every third year a census of overseas assets is taken and reported in a *Supplement* to the Monitor. Summary results are also given in *British Business*. The series were initiated in *Board of Trade Journal* 1963, pp.877–83, providing annual data back to 1958 but in less detail than now published. Annual series of overseas earnings by British contractors are included in the *United Kingdom Balance of Payments* (the 'Pink Book') – see Chapter 6 (Section 6.7).

12.3 LOCAL AUTHORITY DIRECT LABOUR ORGANIZATIONS FINANCIAL STATISTICS

The Local Government, Planning and Land Act 1980 requires local authorities in England and Wales to treat their DLO operations on a formal quasi-trading basis and sets down certain accounting requirements (including the preparation of a balance sheet, a revenue account and a statement of rate of return). Subordinate legislation has prescribed the method of determination of the rate of return and certain additional information which authorities have to include in an Annual Report on their DLO operations. The revenue account and statement of rate of return have to be prepared for each of four specified descriptions of construction and maintenance work (general highways works, major works of new construction, minor works of new construction and general maintenance work). The legislation covers not only local authorities but also Joint Committees and Development Bodies, including New Town Development Corporations, and applied from 1 April 1981. Similar legislation applied in Scotland from 1 April 1982.

Statistics based on the accounts and supporting statements are compiled by CIPFA and published in *Direct Labour Organizations Statistics...[year]...Actuals.* The first report for 1981–82 covered England and Wales; subsequent annual reports will cover Great Britain. Results are presented for each authority *from which returns were received,* grouped into appropriate categories and summarized by type of authority. The statistics show summaries of the revenue account (including items of expenditure and income), the appropriation account, the calculation of the rate of return on capital for each of the specified categories of work and in total, and supplementary statistics: manpower (direct and indirect employment), methods of charging for direct labour work and statistics on the proportion of work (by category and in total) undertaken by the DLO relative to that carried out for the authority in total (including private contractors).

12.4 BANK LOANS AND ADVANCES

Analyses of loans, advances and acceptances to construction and other industries are prepared quarterly by the Bank of England and cover advances etc. to UK residents by banks in the UK. Classification is made according to the main activity of the borrower following the principles of the SIC. Detailed background notes are provided in *Financial Statistics – Explanatory Handbook* (CSO, annually). The data are first published in a *Press Notice* by the Bank of England and reproduced in *Financial Statistics.* They are available for the whole of the period since the end of the Second World War but a new series was introduced in May 1975 (an explanation of the principal changes was given in *Bank of England Quarterly Bulletin* December 1975 – notes to Table 10 – and in the *Explanatory Handbook* referred to above). Quarterly series for the periods 1946–69 and 1970–February 1975 were brought together in the *Bank of England Statistical Abstract,* Nos 1 and 2.

12.5 R & D EXPENDITURE

12.5.1 Background and available data

Surveys of expenditure on R & D have been conducted for many years but data for the construction sector are not available until 1966/67. Currently there are two R & D enquiries carried out by the DTI: an annual inquiry addressed to all government departments and a biennial industrial inquiry. The latter had been carried out triennially from 1969 to 1981 but under the current system full-scale inquiries are to be carried out less frequently (the next one will be for 1985) and coupled with smaller-scale 'mini-surveys' (first conducted for 1983) to provide biennial estimates of major aggregates. The full surveys provide details of current expenditure by type of expenditure (wages and salaries, materials, etc.) and by type of work (i.e. type of research – 'basic'/'applied'/'development'), capital expenditure (analysed, in some enquiries, by type of asset) and sources of finance. They also provide information about employment on R & D (see Chapter 8). The surveys cover not only private industry but also public corporations and research associations, but are confined to firms affirming, in response to an earlier enquiry, that they carry out R & D work (generally larger firms). Data are given separately for each of these categories. The new mini-surveys provide, as far as construction is concerned, figures for total expenditure only. The relevant data for construction obtained in the surveys of central government appear currently in analyses of expenditure according to 'European Community objectives' (categories for 'construction and planning of buildings' and 'civil engineering') and formerly in analyses by function. This series may be carried back to 1964–5 in *Statistics of Science and Technology,* 1967. Other publication sources are given below.

12.5.2 Publication sources

The results of the first five surveys from 1966/67 have been brought together in two overlapping summary reports which include revisions of earlier figures as well as detailed notes on the definition and scope of R & D and the execution of the surveys. These are *Research and Development Expenditure* (1973) which covers the four annual surveys from 1966/67 to 1969/70 and *Research and Development Expenditure and Employment* (1976) which covers the surveys for 1969–70 and 1972/73. The results of subsequent full-scale inquiries (1975/76, 1978 and 1981) appear in the *Business Monitor MO14* series. The results of the central government surveys (coupled with those for industry) appear in an annual article in *Economic Trends* (the latest results, for 1983, appeared in August 1985). The results of the first industrial mini-survey for 1983 were given in *British Business,* 18 January 1985, pp.130–2 and also incorporated in the article in *Economic Trends.*

12.5.3 Interpretation

With regard to interpretation, it is emphasized in the case of construction that the figures do not include the sums for 'the appreciable development work undertaken on sites, particularly work undertaken in civil engineering'. It should also be appreciated that much R & D work of relevance to construction is undertaken in building materials industries.

12.6 COMPANY LIQUIDATION AND BANKRUPTCY (INSOLVENCY) STATISTICS

12.6.1 Background and available series

Insolvency, which normally occurs when a person or company is unable to pay debts on a due date, is recorded in statistics only when it has been acknowledged voluntarily or has been determined by the courts. A distinction is drawn between persons and companies for they are dealt with under separate legal arrangements. Insolvent persons are said to become bankrupt and are dealt with under the Bankruptcy Act 1914 or they may make arrangements with their creditors under the Deeds of Arrangement Act 1914. Insolvent companies are said to go into liquidation and are dealt with under the Companies Acts of 1948 and 1967. Insolvent partnerships are dealt with in conjunction with the insolvencies of the individual partners under the Bankruptcy Acts: if orders are made against each member of a partnership these are consolidated into a single order before being administered. The statistics of the number of bankruptcies and company liquidations analysed according to industry have been compiled for many years on an annual basis, and for the period since 1969 on a quarterly basis (England and Wales only).

(a) *Company liquidations*

There are two types of company liquidation that involve insolvency: company liquidations which stem from winding-up orders by the Courts following petitions to them, and creditors' voluntarily liquidations in which the company and its creditors come to terms without Court proceedings. Separate statistics of the number of liquidations under these two categories for England and Wales and for Scotland separately are published in annual reports by the DTI entitled *Companies in...[year]*. Quarterly series for England and Wales only, of *total* liquidations is published, together with the quarterly bankruptcy statistics noted below, in *British Business* (series for the period 1969–74 appeared in *ET,* March 1975). These statistics do not cover, it should be noted, members' (i.e. shareholders') voluntary liquidations, in which the company winds up for reasons other than insolvency. Summary data are currently reproduced in *HCS* (annual).

(b) *Bankruptcy*

Statistics are available for England and Wales only. Annual figures are published by the DTI in *Bankruptcy, General Report for Year...* and provide analyses of the number of failures and the value of assets and liabilities divided between 'receiving orders' (under the bankruptcy arrangements) and 'deeds of arrangement'. Quarterly series show the number of failures only (not differentiated as above); these were published for the first time in *ET* March 1975 covering the period 1969–74 and since then have been carried forward quarterly in *Trade and Industry* and its successor *British Business.* Summary data are reproduced currently in *HCS* (annual). The analysis by trade, it should be noted, relates to self-employed workers. Employees who go bankrupt are not so classified.

12.6.2 Interpretation

A guide to the nature of the information and the way it is compiled, which is useful for interpretative purposes has been provided by the DoI (1975). Reference should also be made to the Notes published with the data in *British Business*. As far as the construction industry is concerned, one matter that is worthy of emphasis in the context of inter-industry comparisons of insolvency is the need to consider the number of insolvencies in relation to the number of businesses at risk in each sector. The construction industry generally records a higher number of failures than any other industry and this fact alone often seems to be taken in isolation as a fact of some significance, although the number of businesses in the industry is also much larger than all or most other industries. For a comparison of company liquidations in relation to the number of companies, see *British Business*, 7 August 1981, p.680; see also Hillebrandt (1977).

12.7 TAXATION STATISTICS

Taxation statistics are considered in two sections. One section covers all statistics prepared by the Inland Revenue arising from its work in the collection of income and corporation taxes levied on the construction industry and the persons who work in it. The second section covers information about value added tax.

12.7.1 Personal and business income taxes

(a) *The published analyses*

Since 1970 analyses of income and tax assessments classified by industry have been published for each financial year in *Inland Revenue Statistics*. Before 1970 they were included in *Annual Reports of the Commissioners of HM Inland Revenue* (Command Papers). The statistics cover the UK as a whole but some country and regional analyses are available.

PERSONAL TAXATION – PAYE STATISTICS. Current analyses refer to income from employment and cover all *employees* in employment who are liable to tax and/or national insurance (NI) contributions.

Thus coverage is confined to employees with pay above PAYE and NI contributions levels.* Analyses of income from self-employment were discontinued after 1979 (last published in *Inland Revenue Statistics 1982*).

An important development in PAYE statistics occurred with effect from 1976–77 with the initiation of a 1% sample system of PAYE records in place of the former manual count of all records. An account of the new system and prospective developments, together with analyses not previously published has been given by Staton (1984). The analyses presented for construction and other industries show:

1. Aggregate amounts of pay and tax deducted (annually from 1976–77 to 1981–82)
2. Estimated number of 'full-year equivalents' (an approximate indicator of employees in employment) for 1980–81 and 1981–82
3. Tax and NI deductions (separately) as a percentage of pay for 1976–77 to 1981–82
4. Year-on-year comparison of movement between employers of individuals remaining in the same region between 1979–80 and 1980–81.

In addition industrial analyses of pay averages are prepared (not published, but available on request) and certain other tabulations – see Staton (1984) Annex C.

BUSINESS TAXATION. Currently industrial analyses are made for the following categories:

1. Company income – number of assessments and analyses of 'agreed assessments' (including gross trading profits, other income etc.), net amount chargeable to tax and tax deducted
2. Capital allowances – analyses for sole traders and partnerships and for companies
3. Dividends etc. – estimated distributions (dividends etc.) and annual payments made by companies in construction and other trade groups under the corporation tax system.

* The collection of NI contributions was integrated with the PAYE system with effect from 1961 in respect of the graduated scheme and April 1985 in respect of the earnings-related scheme.

(b) *Interpretation*

INDUSTRIAL CLASSIFICATION. Trade groupings are made as far as possible in accordance with the SIC, but the basis of the classification is the Inland Revenue Trade Classification in which each PAYE scheme (i.e. a financial unit) is classified according to the main activity carried out by the employees covered by the scheme. These financial units do not necessarily correspond to 'establishments' used for the classification of output and employment statistics (see Chapter 5). It should be noted that the Inland Revenue retain the title 'building and contracting' rather than 'construction' for the industry.

COVERAGE. The statistics for income from employment and self-employment (to 1979) need to be interpreted in the light of the growth in self-employment in the construction industry that occurred especially in the 1960s and 1970s and which was accompanied by tax evasion on a scale which may be regarded as substantial. A special tax deduction scheme was introduced in April 1972 (under the Finance Act 1971) to combat evasion by self-employed workers working under labour-only sub-contract, under which contractors making payments to sub-contractors had to deduct tax and pay it to the Inland Revenue as an advance of the sub-contractor's personal liability, unless the sub-contractor was a limited company or other corporate body or had been issued with a sub-contractors' tax certificate. The scheme was widened and tightened up in the Finance No. 2 Act 1975. Details of the initial scheme will be found in Inland Revenue (1971a,b) and of the modified scheme in Inland Revenue (1976). It is possible that tax evasion may subsequently have declined partly as a result of this scheme but also as self-employment in the industry has declined partly as a result of the marked decline in construction activity.

12.7.2 Valued Added Tax (VAT)

VAT was introduced on 1 April, 1973. Throughout the whole period since then it has not been payable on new construction work (zero rated) but it has been payable at the standard rate on repairs and maintenance work. In the 1984 Finance Act liability was extended to 'improvements' work which had hitherto been treated as equivalent to new work, rather than repairs and maintenance, and thus also zero rated. The tax has to be paid by all registered 'persons', the registration requirement extending to all persons with a turnover above a defined cut-off limit. The level of the limit is low but is changed from time to time – details are given in the reports cited below. The registration statistics themselves, constitute an important source of information about the size and structure of industry. This aspect of the data is considered in Section 11.5. The available statistics about the tax itself show, in addition to the number of 'registered persons', details of tax due, tax deductible (i.e. tax paid on inputs) and net tax payable for construction and other industries. These are published in annual *Reports of the Commissioners of HM Customs and Excise* (Command Papers).

13
CONSTRUCTION COSTS, PRICES AND PRODUCTIVITY

This chapter falls into two parts. The first part covers the information currently produced to measure changes in the costs or prices of construction output over time. Information about the costs and prices of specific construction inputs, as opposed to outputs, is covered separately in other chapters (labour costs in Chapter 10 and materials prices in Chapter 14) but composite input cost indices are referred to here. Information about average house prices (new and non-new) is considered separately in Chapter 4 along with other housing statistics but indices of housebuilding costs and prices are considered here. The second part of this chapter considers the problems involved in productivity measurement for the construction industry and the limited information that is available.

13.1 INDICES OF CONSTRUCTION COSTS AND PRICES

Use of the terms 'costs' and 'prices' requires some explanation because they are sometimes used synonymously and at other times not. The term 'construction costs' may be used to refer to the costs incurred by contractors covering labour, materials, plant and possibly overheads but excluding profit. The term 'prices', by contrast, represents the amount paid by contractors' clients and naturally includes profits. From a client's point of view, the price paid represents his 'costs of construction' and it is in this sense that the two terms may be used synonymously. In this chapter we use the terms interchangeably in this way (unless indicated otherwise) but index numbers of costs or prices are clearly differentiated.

The attempt to measure changes in construction costs and prices over time raises a number of conceptual and practical problems. In response to these problems various methods of measurement have been employed and a variety of different series have been devised. Interpretation of the available series must rest upon an appreciation of these problems and the different methods of measurement. First, therefore, we discuss these matters before proceeding to define the series available (Section 13.1.2). This is followed by an appraisal of the series in the context of the uses to which the information may be put (Section 13.1.3).

13.1.1 Problems and methods of measurement

The basic measurement problem that has to be faced arises from the extremely varied nature of the work carried out by the construction industry. This includes the construction of a wide variety of building and civil engineering works and a wide variety of repair and maintenance jobs. New construction projects vary not only according to type but also in size, design, specification, complexity and methods of construction etc.; even similar jobs vary according to differences in site conditions with a consequential influence upon costs of construction. In some sense, therefore, each job tends to be unique. Thus from the point of view of measuring changes in costs over time there is no single standard of comparison. Another factor to bear in mind is that construction projects often take a considerable period of time from start to finish and that costs may be measured at different stages of the process. They may refer to prices for work yet to be carried out, that is to say, tender prices, or to the level of costs for work currently being executed, or to the costs or prices of work which has been completed – i.e. complete projects ready for use. Clearly, measurements which relate to these three stages may be expected to differ and likewise the rates of change over time of such measurements may not be equivalent.

We now turn to consider the methods of measurement which may be used. The distinctions we draw are then used in the next section as a means of classifying the indices available. Broadly speaking, there are two approaches to the problem of devising an index of construction costs or prices. One is to use price data for actual contracts. The other is to use the information about changes in factor costs, i.e. the costs of the factors of production which go to determine price, namely labour and material costs, overheads and profits after allowing for the influence of productivity changes on prices. Within each of these two broad approaches, certain variants may be defined as follows:

(a) Actual price data
(i) Total prices
(ii) Unit rates and the repricing of tenders
(b) Factor costs
(i) Factor cost indices
(ii) Repricing aggregate factor costs
(iii) Published unit rates.

We comment on each of these in turn.

(a) *Use of actual price data*

TOTAL PRICES. Only brief remarks are necessary here because this method is not in current use. The main problem confronting the use of this method is the lack of a standard product so that it is difficult, if not impossible, to make comparisons of building prices on a like-for-like basis covering the whole range of construction outputs. One index, the 'Venning index' – was based informally on information about total tender prices but its compilation was ended in 1975 (see Fleming 1966, 1980a for further details). A possible way of overcoming the problem of the lack of a standard product would be to invite tenders periodically from builders for a building of a standard design and specification, even though it was not intended to erect the building. Such a method would be faced, of course, with the need to allow for the changes in standards that do take place over time and with the more severe problem that, since the builders tendering would have no prospect of gaining a contract, there could be no assurance that the prices quoted were reasonable reflections of current cost levels and the tendering climate. The method has not been used in this country. A further approach to the problem of a non-standard product using actual price data is to employ the

statistical technique of multivariate regression analysis to devise
a statistical model allowing prices to be predicted on the basis of
information about the physical characteristics of buildings. Given
information about the latter, 'standardized' price comparisons
can be made over time. The method is used to compile an index
of house prices in the UK (Fleming and Nellis, 1984, 1985) but
has not been used to produce a general construction index. The
housing index is discussed further in Chapter 4 (sub-section
4.1.2).

UNIT RATES AND THE REPRICING OF TENDERS. Instead of using information about the total price of a contract, it is possible to use
information about the unit rates for particular categories of work
used in building up the total contract price. These are available
from the priced bills of quantities of accepted tenders. Such rates
refer to specific construction operations and they therefore have
the advantage of being directly comparable. Naturally, use of
the method requires access to a representative selection of bills
and also a reasonably large number because the rates inserted by
different builders vary considerably not only because of differences in their levels of efficiency and in the labour, materials and
plant costs used by the estimator, but also because of differences
in the practices adopted by firms in arriving at a total tender
price. Use of the method has been increasingly favoured in Great
Britain where, unlike other countries, the use of bills of quantities
for tendering purposes provides an extremely valuable data
source.

There are basically two ways in which the method may be
applied in practice. One is to measure the percentage change in
the rates quoted in current tenders compared with base-period
tenders (a price relative) and to take an appropriately weighted
average of these. This way of using the method is used to obtain
a price index for public sector housebuilding but not for building
costs in general. The other way of applying the method – and
one used in several indices of tender prices – is not to compare
unit rates directly but to use the rates to re-price tenders. Here,
again, two basic approaches are possible: either to use standard
rates from a base period to re-price current bills or to use the
current rates to re-price a standard bill. Comparison of the
values of the bill at base-period and current prices yields an

index of price change for each bill. These 'bill indices' then have to be averaged over several bills to produce a single index.

A method analogous to the use of rates extracted from priced bills is to use unit rates published in builders' price books. Such rates, however, are only estimates built up on the basis of certain standardized formulae for combining input costs and as such are more appropriately considered later.

The use of methods based on actual prices has a disadvantage from the point of view of studies concerned with total construction work, in that it will be generally possible to cover only certain well-defined classes of work, the price movements for which may not be representative of all work. Studies concerned with construction work as a whole require a more general measure of price movements. Until a few years ago, such a measure was built up on the basis of changes in factor costs. In 1978 'output price indices' were introduced by the DoE which use an alternative methodology incorporating the information about tender prices referred to above. The methodology is best defined when considering the available series below (Section 13.1.2). Several series of index numbers based upon factor costs remain, however, as a measure of the movement of construction costs for the contractor.

(b) *Use of factor cost data*

WEIGHTED AVERAGES OF FACTOR COST INDICES. This method basically consists of taking a weighted average of indices of labour and material costs coupled possibly with allowances for changes in productivity, overheads and profits. Failure to allow for changes in profits means that the index will be insensitive to changes in market conditions and will be a measure of costs to the builder (treating profits as a residual rather than a factor cost), rather than prices to the client. The failure to allow for changes in productivity means that, other things being equal, the index over-estimates price changes when productivity is rising and vice versa. Information about changes in the costs of construction labour and materials is available from official sources (considered in Chapters 10 and 14 respectively), but no adequate data are available about overheads, profits and productivity. With regard to overheads and profits, the only official information is that available retrospectively in the annual censuses of production (see Chapter 6, Section 6.2) or from Inland Revenue taxation statistics (see Chapter 12). With regard to productivity, no satisfactory index exists – see Section 13.2. Despite these difficulties, the method was used by the DoE to compile the official 'CNC' index of construction costs until it was replaced by the new series of 'output price indices' in 1978. As the CNC index is no longer produced, no further details are given in this book – a critical appraisal will be found in Fleming (1966, 1980a).

REPRICING AGGREGATE FACTOR COSTS. Briefly, this method consists of taking aggregate information about the cost of factor inputs (of the kind obtained in the annual census of production) and deflating it to base-year price levels through the use of appropriate factor cost indices. Comparison of the sum of factor costs at current and base-period prices yields an index of the change in output prices. The method was used by the author to devise an index for Northern Ireland (Fleming, 1965) but it has not been used in Great Britain and no further discussion is offered here.

USE OF PUBLISHED UNIT ('MEASURED') RATES. This method is analogous to that using unit rates extracted from priced bills of quantity, described above, the difference being that the rates used are those published in builders' price books or trade journals. These rates are meant to represent the going rates for carrying out specific items of building work. *To the extent to which this is the case* they possess certain advantages from the point of view of devising an index. As with unit rates from priced bills, they facilitate the maintenance of a comparable standard over time reflecting both changes in costs and productivity and incorporating a built-in weighting of labour and materials (they do not eliminate the comparability problem because steps still have to be taken to cope with technical change). By taking suitable combinations of rates, it is possible to devise measures of costs for different types of building and construction work. However, the problem of allowing for changes in productivity and other market conditions is not so readily overcome as the description above appears to promise. In practice, published rates are built up on the basis of labour and materials 'constants' (i.e. the quantities of materials, the estimated man-hours and possibly plant-hours required to carry out the item of work in question). Changes in productivity may be allowed for when rates, or more particularly the constants are revised but in practice this is likely to be infrequent: a study by the author of one series going back to the nineteenth century has shown that it was rare for the constants to be changed (Fleming, 1978). Overheads and profits are commonly allowed for in these rates through the addition of a fixed percentage. Consequently, these rates are insensitive to changes in market conditions and are more likely to reflect changes in contractors' basic factor costs rather than output prices.

13.1.2 The available indices of construction costs and prices

We now turn to examine the indices that are available in the light of the various methods of calculation discussed above. Apart from differences in methods of calculation, three other distinctions need to be drawn. First, there is a timing distinction between indices which attempt to reflect changes in the costs or prices of current *output* as opposed to those which reflect changes in the current level of *tender* prices. Secondly, there is the distinction referred to at the outset, between costs to the contractor and costs to the client. Thirdly, there is a distinction between indices which attempt to cover construction work generally and those which refer to particular types of work or particular sectors. We confine our attention here to indices that are currently compiled. For details of the series which have been discontinued, including long-run series extending back to the nineteenth century, reference should be made to Fleming (1966, 1980a).

Altogether fifteen series are currently produced (not counting sub-categories of these series separately and excluding the indices of house prices considered in Chapter 4). Each of these is discussed in turn below but a concise summary giving details of the organizations responsible for their production, starting dates of the series, frequency of publication, publication sources and brief details of the method of calculation and other remarks is given in Table 13.1. It is convenient to consider the available series under three broad headings:

A. Output price indices
B. Tender price indices
C. Cost indices.

These headings are used for classification purposes in Table 13.1. Before turning to examine each index in turn, we may usefully observe, perhaps, that of the potential methods of measurement outlined above, most use is made of two methods. Unit rates extracted from priced bills are used directly to compile tender price indices for six of the fifteen series and, in addition, a seventh series (the output price indices – Series No. (1)) are themselves based indirectly on tender price series. Labour and materials cost information is used in various ways to compile all of the other series. We now examine each index in turn. For ease of reference, each is numbered according to the number given in the first column of Table 13.1.

(1) *DoE output price indices*

These indices – a general index and five sub-indices for different categories of work, as shown in Table 13.1 – were specially devised by the DoE for the purpose of converting values of construction output from current to constant prices. They were introduced in 1978 and carried back retrospectively to 1970. They replaced an index based upon factor costs – the CNC index – which was open to potentially serious errors when used for output-deflation purposes (a critical appraisal will be found in Fleming 1966, 1980a).

The problem that has to be faced in devising an index which reflects the price of work carried out in particular time periods (e.g. quarterly) is that the available price information (tender prices) relates naturally to whole contracts, the completion of which normally extends over several such time periods. The approach adopted in producing the output price indices, there-fore, is one which marries the available information about tender prices with other information about the value, duration and phasing of contracts. In brief, the method combines information about the value of contracts awarded which is collected in the new orders enquiry (Chapter 7) with estimates of contract dura-tion and the phasing of work to give an estimate of the contri-bution made to current output by orders placed in preceding

Table 13.1 Currently compiled indices of construction costs and prices* (all indices relate to Great Britain except where indicated otherwise)

Ref No	Series	Starting date	Frequency	Sub-indices	Publication reference	Basis of index and other remarks
A. OUTPUT PRICE INDICES						
1.	DoE output price indices: (a) New housing – public (b) New housing – private (c) Other new work – public (d) Other new work – private industrial (e) Other new work – private commercial (f) All new construction	1970	Q	By type as shown	*Housing and Construction Statistics*	The 'all new construction' index is a base-weighted combination of the five separate indices labelled (a) to (e). For further details see text.
B. TENDER PRICE INDICES						
2.	DoE public sector building	1968	Q	VOP/FP contracts	*Housing and Construction Statistics*	Based on unit rates extracted from tenders accepted for work in the public sector. The scope of the index was extended from 1975 – see text.
3.	BCIS (RICS) tender price index	1974	Q	VOP/FP contracts – see remarks	*BCIS Quarterly Review of Building Prices*	Based on unit rates extracted from accepted tenders in both public and private sectors. Sub-indices for VOP and FP tenders are provided to BCIS subscribers.
4.	DoE road construction tender price index	1970	Q	By type of road and contract	*Housing and Construction Statistics and Transport Statistics*	Based on unit rates extracted from accepted tenders.
5.	DoE price index of public sector house-building (PIPSH) (E & W)	1964	Q	VOP/FP contracts	*Housing and Construction Statistics*	Based on rates extracted from accepted tenders for dwellings of traditional construction in blocks of up to four storeys in the public sector from 1979. Before 1979 the index was more narrowly based – see text.
6.	SDD housing tender price index (HTPI) (Scotland)	1970	Q	–	*Scottish Housing Statistics*	Based on rates in accepted tenders for 1–3 storey public sector housing contracts in mainland Scotland. Methodology as for PIPSH above.
7.	DB & E (Spon's) tender price index	1966	Q	–	*Spon's Architects' and Builders' Price Book and Architects' Journal*	Based on rates extracted from accepted tenders for new work in the London area handled by the firm of Davis, Belfield and Everest (chartered quantity surveyors).

C. COST INDICES

	Base year	Freq.	By type of building and input – see remarks	Source	Remarks
8. BCIS (RICS) general building cost index	1971	Q		BCIS Quarterly Review of Building Prices	Based upon the PSA price adjustment formulae indices – item 15 below (see text for further details). Sub-indices are provided to BCIS subscribers – see text.
9. Spon's cost indices: (a) Building costs	1956	Q	–	Spon's Architects' and Builders' Price Book and Architects' Journal	Based on changes in labour (wage rates) and material costs weighted in the ratio 40:60.
(b) M & E services costs (c) Electrical services costs	1965 1965	Q Q	– –	Spon's Mechanical and Electrical Services Price Book and Architects' Journal	Based upon appropriate labour (wage rates) and materials costs weighted 30:70 in the case of mechanical services and 50:50 in the case of electrical services.
(d) Civil engineering costs	1970	Q	–	Spon's Civil Engineering Price Book	Composite of PSA price adjustment formula indices (see item 15).
(e) Landscaping cost index	1976	Q	–	Spon's Landscape Price Book	Composite of PSA price adjustment formula indices (see item 15).
10. *Building* housing cost index	1973 (Dec.)	M	–	Building	Weighted average of specific labour and materials costs, together with an allowance for site and head office overheads, based upon specification of a two-storey, three-bedroomed, semi-detached house of traditional construction.
11. SDD housing costs index (Scotland)	1970	Q	–	Scottish Housing Statistics	Composite of PSA price adjustment formulae indices (See item 15) applied to typical Scottish public sector housing contract.
12. BIA/BCIS house rebuilding costs index (UK)	1978–80 1981	Q M	– –	See remarks	Prepared for insurance valuation purposes – see text. The latest index numbers are available on subscription; they are subsequently published in *Chartered Surveyor Weekly* and in various insurance publications. The series is given in the annual *Guide to House Rebuilding Costs for Insurance Valuation*.

(continued overleaf)

Table 13.1 (*continued*)

Ref No	Series	Starting date	Frequency	Sub-indices	Publication reference	Basis of index and other remarks
13.	Association of Cost Engineers – erected process plant cost indices	1958–74 1975–	Q M	4 indices	*Cost Engineer* and *Spon's Mechanical and Electrical Services Price Book*	Based upon labour and materials costs for the erection of process plants (chemical, petrochemical and petroleum projects) in the UK. Indices are prepared for four typical plants.
14.	BMCIS (RICS) maintenance costs	1970	Q	3 sub-indices	Available on subscription only†	Based upon official indices of materials costs plus VAT and official earnings and wage rates data and ancillary labour costs. The general maintenance costs index is a weighted average of separate indices for redecoration, fabric maintenance and service maintenance.
15.	PSA price adjustment formulae indices (see remarks)	1974	M	see remarks	*Price Adjustment Formulae for Construction Contracts, Monthly Bulletin of Indices* and *Press Notice: Indices for Use with Price Adjustment Formulae*	No general construction cost index is given in the *Bulletins;* they contain sets of index numbers for 'work categories' and for labour, materials and plant (compiled for cost reimbursement purposes in VOP contracts). Composite construction cost indices based upon this information are prepared by the BCIS (item 8 above) and also by the PSA for its own use (APSAB indices – see text).

E & W = England and Wales. M = monthly. Q = quarterly.

* Statistics relating to the selling prices of new and second-hand houses are considered separately in Chapter 4 (see Table 4.1).

† Royal Institution of Chartered Surveyors, Building Maintenance Cost Information Service, 85/87 Clarence Street, Kingston-upon-Thames, Surrey, KT1 1RB.

periods. These estimates are made first at current prices and then at constant prices by using indices of tender prices for deflation purposes. The calculation is carried out for different sorts of work and using different tender price indices: mainly the tender price indices numbered (2) to (6) in Table 13.1 (for private non-housing work unpublished indices, produced by the BCIS, are used). Dividing the estimate of output at current prices by the estimate at constant prices produces an output price index for the current period.

In practice, orders are sub-divided into three groups according to expected duration (short, medium or long) and the contribution of each to output in the current period is calculated separately using different time-profiles. A distinction is also made by type of work and between fixed price (FP) and variable price (VOP) contracts. Since the value of the contribution to output made by VOP contracts is affected after the contract is awarded by changes in the costs of labour and/or materials for which the contractor may be reimbursed, these contracts are revalued on the basis of estimates of the proportions of labour and materials adjustable for cost changes and indices of labour and materials costs. An official description of the indices published upon their introduction was provided by Butler (1978).

(2) DoE public sector building tender price index

This index is prepared by the Directorate of Building and Quantity Surveying Services of the Property Services Agency (PSA), which is a part of the DoE, and measures the movement of prices in competitive tenders for building contracts in the public sector. However, it does not include contracts for housing work, work of a mainly civil engineering nature, mechanical and electrical work nor alterations and extensions. Currently, the principal contributors to the sample from which the index is produced are the PSA, Scottish Development Department, Department of Health and Social Security, Home Office, and Department of Education and Science. Examples of building work covered in the index include schools, hospitals, telephone exchanges, prisons, courts, police stations, government offices, military barracks etc. Until the second quarter of 1979 the index was based solely on contracts let by the PSA; its scope was then widened to cover other contracts, as indicated above, and the new index carried back to 1975. However, an index based solely on PSA contracts has been continued as the 'QSSD Index of Building Tender Prices' and published in *Quantity Surveyors Information Notes.*

The method used is that of repricing bills of quantities for current tenders on the basis of standard base rates. Full repricing, however, is not carried out: for each bill examined, a sample of items is selected for repricing from each trade or section of the bill according to their relative importance (in terms of value) to represent a total value of 25% of each trade or section. These trades or sections are then weighted according to the total value of each trade or section relative to the total value of the bill (i.e. the weights are current weights and peculiar to each bill). Preliminaries and other general charges are spread proportionately over each item of the bill of quantities. For each bill an index of price change is computed – representing the current bill as a percentage of the bill as revalued on base-period prices, as described above. These 'bill indices' are then averaged (as a geometric mean up to 1979 but then as an arithmetic mean) to produce an overall index.

Sub-indices for contracts with and without VOP clauses are compiled in a similar manner. Since 1974 an increasing proportion of contracts have been let on VOP bases and this will have tended to influence the overall series in a downward direction. Prior to 1978 the VOP/Firm Price indices were derived from PSA contracts only, although the overall index covers the whole of the public sector.

As explained earlier, the great virtue of the method is the fact that it relies on actual price data and the fact that, since it is based on the comparison of quotations for comparable items of work from each trade or section of the bill of quantities, it is able to meet the problem of the non-standard product. A potential difficulty is the fact that the rates inserted by different contractors in the bills for tendering purposes may differ considerably, for a variety of reasons, and thus introduce an erratic influence, unless the index is based on a large sample of bills. The aim has been to base the analysis on at least 80 contracts each quarter but this has not always been possible in the period since 1980 and an amended form of analysis has had to be used to derive the overall index from the individual bill indices. This consists of dividing them into four groups according to type of building and type of contract and then combining the median index from each group as a weighted average. An official description of the index published soon after its introduction was given by Mitchell (1971). A brief description is also regularly included in *HCS* (annual).

(3) *BCIS (RICS) tender price index*

The methodology used for this index is the same as that used by the DoE for its tender price index discussed above. It should be noted, however, that it covers building work in both the public and private sectors with contract sums over £50 000 which have been priced in competition or by negotiation – the priced bills for analysis being supplied by BCIS members. The attempt is made to obtain a sample size of at least 80 bills each quarter in order to reduce sampling error, but over recent years this has often proved impossible. Sub-indices are calculated for VOP and FP contracts (made available to subscribers only), but it is emphasized that these are less reliable because of the smaller sample sizes on which they are based. Further details are issued by the BCIS to subscribers. This index superseded price indices for buildings and building elements based on factor costs adjusted for 'market conditions' compiled from 1950 to 1976 – see Fleming (1980a).

FORECAST TENDER PRICE INDEX. An attempt is also made to forecast the likely quarterly movement of the tender price index for a period two years ahead. The results together with details of the underlying assumptions about market conditions and cost movements are given in the *Quarterly Review of Building Prices*.

(4) *DoE road construction tender price index*

As in the case of the DoE and BCIS building tender price indices, this index uses the partial repricing method using information in bills of quantities for accepted tenders. It is based currently on new contracts with a works cost of £250 000 or more (before 1979 the lower limit was £100 000 in England and Wales and £25 000 in Scotland). The following description is based on that included in *HCS* (annual). The index is produced by repricing, using a schedule of 1979/80 prices, a selection of the most important items in bills of quantities for accepted tenders. For each contract, the total cost of the selected items is divided by their cost at 1979/80 prices to produce a price relative and these price relatives are each given a weight proportionate to the base year (1979/80) cost in order to calculate weighted average price relatives. As an average calculated from a single quarter's contracts, which are often relatively few in number, would be over-sensitive to tender prices of individual large schemes, each quarterly index value is the average price relative for contracts let in that quarter and in the preceding and following quarters. Sub-indices are produced as follows:

Type of road	Type of contract
Trunk motorways	VOP contracts
Trunk roads	FP contracts
Principal roads	

(5) *DoE price index of public sector housebuilding (PIPSH)*

The methodology for this index is again similar to the other tender price indices discussed above in being based upon the prices quoted for particular items of work in bills of quantities for accepted tenders compared with comparable items at base-period prices. In this case the index provides a measure of the change in tender prices for the construction of public sector housing in England and Wales. It has superseded, from 1979, the price index of local authority housebuilding (PILAH) which was produced until the fourth quarter of 1978. PILAH was itself a revision of a former 'Constants Standards Cost Index' introduced in *Housing Statistics* No. 10, pp.79–80. It was based on tenders accepted for traditionally built one- and two-storey local authority housing, excluding Greater London. Its coverage was extended from 1979 to include contracts let by London boroughs, GLC, new towns and housing associations and to include dwellings in three- and four-storey blocks. The new index, therefore, is an index for the whole of public sector housebuilding in England and Wales and its name was changed accordingly. The methodology remained the same but the base prices and weights used in PILAH were revised. A description of PILAH is given in Osborn (1973) and a description of PIPSH in Griffiths (1979).

The price data used are extracted from the bills of quantities of successful tenders for housing contracts described above. Within this field the price changes are measured from the prices of 23 items which occur in most such bills of quantities. Each item is selected to represent all the work in the particular trade section so that price movements of the other work in a trade section are assumed to be broadly similar to those of the representative item. Details of the items and the weights will be found in the references cited above. The index is calculated in two stages in order to allow for changes in the regional pattern of building and its consequential influence upon average prices because of different regional price levels and rates of change in prices. First, an index is computed for each region or sub-region, as a weighted arithmetic average of the price relatives for each item in the current quarter, relative to the base year. These indices are then combined in the second stage of the calculation using fixed regional weights. Separate figures are published for VOP and FP contracts, but the regional indices referred to above are not published. PILAH and PIPSH series were linked on the fourth quarter of 1978 by computing both series for this period.

(6) *SDD housing tender price index (Scotland)*

This index measures the movement of tender prices for public sector housebuilding of 1–3 storeys in mainland Scotland (remote areas are excluded). The same methodology is used as for the PIPSH index referred to above. All successful tenders are covered including those resulting from negotiation. From the beginning of 1974 a mixture of FP and VOP contracts are covered by the index. Before 1974 it was exclusively firm price. A separate housing cost (as opposed to price) index is also compiled – see item (11) below.

(7) *DB & E (Spon's) tender price index*

This index is produced by Davis, Belfield and Everest, a London-based firm of chartered quantity surveyors, using the same basic methodology as that used for the DoE and BCIS tender price indices but using VOP contracts only. The data used are drawn from contracts handled by the firm and it should be noted that these are confined to new work in the London area, mainly (but not solely) for housing, over a certain value (originally £30 000 but now £200 000). Work of mainly a civil engineering nature, mechanical and electrical work, complex work of alterations and extensions and negotiated contracts are excluded.

For repricing purposes, base-period rates published in *Spon's Architects' and Builders' Price Book* are used. As before, individual bill indices are compiled and these are combined as an arithmetic mean, each bill index being based on a sample of items selected from each trade or section of the bill of quantities up to 25% of the value of the trade or section (these themselves being weighted according to the value of the trade or section as a proportion of the total value of the bill). Preliminaries and other charges are spread proportionately over each item in the bill of quantities. One reservation that should be noted is that the index is based on a smaller number of tenders than the DoE and BCIS tenders and the results, therefore, may be subject to a greater degree of sampling error.

FORECAST PRICE MOVEMENTS. DB & E also attempt to forecast the movement of this index for a period two years ahead and the results published, in the form of 'minimum' and 'maximum' limits, quarterly in the *Architects' Journal*. The series and methodology were introduced in the issue of the *Journal* for 12 November 1975, pp.1017–8. No formal statistical model is employed.

(8) *BCIS (RICS) building and input cost indices*

BUILDING COST INDICES. Unlike the tender price indices referred to above, these indices reflect changes in cost to the builder rather than costs to the client (i.e. prices). In addition to a General Building Cost Index (referred to in Table 13.1) four sub-indices by building type are prepared for BCIS subscribers:

1. General building cost (excluding M & E) index ·
2. Steel-framed construction cost index
3. Concrete-framed construction cost index
4. Brick construction cost index.

The general indices are averages of the steel-framed, concrete-framed and brick construction indices weighted in the ratio 1:1:2. All of the indices represent weighted averages of the PSA price adjustment formulae indices (see item (15) below) which are based upon changes in the costs of the labour, materials and plant required for different construction operations or 'work categories'. The weights for the BCIS indices were derived from an analysis of 40 bills of quantities for steel-framed, concrete-framed and brick construction contracts. A detailed description of the calculation of the indices is made available to subscribers; an account was also included in Tysoe (1981).

INPUT COST INDICES. These indices (made available to BCIS subscribers) are the constituents of the building cost indices referred to above. They are as follows:

1. Mechanical and electrical engineering cost index
2. Basic labour cost index
3. Basic materials cost index
4. Basic plant cost index.

FORECAST BUILDING COST INDEX. The BCIS also publish a quarterly forecast of the general building cost index, along with a forecast of the tender price index, for a period two years ahead in the *BCIS Quarterly Review of Building Prices*. The assumptions about labour and material cost movements etc. built into the forecasts are also set out in the publication.

(9) *Spon's cost indices*

As we indicate in Table 13.1, five indices are produced reflecting changes in the costs of: building, M & E services, electrical services, civil engineering and landscaping (hard surfacing and planting) respectively. The calculations are made by Davis, Belfield and Everest (DB & E), the London-based firm of chartered quantity surveyors which also compiles the tender price index listed under reference no. 7 in Table 13.1.

Each index is a composite index based *solely* on movements in the costs of labour (wage rates and labour on-costs) and materials (official price indices) and, where appropriate, plant use. No allowance is made for changes in productivity, overheads, profits or for payments to labour additional to the basic rates. It will be appreciated, therefore, that these indices merely reflect general changes in contractors' primary factor costs and not current costs of construction nor tender prices. The civil engineering and landscaping indices are weighted averages of the PSA price adjustment formula indices (see item 15 below).

DB & E BUILDING COSTS FORECAST. As with the tender price index, DB & E also attempt to forecast the movement of the cost indices for a period two years ahead. The results are published in the *Architects' Journal* (introduced in the issue for 12 November 1975, pp.1017–8 to which reference should be made).

(10) *Building housing cost index*

This index, like the other cost indices referred to above, is meant to reflect changes in the primary factor costs incurred by builders, but in this case related specifically to the costs of housebuilding. In particular, it is based upon an analysis of the constructional requirements of a two-storey, three-bedroomed, semi-detached house of traditional construction which was taken to be representative of the majority of houses being constructed in the early 1970s.

A brief description of the methodology was published in *Building* 3 January 1975, pp.41–4. In brief, the index is devised as a weighted average of cost changes for individual items of labour and materials. The weights were derived from the analysis of an approximate bill of quantities for a typical house of the type defined above, each bill item being split down into labour and materials constituents which were then re-grouped and priced at base-period prices. The weights themselves represent the relative contribution to total costs made by each item. An additional allowance is made for site and head-office overheads, the latter as a fixed percentage but the former by monitoring changes in representative items. Included in the overheads is an allowance for increased costs of a notional 15-months contract period: 'in this way, the index applies equally to a builder/developer or a builder tendering on a firm price basis'. It should be noted, however, that no allowance is made for land prices or the profit element in building or development, so that the index does not necessarily reflect, therefore, movements in house prices (actual house price series are considered in Chapter 4).

(11) *SDD housing cost index (Scotland)*

This index is meant to reflect changes in building *costs* (as opposed to prices) for traditional public sector housebuilding in

Scotland. It is a composite of the indices prepared for use with the price adjustment formula for building contracts (see item 15 below); these indices reflect cost movements throughout the UK and thus, in this context, it is assumed that they are representative of factor cost movements in Scotland.

(12) *BIA/BCIS house rebuilding cost index*
This index is prepared by the BCIS for the British Insurance Association (BIA). It is intended to update the estimates of house rebuilding costs published annually in the *Guide to House Rebuilding Costs for Insurance Valuation*. This *Guide* gives figures in money terms for rebuilding houses of different types, ages, sizes and quality in different parts of the UK to reflect 'the costs of demolishing and clearing away the existing structure and rebuilding it to its existing design in modern materials, using modern techniques, to a standard equal to the existing property and in accordance with current Building Regulations and other statutory requirements' (1983/84 edition, p.6). Prior to September 1982 the index monitored the rebuilding cost of a modern, small, basic quality, semi-detached house. Since then all house categories, as indicated above, have been covered.

(13) *Association of Cost Engineers – erected process plant cost indices*
Four indices are compiled which are meant to reflect changes in the erection costs of typical process plants in the chemical, petrochemical and petroleum industries in the UK. They are based on changes in the costs of labour (erection and other), materials, construction equipment and transport. An allowance is made for changes in productivity but no other allowances for the influences of market conditions on price levels. The indices are base weighted reflecting the pattern of costs of typical plants in the base period and therefore do not reflect subsequent changes in technology or standards etc. Full details of the method of calculation and data sources are given in Eady and Boyd (1964) for the original series and in Kay *et al.* (1981) for the current, revised, series based on 1975.

(14) *BMCIS (RICS) maintenance cost indices*
Four series are produced: a general index and three sub-indices (see Table 13.1) which are meant to reflect movements in the

costs of various types of building maintenance as distinct from new construction. Each is compiled as a weighted average of materials and labour costs. No adjustments are made for changes in productivity or overheads and profits. It is important to recognize, therefore, as with other cost indices, that these series will not necessarily reflect price movements for maintenance work. It is sometimes argued that the scope for productivity improvement on maintenance work is limited and that cost movements, therefore, will more nearly match price movements than in the case of new construction. While there may be some substance in such a view, it is doubtful whether the scope is so limited as to offer no improvement at all over time, especially in the context of innovations in materials and fixing methods. With regard to the impact of market conditions on prices, there is, of course, no reason why these should not influence maintenance work prices as they do for new work. A further difficulty in the case of maintenance work is the determination of a suitable weighting pattern because of wide differences in the pattern of maintenance expenditure on individual buildings. The indices can only be expected, therefore, to give a broad indication of cost/price changes and need to be interpreted with these potential limitations in mind. More detailed information about the method of compilation, which is useful for interpretative purposes, is made available to subscribers.

(15) *PSA price adjustment formulae indices*

These indices (formerly known as NEDO price adjustment formulae indices) are compiled by the PSA for use in the adjustment of prices in contracts let under price variation arrangements as an alternative to the conventional method, in which reimbursement for price changes requires the repricing of each item of work involved separately. Under the 'formula method', reimbursement is merely calculated by reference to the movement of the appropriate index numbers. These index numbers relate to particular 'work categories' or labour, materials and plant input costs. They do not provide a composite measure of construction costs in general but the information has been used for this purpose and the results published elsewhere – see below.

Three sets of indices are compiled as part of 'building', 'specialist engineering' and 'civil engineering' formulae respectively. Currently they are as follows:

Building formula
Work category indices (49 series)
Labour indices (5 series)
Scaffolding indices (2 series)
Plant index

Specialist engineering formulae
Electrical installations (2 series: labour, materials)
Heating and ventilating and sprinkler installations (2 series: labour, materials)
Lift installations (4 series: labour, materials)
Catering equipment (4 series: labour, materials)
Structural steelwork (2 series: labour, materials).

Civil engineering formula
Civil engineering works (12 series: labour, plant, materials)
Structural steelwork (2 series: labour, materials)

The 'work-category' indices are meant to reflect changes over a base period in the current costs of specific items of work arising from changes in the cost of labour, materials and the cost of using plant and are composite indices for these items weighted together according to their relative contribution to costs in a base year. They do not reflect, and are not meant to reflect, changes in overheads, profits and productivity over time. The changes in labour costs are assessed by reference to the movement of wage rates rather than earnings (except in the case of engineering categories where there was no national wage agreement applicable to the labour) and other costs based on *national working rules* applicable to various sectors of the construction industry. The changes in materials and plant costs are based on the official DTI series considered in Chapter 14.

The price adjustment formulae were introduced into building contracts for the first time in 1974. The indices themselves were reviewed and new series introduced in 1977. Full details of the methods used for compiling and maintaining the series are given in NEDO (1974) for the original series (Series 1) and PSA (1977a, 1979a) for the revised series (Series 2). Current guides to the practical application of the indices will be found in PSA (1977b, 1979b).

COMPOSITE CONSTRUCTION COST INDICES (APSAB). Apart from their
use for cost reimbursement purposes, the formulae indices offer
obvious potential for use in the compilation of a single general
index, albeit one measuring costs rather than price changes.
They have been put to such use by the BCIS to devise several
building cost indices (discussed above under reference no. 8)
and also by the PSA itself for its own internal use. The PSA index
– known as the APSAB (Average PSA Building) costs index – is
a weighted average of three separate indices for building, heating,
ventilating and air conditioning, and electrical work. They are
published in *Quantity Surveyors Information Notes.* Details of the
index and series for the period 1970–80 (first quarter) are given
in Tysoe (1981). The price adjustment formulae indices are also
used as the basis of the SDD housing cost index (series 11) and
the Spon's civil engineering and landscaping indices (series 9(d)
and 9(e)).

13.1.3 Appraisal: the interpretation and use of the available indices

We indicated at the beginning of this chapter that major improvements have taken place in the indices available over the last 10 to
20 years, particularly in the development of indices based directly
on actual price data. The great potential offered by the information contained in priced bills of quantities was argued by the
author in 1966 (Fleming, 1966). At that time the available indices
were mainly based on factor costs. All of these indices have now
been replaced by tender price series standardized through the
use of comparable unit rates extracted from priced bills. As
indicated above, there are now six tender price series and a
seventh set of index numbers based indirectly on tender price
data. These now represent the primary indicators of construction
price movements. At the same time, series based upon factor
costs have continued to be compiled – indeed the number of
series has grown – but limited in scope to measuring movements
in costs to the contractor, no attempt now being made to trans-
mute such series into surrogate measures of price movements.

Interpretation of the available indices obviously needs to take
account of the inherent problems involved in attempting to
produce a single measure of price or cost changes for such a

heterogeneous mixture of non-standard products, and the nature of the methods and sources of information used. These have been fully discussed above. It is inevitable that potentially large margins of error must adhere to any single measure.

Use of the available series must also depend partly upon the purpose for which the index is required. Broadly speaking, four purposes may be distinguished:

1. For converting value series expressed in terms of current prices to an equivalent volume (i.e. constant price) series by eliminating from it the effect of price changes
2. For converting figures of construction costs or tender prices for a particular building or category of construction work from one time base to another
3. For the calculation of price adjustments in contracts including VOP clauses
4. For studying price movements as such, as in studies of building cycles and economic fluctuations or comparative studies of industrial performance and trends.

Except for the third, rather specialised use, each of these purposes may be said to require an index of prices rather than costs, although the fourth purpose identified above might also find information about costs useful.

The first use defined above, mainly concerns the government statisticians responsible for compiling official economic statistics for the construction sector, although contractors may also find it useful for the analysis of trends in their own activities over time. A distinction may be made between series of the value of work done (output) and work to be done (new contracts and orders). Both require indices coincident in timing with the valuation of the work. Thus in so far as building output statistics record the value of work at the time it is done (as distinct from the time when the whole contract is complete), as is the case in Great Britain, the index required for deflation purposes is one reflecting current costs as defined above. The output price indices introduced by the DoE in 1978 (Table 13.1, Series No. 1) are expressly designed for this purpose. The deflation of value series of new orders, on the other hand, requires an index of tender prices allowing for the incidence of FP and VOP contracts. The official new orders statistics have been deflated by tender price indices since 1973 when the series were retrospectively revised back to 1963 (see Chapter 7).

The second purpose identified above mainly concerns the construction client and his advisers. The index required for this purpose would generally be one reflecting changes in tender prices and thus one of the tender price indices now compiled would seem the most suitable. On the other hand, in this particular use, one is concerned with the repricing of a particular building, or building type, in a particular location and it is essential to recognize that the available tender indices do not necessarily apply equally to different building types and locations. Again, therefore, their use must unavoidably involve potentially substantial margins of error. A useful discussion of the use of price indices in this context has been provided by Azzaro (1976).

The use of indices for the third purpose is an innovation of the 1970s and has involved the compilation of factor cost indices especially for the purpose – the PSA price adjustment formulae indices (Series No. (15)). Given the general nature of index numbers, it is, of course, virtually inevitable that their use to calculate cost reimbursement payments on an individual contract will not yield amounts which exactly equal the cost increases the contractor has actually incurred on that contract: both under-recovery and over-recovery of cost increases will occur. In principle, this should even out in the aggregate over several contracts. This depends in part upon the reliability and 'representativeness' of the data and methods used to calculate the index numbers and, in part, upon the way the contractor prepares his tender. Useful appraisals of the sensitivity and limitations of the price adjustment formulae indices for adjusting prices on particular contracts have been provided by Barnes (1975) and Jones (1975). A comparison of the reimbursement provided by the Series 1 and Series 2 PSA formulae has been provided in a study by Neale and Light (1981).

With regard to the fourth purpose – studies of economic fluctuations and comparative performance – cost and price indices may be not so much intermediate tools of analysis as the subject of analysis themselves. In this context particularly long-run series may be required but the further back the series are extended the less satisfactory they become because of deficiencies in the available data, and important qualifications must be attached to them. Of the indices prepared currently, the tender price indices would again seem to offer the more reliable source of evidence bearing in mind their potential limitations in scope across the industry. However, none of the currently-compiled tender price indices can be carried back earlier than 1964. For earlier periods, therefore, resort must be had to series which have now been discontinued – full details of these will be found in Fleming (1966, 1980a).

13.2 PRODUCTIVITY

13.2.1 Productivity movements

By 'productivity' is meant the ratio between output and the inputs required to produce it. Studies of productivity *levels*, as opposed to *movements* over time, for particular types of construction work are made from time to time. But considerable problems are involved in trying to devise a satisfactory indicator of productivity change for the construction industry *as a whole* and there is no official index. The purpose of measurement is, of course, to measure improvement in the efficiency with which resources are used by the industry. The term is most commonly used without further qualification, to refer to the ratio between labour inputs and outputs – strictly a measure of labour productivity as opposed to total factor productivity.

It is a simple matter, of course, given statistics of the value of output and employment for the industry and a price index, to calculate an index of output per man at constant prices, and it is not uncommon to see the results of such calculations in various publications. The results of such calculations, however, raise more questions of interpretation than they provide answers about efficiency. First, estimates of the value of gross output per man, or per man-hour, are not an indicator of changes in the productivity of the construction industry as such, because they also reflect changes in the inputs of materials and components from other industries and thus the degree of off-site prefabrication etc. Since the input of materials is a large proportion of total output, the ratio is critically dependent upon changes in the proportion they represent. Therefore, other things being equal, measures of *net* output per man or per man-hour, are more appropriate. But, secondly, the use of such broad measures as gross or net output which, for the construction industry as a whole, encompass such a heterogeneous mixture of work is also inherently misleading, for differences in the labour and material requirements of different sorts of work (e.g. road building versus hospitals) means that the 'productivity' index may change merely in response to changes in the output mix. As with the measurement of price movements over time, comparisons of productivity untarnished by other factors, can only be made on a like-for-like basis. Thirdly, at a practical level, data limitations introduce their own problems of interpretation so that movements in a productivity index may reflect deficiencies in the data bases rather than any underlying reality. The principal (DoE) output and employment series have been affected by deficiencies in coverage varying in their incidence over time and in their effects on one series as against the other (see Chapters 6 and 8). Quite apart from deficiences in coverage that have arisen, the restriction of employment series to 'employees' increases the problems of interpretation because the latter have declined as a result of substitution by self-employed labour. Ratios of output per *employee,* even disregarding all other problems, provide no indication by themselves of productivity change. Further, the calculations are critically dependent on the price index used for deflating current output to constant price values. Whilst improvements have been made to the measurement of price trends over recent years, the inevitable margins of error that remain must cast doubt on whether productivity movements can be independently distinguished with any assurance. A fuller discussion of these matters is given in Fleming (1980a), pp.280–1.

13.2.2 Productivity levels

As noted above, studies of productivity *levels,* as opposed to *movements* over time, for particular sectors of the industry are carried out from time to time. These sometimes provide information in physical terms, e.g. man-hours per house or per 1000 square feet of floor area etc. The most important source of information here is the Building Research Establishment. Recent studies have been concerned with measuring labour requirements for various unit measures of construction work (per £1000 of contract value, square metres of floor area, or functional units such as dwellings, pupil places in schools) for various types of construction output: new housing and housing improvements, educational buildings, hospitals, PSA contracts, industrial buildings, roads, harbours, water and sewerage. Details have been given by Lemessany and Clapp (1980). Details of earlier studies will be found in Fleming (1980a), p.281.

14
CONSTRUCTION MATERIALS AND PLANT

This chapter is divided into two parts, one dealing with statistics relating to production, consumption etc. of materials and the production or use of contractors' plant and the other dealing with information about their prices.

14.1 CONSUMPTION, PRODUCTION AND OVERSEAS TRADE

As with any production activity, statistics about the materials used could be collected either from their suppliers (producers) or direct from their users. In the case of construction, however, the collection of data from producers is confronted by the problem that construction uses a great variety of materials and components drawn from a very wide range of industries and that many of them are not specific in use to construction: they may be suitable for use in construction but are not used solely for construction purposes and the producer may not be able to specify the end-uses of the materials he supplies. The only useful information from the production side, therefore, is confined to that relating to well-defined construction materials. Information is collected from the consumption end – i.e. from contractors – but this is generally limited to information about the total value of materials purchased; it is rarely broken down by type of material. We now turn to examine the information available in these two areas of consumption and production, first dealing with materials and then plant.

14.1.1 Construction materials

(a) *Consumption and use of construction materials*
Information is available from the following sources each of which we consider in turn:

(i)   Censuses of production
(ii) Input–output analyses
(iii) *Ad hoc* surveys and estimates
(iv) Manufacturers' sales statistics.

CENSUSES OF PRODUCTION. The censuses of production are considered fully in Chapter 6, Section 6.2 and reference should be made to that for full details. It will be noted that in the current system of censuses, conducted by the BSO annually since 1974 in the case of construction, that only total figures are collected for the purchase of materials and fuel etc. as follows:

1. Purchases of materials for use in construction
2. Cost of fuel and electricity
3. Purchases of goods for merchanting or factoring
4. Other purchases.

Under the previous system of censuses, a 'detailed' census was taken every few years in which a breakdown of materials purchased was requested. The last such detailed census took place in 1968. Full details of these censuses back to 1946 are given in Fleming (1980a). Under the new system of censuses, detailed information about goods purchased is collected periodically in supplementary 'purchases enquiries' but these do *not* cover the construction industry.

INPUT–OUTPUT ANALYSES. Input–output tables set out to show the interrelationships between industries in the whole economy and show therefore the inputs into construction supplied by every other industry. These tables are based on the census of production data and are considered in Chapter 6, Section 6.4. It is important to note that the figures for construction involve a large element of estimation and relate to broad industry groups as opposed to specific materials.

AD HOC SURVEYS AND ESTIMATES. We refer here only to studies

published since 1970, references to earlier studies will be found in Fleming (1980a), p.316. The most recent general study is one carried out by NEDO (1978). This provides estimates of the uses of some 80 materials in the period 1974–5 in various types of work made on the basis of invoice analyses and 'informed guesses'. Studies at the Building Research Station have provided estimates of the overall usage of aggregates (Lemessany, 1976) and some limited information about the use of timber (Carruthers and Harding, 1976). Further research is being undertaken into the usage of materials in a range of different building types but, as yet, no results have been published.

SALES AND DELIVERIES OF SPECIFIC MATERIALS. The data falling within this heading are considered below because the data are collected from manufacturers along with production data.

(b) *Production, sales and deliveries of construction materials*

Two sets of data are available: one in physical units and one in monetary units. We consider each separately.

DATA IN PHYSICAL UNITS. Details of the current series and publication sources are set out in Table 14.1. The most detailed source, generally speaking, is *Monthly Statistics of Building Materials and Components (MSBMC)*, but many of the series are reproduced in 'secondary' sources and in some cases these include series not given in *MSBMC*.

As noted in Table 14.1, the production of aggregates and other minerals has been covered in an annual Minerals Enquiry since 1974. The results, published in *Business Monitor PA 1007*, provide breakdowns by type of mineral and end-use. *UK Mineral Statistics* brings together data from a wide range of sources (including the annual minerals enquiry) and provides estimates for the usage of some minerals not available elsewhere. Further valuable sources of reference with regard to the production and use of minerals are a series of *Mineral Dossiers* prepared for the Mineral Resources Consultative Committee: the main reports of relevance are listed under this committee in the References at the end of the book. They contain long-run series going back, in some cases, to the nineteenth century and provide useful commentaries on the resources and uses of the minerals and about the statistics themselves. The supply of, and demand for, aggregates in particular have long been subjects of special attention. Detailed supply statistics for marine-dredged and land-won production (by type) according to country, county and region (EPRs and Scottish regions) are now published in *Business Monitor PA 1007* referred to above. Until 1981 (data for 1979) they were published in *Production of Aggregates*.

DATA IN MONETARY UNITS. These data are collected in quarterly (and in a few cases monthly) enquiries into manufacturers' *sales* conducted by the BSO and published in *Business Monitors* bearing the prefix PQ or PM respectively. A guide to the enquiries is given in *Business Monitor PO 1001*. As far as construction materials are concerned, the principal reports are those listed below. For further assistance in tracing information about particular materials reference should be made to the *Index of Commodities: Business Monitor PO 1000*. Unlike most of the data referred to in Table 14.1, these statistics relate to the United Kingdom. It should be noted that small producers are excluded from the enquiries.

Business Monitor	Title
PQ 2245	Aluminium and aluminium alloys
PQ 2246	Copper, brass and other copper alloys
PQ 2310	Extraction of stone, clay, sand and gravel
PQ 2396	Miscellaneous minerals
PQ 2410	Structural clay products
PQ 2420	Cement, lime and plaster
PQ 2436	Ready-mixed concrete
PQ 2437	Miscellaneous building products of concrete, cement or plaster
PQ 2440	Asbestos
PQ 2450	Working of stone and miscellaneous non-metallic minerals
PQ 2471	Flat glass
PQ 2489	Ceramic goods
PQ 2551	Paints, varnishes and painters' fillings

Table 14.1 Sources of building materials production and related statistics – Great Britain (unless indicated otherwise)*

Material	Frequency†	MSBMC	HCS	MDS	AAS	UK.Min. Stats.‡	Remarks
Aggregates							
Sand and gravel	Q	P/S	P/S	P/S	P/S	P/S	Primary source is annual Minerals Inquiry – *Business Monitor* PA1007‡ – see text. Production data, based on sample enquiries, to end 1979; then total sales. All except MDS contain breakdowns by type (building/concreting/gravel). *MSBMC* and *HCS* provide analyses by country, region and county (land-won/marine dredged). Analyses by type in *HCS* and *AAS*.
Crushed rock aggregates	A		P		P	P	
Mftd lightweight aggregates					P	P	
Asbestos cement products	Q	P.D.St.	P.D.	P	P	P	Analyses by type in *MSBMC* (P.D.) and in annual *HCS* (P.) and *AAS* (P.).
Bricks	Q	P.D.St.	P.D.St.		P	P	*MSBMC* includes analyses by type (commons/facings/engineering); by type of material (clay/sandlime/concrete) and deliveries from each country and region. The annual *HCS* gives production data by type and material type as above and deliveries as above. *UK.Min. Stats.* gives analyses by type of material. *MSBMC* includes analyses by type (as above), country and region. First issued (P.D.St. data) as a *DoE Press Notice*.
	M	P.HD.St.E.	P.HD.St.	P.St.			
	M			P.St.			
Cement	Q	§	P.HD.St.		P	P	UK. Exports are of cement and cement clinker. First issued (P.HD.St.) as a *DoE Press Notice*.
Cement clinker	M	P.St.	P.St.	P.St.		P	*MSBMC* and annual *HCS* include analyses of HD (sales incl. imports) into standard regions and countries of UK.
Clay roofing tiles	A				S	S	UK. Unglazed floor quarries, glazed/unglazed tiles.
Clay tiles	A				S	S	

Material	†						Remarks
Concrete building blocks	M	P.D.St.	P.D.	P	P	P	Analyses by type in MSBMC, HCS, AAS and UK.Min.Stats.
Concrete pipes	Q	P			S	S	Analyses by country and region in MSBMC.
Concrete roofing tiles	A	P.D.St.	P.D.St.	P.St.	P		
Gypsum	Q	Mined	Mined	Mined	Mined	Mined	
Metals							
Finished steel	Q	See remarks					Receipts, consumption and stocks. Primary source is *Iron and Steel Industry Monthly Statistics* (also *Iron and Steel Industry Annual Statistics*).
Cast iron pipes and fittings	A						
Pressure pipes and fittings	A				P	P	
Copper and brass tubes	Q	P			P	P	Copper/Brass/Other copper alloys for all purposes.
Copper tubing	A				P		
Plaster	M	P.D.	P.D.	P	P	P	Excluding plaster used in production of plasterboard.
Plasterboard	M	P.HD.St.E.	P.D.St.	P.St.	P	P	
Ready-mixed concrete	Q	P	P	P	P	P	UK.
Slate	Q	P.D.St.	P.D.St.	P.St.	P	P	Analyses by type in MSBMC and annual HCS (P only) and UK.Min.Stats.
Timber							
Imported softwood	M	D.St.					
Imported hardwood	M	D.St.					
Wood chipboard	M	P.D.St.					Home produced.
Imported particle board	M	D.St.					
Imported plywood	M	D.St.					
Hardboard and insulation board	A					S	UK.

Data available are indicated by the following abbreviations: P=production; D=deliveries; HD=home deliveries; S=sales; St=stocks; E=exports.

* Excluding manufacturers' sales enquiries reported in *Business Monitor* PQ series and foreign trade statistics, except where collected with production data – see text.

† The greatest frequency is shown in this column: the annual *HCS*, *AAS* and *UK.Min.Stats.* contain annual series only and the quarterly *HCS* contains quarterly series.

‡ *Business Monitor PA 1007* and *UK.Min.Stats.* also give analyses of sales by broad end-use and area of origin for: sandstone, igneous rock, limestone, dolomite, chalk, clay and shale, and crushed rock. The *Business Monitor* also contains detailed analyses for sand and gravel for construction.

PQ 3111   Iron castings
PQ 3142   Metal doors, windows etc.
PQ 3169   Miscellaneous finished metal products
PQ 3204   Fabricated constructional steel work
PQ 3284   Refrigerating, space heating, ventilating and air-conditioning equipment
PQ 4620   Semi-finished wood products; preservation and treatment of wood
PM 4621   Wood chipboard
PQ 4630   Builders' carpentry and joinery
PM 4710
PQ 4710   } Pulp, paper and board
PQ 4721   Wallcoverings
PQ 4833   Plastics floor coverings
PQ 4834   Plastics building products

(c) *Overseas trade in construction materials*

The most convenient source of information about the value of imports and exports of materials and components suitable for use in construction is *MSBMC* and the annual *HCS* which include quarterly and annual series respectively for (currently) over 40 different commodities. The data are extracted from the official publications covering all UK trade. These are: *Overseas Trade Statistics of the United Kingdom,* published monthly, and the *Annual Statement of Overseas Trade of the United Kingdom* which is published annually and provides information in somewhat greater commodity detail.* A description and guide to the classification used is provided in HM Customs and Excise (annually). In addition to these sources, information in physical terms for the exports of cement and plasterboard are collected separately as part of deliveries statistics (Table 14.1 refers). Also of possible interest are quarterly analyses of *Overseas Trade Analysed in Terms of Industries* and *Import Penetration and Export Sales Ratios* published in *Business Monitor MQ 10* and *MQ 12* respectively, although the classification is by broad industry grouping and not by specific materials. With regard to the interpretation of these data, reference should be made to *ET* February 1975 and August 1977 respectively.

* More detailed information than that published is available, subject to rules regarding disclosure, from the Statistical Office of HM Customs and Excise, Bill of Entry Service, Portcullis House, 27 Victoria Avenue, Southend-on-Sea, SS2 6AL.

14.1.2 Construction plant and equipment

(a) *Use of plant and equipment in the construction industry*

Statistics of the capital expenditure by contractors (excluding direct labour organizations) on plant and equipment are a constituent series of the official statistics of GDFCF, published in the *UK National Accounts* Blue Book, which were considered earlier in Chapter 6 (Section 6.5). Information on capital expenditure sub-divided by trade of firm (on which the GDFCF figures are based) is given in the annual census of production report for construction *Business Monitor PA 500* – see Section 6.2 for further details. The census of production also gives figures on the payments *received* by firms in the industry for plant hire and, for larger undertakings only (those employing 100 or more persons) payments *made* for the hire of vehicles, plant and machinery.

(b) *Production and overseas trade statistics for contractors' plant*

Statistics of the production and sales of particular types of plant and equipment are collected in the quarterly BSO manufacturers' sales enquiries referred to earlier, and published in the PQ series of *Business Monitors*. The principal reports are as follows:

PQ 3254   Construction and earth-moving equipment
PQ 3255   Mechanical lifting and handling equipment
PQ 3283   Compressors and fluid power equipment
PQ 3285   Scales, weighing machinery and portable power tools.

For further details reference should be made to the *Index of Commodities – Business Monitor PO 1000*. The sources of overseas trade statistics for contractors' plant and equipment are the same as for construction materials considered in Section 14.1.1 except that summaries are *not* included in *MSBMC* or *HCS*.

14.2 PRICES OF CONSTRUCTION MATERIALS AND PLANT

14.2.1 Construction materials prices

(a) *Price indices for materials purchased by the construction industry*

THE SERIES AVAILABLE. Price index numbers, designed to measure the change in price over time, for a wide range of commodities relevant to all industries are compiled by the DTI. These indices are published in *British Business* as part of a set of 'Producer Price Indices' (known as 'Wholesale Price Indices' until August 1983) and are available monthly back to 1946.* They cover a large number of individual construction materials and four general indices in which the individual price indices are combined to produce weighted averages reflecting the relative importance of different materials in different sectors of construction activity as follows:

1. All work ('Construction materials')
2. New housing ('House-building materials')
3. Other new work
4. Repairs and maintenance

Only the first two series are formally part of the set of Producer Price Indices and many publications, therefore, include these series only. The main publication sources are listed below.
First two series only:
> *Press Notice. Producer Prices Indices:* monthly
> *British Business:* monthly
> *MDS:* monthly
> *AAS:* annual.

All four series:
> *MSBMC:* monthly
> *HCS:* quarterly and annual.

The price indices for specific construction materials refer to 'commodities produced in the UK (home sales)'. A separate, much more limited, set of indices is presented for 'commodities wholly or mainly imported into the UK' (the main items of relevance to construction are wood and wood manufactures). The currently-published price indices and publication sources are listed in Table 14.2.

INTERPRETATION. The purpose of the general indices is to measure movements in the purchase prices of the materials used. It is important to note, however, that none of the price data is obtained from users. In practice a mixture of ex-works and delivered prices is used (the distance and area of delivery vary)

---

* Earlier series of a comparable nature were compiled by the MoW back to 1939 – details will be found in Fleming (1980a) pp.326–7 and the series themselves in Fleming (1980b).

the latter usually including discount appropriate to the firms' most common selling quantities. The prices are obtained in the main from producers but some are obtained from trade associations and importers and a few from trade publications. All prices are taken exclusive of relevant taxes (i.e. VAT and, before its abolition, purchase tax). In practice, of course, the prices actually paid in particular transactions may be affected by rebates and discounts from list prices which may vary with size of order and may be special to particular customers. They are thus difficult to incorporate in the price-reporting system. As noted above, however, the attempt is made to obtain quotations net of the contributors' typical level of discounts. A further problem for the construction sector is the fact that many materials are obtained through builders' merchants rather than direct from producers. As a measure of the movement of materials input costs, therefore, the assumption is implicit that the movement of the price quotations will faithfully reflect the movement of actual transaction prices. Particular problems in this respect may have been experienced following the development of more fluid trading conditions after the ending of producer price cartels and resale price maintenance in some industries from the mid 1950s onwards – for further discussion see Fleming (1980a), p.325. The use of ex-works prices for some materials is an important limitation in principle in the case of construction, given the necessity for distribution to sites throughout the whole country and the importance of transport costs for many of the materials used. Delivered prices are preferable but need to reflect the geographical pattern of construction activity. Information collected directly from users (contractors) would be better still but, of course, would be more difficult and costly to collect. A detailed account of the principles and methodology involved in the compilation of the series is given in CSO (1980).

(b) *Price indices for stocks held by builders' merchants and building materials producers*

Following the report of the Sandilands Committee on *Inflation Accounting* (Cmnd 6225) a variety of special indices were introduced for current cost accounting (CCA) purposes. In the context of construction materials, two 'industry-specific' indices – intended to reflect the price movements of stocks of materials

Table 14.2 Construction materials price indices

Material	Price index series	1980 SIC Ref. No.	Principal publication sources*			
			BB	MSBMC	HCS†	AAS
Aggregates	Uncoated sand and gravel	2310	x		x	x
	Granite and other chippings, aggregates and roadstone		x	x		x
	Uncoated limestone roadstone and aggregates	2450	x	x		x
	Coated granite and whinstone, roadstone		x	x	x	x
	Coated limestone roadstone		x	x		x
Bricks	All bricks (common, facing and engineering)		x	x	x	x
	Flettons (delivered)					
	Facing		x	x	x	x
	Common	2410	x	x	x	x
	Non-flettons (ex-works)					
	Facing		x	x	x	x
	Common		x	x	x	x
	Engineering				x	
Cement	Calcareous cement (other than clinker)			x		x
	Delivered (25 miles)	2420				
	– in bulk		x			x
	– in bags		x			x
Clay products (other)	Vitreous china sanitary ware	2489		x	x	x
	Wash basins, all types		x			x
	WC pans, all types		x			x
	Roofing tiles	2410	x	x		x
Concrete	Ready-mixed concrete	2436	x	x		x
Concrete products	Flagstones		x	x	x	x
	Kerbs and edgings	2437	x	x	x	x
	Pipes to BS 556		x	x	x	x
Felt	Bituminous and flat felts (including sarking and sheathing felts)	2450	x	x	x	x
Heating apparatus	Electric heating apparatus	3460	x	x	x	x
	Space-heating apparatus		x			x
Insulation materials	Insulating materials for thermal or acoustic purposes	2450	x	x	x	x
	Mineral wool (rock and slag)		x			x

Key:
BB = British Business. MSBMC = Monthly Statistics of Building Materials and Components
HCS = Housing and Construction Statistics. AAS = Annual Abstract of Statistics.

* The PQ series of *Business Monitors*, which report the results of manufacturers' sales enquiries, also include the relevant indices for particular commodities; each volume is identified by the SIC reference number given in the third column.

Material	Price index series	1980 SIC Ref. No.	Principal publication sources*			
			BB	MSBMC	HCS†	AAS
Metals and metal products	Iron and steel‡					
	Finished rolled products		x			
	Railway material					
	– heavy permanent		x			x
	– light permanent		x			x
	Sheet piling		x			x
	Beams and sections	2210	x			x
	Bars and rods		x			
	Hot rolled narrow strip		x			x
	Hot rolled coil plate and sheet		x	x	x	x
	3 mm to 4.75 mm		x	x	x	x
	Steel for reinforcement, cut, bent and delivered		x			x
	Steel tubes	2220	x	x	x	x
	Iron castings	3111	x	x	x	x
	Aluminium plate, sheet, strip circles and blanks	2245	x	x	x	x
	Copper tubes		x	x	x	x
	Copper sheet and copper strip	2246	x	x	x	x
	Metal doors, windows etc.	3142	x	x	x	x
	Sanitary ware and plumbing fixtures and fittings		x	x	x	x
	Bath, basin, sink taps	3169	x			x
	Plumbers' brassware				x	
Paint etc.	Paints, varnishes and painters' fillings		x		x	x
	Building, structural, preservative and decorative products – non-aqueous, oil and/or synthetic-based	2551	x			x
	Filling and sealing compounds of all types		x			x
Plaster	Plaster, gypsum	2420			x	
Plasterboard	Plasterboard	2437	x	x	x	x
Plastic products	Pipes and fittings		x	x	x	x
	Soil waste pipes and fittings	4834	x			x
	Rainwater pipes and fittings		x	x	x	x

† Annual volume.
‡ Currently 36 series are published under this heading (SIC serial 2210), selected series only are listed here.

(*continued overleaf*)

Table 14.2 *(continued)*

Material	Price index series	1980 SIC Ref. No.	BB	MSBMC	HCS†	AAS
			Principal publication sources*			
Timber and manufactured joinery	Homegrown hardwood (sawn)	4610	x	x	x	x
	Imported hardwood		x		x	x
	Imported softwood		x		x	x
	Imported plywood and blockboard		x		x	x
	Builders' carpentry and joinery**	4630	x			x
	Builders' woodwork and prefabricated building structures		x		x	x
	Doorsets, leaves and frames and window frames		x			x
	Doorsets, leaves and frames		x			x
	Door leaves flush		x	x		x
	Other door leaves including louvred doors		x	x		x
	Window frames		x	x		x

Key: BB=*British Business*. MSBMC=*Monthly Statistics of Building Materials and Components* HCS=*Housing and Construction Statistics*. AAS=*Annual Abstract of Statistics*.

* The PQ series of *Business Monitors*, which report the results of manufacturers' sales enquiries, also include the relevant indices for particular commodities; each volume is identified by the SIC reference number given in the third column.

† Annual volume.

‡ Currently 36 series are published under this heading (SIC serial 2210), selected series only are listed here.

** Separate import price series also given.

held – are of relevance, namely for builders' merchants and the 'building materials and minerals extraction industry'.* In the case of the latter, two series are produced: one for 'stocks held as materials and fuel' and one for 'stocks of goods on hand for sale'. Each index represents a base-weighted average of appropriate combinations of indices in the family of producer price index numbers referred to above. The series, running from 1970 were initially published by CSO in *Price Index Numbers for Current Cost Accounting (PINCCA)* until 1981. They are now published by BSO each month in *Business Monitor MM 17;* a summary volume – *Business Monitor MO 18* – gives the whole series for the period 1974–82.

It should be appreciated that these indices are prepared for the convenience of companies who wish to use them for CCA purposes. Warnings are expressed in the published reports about the possible inappropriateness of the indices for individual companies. This can only be judged by individual companies themselves by comparing the composition of their own stock in relation to that taken as representative in the published indices themselves. The use of ex-works, as against delivered prices, may also be an additional limitation for some companies.

(c) *Actual price data*

Actual prices for a range of construction materials are regularly quoted (as either ex-works prices or prices delivered to certain areas) in the trade press and builders' price books. The principal journal is *Building;* the most well-known and long-established price books are *Laxton's Building Price Book* and *Spon's Architects' and Builders' Price Book.* In the context of the discussion of the official price indices above, it will be appreciated that the prices quoted in these sources are not necessarily representative either of prices in different parts of the country nor of the prices which buyers autually pay: many of the quotations are representative list prices quoted either ex-works or delivered to a particular town (generally London). A more comprehensive source of infor-

* Defined, currently as 'Activities' 2310–2460 of the 1980 SIC namely: building products of concrete, cement, plaster; crushed stone and other non-metallic minerals; structural clay products; asbestos goods; stone, clay, sand, gravel; abrasive products; cement, lime, plaster; ready-mixed concrete; other minerals not elsewhere specified.

mation about *list prices* is lists prepared by Building Materials Market Research Limited (based in Brighton, Sussex); these are made available to subscribers only.

14.2.2 Construction plant prices

Price indices for construction plant and equipment are compiled by the DTI currently as part of the same Producer Price Indices series of which the construction materials price indices, discussed above, form part. They are published in *British Business,* in the PQ series of *Business Monitors* and as part of a set of 'asset-specific' indices developed for CCA purposes and published, currently, in *Business Monitor MM 17* (formerly in *PINCCA*). The CCA set of index numbers also include general 'industry-specific' indices, including one for capital expenditure on plant and machinery by the construction industry (quarterly series from 1956 to 1971 and then monthly), constituting base-weighted averages of appropriate indices in the family of producer price indices. Finally, it may be noted that indices covering the costs of providing, operating and maintaining constructional plant and equipment are compiled as part of the series devised for use with the PSA price adjustment formulae; these are considered in Chapter 13.

INTERPRETATION. It will be appreciated that, as in the case of the construction materials indices, the appropriateness of these indices for use by a particular company depends on how well the pattern of weights match the particular pattern appropriate to that particular company, as well as the reliability of the underlying price information. Details of the composition and weights are given in the published reports.

15
CONSTRUCTION
PROFESSIONS

15.1 INTRODUCTION

The professional activities related to construction are architecture, surveying (particularly quantity surveying) and the various kinds of engineering that are related to the design of buildings, other construction works and engineering services installations. The range of information available is limited and uneven. There are few general sources covering all three professional areas: most of the data are collected by the professional associations themselves and naturally relate to their own members. The architectural profession is much better documented than others. There are perhaps five main subjects of interest and we consider each of these in separate sections as follows:

15.2 Manpower
15.3 Work done
15.4 Average earnings
15.5 Professional practice costs and incomes
15.6 Organization and structure of professional practices.

15.2 MANPOWER

With regard to manpower, it is important to draw distinctions between the professionally qualified and unqualified and, amongst the former, between those employed in a professional capacity and those who are not. It should also be borne in mind that the provision of professional services may not necessarily be confined to those with professional qualifications.

15.2.1 General sources

(a) *Censuses of population*

The one *general* source for the numbers in professional occupations is the Census of Population. This has recorded the occupations of individuals since 1841 and, from 1961, it has recorded additional information about qualifications. We confine our attention here to the five censuses taken since the Second World War: 1951, 1961, 1966, 1971 and 1981. For details of earlier censuses see OPCS and GRO(S) (1977); see also Fleming (1980a), p.350.

OCCUPATIONAL ANALYSES. In the latest (1981) census only two relevant categories are distinguished: architects, town planners, quantity, building and land surveyors as one category and civil, structural, municipal, mining and quarrying engineers as another. In the earlier post-war censuses the classification varied. Architects were grouped with town planners in 1951 and 1971 and with surveyors in 1961 and 1966. Surveyors were reported separately in 1951 and 1971 but not sub-divided by type. Civil, structural and municipal engineers were treated as one category in each census from 1951 to 1971. An official guide to the *Classification of Occupations* is published for each census: GRO (1956, 1960, 1966) and OPCS (1970, 1980). The data are published in 'Economic Activity' reports for the most recent censuses and 'Occupation Tables' for earlier censuses – for details see the List of statistical sources at the end of this book under 'census'. The effect of reclassification in the latest census may be studied in the *Census 1981 Economic Activity* report which gives comparisons of the 1981 data recoded according to the 1970 classification, and 1971 data recoded according to the 1980 classification.

QUALIFIED MANPOWER. Qualified manpower analyses available from the Census of Population and other sources are considered in Chapter 8 (Section 8.9).

(b) *Surveys of contractors and direct labour organizations*

A return of 'architects, surveyors and engineers' (not further defined) employed by contractors in scope to the CITB has been obtained annually since 1977. Details are given in Chapter 8

(Section 8.4). Before 1977 corresponding data were collected by the DoE from 1965 in the case of contractors (broken down by type of staff: architects, surveyors, engineers until 1974) and from 1968 to 1980 in the case of direct labour organizations – further details are given in Chapter 8 (Section 8.1).

15.2.2 The architectural profession

(a) *The ARCUK Register*

A statutory registration body, the Architects' Registration Council of the United Kingdom (ARCUK) was established in 1931. In 1938 the legal use of the title of 'architect' was restricted to those who are legally registered, registration being limited to those who are suitably qualified, but no restriction was imposed on the provision of architectural services. The ARCUK register, therefore, provides a good source of information about the numbers qualified to practise as 'architects'. However, persons on the register will not necessarily be practising in the UK and some may not be practising at all. Further, some persons who satisfy the qualification requirements may not register. The Council publishes an annual list of names and addresses of persons on the register together with a note on the numbers added and removed in the year (ARCUK, annually).

(b) *RIBA membership statistics and survey data*

The principal professional association for architects is the Royal Institute of British Architects (RIBA) and it is the only examining body recognized by the ARCUK other than the 'Schools' of architecture (mainly in universities and polytechnics) which are themselves 'recognized' by the RIBA. Statistics of RIBA corporate and student membership are published in *Annual Reports* (RIBA, annually) and an annual *Architects' Employment and Earnings* survey (referred to below) includes percentage analyses by 'employment activity' and age.

ARCHITECTS' EMPLOYMENT AND EARNINGS SURVEYS. These surveys are based on a sample drawn from the ARCUK register each year. Apart from the analysis of RIBA membership, referred to above, they provide regular information on employment and earnings and periodic coverage of particular employment issues (the latest, 1984, survey for example, covered the allocation of time to various activities and holiday entitlements). The employment data provide information on employment activity, fields of employment, age, sex, full-time and part-time employment, unemployment, and also information on under-employment.

EMPLOYMENT IN PRIVATE PRACTICE. Information on employment levels in private offices has been collected as part of quarterly workload surveys since 1977. It is published currently as an index for three categories of staff (Principals, salaried architects and other architectural staff) in the *RIBA Quarterly Statistical Bulletin.* Information on employment in private practices is also obtained in periodic censuses by the RIBA – see Section 15.5.

LOCAL AUTHORITY STAFFING. A survey of local authority architects' departments was made by the RIBA in 1981 and published in *Local Authority Staffing.* The results show the number of architects and architectural assistants employed on 1 January 1980 and 1981 and predictions for 1982 according to type of authority and region. See also sub-section 15.6.1.

STUDENT STATISTICS. Education statistics are collected annually by the RIBA from all of the architectural schools in the country and published in *Education Statistics.* They provide information on numbers of students and examination results. In addition, special student surveys are conducted from time to time. The latest surveys are *Student Employment Survey 1978* (a survey of students who completed their Part II examination in the previous year) and *Student Survey 1979* which was a complementary survey of students at an earlier stage of their course, namely towards the end of their first year of practical training (most of whom had sat their Part I examination).

15.2.3 The surveying professions

The professional association for surveyors is the Royal Institution of Chartered Surveyors (RICS) covering a wide range of surveying specializations. In 1983 a separate Institute of Quantity Surveyors (IQS) which represented in the main the quantity surveyor in employment with contractors, merged with the RICS. Unlike architecture, there is no statutory registration body and no restriction on the use of the term 'surveyor'. Quantity surveyors may practise, therefore, without formal qualification or membership of professional associations. It may be noted too that some architects offer quantity surveying services as do civil engineers and mechanical and electrical engineers in their respective fields. An account of the development and organization of the profession will be found in Thompson (1968).

Membership statistics of the RICS according to professional practice division are given in the *RICS Yearbook* (RICS, annually). The only other information comes from occasional surveys. The results of the latest such survey were published in 1984 in *A Study of Quantity Surveying Practice and Client Demand*. This gives details of employment of chartered quantity surveyors by field of employment in 1972, 1981 and 1983. Details of earlier surveys carried out by the RICS, IQS and other bodies will be found in Fleming (1980a), pp.353–4.

15.2.4 The engineering professions

The principal associations for the engineering professions related to construction are the Institution of Civil Engineers (ICE), the Institution of Structural Engineers, the Institution of Municipal Engineers (prior to merging with the ICE in 1984), and the Chartered Institution of Building Services (CIBS) – formerly the Institution of Heating and Ventilating Engineers (IHVE). Members of other institutions, such as the Institution of Mechanical Engineers and the Institution of Electrical Engineers may also carry out work relating to construction but, of course, their members are not primarily concerned with construction activities. There is no statutory registration body but in 1962 a Council of Engineering Institutions (CEI) was established as a federation of some 14 professional engineering institutions which have a qualifying function (including all those mentioned above with the exception of IHVE), and it established an Engineers' Registration Board in 1971 to operate a register of chartered engineers, technician engineers and engineering technicians. In 1981 the CEI was replaced by the Engineering Council. The Engineers' Registration Board was wound up at the end of 1983 and its functions transferred to the Engineering Council. A further association of relevance in the context of construction is the Association of Consulting Engineers (ACE) to which many of the consulting engineers in private practice belong.

(a) *Membership statistics*

Details of membership of the institutions are given in annual reports or yearbooks prepared by the institutions (these are listed in the References at the end of the book). It must be remembered that the membership figures will include not only members who are in employment but also those who are unemployed or retired and, amongst those who are active, those who are active overseas and some who are active in fields other than construction. Also it must be remembered that the membership of some institutions may overlap.

(b) *Membership surveys*

Surveys of Chartered Engineers and Technician Engineers are conducted every other year by the Engineering Council in continuation of a series initiated in 1966. The results are published in *The Survey of Professional Engineers.* The primary topics covered are employment, income and age but the full range of analyses are not made by industry as such. With reference to construction, the latest survey (1983) provides analyses of employment, income and age by occupation (including 'construction, installation') and by 'field of employment' (i.e. industry); analyses, by institution, of trade union membership, salary determination, earnings, and Chartered Engineers by qualification; and unemployment by field of work. For civil engineers, the ICE has conducted annual salary surveys of its members since 1976 (apart from 1981 and 1982); these include details of fields of employment, type of work and location. The results are published in *New Civil Engineer* (e.g. 23 February 1984, pp.20–6 which gives the 1983 survey results). Details of *ad hoc* surveys carried out in the past will be found in Fleming (1980a) pp.355–6.

15.3 WORK DONE BY THE CONSTRUCTION PROFESSIONS

15.3.1 Private architects' design work

Statistics of the value of private architects' design work for building in Great Britain have been collected by the RIBA

from a sample of private architectural practices for many years –
the principal series go back to 1958. The current analyses,
published in the RIBA *Quarterly Statistical Bulletin* are as follows:

1. Quarterly statistics of the value of new commissions and
   work entering the production drawings stage. These are
   analysed by type of building (housing and other building)
   by sector at both current and constant prices and total work
   is analysed by region (based on *location of architects' office*) at
   current prices only
2. Quarterly analyses of the value of rehabilitation work (i.e.
   work exceeding £2500 in value carried out on existing buildings) as a percentage of new commissions by type of building
3. Quarterly figures of the proportion of work abandoned or
   postponed (given in introductory notes to the tables)
4. Annual figures for the value of work certified, analysed by
   type of work and sector, and by building type (distinguishing
   new building from rehabilitation).

It will be appreciated that all of these data are subject to sampling
error and are affected by the normal uncertainties of the estimation of values at early stages of the design process. Likewise the
revaluation to constant prices also presents difficulties at this
stage (the price indices employed are implicit deflators derived
from the DoE series of new orders at current and constant prices
– see Chapter 7). For further details and discussion see Fleming
(1980a), pp.361–72.

15.3.2 Work undertaken by private chartered quantity surveyors

The only data collected regularly are obtained in qualitative workload returns made to the RICS by quantity surveying practices in
England and Wales in which they indicate whether the volume
of the total work in hand is 'more', 'the same', or 'less' in the
current quarter compared with the previous quarter. The results
are published in *Chartered Surveyor Weekly* and show simply the
percentage of firms reporting in each category.

15.3.3 Work undertaken by consulting engineers

Only limited information is available. The journal *New Civil
Engineer* conducts an annual survey of consulting engineers

seeking information about workload and other subjects. The workload enquiry is qualitative, the results being presented as the percentage of firms expecting an increase or decrease over the previous year. Information is also presented separately for each firm showing size of firm, percentage of staff involved in civil and structural engineering, percentage of overseas work, countries of work and types of work. The latest results at the time of writing were published in *New Civil Engineer* for 22 March 1984 (pp.20–4).

The only other statistics collected regularly are for overseas contracts obtained by members of the ACE, details of which are listed annually in *Overseas Work Entrusted to Members*. In addition, a commentary on some of the major projects is included as part of an article on 'Construction Overseas' published once a year in *British Business*.

15.4 AVERAGE EARNINGS

We are concerned here with information about the earnings of individuals employed in the professional sector (whether professionally qualified or not). Information about the *total* income of private practices and total income earned overseas is considered in Section 15.5. We first consider general sources and then those sources which are specific to each of the main professions. Current sources only are considered – full details of historical sources are given in Fleming (1980a), pp.359–67.

15.4.1 General sources

Currently there are two *general* sources of information. Until 1979 a third source was provided by the Inland Revenue in analyses of income from self-employment for Architects and for Engineers (last published in *Inland Revenue Statistics 1982*).

(a) *The New Earnings Survey*

This is a sample survey of earnings of *employees* only recorded in a single week each year. Separate figures are given for architects and planners; quantity surveyors; civil, structural and municipal engineers; and town planning assistants, architectural and building technicians. Further details are given in Chapter 10 (sub-section 10.2.3).

(b) *Reward Regional Surveys*

Biannual salary surveys are made for construction and other sectors which provide analyses according to various functional and job categories and by qualification. Further details are given in Chapter 10 (sub-section 10.2.6).

15.4.2 Architectural profession

The RIBA collect data on earnings in an annual sample of architects on the ARCUK register with UK addresses. Information is obtained for both salaried architects and Principals. The results, published in *Architects' Employment and Earnings* provide analyses according to field of employment (separately for Principals and employees), by region and experience, by size of practice, by age and sex.

15.4.3 Surveying profession

There are no current sources of earnings data other than those referred to in sub-section 15.4.1 and no source of private practice costs and incomes data. Details of a survey of salaries and other benefits carried out in 1979 by Building Business Unit are given in Chapter 10 (sub-section 10.2.6). Details of earlier *ad hoc* surveys will be found in Fleming (1980a), pp.362–7.

15.4.4 Engineering professions

Apart from the general sources referred to in sub-section 15.4.1, there are three specific sources of information, two of which have already been referred to (sub-section 15.2.4): one is the biennial *Survey of Chartered and Technician Engineers* conducted currently by the Engineering Council; the other is the ICE Salary Surveys published in *New Civil Engineer*.

The former covers chartered engineers who are members of the 16 constituent institutions of the Engineering Council and also technician engineers. Analyses relevant to construction include median income by institutional sector and by broad class of employment and occupation, and average earnings by age and institutional membership. The overall sample is large but, unfortunately, the much smaller sample sizes for sub-categories are not given. The ICE analyses of salaries (distributions and medians) focus on level of membership, age, qualification, size of company and level of responsibility.

The third source is an annual survey of consulting engineering firms carried out by Reward Regional Surveys since 1983 and published as *Consulting Engineers Salary Survey*. This covers a large sample of companies and individuals ranging from Director/ Partner to trainee draughtsman/tracer. Coverage has increased over time. Analyses of pay, covering basic and total remuneration, are made by rank, function, age, qualification and discipline.

As for the surveying professions, earlier one-off surveys are considered in Fleming (1980a), pp. 362–7.

15.5 PROFESSIONAL PRACTICE COSTS AND INCOMES

The only information obtained on a regular basis relates to private architectural practice and annual estimates of overseas earnings. Details of *ad hoc* surveys for each profession carried out in the past are given in Fleming (1980a), pp.362–7.

15.5.1 Private architectural practices

The RIBA conduct periodic surveys of private practices in which it obtains *annual* data on the following subjects: fee income (turnover), unit costs and profit margins, profits per principal, fee income per member of staff and a breakdown of costs. Full details about the surveys are given in the published reports which are issued under the title *Costs and Profitability of Private Architectural Practice.*

15.5.2 Overseas earnings

Official estimates of the sums earned by consulting engineers, process engineers and by chartered surveyors for overseas work are given annually in the *United Kingdom Balance of Payments.* A commentary on major contracts is given in an article on 'Construction Overseas' published in *British Business* towards the end of each year.

15.6 ORGANIZATION AND STRUCTURE OF PROFESSIONAL PRACTICE

The only information currently obtained on a regular basis relates to architectural practices and is obtained by the RIBA in periodic censuses of private practices and surveys of local authority offices. For the other professions information is obtained only on an *ad hoc* basis.

15.6.1 Architectural practice

(a) *Private architectural practices*

The most recent report is *Census of Private Architectural Practices 1980.* This includes comparisons back to 1968 of the number of architectural practices and the number of staff employed (by type) by size of practice and by region in the UK. Details of a variety of earlier surveys are given in Fleming (1980a), pp.357–8.

(b) *Local authority offices*

A report on a *Survey of Local Authority Offices* was published by the RIBA in 1982. This provides information about the number of architects employed, the extent to which work is carried out by private consultants and on the value of programmes for new building work and for maintenance. Details of earlier sources of information are again given in Fleming (1980a), pp.358–9.

15.6.2 Surveying practices

Data are available only from *ad hoc* studies. The most recent information comes from a survey of private practices and other organizations in which quantity surveyors were employed which was conducted for the RICS and published in 1984 as *A Study of Quantity Surveying Practice and Client Demand.* This report draws comparisons with an earlier study published in 1974 *(A Study of Quantity Surveying Practice)* but it should be noted that the comparisons are affected by the merger between the RICS and the IQS in 1983. The 1984 study provides separate analyses for private practices, public service organizations and quantity surveying departments of contractors. The main topics covered are: the number of practices or departments by size, the distri-

bution of the workload according to type of client, and the types
of service provided. For private practices information is also
given about staffing, year of establishment, mergers and overseas offices. Other topics covered include the nature of client
demands, the use of computers and the education of recently-
qualified quantity surveyor employees. Details of the 1974 study
and other sources will be found in Fleming (1980a), p.359.

15.6.3 Engineering practices

The only regular source of relevant information is surveys of
consulting engineers conducted by *New Civil Engineer* which lists
individual firms and the number of staff employed (the latest
survey at the time of writing was published on 22 March 1984,
pp.20–24). No major inquiry has been carried out since 1972:
*Report of Reddaway Inquiry into Consulting Engineering Firms' Costs
and Earnings* which contains analyses of the number of firms and
staff employed analysed by size of firm and specialization as
well as financial data.

PART 3
THE CONSTRUCTION STOCK AND THE PROPERTY MARKET

16
THE CONSTRUCTION STOCK

This chapter is concerned with all statistics relating to the stock of buildings and works other than housing which is considered in Chapter 2. The chapter is arranged in two sections as follows:

16.1 Size, composition and characteristics of the construction stock
16.2 Changes to the stock

Related information about stock transactions and the operation of the property market is considered in Chapter 17.

16.1 SIZE, COMPOSITION AND CHARACTERISTICS OF THE CONSTRUCTION STOCK

16.1.1 The total stock of buildings and works

There are two sets of relevant data:

(a) Estimates of the replacement cost of buildings and works incorporated as a component of the official estimates of the national stock of fixed assets (capital stock), and
(b) Estimates of the market value of land, buildings and works incorporated in 'national balance sheets' for the UK.

It should be noted that these estimates differ in coverage (the inclusion and exclusion of land), in the basis of valuation (replacement costs *v.* market values) and in the methods of estimation used. We consider each in turn.

(a) *The stock of buildings and works at replacement cost*

BACKGROUND. Measurement of the total stock of buildings and other construction works may be obtained *directly* by means of a census or *indirectly* by a perpetual inventory method. The official statistics for the UK use the latter method. It involves the maintenance of a total stock figure, starting from a benchmark year, by adding in new investment each year and subtracting an allowance for capital that has reached the end of its life ('retirements'). In practice, severe practical and technical difficulties are involved and the series, especially for buildings and other construction works, is acknowledged to be open to very wide margins of error. For further discussion see below under 'Interpretation'. For further details of the methods of calculation reference should be made to CSO (1985), Griffin (1975, 1976) and Hibbert *et al.* (1977).

THE SERIES AVAILABLE AND SOURCES. The series are prepared annually and published in the Blue Book *(United Kingdom National Accounts)* as follows:

1. Gross capital stock at replacement cost (constant prices) from 1948:
    (a) by type of asset distinguishing 'dwellings' and 'other buildings and works', and
    (b) by asset (distinguishing 'buildings other than dwellings') by industry (manufacturing industries only after 1981)
2. Net capital stock at current replacement cost from 1948 by type of asset (dwellings/other buildings and works) by sector
3. Capital consumption at current and constant prices. Currently only dwellings are distinguished as a separate type of asset. Other buildings and works were distinguished until 1974. First published in the Blue Book 1956 edition but subsequently revised
4. Capital retirements – dwellings only – from 1965 to 1980. First published in Blue Book 1976 edition. The reason for the discontinuation of the series is given in the 1983 edition, p.114.

INTERPRETATION. The gross stock estimates are derived, as explained earlier, by summing series for GDFCF and subtracting estimates of capital 'retirements', the latter being based on assumptions about the length of life of different assets. Net capital stock figures are net of capital consumption which is an estimate of the replacement value of capital used up in current production/service. Capital consumption, therefore, is analogous to the concept of depreciation, but it is not the same as the figures recorded in company accounts etc. For the purpose of national income accounting, the figures are obtained by dividing for each asset type the gross capital stock figure by the length of life assumed (i.e. the straight line method of depreciation).

In the light of the brief discussion above, it will be appreciated that the estimates are open to error for a number of reasons including errors in the original 'benchmark' estimates of the total stock, in the GDFCF series, in the assumptions about length of life (and hence the associated estimates of capital retirements and capital consumption) and in the price indices used to convert current-price series to constant prices. Over time, of course, errors associated with the original benchmark figures become less important as assets are retired and the total stock figure comes to consist more and more of directly measured GDFCF figures. Official series for the latter are available from 1948 (Chapter 6, Section 6.5 refers). Buildings and other construction works, however, have very long lengths of life (up to 120 years is assumed for some types of buildings) and thus part of the current stock figures consist of elements that predate the collection of official statistics. Recently it has been decided that the lives assumed for some assets including buildings in manufacturing industry have been too long and revised estimates of capital consumption and capital stock have been made (see Blue Book 1983 edition, p.114). Further errors may arise because of the difficulty of measuring changes in construction prices over the long periods required here (see Chapter 13).

It should also be appreciated that certain parts of the construction stock are not included in the figures because it was impossible to estimate them by the perpetual inventory method. This part covers the buildings and works that have survived from the distant past such as 'historic buildings' (cathedrals, castles etc.) and public works such as embankments.

Official assessments of the reliability of the estimates are not subdivided by type of asset, except for dwellings at constant replacement cost, for which a margin of error in excess of 20% is suggested (CSO, 1985), p.202. The margin of error for the total gross capital stock (all assets) of the construction industry itself (excluding DL organizations) is put at 10–20%. All capital consumption figures are regarded as having an error of more than 10% (CS0, 1985, p.201). Further details of the grading system itself are given in Chapter 3, sub-section 3.7.1(b).

For fuller discussion and references to unofficial historical estimates predating the official series, see Fleming (1980a).

(b) *The stock of land, buildings and works at market value*

BACKGROUND. These estimates are made as part of national and sector balance sheets for the UK which, unlike the capital stock statistics referred to above, cover not only fixed assets but also other tangible assets and financial assets and liabilities (the net total being defined as net wealth). Apart from the difference in valuation, noted earlier, the main difference as far as housing and construction are concerned is the inclusion of land.

AVAILABLE SERIES AND SOURCES. Up-to-date series (one for dwellings and one for other land, buildings and works) are produced for the personal sector only. Official annual estimates for the period 1966–1976 were published in CSO (1978a) and for 1976–1983 in *Financial Statistics* (February 1985, Table S2); these continue unofficial estimates made by Revell (1967) and Roe (1971) for the years 1957–1966. Comprehensive estimates covering all sectors for every third year from 1957 to 1975 (incorporating the unofficial figures referred to above) were published in Pettigrew (1980); this also included a sub-division of the 1975 estimates according to seven sectors of ownership. The work of Revell (1967) and Roe (1971) also include detailed asset and sectoral breakdowns.

METHODOLOGY AND INTERPRETATION. In contrast to the indirect, perpetual inventory, method used for the capital stock series, a direct method of estimation is used based on rating statistics (see sub-section 16.1.2). As rateable values represent annual net rental values it is possible to estimate market values by capitalizing the rateable values and adjusting to a gross basis. In the case of unrated property, separate estimates are made. The work is carried out by the CSO, in continuation of the pioneering work done by Revell (1967) and Roe (1971). Descriptions are given in CSO (1978a), dealing with the personal sector, and Hibbert (1981).

With regard to interpretation, apart from the points about coverage and valuation noted above, the essential matter to bear in mind is that the estimates are again open to very wide margins of error. The land and buildings elements in particular are regarded as the least reliable parts and indeed have been referred to as being 'rather shaky' (Pettigrew, 1980, pp.97 and 99). In general the figures should be regarded as providing no more than indicators of broad orders of magnitude.

16.1.2 Stock statistics for particular types of buildings

The total stock statistics considered above, are necessarily measured in monetary units. This section brings together references to other sources, all of which provide data for specific types of buildings in physical units. As mentioned above, how-ever, data on the housing stock are considered separately in Chapter 2.

(a) *Commercial and industrial floor space statistics*

These statistics are derived from records of the valuation of properties prepared by the Inland Revenue for rating purposes. Complete analyses of the records (stock counts) were made in 1967 and 1974 (following the revaluation of 1973). In the years between stock counts, returns are produced annually to show the changes in floor space. Analyses are made to show: the number of hereditaments* and floor space for six non-domestic use-classes (including industrial, warehouses, commercial offices and shops) and analyses of changes to the stock according to whether they are the result of demolition, extension, new development or change of use, all analysed by size group by region. In addition, the estimated number of hereditaments and stock of floor space is given by county and district. The primary publication source is *Commercial and Industrial Floor Space Statistics* (single volume for England and Wales to 1981, then separate

* A rateable hereditament is a unit of occupation (or in appropriate cases 'owner-ship') for rating purposes. Often it is a single building but it may be just part of a whole building or it may comprise a number of whole buildings on the same site.

volumes). Summary data for Wales are given in *DWS*. Background information about the data is contained in the reports cited. Reference may also be made to Coppock and Gebbett (1978).

VACANT INDUSTRIAL FLOORSPACE. There are no official statistics about vacant properties but useful surveys have been conducted by King and Co, a London-based firm of chartered surveyors, three times a year since August 1975. The results, published in *Industrial Floorspace Survey*, provide figures of the area of floorspace vacant and which is available to let or for sale, in warehouses and factories (separately) in premises of 5000 square feet or more in size in each region of England and Wales. It is difficult to judge how comprehensive the surveys are (the information is collected from agents throughout the country) but it is thought that all new buildings are covered and a very high proportion of non-new buildings so that the figures are considered to provide a reasonably reliable indicator of trends.

(b) *Rating statistics*

The rating valuation records, upon which the floor space statistics referred to above are based, have been analysed for a longer period to show total rateable value for a large number of difference use-classes (currently over 40) and, for England and Wales, related information about the number of hereditaments all broken down by local authority districts. Since 1970 the primary publication source for England and Wales is *Inland Revenue Statistics*; before 1970 the data were included in *Annual Reports of the Commissioners of HM Inland Revenue* (Command papers). Rateable values for broad use-classes for each local authority area in England and Wales are given in *Local Government Financial Statistics*. Separate data for Wales and for Scotland are given in *Welsh Local Government Financial Statistics* and *Scottish Local Government Financial Statistics* respectively. Statistics about rates are also compiled by CIPFA – see Chapter 3, sub-section 3.5.6.

INTERPRETATION. In the context of the construction stock, perhaps the most important point to bear in mind about the rateable value statistics is that they relate to the land on which buildings stand as well as the buildings themselves. Background information about the rating system is contained in the references cited above. Reference may also be made to Revell (1967) in which use is made of the statistics to obtain estimates of the total market value of land and buildings (considered in sub-section 16.1.1), and which provides an appraisal of the nature of the data.

(c) *Hospital buildings*

No systematic data are published but summary details about the age of the stock in England, obtained in an unpublished DHSS study of 1972, are reported in the Report of the Royal Commission on the National Health Service in 1979 (Cmnd 7615), para. 10.67.

(d) *Schools*

Official surveys of school buildings in England and Wales were carried out in 1962 *(The School Building Survey 1962)* and 1975–6 (reported in *A Study of School Building* and *Statistics of Education SS5 School Building Surveys 1975 and 1976).* Both provide information about the age and condition of the stock and the cost of making good deficiencies. The latter also provides data on characteristics such as site area, playing fields, number of storeys, outside WCs etc., and an estimate of replacement value of the stock. Time series of the number of schools by size (in terms of number of pupils) will be found in *Statistics of Education* for England and Wales, *Statistics of Education in Wales* for Wales and in the *SAS* for Scotland. Summary data for each country is also given in *Education Statistics for the UK* and in the *AAS*.

(e) *Distribution and services*

Information on distribution and services outlets (number of shops etc.) is available from censuses of distribution and other inquiries conducted by the BSO. Details are given in Chapter 6 (Section 6.6). Details of the number of establishments registered under the terms of the Office, Shops and Railway Premises Act, 1963 are given in annual reports under the Act (Command papers).

(f) *Hotels*

Two studies: *Hotel Prospects to 1980* and *Hotel Prospects to 1985* provide detailed analyses of hotel capacity *inter alia* in 1970 and 1976 respectively. Some information about additions to the stock are published in *New Hotels in England* and *Scotland, New Hotel Capacity*.

(g) *Leisure facilities*

For information on this very broad and wide-ranging subject, reference is best made to Lewes (1975) and a large number of sources of information listed in the *Guide to Official Statistics* (CSO, biennially).

(h) *Transport facilities*

ROADS. Statistics of the lengths of various types of road are given in a number of publications: the most detailed source (containing data by type of road by region throughout Great Britain) is *Transport Statistics*. Data for all four countries of the UK and English regions are included in *Regional Trends*. For Wales detailed data are given in *Statistics of Road Lengths in Wales* with summary data in *DWS* and for Scotland in *SAS*. Data for Great Britain are also reproduced in the *AAS*. Information about the physical condition of roads is obtained in an annual survey by the Department of Transport and reported in *National Road Maintenance Condition Survey*. This shows defects levels, a summary defects index, road lengths by residual life, road lengths resurfaced or reconstructed, trends in maintenance expenditure by operation (at constant prices) and road lengths receiving treatment. The estimates of the residual lives of roads and the defects index of road condition are reproduced in *Transport Statistics*.

OTHER TRANSPORT FACILITIES. Information available for rail and sea transport and for ports, inland waterways and airports is considered in Aldcroft and Mort (1981) and Baxter and Phillips (1979) respectively. Reference should also be made to *Guide to Official Statistics* (CSO, biennially).

16.2 CHANGES TO THE STOCK

Information about changes to the stock is very limited; most sources have been referred to elsewhere in this book but they are drawn together here for convenience.

ADDITIONS TO THE STOCK. Direct information is available from the commercial and industrial floor space statistics considered in Section 16.1. Data for the housing stock are considered in Chapter 2. Other sources of new building statistics are considered in Chapter 6.

LOSSES FROM THE STOCK. Information about commercial and industrial floor space lost by demolition is considered in Section 16.1. Housing demolitions are considered in Chapter 2. Conventional allowances of 'consumption' and 'retirements' from the construction stock are computed by the CSO for the purposes of the national accounts but they are not based on direct statistical evidence and are subject to wide margins of error – again see Section 16.1.

CHANGES OF USE. Statistics in this field are extremely limited. Planning statistics provide figures of the number of applications for change of use granted or refused but indicate only the use *to which* the application refers. The statistics for England and Wales are published in *Development Control Statistics.* For Scotland figures appeared in *Scottish Development Department, Annual Report* until 1979 when publication ceased. Figures on the numbers of development applications considered by each local authority are published by CIPFA in *Planning and Development Statistics.* For further discussion see Coppock and Gebbett (1978).

17
THE PROPERTY
MARKET

In contrast to the previous chapter, which was concerned with data on the total construction stock and stock changes, this chapter is concerned with information relating to the flow of stock transactions, and related aspects of the property market including the level of activity, institutional investment, building rents and occupancy costs, measures of property investment performance and the activities and performance of property companies. It should be noted, however, that the operation of the housing market is treated separately in Part I and that no attention is devoted to transactions in agricultural property as this is a specialized sector beyond the scope of this book.

The chapter is arranged in four sections as follows:

17.1 Activity indicators – property transactions and investment
17.2 Building rents and occupancy costs
17.3 Property investment performance indicators
17.4 Property companies.

17.1 ACTIVITY INDICATORS – PROPERTY TRANSACTIONS AND INVESTMENT

This section is divided into three sub-sections which cover in turn: transactions in land and existing buildings, investment in new construction and improvements, and statistics of property investment by institutions.

17.1.1 Sales and purchases of existing buildings

(a) *Surveys of conveyancing in England and Wales*

These surveys provide the principal source of information but they are limited to activity in one week only each year. They have been carried out by the Inland Revenue in February 1968 (reported in *Inland Revenue Statistics*, 1970 edition, p.210) and then annually from 1973, the results being reported in *Economic Trends* each year (various issues from May 1974); currently these reports appear under the title 'Trends in sales of land and buildings...'. They provide information about the number and value of transactions by price range, by type of property (land, residential, commercial) and by tenure (freehold/leasehold) together with analyses by region and by sector of buyer and sector of seller. Relevant information about the interpretation of the data is provided in the reports themselves. Separate data for Wales appear in *DWS*.

(b) *Other sources of data on the acquisition and disposal of land and existing buildings*

Information on house prices and housing land are considered in Chapter 4. Information about the non-housing private sector has been regularly collected in censuses of production from 1959, censuses of distribution from 1961 to 1971 and in smaller-scale enquiries at various dates from the early 1960s as a constituent part of information on capital expenditure. Prior to these dates such expenditure was not separately distinguished from expenditure on *new* buildings. Publication references to these sources are given in Chapter 6 (Sections 6.2 and 6.5 respectively). In the public sector, annual series for local authorities in England and Wales from 1969–70 have been published in *Local Government Financial Statistics* and for Wales alone in *Welsh Local Government Financial Statistics* since 1977.

(c) *The treatment of land and existing buildings in the National Accounts*

The statistics referred to above are used by the CSO in the compilation of the capital accounts in *United Kingdom National Accounts* (the Blue Book). In the aggregate, of course, expenditure on the purchase of land and existing buildings would net out with sales were it not for the inclusion of transfer costs in the

costs of acquisition. These costs are included as part of gross
domestic fixed capital formation and appear as a separate item
in these accounts as 'purchases less sales of land and existing
buildings'.

17.1.2 Investment in new construction and improvements

Statistics of expenditure on new construction and improvement
constitute the series of gross domestic fixed capital formation
compiled for the *UK National Accounts* by the CSO. As an important indicator of construction activity they are considered fully
in Part 2 (Chapter 6, Section 6.5).

17.1.3 Institutional investment

Official statistics of the net acquisition of UK land, property and
ground rents by institutional investors are compiled quarterly
and published in *Financial Statistics* in a quarterly supplementary
table entitled 'institutional investment'. This gives separate
figures for pension funds, insurance companies, investment
trusts, unit trusts and property unit trusts, trustee savings banks
and building societies. For insurance companies and super-
annuation funds the statistics are included in each monthly issue
together with annual figures of the market value of holdings in
these assets. Further particulars of investment by insurance
companies and pension funds is given in *Business Monitor MQ5*.

17.2 BUILDING RENTS AND OCCUPANCY COSTS

17.2.1 Aggregate rent income

Rent is, of course, a major form of factor income and as such
constitutes an important component of the *United Kingdom
National Accounts* and is identified in various analyses by sector.
In this context it denotes gross receipts from the ownership of
land and buildings *less* actual expenditure by the owners on
repairs, maintenance and insurance. An imputed income is
included for owner-occupied dwellings and farmhouses provided
rent-free by employers and houses owned by general government. Imputed income from owner-occupied trading property is

not counted as part of rent but is included as part of trading income. A detailed account of the treatment of rent in the *National Accounts* and the sources of information used is given in CSO (1985), pp.247–9.

17.2.2 Commercial and industrial rent levels and trends

The measurement of rent levels and trends for different types of commercial and industrial property raises severe statistical problems because the great diversity of different types of buildings in different locations means that it is difficult to define a standard of comparison which is comparable between different locations and one which can be maintained over time. The rent that may be obtained for a building is influenced critically not only by the characteristics of the building itself in terms of size, its standard of construction and the facilities it offers etc. but also by its location. Location, in particular, is critical not only from the point of view of differences between towns and regions but also between sites within a town. A further factor to take into account is the difference between rent levels surviving from leases fixed in the past and current levels determined on review and in leases for new buildings.

The main problem from a statistical point of view, therefore, is to devise a suitable standard of comparison for different categories of building allowing for the twin influences of building and locational characteristics. Any general approach which attempts to cover the whole market comprehensively, confronts the problem of how to combine the data in such a way as to maintain comparability from one time period to the next in the face of a changing mix of buildings and locations. The obvious alternative approach is a selective one in which a standard of comparison is defined in terms of particular building types and locations at the outset and data are collected which correspond to the defined criteria. However, this approach itself raises problems in terms of the appropriate criteria to adopt (as several standards of comparison may be defined), the problem of obtaining adequate sample sizes for each category and how best to combine data for specific buildings in specific locations into a single summary measure.

In the light of these problems, it is not surprising to find that a

Table 17.1 Commercial and industrial property rent statistics

Source	Property categories	Geographical coverage	Period covered	Frequency*	Nature of data	Publication source
A. RENTAL VALUES (£ PER UNIT FLOORSPACE)						
1. Inland Revenue	Shops Offices Factories and Warehouses	Various towns in GB	1983–	BA (Apr and Oct)	Typical rental values for new leases and rates	*Valuation Office Property Market Report*
2. Jones Lang Wootton (JLW)	Offices Industrial	50 centres in E & W	1969– 1979–	BA (Mar and Sept)	Top rents for prime properties	*50 Centres – A Guide to Office and Industrial Rental Trends in England and Wales*
3. MLP–CIG	Shops ('Retail') Offices Industrial	GB×region	1962–	BA (Jan and Jul)	Achieved rack rents	*MLP–CIG Property Index*
4. Healey & Baker	Offices Industrial	Various centres in GB	1977–	BA (Jun and Dec)	Estimated prime rents	*PRIME – Property Rent Indices and Market Editorial and Guide to Rental Values*
5. Debenham Tewson & Chinnocks	Shops Offices Industrial	Various centres in GB	1978– 1973/74– 1973/74–	A	Estimated prime rents and rates	*Shop Rents and Rates.* *Office Rents and Rates.* *Industrial Rents and Rates.*
6. Kenneth Ryden & Partners	Shops Offices Industrial	Scotland – various centres Scottish cities Scotland – various locations	1978–	BA	Estimated prime pitch values – see remarks. Selected values for new leases. Actual rents.	*Scottish Industrial and Commercial Property Review*

* A = Annual, BA = Biannual, Q = Quarterly

Remarks

1. Based upon the information available to District Valuers, but it is emphasized that the data should be regarded as indicative rather than definitive. Earlier series of index numbers drawn from this source were published by DoE in *Commercial and Industrial Property Statistics* for offices (1962–1979), shops (1965–1976) and factories (1969–1979). This publication also gives details of the nature of the series.

2. Based upon actual transactions known to JLW. Technical details published in *50 Centres Guide* (JLW, 1984a). An estimated rental growth index for an institutional property portfolio is also compiled – see table 17.2.

3. Based on actual market transactions. National figures are weighted averages of regional figures drawn from 17 urban centres weighted to reflect the mix of institutional portfolios.

4. Estimates for prime institutional properties (standard shop and industrial units and new high specification offices) in the best locations in various centres.

5. Estimates based on hypothetical standard properties in prime locations – details are given in the publications cited.

6. Overall index also quoted.   Offices – Figures for Edinburgh, Glasgow and Aberdeen.   Industrial – Rental values for specified new developments of industrial and warehouse accommodation.

Table 17.1 (continued)

Source	Property categories	Geographical coverage	Period covered	Frequency*	Nature of data	Publication source
B. INDEX NUMBERS OR GROWTH RATES						
7. RICS – Institute of Actuaries City Office Rent Indices	Offices	Five centres – see remarks	1972–77 1978–	A Q	Assessed rental values for typical units	Chartered Surveyor Weekly
8. Investors Chronicle Hillier Parker (ICHP)	Shops Offices Industrial All	GB×region (or area within London)	1965–	BA (May and Nov)	Estimated current market rental levels for "good 'average' modern buildings"	Investors Chronicle and Investors Chronicle – Hillier Parker Rent Index
9. Richard Ellis	Shops ('Retail') Offices Industrial All	GB×region	1978–	A (Mar)	Estimated rental values – see remarks	Richard Ellis Annual Investment Review and Property Market Indicators
10. Healey & Baker	Shops Offices Industrial	GB×region	1977–	BA (Jun and Dec)	Estimated prime rents	PRIME – Property Rent Indices and Market Editorial and Guide to Rental Values
11. RICS–FT Property Indicators	Shops Offices Industrial	UK×region	1976–	Q	Qualitative view of trends – see remarks	Financial Times

* A = Annual, BA = Biannual, Q = Quarterly

Remarks

7. Based on reports by panels of chartered surveyors in private practice and financial institutions in each centre. Current open market rental values are assessed by each surveyor for specified buildings falling within defined categories assuming full repairing and insuring leases with five-yearly reviews. Index numbers are prepared for each category of building based on simple averages of the surveyors' valuations. An all buildings index is compiled as a simple average of the category indices. The areas covered are City of London, West End of London, Liverpool, Newcastle, Birmingham. It is planned to extend the coverage to Bristol, Leeds and Cardiff. Annual series from 1972 are available for City of London only. A short technical account of the methodology was published in *Chartered Surveyor Weekly*, 17 October 1985, p.253.

8. Based on estimates of open market rental values of buildings at 189 'rent points' covered in Hillier Parkers' own records. Not a static sample of buildings. National indices are weighted averages of regional indices which, in turn are weighted averages of evidence for the 'rent points'. The aggregate index for all properties is weighted (shops 30%, offices 45%, industrials 25%) to reflect institutional views on an ideal mix in an investment portfolio. A technical account is given in *ICHP Rent Index Bulletin No.4*, May 1979.

9. National index and regional growth rates. Based upon valuations of institutional portfolios with valuation dates at or around the end of March (39 in 1984) to which Richard Ellis act as advisers, managers or valuers. Covered 1015 properties in 1984. In order to reflect demand and supply, rather than other factors affecting rental and capital values, properties not conforming to certain criteria are excluded (eg those affected by refurbishment and other monetary injections, short leaseholds, lease restructuring etc.). Each property equally weighted in each sector. Aggregate index is weighted average of sector indices (with their respective capital values as weights). Technical details given in *Property Market Indicators 1984*.

10. See item (4) above. The regional indices for each sector are unweighted averages of location indices and national indices are unweighted averages of regional indices.

11. RICS member firms and investing institutions are asked if there is a rising, falling or static trend in rents (and also investment yields, capital values and investment activity) for five classes of commercial and industrial property (offices, prime regional shops, secondary shops, modern factories, modern warehouses).

variety of indicators are prepared by different organizations. Most of the sources are large London based firms of chartered surveyors which provide services to property investors. As a consequence, the focus of the analyses is often directed towards those which would be of most direct use and interest to property investing institutions, the aim being to provide a property performance yardstick against which particular funds could measure the performance of their own portfolio, as well as one which could be used to measure property performance against that of alternative investments, in particular equities and gilts. The performance measures cover not only rental values but also capital values, yields and total returns. The latter are considered separately in section 17.3. All the measures reflect, however, differences in approach and differences in the underlying data base available to the organizations which compile them.

A summary guide to what would appear to be the main regular sources of data about commercial and industrial rents (shops, offices and industrial buildings) is set out in Table 17.1. It will be seen that we group the sources according to whether they provide data in the form of rental values or as index numbers (or growth rates) measuring changes over time.

The one official source, based on data provided by Inland Revenue District Valuers, gives figures of typical rental values in new leases (item 1 in the table). This must be regarded as the most comprehensive source, not only because of the direct involvement of District Valuers in the property market throughout the country but also because of the information about transactions available to them from the 'Particulars of Deposit' procedure for stamp duty purposes. Nonetheless the returns made by District Valuers retain an element of subjectivity and it is stressed that the data should be regarded as indicative rather than definitive. Comparisons over time of the 'typical values' that are reported are obviously affected by differences in the properties that are regarded as 'typical' at different times and the regional pattern of transactions. Indeed, values are only quoted for particular towns etc., no attempt being made to compile overall measures.

The other sources vary for a variety of reasons relating to methodology and the data base. Comparison of one source with another is complicated by differences in the criteria used to define comparable building categories and by differences in geographical coverage. It will be noted too that some sources are confined to prime rents rather than rents in general. Another factor to bear in mind is that some of the data are based on actual transactions but in other cases estimates are made, either for the purpose of the statistical analysis or in connection with portfolio valuations. It is well known that valuation is an inexact art, rather than a science, subject to large margins of error – see Sykes (1983), Hager and Lord (1985).

With regard to the measurement of trends over time, perhaps the most refined source is the RICS – Institute of Actuaries Office Rent Indices. These maintain a standard of comparison by obtaining independent valuations of the *same* set of buildings in different time periods by several surveyors. But it will be seen that coverage is limited to a few cities only.

Table 17.1 attempts to set out information about the scope and nature of the data in as comparable a form as possible. We would stress, however, that coverage of unofficial sources is limited to the major sources provided by the big firms and the RICS.

17.2.3 Building occupancy costs

A further aspect of the property market is the occupancy costs of buildings, that is expenditure on the upkeep and associated operational and running costs of buildings – cleaning, lighting, heating etc. A large volume of resources is devoted to these purposes but there are no comprehensive statistics. The best source of reference is the BMCIS*, one of whose functions since it was established in 1971 has been to develop a data bank of analyses about the full range of property occupancy costs for particular buildings in a comparable, standardized, form on the basis of data submitted by subscribers to the service.

Three reports are made available to subscribers annually. These are an *Average Occupancy Costs Study*, which gives average analyses for groups of buildings by type, secondly a *Cost Analyses* study, which provides detailed cost breakdowns of property occupancy for individual buildings over a number of years and,

---

* Building Maintenance Cost Information Service, 85/87 Clarence Street, Kingston-upon-Thames, Surrey KT1 1RB.

Table 17.2 Commercial and industrial property investment yields and capital values statistics

Source (Numbered as in Table 17.1)	Data	Property categories*	Geographical coverage	Period covered	Frequency†	Nature of data	Publication source
1. Inland Revenue	(a) Yields	O.S.I.	E & W × Region	1983–	BA	Actual transactions – see remarks	Valuation Office Property Market Report
	(b) Capital values	Factories and warehouses	Selected towns in E & W	1983–	BA	Typical values	Valuation Office Property Market Report
2. Jones Lang Wootton (JLW)	Capital and income growth indexes	All / O.S.I. Ag	GB	1967-77 / 1977–	A / Q	Portfolio valuations	JLW Property Index
3. MLP – CIG	(a) Capital growth / Income return / Total return	O.S.I. see remarks	UK	1978–	Q / A / A	Portfolio data	MLP–CIG Property Index
	(b) Yields / Capital values	O.S.I.	GB	1962–	BA	Actual transactions	MLP–CIG Property Index
4. Healey & Baker	Yields	5 sectors – see remarks	GB	1971–	Q	Prime institutional properties	Investment Report
8. Investors Chronicle – Hillier Parker	Average yields / Prime yields	O.S.I. all / All	GB × region / GB	1972– / 1972–	Q / A	Valuation data – see remarks	Investors Chronicle – Hillier Parker Average Yields
9. Richard Ellis	Capital index and growth rates / Prime yields	O.S.I. all	GB × region	1978–	A	Valuation date – see remarks	Richard Ellis Annual Investment Review and Property Market Indicators
	Prime yields	O.S.I.	GB	1975–	Q		
	Average and prime yield changes / Total returns	O.S.I. / All	GB / GB	1978– / 1978–	A / A		
11. RICS-FT Property Indicators	Yields / Capital values		UK × region	1976–	Q	Qualitative view of trends	Financial Times

* O=Offices, S=Shops, I=Industrial. Ag=Agricultural.   † A=Annual, BA=Biannual, Q=Quarterly

Remarks

1(a) District valuers are asked to provide in respect of each class of property details of three transactions relating to investment by direct purchase at prices in excess of £100000. Figures are for initial yields (or their equivalent in cases of reversionary income) and are quoted as ranges and as value-weighted averages. Figures are also given of the number of transactions, the proportion these represent of total transactions and the value of total transactions.

1(b) Typical capital (and rental) values are given for two sizes of unit (under/over 230 m²). They do not relate to any particular property and it is stressed that they should be regarded as indicative, not definitive.

2. Several indexes are compiled. The main index is the JLW Property Index which is a combined index of capital and income showing the overall performance of a property portfolio. Other indexes show component parts of the main index: a capital growth index measuring the change in capital value, a net income index measuring the actual income flow, and a rental value index measuring the rate of growth in estimated rental values (assuming open market transactions). The properties constituting the portfolio are drawn from the portfolios of investment institutions (as opposed to development companies and private owners) with funds advised and managed by JLW (over 20 funds). They are selected to represent a 'typical' institutional portfolio in terms of the distribution of capital value by region and property type. The fund is 'actively managed' so that it does not retain a static composition and it incorporates the investment of new monies. A technical account is given in *JLW Index – Explanatory Notes* (JLW, 1984b).

3(a) Data given as indexes and annual rates of return. Based upon portfolio data from a wide range of institutions supplied to CIG in confidence giving the open market value of entire portfolio split by property category (O,S,I) and purchases, sales and rental income (not split). Data are claimed as representative of UK institutional property holdings. Capital growth is measured as end value less one half of net purchases as a percentage of start value plus a half of net purchases. The income return represents net income as a percentage of valuation of portfolio at start of period plus one half of net purchases, where net income represents rents received less unavoidable expenses involved in holding the portfolio (e.g. ground rents and property outgoings). The total return combines the income return and capital growth. The formulae assume that net new purchases are made equally throughout the period. Technical account given in *MLP–CIG Property Index 1978–1984* (Appendix I).

3(b) Based upon data, collected by CIG, on achieved rack rents (see Table 17.1) and yields in 17 urban centres to represent eight regions. Capital values represent capitalized rents obtained by applying average, not prime, yields. National figures are weighted averages of regional figures. Technical details are given in *MLP–CIG Property Index 1978–84* (Appendix III).

4. Initial yields achieved by sales of town centre shops, offices, industrial buildings and warehouses, high technology buildings and retail warehouses in a sample of centres (unspecified).

8. Average yields are derived from valuations of properties at the 189 rent points used in the ICHP rent index (see Table 17.1). National and regional averages are constructed using the same method and weights. Prime yields at each rent point were assessed for a rack rented freehold let on full repairing and insuring terms to a good covenant with upward only rent reviews every fifth year. Technical details are given in *Average Yields* November 1984. Capital values index is available through Datastream.

9. Same data base as used for the rental index – see Table 17.1. The capital growth figures are broken down into estimated component elements. Long-run measures of changes are obtained by chain-linking annual indicators. Technical details are given in *Richard Ellis Property Market Indicators 1984*.

11. See remarks to Table 17.1. For trends in capital values a sixth property category – industrial land – is distinguished.

thirdly, a *Study of Energy in Buildings,* which gives average energy consumption costs for a range of building types. In addition special studies are prepared from time to time which are published as occasional papers as well as the regular analyses of building maintenance cost trends referred to earlier (Chapter 13). Full details are available from BMCIS.

17.3 PROPERTY INVESTMENT PERFORMANCE INDICATORS – YIELDS AND CAPITAL VALUES

The calculation of summary measures of property yields and capital values is subject to the same statistical problems as the derivation of summary measures of property rents. These were considered in sub-section 17.2.2 and reference should be made to the discussion there. In brief, the problems arise out of the great heterogeneity of buildings, the importance of locational factors and the influence of leasing arrangements (terms and revision arrangements etc.) on rental and capital values. Much of the information available is compiled by the same firms of chartered surveyors who act as advisers, agents and managers for property investing institutions and is consequently focused on measuring the performance of property as an investment in those sectors of the market of particular interest to property investing institutions. It is important to appreciate, therefore, that these sources may not be representative of the market in general.

The appraisal of one source as against another needs to take account of differences in the scope and nature of the primary information available to different organizations and in the methods of analysis used. A summary of the main sources together with details of the nature of the data and statistical methodologies used is set out in a reasonably comparable format in Table 17.2. The most generally representative source is that provided by Inland Revenue District Valuers, though the limitations of the data as indicative rather than definitive series are again stressed (as with the official analyses of rents – see Table 17.1). All the other sources are unofficial with a particular interest in measuring the performance of property as an investment. Technical differences among these sources, however, still leaves the comparison of one with another problematic. Apart from the differences in the scope of the underlying primary data inputs in each case, principal differences are the reliance on property valuations in some cases but actual market transactions in others, and the restriction of some analyses to prime properties. Another important difference is between sources which measure investment performance in terms of an 'actively managed', and thus changing, portfolio (as in the case of JLW) and others which attempt to maintain a standard of comparison from one time period to another by excluding properties that do not satisfy certain criteria (as in the case of Richard Ellis).

17.4 PROPERTY COMPANIES

17.4.1 Finance

Statistics of capital issues and redemptions in the UK by property companies and of bank loans and advances to property companies, are compiled quarterly by the Bank of England and published in *Financial Statistics*. Background information on the data is given in *Financial Statistics Explanatory Handbook* (CSO, annually).

17.4.2 Financial performance

The financial performance of property companies is probably best monitored by reference to the component series included as part of the FT-Actuaries Share Indices published in the *Financial Times*. For each sector (property companies constitute one sector) daily information is published on the earnings yield, the dividend yield and the price/earnings ratio as well as the share price index number, the day's change and highs and lows for the year and since compilation. Full technical details will be found in Bell and Greenhorn (1984). Complementary analyses giving summary financial results of the companies included in the FT-Actuaries indices are also given in a quarterly table entitled 'Trend of Industrial Profits'. The results for individual companies are summarized in biannual property supplements to the *Investors Chronicle*.

STATISTICAL SOURCES

Listed alphabetically by title

Title	Organization responsible or author	Publisher	Frequency or date of publication	Remarks
Annual Abstract of Greater London Statistics	GLC Intelligence Unit	GLC, London	Annually	
Annual Abstract of Statistics	Central Statistical Office	HMSO, London	Annually	
Annual Bulletin of Statistics, continued as Annual Bulletin of Construction Statistics	Ministry of Works and successor Departments*	The Ministry or Department, London	Annually from March 1960 (No. 1) to the issue for 1970 (No. 12)	Replaced by Housing and Construction Statistics
Annual Report, Advisory, Conciliation and Arbitration Service	ACAS	ACAS, London	Annually	From 1976 (Report for 1975)
Annual Report of the Certification Officer	Certification Office for Trade Unions and Employers' Associations	HMSO, London	Annually	From 1977 (Report for 1976)
Annual Report of HM Chief Inspector of Factories	HM Chief Inspector of Factories	HMSO, London	Annually to Report for 1974	Replaced by Health and Safety Statistics
Annual Statement of Overseas Trade of the United Kingdom	HM Customs and Excise	HMSO, London	Annually	

* The Ministry of Public Building and Works from July 1962 to November 1970 and then the Department of the Environment.

Architects' Employment and Earnings	RIBA	RIBA, London	Annually	
Architects' Journal	Architectural Press Ltd	Architectural Press Ltd, London	Weekly	
Attitudes to Letting in 1976	B. Paley, OPCS	HMSO, London	1978	
Average Occupancy Costs Study	BMCIS	BMCIS, Kingston-upon-Thames	Annually	
Bank of England Statistical Abstract	Bank of England	Bank of England, London	1971 and 1975	
BCIS Quarterly Review of Building Prices	BCIS (RICS)	BCIS, Kingston-upon-Thames	Quarterly	
BMCIS Quarterly Briefing of Maintenance Costs	BMCIS (RICS)	BMCIS, Kingston-upon-Thames	Quarterly	
BMP Information	NCBMP	NCBMP, London	Monthly	
BMP Statistical Bulletin	NCBMP	NCBMP, London	Weekly	
British Business	Department of Trade and Industry	HMSO, London		Formerly *Trade and Industry*
British Labour Statistics, Historical Abstract 1886–1968	Department of Employment and Productivity	HMSO, London	1971	
British Labour Statistics Yearbook	Department of Employment	HMSO, London	Annually from 1971 to 1978	Yearbooks for 1969 to 1976
BSA Bulletin	BSA	BSA, London	Quarterly	Called *Facts and Figures* before 1975

List of statistical sources (*continued*)

Title	Organization responsible or author	Publisher	Frequency or date of publication	Remarks
Building	Building (Publishers) Ltd	Building (Publishers) Ltd, London	Weekly	Formerly *The Builder*
Building Society Fact Book 1984	BSA	BSA, London	1984	Formerly issued annually from 1980 as *Building Societies in ... [year]*
Building Societies Year Book	BSA	Franey & Co., London	Annually	
Bulletin of (Construction) Statistics Supplements	DoE and Predecessor Depts	DoE, London	1959–65 (Annually) 1965–70 (Biannually)	In 1963 a separate *Addendum* was published containing the September 1963 census results
Business Monitor MA3 Company Finance	Business Statistics Office	HMS0, London	Annually	From 1969. Formerly *Monitor M3*
Business Monitor MA4 Overseas Transactions	Business Statistics Office	HMSO, London	Annually	From 1977. Formerly *Monitor M4*
Business Monitor MM17 Price Index Numbers for Current Cost Accounting (Monthly Supplement)	Business Statistics Office	HMSO, London	Monthly	From 1980
Business Monitor M014 Industrial Research and Development Expenditure and Employment	Business Statistics Office	HMSO, London	Occasional	

Title	Publisher	Place	Frequency	Notes
Business Monitor MO18 Price Index Numbers for Current Cost Accounting, Summary Volume 1974–82	Business Statistics Office	HMSO, London	1983	
Business Monitor MQ5 Insurance Companies' and Pension Funds' Investments	Business Statistics Office	HMSO, London	Quarterly	
Business Monitor MQ7 Acquisitions and Mergers of Industrial and Commercial Companies	Business Statistics Office	HMSO, London	Quarterly	From 1971. Formerly *Monitor M7*
Business Monitor MQ10 Overseas Trade Analysed in Terms of Industries	Business Statistics Office	HMSO, London	Quarterly	
Business Monitor MQ12 Import Penetration and Export Sales Ratios for Manufacturing Industry	Business Statistics Office	HMSO, London	Quarterly	
Business Monitor PA series: Census of Production Reports*	Business Statistics Office	HMSO, London	Annually	From 1971. C Series in 1970

* Each publication in the series has a numerical identification based on the Standard Industrial Classification.

List of statistical sources (*continued*)

Title	Organization respon-sible or author	Publisher	Frequency or date of publication	Remarks
Business Monitor PA 500, Report on the Census of Production.... [year] Construction	Business Statistics Office	HMSO, London	Annually	From 1976 (Report for 1974
Business Monitor PA1002 Summary Tables	Business Statistics Office	HMSO, London	Annually	
Business Monitor PA1004 Input–Output Tables for the United Kingdom	Business Statistics Office	HMSO, London	Irregularly	From 1974 (Tables for 1970)
Business Monitor PA1007 Minerals	Business Statistics Office	HMSO, London	Annually	From 1976 (Report for the years 1974 and 1975)
*Business Monitor PM series**	Business Statistics Office	HMSO, London	Monthly	Introduced at various dates from 1962 onwards
*Business Monitor PQ series**	Business Statistics Office	HMSO, London	Quarterly	Introduced at various dates from 1962 onwards
Business Monitor SD series	Business Statistics Office	HMSO, London	Various	From 1970
Business Monitor SDO 10–23 Census of Distribution and Other Services 1971	Business Statistics Office	HMSO, London	Various dates from 1974	13 Parts plus supplement
Capital Expenditure of County Councils... [year]	Society of County Treasurers	The Society, Shire Hall, Reading	Annually to 1981	Issue for 1980–81

	CIPFA	CIPFA, London	Annually	
Capital Expenditure and Debt Financing Statistics	CIPFA	CIPFA, London	Annually	
Census 1951, England & Wales. General Tables	General Register Office	HMSO, London	1956	
Census 1951, England & Wales. Housing Report	General Register Office	HMSO, London	1956	
Census 1951, England & Wales, Industry Tables	General Register Office	HMSO, London	1957	
Census 1951, England & Wales. Occupational Tables	General Register Office	HMSO, London	1956	
Census 1951, Scotland. Occupations and Industries	General Registry Office	HSMO, Edinburgh	1956	
Census 1951, Scotland. General Volume	General Registry Office	HMSO, Edinburgh	1954	
Census 1961, England & Wales, Education Tables	General Register Office	HSMO, London	1966	
Census 1961, England & Wales, Housing National Summary Tables	General Register Office	HSMO, London	1964	An advance publication containing selected tables reproduced in the main volume referred to below

* Each publication in the series has a numerical identification based on the Standard Industrial Classification.

List of statistical sources (*continued*)

Title	Organization responsible or author	Publisher	Frequency or date of publication	Remarks
Census 1961, England & Wales, Housing Tables	General Register Office	HMSO, London	1965	
Census 1961, England & Wales. Industry Tables: Parts I and II	General Register Office	HMSO, London	1966	
Census 1961, England & Wales. Occupation Tables	General Register Office	HMSO, London	1966	
Census 1961, England & Wales. Workplace Tables	General Register Office	HMSO, London	1966	
Census 1961, Great Britain. Migration Tables	General Register Office	HMSO, London	1966	
Census 1961, Great Britain. Scientific and Technological Qualifications	General Register Office	HMSO, London	1962	
Census 1961, Great Britain. Summary Tables	General Register Office	HMSO, London	1966	
Census 1961, Scotland. Housing and Households	General Register Office	HMSO, London	1966	
Census 1961, Scotland. Housing National Summary Tables	General Register Office	HMSO, London	1964	An advance publication containing selected tables reproduced in the main volume referred to above

Census 1961, Scotland. Internal Migration	General Register Office for Scotland	HMSO, Edinburgh	1966
Census 1961, Scotland. Occupation, Industry and Workplace Tables	General Register Office for Scotland	HMSO, Edinburgh	1966
Census 1961, Scotland. Terminal Education Age	General Register Office for Scotland	HMSO, Edinburgh	1966
Census 1966, England & Wales. Housing Tables	General Register Office	HMSO, London	1968
Census 1966, England & Wales. Migration Regional Reports	General Register Office	HMSO, London	1968
Census 1966, England & Wales. Migration Summary Tables	General Register Office	HMSO, London	1968–9
Census 1966, England & Wales. Workplace and Transport Tables	General Register Office	HMSO, London	1968
Census 1966, Great Britain. Economic Activity Tables	General Register Office	HMSO, London	1968–9
Census 1966, Great Britain. Qualified Manpower Tables	OPCS	HMSO, London	1971
Census 1966, Great Britain. Scientific and Technological Qualifications	OPCS	HMSO, London	1971

List of statistical sources (*continued*)

Title	Organization respon-sible or author	Publisher	Frequency or date of publication	Remarks
Census 1966, Scotland. Economic Activity, County Tables	General Register Office for Scotland	HMSO, Edinburgh	1969	
Census 1966, Scotland. Housing Tables	General Register Office for Scotland	HMSO, Edinburgh	1968	
Census 1966, Scotland. Migration Tables	General Register Office for Scotland	HMSO, Edinburgh	1968–9	
Census 1966, Scotland. Workplace and Transport Tables	General Register Office for Scotland	HMSO, Edinburgh	1968	
Census 1971, England & Wales. Housing Tables	OPCS	HMSO, London	1974	
Census 1971, England & Wales. Workplace and Transport to Work Tables	OPCS	HMSO, London	1975–6	
Census 1971, Great Britain. Economic Activity Tables	OPCS	HMSO, London	1975	
Census 1971, Great Britain. Housing Summary Tables	OPCS	HMSO, London	1974	
Census 1971, Great Britain. Migration Tables	OPCS and General Register Office, Edinburgh	HMSO, London	1977	

Census 1971, Great Britain. Qualified Manpower Tables	OPCS	HMSO, London	1976	
Census 1971, Scotland. Economic Activity Tables	General Register Office, Edinburgh	HMSO, Edinburgh	1978	
Census 1971, Scotland. Housing Report	General Register Office, Edinburgh	HMSO, Edinburgh	1975	
Census 1971, Scotland. Qualified Manpower Tables	General Register Office for Scotland	HMSO, Edinburgh	1978	
Census 1971, Scotland. Migration Tables	General Register Office for Scotland	HMSO, Edinburgh	1977	
Census 1971, Scotland. Workplace and Transport Tables	General Register Office for Scotland	HMSO, Edinburgh	1976	
Census 1981, England & Wales. Household and Family Composition	OPCS	HMSO, London	1984	Code CEN 81 HFC
Census 1981, England & Wales. Housing and Households	OPCS	HMSO, London	1983	Code CEN 81 HH
Census 1981, England & Wales. New Towns Report	OPCS	HMSO, London	1983	Code CEN 81 NT
Census 1981, England & Wales. Workplace and Transport to Work	OPCS	HMSO, London	1984	Code CEN 81 WT

List of statistical sources (*continued*)

Title	Organization responsible or author	Publisher	Frequency or date of publication	Remarks
Census 1981, Great Britain. Economic Activity	OPCS	HMSO, London	1984	Code CEN 81 EA
Census 1981, Great Britain. Definitions	OPCS	HMSO, London	1981	Code CEN 81 DEF
Census 1981, Great Britain. National Migration	OPCS	HMSO, London	1983	Code CEN 81 NM
Census 1981, Great Britain. National Report	OPCS	HMSO, London	1983	Code CEN 81 NR
Census 1981, Great Britain. Regional Migration	OPCS	HMSO, London	1983–4	Code CEN 81 RM
Census 1981, Great Britain. Report for Wales	OPCS	HMSO, London	1983	Code CEN 81 RW. Published in English and Welsh language versions
Census 1981, Great Britain. Qualified Manpower	OPCS	HMSO, London	1984	Code CEN 81 QM
Census 1981, Key Statistics for Urban Areas	OPCS	HMSO, London	1984	Code CEN 81 KSU A1–5. Volume for Scotland published separately – see below

Census 1981, Scotland. Economic Activity	Registrar General Scotland	HMSO, Edinburgh	1984	
Census 1981, Scotland. Household and Family Composition	Registrar General Scotland	HMSO, Edinburgh	1984	
Census 1981, Scotland. Housing and Household Report	Registrar General Scotland	HMSO, Edinburgh	1984	
Census 1981, Scotland. Migration	Registrar General Scotland	HMSO, Edinburgh	1983–4	
Census 1981, Scotland. New Towns	Registrar General Scotland	HMSO, Edinburgh	1983	
Census 1981, Scotland. Scottish Summary	Registrar General Scotland	HMSO, Edinburgh	1983	
Census 1981, Scotland. Workplace and Transport to Work	Registrar General Scotland	HMSO, Edinburgh	1984	
Census 1981, Key Statistics for Urban Areas, Scotland. Localities	Registrar General Scotland	HMSO, Edinburgh	1984	
Census of Private Architectural Practices	RIBA	RIBA, London	Irregular	Latest census is for 1984

List of statistical sources (*continued*)

Title	Organization responsible or author	Publisher	Frequency or date of publication	Remarks
Changes in Rates of Wages and Hours of Work	Department of Employment	HMSO, London	Monthly from May 1966 to Dec. 1982	From Jan. 1983 the information contained in this publication is available from DE Statistics Division A4, Watford, Herts Research Report No. 5
The Characteristics of London's Households	GLC	GLC, London	1970	
Chartered Institute of Building Yearbook and Directory of Members	CIOB	CIOB, Ascot	Annually	
Chartered Institution of Building Services Annual Report and Accounts	CIBS	CIBS, London	Annually	
Chartered Surveyor Weekly	RICS	RICS Journals Ltd, London	Weekly	Formerly *Chartered Surveyor*
CITB Annual Report	CITB	CITB, London	Annually	
Commercial and Industrial Floorspace Statistics	DoE	HMSO, London	Annually	From 1978 (covering period 1974–7). Formerly *Statistics for Town and Country Planning. Series II Floorspace* (q.v.)

Title	Organisation	Publisher/Place	Frequency	Notes
Commercial and Industrial Floorspace Statistics: Wales	Welsh Office	Welsh Office, Cardiff	Annually	
Commercial and Industrial Property Statistics	DoE	HMSO, London	Annually 1978–80	Issues for 1977 to 1979 Discontinued
Compendium of Building Society Statistics	BSA	BSA, London	Irregular	Fifth edition published in 1984
The Condition of London's Housing – A Survey	GLC	GLC, London	1970	Research Report No. 4
Construction Forecasts	NEDO	HMSO, London	Biannually	Available on subscription only. Issued by NEDO prior to 1975
Consulting Engineers Salary Survey	Reward Regional Surveys	Reward Regional Surveys Ltd, Stone, Staffs	Annually from 1983	
Cost Analyses	BMCIS	BMCIS, Kingston-upon-Thames	Annually	
Costs and Profitability of Private Architectural Practice	RIBA	RIBA, London	Irregular	Two reports have been published to date, one for the years 1971–1977 (1978) and one for the years 1978–80 (1981)

List of statistical sources (*continued*)

Title	Organization responsible or author	Publisher	Frequency or date of publication	Remarks
Department of Employment Gazette	DoE	HMSO, London	Monthly from Jan. 1971 to December 1979	Continued as *Employment Gazette* Formerly *Employment and Productivity Gazette*
Development Control Statistics	DoE, Welsh Office	The Department, London	Annually	From 1976 (for 1974/5). Formerly *Statistics for Town and Country Planning. Series I Planning Decisions*
Digest of Statistics, Northern Ireland	Department (formerly Ministry) of Finance	HMSO, Belfast	Biannually, 1954–81	Continued as *Northern Ireland Annual Abstract of Statistics*
Digest of Welsh Statistics	Welsh Office (formerly Home Office)	HMSO, Cardiff	Annually	From 1954
Direct Labour Organisations Statistics	CIPFA	CIPFA, London	Annually	
Earnings in the Building Industry. A Survey of Operatives' Earnings and Hours in May 1973	EDC for Building	NEDO, London	1974	

Economic Outlook	LBS, Centre for Economic Forecasting	Gower, Aldershot	Monthly	
Economic Trends	CSO	HMSO, London	Monthly	
Economic Trends Annual Supplement	CSO	HMSO, London	Annually	From 1975
Education Statistics	CIPFA	CIPFA, London	Annually	Two volumes: *Estimates* and *Actuals*
Education Statistics	RIBA	RIBA, London	Annually	
Education Statistics for the United Kingdom	Department of Education and Science	HMSO, London	Annually	From 1970 (issue for 1967)
Employment Gazette	Department of Employment	HMSO, London	Monthly from January 1980	Formerly *Department of Employment Gazette*
Employment and Productivity Gazette	Department of Employment and Productivity	HMSO, London	Monthly from June 1968 to December 1970	Continued as *Department of Employment Gazette*. Formerly *Ministry of Labour Gazette*
Empty Housing in England	OPCS	HMSO, London	1980	
English House Condition Survey 1976, Part 1 Report of the Physical Condition Survey	DoE	HMSO, London	1978	Housing Survey Report No. 10
English House Condition Survey 1976, Part 2 Report of the Social Survey	DoE	HMSO, London	1979	Housing Survey Report No. 11

List of statistical sources (*continued*)

Title	Organization responsible or author	Publisher	Frequency or date of publication	Remarks
English House Condition Survey 1981, Part 1 Report of the Physical Condition Survey	DoE	HMSO, London	1982	Housing Survey Report No. 12
English House Condition Survey 1981, Part 2 Report of the Interview and Local Authority Survey	DoE	HMSO, London	1983	Housing Survey Report No. 13
English Housing Trends	J.B. Cullingworth	G. Bell and Sons Ltd, London	1965	
50 Centres – A Guide to Office and Industrial Rental Trends in England and Wales	Jones Lang Wootton	Jones Lang Wootton, London	Biannually	
Family Expenditure Survey	DE	HMSO, London	Annually	From 1957
Financial Statistics	CSO	HMSO, London	Monthly	
Financial Times	Financial Times	Financial Times Ltd, London	Daily	
Financial Weekly	Fleet Financial Publishing Ltd	Fleet Financial Publishing Ltd, London	Weekly	

Title	Source	Publisher	Frequency	Notes
First Destination of Polytechnic Students Qualifying in ...[year]	Polytechnic Careers Advisers: Statistics Working Party	Committee of Directors of Polytechnics, London	Annually	From 1973. Limited coverage until 1976
Guide to House Rebuilding Costs for Insurance Valuation	BCIS, (RICS)	BCIS, Kingston-upon-Thames	Annually	
The General Household Survey	OPCS	HMSO, London	Annually	From 1971
The Government's Expenditure Plans	Command Paper	HMSO, London	Annually	Plans for 1985–6 to 1987–8 published in January 1985 in Cmnd 9428
The Greater London House Condition Survey	GLC	GLC, London	1981	Reviews and Studies Series No. 7
Health and Safety Statistics	Health and Safety Executive	HMSO, London	Annually	From 1977 (Report for 1975)
Highways and Transportation Statistics	CIPFA	CIPFA, London	Annually	Two volumes: *Estimates* and *Actuals*
Historical Record of the Census of Production 1907-1970	BSO	HMSO, London	1979	
Homelessness Statistics	CIPFA	CIPFA, London	Annually	
Homes – People, Prices and Places	Abbey National Building Society	The Society, London	Quarterly	Discontinued in 1985

List of statistical sources (continued)

Title	Organization responsible or author	Publisher	Frequency or date of publication	Remarks
Hotel Prospects to 1980	EDC for the Hotel and Catering Industry	NEDO, London	1972	A summary of this report was published by Sandles (1973)
Hotel Prospects to 1985	EDC for the Hotel and Catering Industry	NEDO, London	1976	
House Condition Survey 1971, England and Wales	DoE	DoE, London	1973	Housing Survey Report No. 9
Housing and Construction Statistics	DoE, SDD and Welsh Office	HMSO, London	Quarterly and Annually	Quarterly in two *Parts* from 1972 and annually (covering a decade) from 1980 (covering 1969–79)
Housing in Clydeside 1970	SDD (J.B. Cullingworth, J.C. Watson)	HMSO, Edinburgh	1971	
The Housing Corporation Report...(year)	Housing Corporation London	The Corporation,	Annually	
Housing Finance	Leeds Permanent Building Society	The Society, Leeds	Quarterly	
Housing Management and Maintenance Statistics	CIPFA	CIPFA, London	Annually	
Housing Market	Anglia Building Society	The Society, Northampton	Biannually	

Title	Author/Organisation	Publisher	Date	Notes
Housing Rents Statistics	CIPFA	CIPFA, London	Annually	
Housing Revenue Account Statistics	CIPFA	CIPFA, London	Annually	Two volumes: *Estimates* and *Actuals*
The Housing Situation in 1960	P. G. Gray and R. Russell	COI, London	1962	
Housing Statistics	MOHLG (DoE)	HMSO, London	Quarterly from March 1966 to February 1972	
The Housing Survey in England and Wales 1964	Myra Woolf	HMSO, London	1967	
Housing Survey Reports:*				
No. 1 West Midlands Conurbation House Condition Survey 1967	MOHLG	HMSO, London	1969	
No. 2 South East Lancashire Conurbation House Condition Survey 1967	MOHLG	HMSO, London	1969	
No. 3 Merseyside Conurbation House Condition Survey 1968	MOHLG	HMSO, London	1969	

* Housing Survey Reports Nos. 9–13 are listed under their main titles: *House Condition Survey* or *English House Condition Survey*.

List of statistical sources (*continued*)

Title	Organization responsible or author	Publisher	Frequency or date of publication	Remarks
No. 4 *Tyneside Conurbation House Condition Survey 1968*	MOHLG	HMSO, London	1969	
No. 5 *West Yorkshire Conurbation House Condition Survey 1969*	MOHLG	HMSO, London	1970	
No. 6 *West Midlands Conurbation Housing Survey 1966*	DoE	DoE, London	1971	
No. 7 *West Yorkshire Conurbation Housing Survey 1969*	DoE	DoE, London	1972	
No. 8 *West Yorkshire Movers Survey 1969*	DoE	DoE, London	1973	
Industrial Floorspace Survey	King & Co	King & Co, London	Three times per year	
Industrial Rents and Rates	Debenham Tewson & Chinnocks	Debenham Tewson & Chinnocks, London	Annually	

Title	Source	Publisher	Frequency/Year	Notes
Inland Revenue Statistics	Board of Inland Revenue	HMSO, London	Annually from 1970	
Input–Output Tables for Scotland	The Fraser of Allander Institute	Scottish Academic Press, Edinburgh and London	1977	
Iron and Steel Annual Statistics	Iron and Steel Statistics Bureau	The Bureau, Croydon	Annually	
Iron and Steel Monthly Statistics	Iron and Steel Statistics Bureau	The Bureau, Croydon	Monthly to December 1982	Ceased publication
Investors Chronicle	FT Business Information Ltd	FT Business Information Ltd, London	Weekly	
Investors Chronicle – Hillier Parker Average Yields	Hillier Parker May Rowden	Financial Times Business Publications Ltd, London	Biannually	
Investors Chronicle – Hillier Parker Rent Index	Hillier Parker May Rowden	Financial Times Business Publications Ltd, London	Biannually	
Investment Report	Healey & Baker	Healey & Baker, London	Quarterly	
JLW Property Index	Jones Lang Wootton	Jones Lang Wootton, London	Quarterly	
Judicial Statistics	Command Paper	HMSO, London	Annually	
Labour Costs in Great Britain in 1964	Ministry of Labour	HMSO, London	1968	
Labour Costs in Great Britain in 1968	Department of Employment	HMSO, London	1971	

List of statistical sources (*continued*)

Title	Organization respon-sible or author	Publisher	Frequency or date of publication	Remarks
Labour Force Survey	OPCS	HMSO, London	Biennially	A report on the first three surveys for 1973, 1975 and 1977 was published in 1980. Separate reports on the 1979 and 1981 surveys were published in 1982
Labour Mobility in the Construction Industry	OPCS Marsh, Alan *et al.*	HMSO, London	1981	
Laxton's Building Price Book	V. B. Johnson & Partners (eds)	Thomas Skinner Directories, East Grinstead	Annually	
Local Authority Staffing	RIBA	RIBA, London	1981	
Local Government Financial Statistics, England and Wales	DoE and Welsh Office	HMSO, London	Annually	
Local Housing Statistics, England and Wales	DoE and Welsh Office	HMSO, London	Annually	
Ministry of Labour Gazette	Ministry of Labour	HMSO, London	Monthly to May 1968	Continued as *Department of Employment and Productivity Gazette*

MLP–CIG Property Index	Michael Laurie & Partners	Michael Laurie & Partners, London	Annually	
Monthly Bulletin of (Construction) Statistics	Ministry of Works and successor Departments*	The Ministry or Department, according to date of issue, London	Monthly from February 1946 to June 1972	
Monthly Digest of Statistics	CSO	HMSO, London	Monthly	An annual *Supplement* includes notes and definitions
Monthly Statistics of Building Materials and Components	DoE	DoE Statistics Construction Division, London	Monthly	Available on subscription only
MSC Annual Reports	MSC	MSC, Sheffield	Annually	
National Bulletin	Halifax Building Society	The Society, Halifax	Monthly	
National Dwelling and Housing Survey	DoE	HMSO, London	1978	Report on Phase I
National Dwelling and Housing Survey, Phases II and III	DoE	HMSO, London	1980	
National Health Service Reorganisation Act 1973, National Health Service Act 1977 and Health Services Act 1980 – Accounts...[year]	House of Commons Papers	HMSO, London	Annually	

* The Ministry of Public Building and Works from July 1962 to November 1970 and then the Department of the Environment.

List of statistical sources (*continued*)

Title	Organization responsible or author	Publisher	Frequency or date of publication	Remarks
National Health Service (Scotland) Act 1978 and Health Services Act 1980, Accounts...[year]	House of Commons Papers	HMSO, London	Annually	
National Income and Expenditure	CSO	HMSO, London	Annually from 1952 to 1983	The Blue Book. Continued as *United Kingdom National Accounts*. Before 1952, issued as a Command Paper (see below)
National Income and Expenditure of the United Kingdom 1938 to 1946	Command Paper Cmd 7099	HMSO, London	1947	
National Income and Expenditure of the United Kingdom 1946 to 1950	Command Paper Cmd 8203	HMSO, London	1951	
National Institute Economic Review	NIESR	NIESR, London	Quarterly	
National Road Maintenance Condition Survey Report	Department of Transport	The Department, London	Annually	

Title	Author/Organization	Publisher	Frequency	Notes
Nationwide Building Society Bulletin	Nationwide Building Society	The Society, London	Quarterly	
New Civil Engineer	ICE	Thomas Telford Ltd, London	Weekly	
New Earnings Survey	DE	HMSO, London	Annually	From 1970 (Report for 1968); subsequent issues relate to the years from 1970 onwards. Since the issue for 1974 the report has been published in six parts (Parts A–F)
New Hotels in England	English Tourist Board	English Tourist Board, London	Annually	
News Release. HVCA State of Trade Enquiry...[date]	HVCA	HVCA, London	Biannually	
Northern Ireland Annual Abstract of Statistics	Department of Finance and Personnel	HMSO, Belfast	Annually from 1982	Formerly *Digest of Statistics, Northern Ireland*
Office Rents and Rates	Debenham Tewson & Chinnocks	Debenham Tewson & Chinnocks, London	Annually	
OPCS Monitor	OPCS	OPCS, London	Various	Various series are issued according to subject. They are available free on request.

List of statistical sources (*continued*)

Title	Organization responsible or author	Publisher	Frequency or date of publication	Remarks
Our Older Homes, A Call for Action	MOHLG	HMSO, London	1966	
Overseas Trade Statistics of the United Kingdom	DTI	HMSO, London	Monthly	Formerly published as *Accounts Relating to Trade and Navigation of the United Kingdom*
Overseas Work Entrusted to Members During ...[year]	Association of Consulting Engineers	The Association, London	Annually	
Persons with Qualifications in Engineering, Technology and Science 1959 to 1968	DTI	HMSO, London	1971	Studies in Technological Manpower No. 3
Persons with Qualifications in Engineering, Technology and Science. Census of Population 1971 Great Britain	DOI	HMSO, London	1976	Studies in Technological Manpower No. 5
Planning and Development Statistics	CIPFA	CIPFA, London	Annually	Two volumes: *Estimates and Actuals*
Policy for Roads: England	Command Papers	HMSO, London	Annually from 1978	Formerly *Roads in England*

Title	Source	Location	Frequency	Notes
Press Notice. Bricks and Cement Production	DoE	DoE, London	Monthly	
Press Notice. BEC State of Trade Enquiry	Building Employers Confederation	BEC, London	Quarterly	
Press Notice. Capital Expenditure by the Manufacturing, Construction Distribution and Financial Industries	DTI	DTI, London	Quarterly	
Press Notice, HBF State of Trade Enquiry	House-Builders Federation	HBF, London	Quarterly	
Press Notice. Homeless Households Reported by Local Authorities in England	DoE	DoE, London	Biannually	Also covers Renovations quarterly and Slum Clearance annually
Press Notice. Housebuilding	DoE	DoE, London	Monthly	
Press Notice. Index of Output of the Production Industries	CSO	CSO, London	Monthly	
Press Notice. Index of Production and Construction for Wales	Welsh Office	Welsh Office, Cardiff	Quarterly	

List of statistical sources (*continued*)

Title	Organization responsible or author	Publisher	Frequency or date of publication	Remarks
Press Notice, Index of Retail Prices	DE	DE, London	Monthly	
Press Notice. Indices for Use with Price Adjustment Formulae	PSA, DoE	PSA, DoE, London	Monthly	
Press Notice. Industry's Investment Intentions for …	DTI	DTI, London	Three times a year	
Press Notice. Joint Manpower Watch	DoE	DoE, London	Quarterly	Covers England. Similar press releases for Wales and for Scotland are issued by the Welsh Office and the Scottish Office respectively
Press Notice. Orders for New Construction in…	DoE	DoE, London	Monthly	
Press Notice. Output and Employment in the Construction Industry	DoE	DoE, London	Quarterly	
Press Notice. Producer Prices for…	DTI	DTI, London	Monthly	

Title	Source	Publisher	Frequency	Notes
Press Notice. RICS News	RICS	RICS, London	Monthly	
Press Release. Building Societies' Monthly Figures	BSA	BSA, London	Monthly	
Press Release. The CBI Industrial Trends Survey	CBI	CBI, London	Quarterly	
Press Notice. Statistics of Planning Applications	DoE	DoE, London	Quarterly	
Price Adjustment Formula for Construction Contracts, Monthly Bulletin of Indices	PSA (DoE)	HMSO, London	Monthly	Formerly published as two separate Bulletins: *Price Adjustment Formulae for Building Contracts (Series 2) Monthly Bulletin of Indices* (to December 1983) and *Monthly Bulletin of Indices, Price Adjustment Formula for Civil Engineering Works* (to November 1983). The former bulletin was itself a combination of separate bulletins for *Building Works (Series 1)* and *Specialist Engineering Installations* issued until March 1982 and April 1982 respectively

List of statistical sources (continued)

Title	Organization respon-sible or author	Publisher	Frequency or date of publication	Remarks
Price Index Numbers for Current Cost Accounting	CSO	HMSO, London	1976–81 (three times a year)	Continued as Business Monitors MM17 and MO18
Prime – Property Rent Indices and Market Editorial and Guide to Rental Values	Healey & Baker	Healey & Baker, London	Biannually	
Private Contractors' Construction Census	DoE	HMSO, London	Annually from 1974 to 1979	Censuses from 1971 to 1978
Private House-Building Statistics	NHBC	NHBC, Amersham	Quarterly	
Privately Rented Accommodation in London. Printed in Report of the Committee on Housing in Greater London (Cmnd 2605)	P.G. Gray & Jean Todd MOHLG	HMSO, London	1965	Social Survey Report SS361
The Privately Rented Sector in 1978	OPCS	HMSO, London	1982	
Production of Aggregates	DoE and former MPBW and MOW	HMSO, London	1973–81 (Annually)	Covered the years 1971–79. Formerly Sand and Gravel Production. Continued as Business Monitor PA 1007

Title	Author	Publisher	Date/Frequency	Notes
Qualified Manpower in Great Britain – The 1966 Census of Population	CSO	HMSO, London	1971	Studies in Official Statistics No. 18
Qualified Manpower in Great Britain – the 1971 Census of Population	CSO	HMSO, London	1976	Studies in Official Statistics, No. 29
Quantity Surveyors Information Notes	PSA	PSA, London	Monthly	Available from PSA Library Sales Office, Croydon, CR9 3LY
Rate Collection Statistics	CIPFA	CIPFA, London	Annually	Scottish data in *Rating Review*
Rates and Rateable Values in England and Wales	DoE and Welsh Office (agency varies)	HMSO, London	Annually	
Rates and Rateable Values in Scotland	Scottish Office (agency varies)	HMSO, Edinburgh	Annually from 1959 (for year 1958/9)	Formerly *Rates in Scotland*
Recently Moving Households	OPCS	HMSO, London	1983	
Regional Bulletin	Halifax Building Society	The Society, Halifax	Quarterly	
Regional Trends	CSO	HMS0, London	Annually from 1981	Formerly *Regional Statistics*
Rents of Public Authority Houses and Rent Rebates and Allowances in Scotland	Command Papers	HMSO, London	Annually until 1977	Final publication (Cmnd 6759) covered the year 1976

List of statistical sources (*continued*)

Title	Organization responsible or author	Publisher	Frequency or date of publication	Remarks
Report of the Chief Registrar	Registry of Friendly Societies	HMSO, London	Annually	
Report of the Commissioners of HM Customs and Excise for the year ended...	Command Papers	HMSO, London	Annually	
Report of the Commissioners of Her Majesty's Inland Revenue for the year ended...	Command Papers	HMSO, London	Annually	
Report on the Census of Distribution and Other Services 1957	Board of Trade	HMSO, London	1959	
Report on the Census of Distribution and Other Services 1961	Board of Trade	HMSO, London	1963–4 and 1971	14 Parts plus supplement
Report on the Census of Distribution and Other Services 1966	Board of Trade	HMSO, London	1970–1	2 vols
Research and Development Expenditure	CSO	HMSO, London	1973	Studies in Official Statistics No. 21
Research and Development Expenditure and Employment	CSO	HMSO, London	1976	Studies in Official Statistics No. 27

Title	Source	Publisher	Frequency/Year	Notes
Retail Prices Indices 1914–1984	DE	HMSO, London	1984	
Reward	PER	Synergy Publishing Ltd, Stone, Staffs	Three times a year from 1975 to 1982 Biannually	
Reward – Salary and Living Cost Report	Reward Regional Surveys	Reward Regional Surveys Ltd, Stone, Staffs		
RIBA Quarterly Statistical Bulletin	RIBA	RIBA, London	Quarterly from 1958	
Richard Ellis Annual Investment Review and Property Market Indicators	Richard Ellis	Richard Ellis, London	Annually	
Roads in England	House of Commons Papers	HMSO, London	Annually to 1976	Replaced in 1978 by new series: *Policy for Roads: England*
Roads in Scotland, Report for…[year]	Command Papers	HMSO, London	Annually	
Roads in Wales	Welsh Office	Welsh Office, Cardiff	Annually	
Salaries and Benefits in Building Contracting	Building Business Unit	The Unit, London	1980	
Salaries and Benefits for Building Surveyors, Quantity Surveyors and Technicians	Building Business Unit	The Unit, London	1980	

List of statistical sources (*continued*)

Title	Organization responsible or author	Publisher	Frequency or date of publication	Remarks
Sand and Gravel Production	DoE and former MPBW and MOW	HMSO, London	1958–72 (Annually)	Covered the years 1954–71. Continued as *Production of Aggregates*
The School Building Survey 1962	DES	HMSO, London	1965	
Scotland – New Hotel Capacity	Scottish Tourist Board	Scottish Tourist Board, Edinburgh	Irregularly	
Scotland's Older Houses	SDD	HMSO, Edinburgh	1967	
Scottish Abstract of Statistics	Scottish Office	HMSO, Edinburgh	Annually from 1971	
Scottish Economic Bulletin	Scottish Office	HMSO, Edinburgh	Biannually from 1971	
Scottish Educational Statistics	Scottish Education Department	HMSO, Edinburgh	Annually from 1966 to 1974	
Scottish Health Service Costs	Scottish Health Board	The Board, Edinburgh	Annually	
Scottish Housing in 1965	SDD. J.B. Cullingworth	SDD, Edinburgh	1967	
Scottish Housing Statistics	SDD	HMSO, Edinburgh	Quarterly to 1982, then Annually	
Scottish Industrial and Commercial Property Review	Kenneth Ryden & Partners	Kenneth Ryden & Partners, Edinburgh	Biannually	

Title	Author	Publisher	Date/Frequency	Notes
Scottish Residential Property Review	Kenneth Ryden & Partners	Kenneth Ryden & Partners, Edinburgh	Biannually	
Scottish Input–Output Tables for 1979	Industry Department for Scotland	Industry Department for Scotland, Edinburgh	1984	Five volumes: (1. Introduction and Summary Tables; 2. Detailed Tables; 3. Further Results and Analyses; 4. Sources and Methods; 5. Comparisons with Scotland 1973 and UK 1979)
Scottish Local Government Financial Statistics	Scottish Office	HMSO, Edinburgh	Annually	
Shops Rents and Rates	Debenham Tewson & Chinnocks	Debenham Tewson & Chinnocks, London	Annually	
Slum Clearance (England & Wales)	Command Paper, Cmd 9593	HMSO, London	1955	
Slum Clearance	Command Paper, Cmd 9685	HMSO, Edinburgh	1956	
Social Security Statistics	DHSS	HMSO, London	Annually	
Social Trends	CSO	HMSO, London	Annually	
Spon's Architects' and Builders' Price Book	Davis, Belfield & Everest (eds)	E. & F.N. Spon Ltd, London	Annually	

List of statistical sources (*continued*)

Title	Organization responsible or author	Publisher	Frequency or date of publication	Remarks
Spon's Civil Engineering Price Book	Davis, Belfield & Everest (eds)	E. & F.N. Spon Ltd, London	1984	First edition
Spon's Landscape Price Book	D. Lovejoy & Partners; Davis, Belfield & Everest (eds)	E. & F.N. Spon Ltd, London	Irregular	First edition 1978; Third edition 1983
Spon's Mechanical and Electrical Services Price Book	Davis, Belfield & Everest (eds)	E. & F.N. Spon Ltd, London	Annually	
Statistical Bulletin HSIU series	SDD	SDD, Edinburgh	See remarks	Quarterly series on housing trends, annual series on public sector rents and sales of public sector houses and occasional issues on special topics
Statistical Bulletin	Scottish Education Department	The Department, Edinburgh	Irregular	Topics covered are: further education; school leavers; schools, pupils and teachers; universities and student awards
Statistics Collected by the Ministry of Works 1941–56. Vols 1 and 2	M.C. Fleming	DoE, London	1980	Vol 1: Construction industry. Vol 2: Building materials, production and prices

Title	Originator	Publisher	Dates	Notes
Statistics for Town and Country Planning Decisions	DoE (MOHLG), Welsh Office	HMSO, London	Annually 1969–74	*Continued as Development Control Statistics. Formerly Statistics of Decisions on Planning Applications*
Statistics for Town and Country Planning. Series II Floor Space	DoE, Welsh Office	HMSO, London	1969, 1972, 1974, 1976	*Continued as Commercial and Industrial Floorspace Statistics*
Statistics of Decisions on Planning Applications: England and Wales	MOHLG	DoE, London HMSO, London	1977 Annually 1962–8	*Continued as Statistics for Town and Country Planning Series I*
Statistics of Education	DES	HMSO, London DES, London	Annually	*HMSO publication to 1979 edition*
Statistics of Education in Wales	Welsh Office	HMSO, Cardiff	Annually from 1976	
Statistics of Education SS3. Surveys of Earnings of Qualified Manpower in England and Wales, 1966–67	DES	HMSO, London	1971	
Statistics of Education SS5 School Building Surveys 1975 and 1976	DES	HMSO, London	1979	
Statistics of Road Lengths in Wales	Welsh Office	Welsh Office, Cardiff	Irregular	

List of statistical sources (*continued*)

Title	Organization responsible or author	Publisher	Frequency or date of publication	Remarks
The Stock Exchange Fact Book	Stock Exchange	Public Relations Department, The Stock Exchange, London	Quarterly	Now incorporated in *The Stock Exchange Quarterly*
Student Employment Survey 1978	RIBA	RIBA, London	1978	
Student Survey 1979	RIBA	RIBA, London	1979	
Study of Energy in Buildings	BMCIS	BMCIS, Kingston-upon-Thames	Annually	
A Study of Quantity Surveying Practice	University of Aston in Birmingham	RICS, London	1974	
A Study of Quantity Surveying Practice and Client Demand	Building Design Partnership	Surveyors Publications, London	1984	
A Study of School Building	DES, Welsh Office	HMSO, London	1977	
Survey of Local Authority Offices	RIBA	RIBA, London	1982	
Survey of Chartered and Technician Engineers	Engineering Council (and former CEI)	The Council, London	Biennially from 1971	Former title: *Survey of Professional Engineers*. Surveys for 1966 and 1968 published by HMSO, London in 1967 and 1970.
Survey of Wages and Conditions in the Construction Industry	GMBATU	GMBATU, Esher, Surrey	1984	

Title	Author/Body	Publisher	Frequency	Notes
The Times 1000	Times Books	Times Books Ltd, London	Annually	
Time Rates of Wages and Hours of Work	DE	HMSO, London	1946–82 (Annually)	Earlier issues were irregular commencing in 1893. Not published in 1953. Replaced by regularly up-dated loose-leaf folder available on subscription
Transport Statistics, Great Britain	Department of Transport	HMSO, London	Annually	Formerly *Highway Statistics*
United Kingdom Balance of Payments	CSO	HMSO, London	Annually	The CSO Pink Book
United Kingdom Mineral Statistics	British Geological Survey	HMSO, London	Annually from 1973	
United Kingdom National Accounts...[year]. The CSO Blue Book	CSO	HMSO, London	Annually from 1984	Formerly *National Income and Expenditure*
University Statistics	UGC	Universities' Statistical Record, Cheltenham	Annually from 1978	Published in three volumes: Vol. 1, Students and Staff; Vol. 2, First Destination of University Graduates; Vol. 3, Finance

List of statistical sources (continued)

Title	Organization responsible or author	Publisher	Frequency or date of publication	Remarks
Valuation Office Property Market Report	Inland Revenue	Surveyors Publications, London	Biannually from Oct. 1983	The first published report bears the number 40. Earlier numbers in the series were internal documents and not published.
Valuer	ISVA	ISVA, London	Ten issues per year	
Welsh Economic Trends	Welsh Office	HMSO, Cardiff	Annually from 1974	
Welsh House Condition Survey 1968	Welsh Office	HMSO, Cardiff	1969	
Welsh House Condition Survey 1973	Welsh Office	HMSO, Cardiff	1975	
Welsh House Condition Survey 1976	Welsh Office	HMSO, Cardiff	1978	
Welsh House Condition Survey 1981	Welsh Office	Welsh Office, Cardiff	1982	
Welsh Housing and Dwelling Survey	Welsh Office	Welsh Office, Cardiff	1981	
Welsh Housing Statistics	Welsh Office	Welsh Office, Cardiff	Annually	
Welsh Local Government Financial Statistics	Welsh Office	HMSO, Cardiff	Annually from 1977	
Welsh Social Trends	Welsh Office	Welsh Office, Cardiff	Biennially	
Woolwich Review	Woolwich Equitable Building Society	The Society, London	Biannually	

REFERENCES

Aldcroft, Derek, H. and Mort, Derrick (1981) *Rail and Sea Transport*, Pergamon Press, Oxford, on behalf of the Royal Statistical Society and the Social Science Research Council.

Alderson, Michael and Whitehead, Frank (1974) *Central Government Routine Health Statistics and Social Security Statistics*, Heinemann Educational Books, London, on behalf of the Royal Statistical Society and the Social Science Research Council.

Allen, Kevin and Yuill, Douglas (1977) The accuracy of pre-1971 employment data (the ER IIs) *Regional Studies*, **11** (4), 253–61.

Allen, Patrick (1982) *Shared Ownership*, HMSO, London.

ARCUK (annually) *The Register of Architects*, ARCUK, London.

Association of Consulting Engineers (annually) *Consulting Engineers Who's Who and Yearbook*, Municipal Publications Ltd, London.

Audit Commission (1985) *Capital Expenditure Controls in Local Government in England*, HMSO, London.

Azzaro, D.W. (1976) Measuring the level of tender prices *Chartered Surveyor Building and Quantity Surveying Quarterly*, **4** (2), 17–19.

Bain, G.S. and Price, R. (1980) *Profiles of Union Growth*, Basil Blackwell, Oxford.

Bannock, Graham (1975) *The Larger Private Company in Britain*, Wilton House Publications, London.

Barnes, Martin and Partners (1975) *The Sensitivity of the Building Price Adjustment Formula*, The NFBTE, London.

Baxter, R.E. and Phillips, Celia M. (1979) *Ports, Inland Waterways and Civil Aviation*, Pergamon Press, Oxford, on behalf of the Royal Statistical Society and the Social Science Research Council.

Beckett, R. and Glass, D. (1984) Revised Northern Ireland construction output data. *Statistical News*, **65**, 65.15–65.17.

Bell, David and Greenhorn, Alan (eds) (1984) *A Guide to Financial Times Statistics,* Financial Times Business Information Ltd, London.

Benjamin, Bernard (1970) *The Population Census,* Heinemann Educational Books, London.

Bielckus, C.L., Rogers, A.W. and Wibberley, G.P. (1972) *Second Homes in England and Wales,* Wye College, Ashford, Kent.

Board of Inland Revenue (1971a) *Income Tax. Subcontracting in the Construction Industry. Explanatory Pamphlet for Contractors,* Pamphlet IR 14, The Board, London.

Board of Inland Revenue (1971b) *Income Tax. Subcontracting in the Construction Industry. Explanatory Pamphlet for sub-contractors,* Pamphlet IR 15, The Board, London.

Board of Inland Revenue (1976) *Income Tax. Construction Industry Tax Deduction Scheme,* Pamphlet IR 14/15, The Board, London.

Board of Trade (1962) *Income and Finance of Public Quoted Companies. Summary and Industrial Group Tables 1949–1960,* Board of Trade, London.

Boleat, Mark (1982) *The Building Society Industry,* Allen and Unwin, London.

Britton, Andrew (ed.) (1983) *Employment, Output and Inflation: The National Institute Model of the British Economy,* Heinemann Educational Books, London.

Britton, Malcolm and Birch, Francis (1985) *1981 Census Post-Enumeration Survey,* HMSO, London.

BSA (1980) *Studies in Building Society Activity 1974–79,* BSA, London.

BSA (1982) *Studies in Building Society Activity 1980–81,* BSA, London.

BSA (1984) *Studies in Building Society Activity 1982–83,* BSA, London.

BSO (1979, 1983) *Business Monitor PO 1000, Quarterly Statistics of Manufacturers' Sales, Index of Commodities,* HMSO, London.

BSO (1984) *Business Monitor PO 1001, Guide to Short Term Statistics of Manufacturers' Sales,* HMSO, London.

Butler, A.D. (1978) New price indices for construction output statistics. *Economic Trends,* No.297, 97–110.

Butler, Rosemary (1977) Qualified manpower statistics. *Statistical News,* No.36, 36.12–36.14.

Buxton, N.K. and MacKay, D.I. (1978) *British Employment Statistics: A Guide to Sources and Methods,* Basil Blackwell, Oxford.

Carruthers, J.F.S. and Harding, T. (1976) British-grown timber and the building and construction industry: current usage and future potential, *BRE Current Paper CP5/76*, BRE, Garston, Herts.

Chartered Institution of Building Services (annually) *Annual Report and Accounts,* The Institution, London.

CITB (annually) *Report and Statement of Accounts for the Year ended ...,* The Board, London, annually from the report for 1972–3. Earlier reports were issued as House of Commons papers (HMSO, London).

Claydon, Sylvia (1980) Counting our skills: The National Training Survey. *Employment Gazette,* November, 1150–54, 1160.

Cmnd 953 (1960) *Report on Safety and Health in the Building and Civil Engineering Industries 1954–1958,* HMSO, London.

Cmnd 3602 (1968) *Older Houses into New Homes,* HMSO, London.

Cmnd 3714 (1968) *Report of the Committee of Inquiry under Professor E.H. Phelps Brown into Certain Matters Concerning Labour in Building and Civil Engineering,* HMSO, London.

Cmnd 5905 (1975) *Housing Costs, Weighting and Other Matters Affecting the Retail Prices Index,* HMSO, London.

Cmnd 6225 (1975) *Inflation Accounting. Report of the Inflation Accounting [Sandilands] Committee,* HMSO, London.

Cmnd 6851 (1977) *Housing Policy, A Consultative Document,* HMSO, London.

Cmnd 6852 (1977) *Scottish Housing, A Consultative Document,* HMSO, Edinburgh.

Cmnd 6999 (1977) *Royal Commission on the Distribution of Income and Wealth Report No.5, Third Report on the Standing Reference,* HMSO, London.

Cmnd 7615 (1979) *Report of the Royal Commission on the National Health Service,* HMSO, London.

Cmnd 8014 (1980) *Standing Commission on Pay Comparability, Report No.10, Local Authority Building Workers,* HMSO, London.

Cmnd 9518 (1985) *Reform of Social Security Volume 2: Programme for Change,* HMSO, London.

Cmnd 9520 (1985) *Housing Benefit Review – Report of the Review Team,* HMSO, London.

Copeman, Harold (1981) *The National Accounts: a Short Guide,* Central Statistical Office, Studies in Official Statistics, No.36, HMSO, London.

Coppock, J.T. (ed.) (1977) *Second Homes: Curse or Blessing?,* Pergamon Press, Oxford.

Coppock, J.T. and Gebbett, L.F. (1978) *Land Use and Town and Country Planning*, Pergamon Press, Oxford, on behalf of the Royal Statistical Society and the Social Science Research Council.

Creigh, S.W. (1984) Strikes in Britain: a selective annotated bibliography. *Quality of Working Life Journal*, **1** (5), 3–12.

Crine, A. and Wintour, J. (1980) HIPs – the vital statistics, *Roof* **5**(2), 52–4.

CSO (annually) *Financial Statistics – Explanatory Handbook*, HMSO, London. First edition 1977 (replaced former *Notes and Definitions* supplement).

CSO (annually) *Monthly Digest of Statistics Supplement – Definitions and Explanatory Notes*, HMSO, London. Annually each January since 1946.

CSO (biennially) *Guide to Official Statistics*, HMSO, London. Fourth edition published in 1982.

CSO (quarterly) *Statistical News*, HMSO, London.

CSO (1948, 1958, 1968) *Standard Industrial Classification*, HMSO, London.

CSO (1967) *Method of Construction and Calculation of the Index of Retail Prices, Studies in Official Statistics No.6*, HMSO, London.

CSO (1970) *Input–Output Tables for the United Kingdom 1963, Studies in Official Statistics No.16*, HMSO, London.

CSO (1973) *Input–Output Tables for the United Kingdom 1968, Studies in Official Statistics No.22*, HMSO, London.

CSO (1976a) *Research and Development Expenditure and Employment, Studies in Official Statistics No.27*, HMSO, London.

CSO (1976b) *The Measurement of Changes in Production, Studies in Official Statistics No.25*, HMSO, London.

CSO (1978a) *Personal Sector Balance Sheets and Current Developments in Inland Revenue Estimates of Personal Wealth, Studies in Official Statistics No.35*, HMSO, London.

CSO (1978b) *Regional Accounts, Studies in Official Statistics No.31*, HMSO, London.

CSO (1979) *Standard Industrial Classification Revised 1980*, HMSO, London.

CSO (1980) *Wholesale Price Index, Principles and Procedures, Studies in Official Statistics No.32*, HMSO, London.

CSO (1985) *United Kingdom National Accounts, Sources and Methods*, 3rd edn HMSO, London.

Daniel, W.W. and Millward, Neil (1983) *Workplace Industrial Relations in Britain, The DE/PSI/SSRC Survey,* Heinemann Educational Books, London.

Dartington Amenity Research Trust (1977) *Second Homes in Scotland,* The Trust, Totnes, Devon.

Dean, Andrew (1980) *Wages and Earnings,* Pergamon Press, Oxford, on behalf of the Royal Statistical Society and the Social Science Research Council.

DoE (1973) Construction industry: revised series of output statistics 1963–72 (Great Britain). *Economic Trends,* No.240, lxi–lxviii.

DoE *et al.* (1976) *Aggregates: The Way Ahead. Report of the Advisory Committee on Aggregates,* HMSO, London.

DoE (1977) *Housing Policy Technical Volumes, Parts I–III,* HMSO, London.

DoI (1975) Insolvency statistics for England and Wales, *Economic Trends* **257**, 111–112.

DoI (1977) *Changes in the Population of Persons with Qualifications in Engineering, Technology and Science 1959 to 1976, Studies in Technological Manpower No.6,* HMSO, London.

Donnison, D.V. (1961) The movement of households in England, *Journal of the Royal Statistical Society, Ser. A,* **124**(1), 60–80.

Downing, P. and Dower, M. (1973) *Second Homes in England and Wales,* Countryside Commission, London.

DTI (1971) *Persons with Qualifications in Engineering, Technology and Science 1959–1968, Studies in Technological Manpower No.3,* HMSO, London.

Durcan, J.W., McCarthy, W.E.J. and Redman, G.P. (1983) *Strikes in Post-War Britain,* Allen and Unwin, London.

Eady, C.W. and Boyd, N.G. (1964) Indices of erected costs of process plants. *The Cost Engineer* (part of *Chemical and Process Engineering),* March, reprinted in *The Cost Engineer,* **20** (2,3), 1981, 11–16.

Erritt, M.J. and Stibbard, P.J. (1978) Industrial and commercial companies financial statistics. *Statistics Users: Conference on Financial Statistics,* Bank of England, London.

Evans, A.W. (1974) Private sector housing land prices in England and Wales. *Economic Trends,* February, xiv–xxxvii.

Evans, A.W. (1975) *The Five Per Cent Sample Survey of Building Society Mortgages, Studies in Official Statistics No.26* (CSO),

HMSO, London.

Farthing, S.M. and Fleming, M.C. (1974) *Housing in Great Britain and Northern Ireland,* Heinemann Educational Books, London, on behalf of the Royal Statistical Society and the Social Science Research Council.

Fleming, M.C. (1965) Costs and prices in the Northern Ireland construction industry, 1954–64. *Journal of Industrial Economics,* **14,** 42–54.

Fleming, M.C. (1966) The long-term measurement of construction costs in the United Kingdom. *Journal of the Royal Statistical Society, Series A (General),* **129,** 534– 56; and Correction *idem.,* **130,** 1967, 282.

Fleming, M.C. (1974) *Housing in Northern Ireland,* in Farthing and Fleming (1974).

Fleming, M.C. (1978) Pricing in construction – the relationship of constants to productivity. *Building Technology and Management,* **16** (11), 5–10.

Fleming, M.C. (1980a) *Construction and the Related Professions,* Pergamon Press, Oxford, on behalf of the Royal Statistical Society and the Social Science Research Council.

Fleming, M.C. (1980b) *Statistics Collected by the Ministry of Works 1941–1956,* 2 vols, Department of the Environment, London.

Fleming, M.C. and Nellis, J.G. (1981) The interpretation of house-price statistics for the United Kingdom. *Environment and Planning A,* **13,** 1109–24.

Fleming, M.C. and Nellis, J.G. (1984a) *The Halifax House Price Index: Technical Details,* Halifax Building Society, Halifax.

Fleming, M.C. and Nellis, J.G. (1984b) How the new Halifax house price index was devised. *Building Societies Gazette,* **116** (1408), 566–8.

Fleming, M.C. and Nellis, J.G. (1985a) Research policy and review 2. House price statistics for the United Kingdom: a survey and critical review of recent developments. *Environment and Planning A,* **17,** 297–318.

Fleming, M.C. and Nellis, J.G. (1985b) The application of hedonic indexing methods: a study of house prices in the United Kingdom. *Statistical Journal of the United Nations Economic Commission for Europe,* **3,** 249–70.

Garside, W.R. (1980) *The Measurement of Unemployment, Methods and Sources in Great Britain 1850–1979,* Basil Blackwell, Oxford.

Government Social Survey (1968) *Workplace Industrial Relations, Report SS 402*, HMSO, London.

GRO (1952) *Census 1951, Classification of Industries*, HMSO, London.

GRO (1956) *Census 1951. Classification of Occupations*, HMSO, London.

GRO (1958) *Census 1951, England and Wales. General Report*, HMSO, London.

GRO (1960) *Classification of Occupations 1960*, HMSO, London.

GRO (1966) *Classification of Occupations 1966*, HMSO, London.

GRO (1968) *Census 1961, Great Britain. General Report*, HMSO, London.

Gray, Percy and Gee, Frances A. (1972) *A Quality Check on the 1966 Ten Per Cent Sample Census of England and Wales*, HMSO, London.

Griffin, Tom (1975) Revised estimates of the consumption and stock of fixed captital. *Economic Trends*, **264**, 126–9.

Griffin, Tom (1976) The stock of fixed assets in the United Kingdom: how to make best use of the statistics. *Economic Trends*, **276**, 130–43.

Griffiths, Bernard (1979) A tender price index for housing. *Chartered Surveyor*, December, 109–10.

Hakim, Catherine (1982) *Secondary Analysis in Social Research*, Allen and Unwin, London.

Hall, M. and Richardson, M. (1979) *Forecasting Housing Booms and Slumps*, Housing Research Foundation, London.

Hansard (daily) *Parliamentary Debates, House of Commons, Official Report*, HMSO, London.

H.M. Customs and Excise (annually) *Reports of the Commissioners of H.M. Customs and Excise*, Command Papers, HMSO, London.

Hager, David P. and Lord, David J. (1985) The property market, property valuations and property performance measurement, *Journal of Institute of Actuaries*, **112**, 19–48.

Hay, Donald A. and Morris, Derek J. (1984) *Unquoted Companies*, Macmillan, London.

Health and Safety Commission (1983) *Consultative Document: Proposals for Revised Arrangements for Reporting Accidents, Ill Health and Dangerous Occurrences at Work*, HMSO, London.

Health and Safety Executive (1978) *One Hundred Fatal Accidents in Construction*, HMSO, London.

Health and Safety Executive (1979) *Fatal Accidents in Construction 1977,* HMSO, London.

Health and Safety Executive (1980) *The Notification of Accidents and Dangerous Occurrences. Health and Safety Series Booklet HS(R)5,* HMSO, London.

Health and Safety Executive (1981) *Fatal Accidents in Construction 1978,* HMSO, London.

Hibbert, J., Griffin, T.J. and Walker, R.L. (1977) Development of estimates of the stock of fixed capital in the United Kingdom. *Review of Income and Wealth,* **23** (2), 117–35.

Hibbert, Jack (1981) National and sector balance sheets in the United Kingdom. *Review of Income and Wealth,* **27** (4), 357–71.

Hillebrandt, Patricia (1977) Going bust: what are the facts? *Building,* **232,** 52–3.

Hoinville, G. and Smith, T.M.F. (1982) The Rayner review of government statistical services, *Journal of the Royal Statistical Society, Ser A,* **145** (2), 195–207.

House of Commons Environment Committee (1980) *First Report, Session 1979-80,* House of Commons Paper 714, HMSO, London.

IDS (annually) *Directory of Salary Surveys,* Incomes Data Services, London. Available on subscription.

IDS (fortnightly) *IDS Reports,* Incomes Data Services, London. Available on subscription.

Institute of Building (1976) *Survey of Home Members, 1975,* The Institute, Ascot, Berks.

Institution of Civil Engineers (annually) *Yearbook,* Thomas Telford Ltd, London.

Institution of Structural Engineers (annually) *Sessional Yearbook and Directory of Members,* The Institution, London.

Interdepartmental Committee on Social and Economic Research (1958) *Guides to Official Sources: No.1 – Labour Statistics,* HMSO, London.

Interdepartmental Committee on Social and Economic Research (1961) *Social Security Statistics,* Guides to Official Sources No.5, HMSO, London.

JWL (1984a) *50 Centres Guide, Technical Paper I, Selection of Centres and Rental Series,* Jones Lang Wootton, London.

JWL (1984b) *JLW Index – Explanatory Notes,* Jones Lang Wootton, London.

Jones, G.P. (1975) *An Appraisal of Formulae Used for Fluctuations in Construction Costs* Institute of Building, Occasional Paper 9, The Institute of Building, Ascot, Berks.

Kay, S.R., White, E.A. and Hall, D.J. (1981) Cost indices of erected cost of process plants. *The Cost Engineer,* **20** (2, 3), 17–23.

Kemsley, W.F.F., Redpath, R.U. and Holmes, M. (1980) *Family Expenditure Survey Handbook* (OPCS), HMSO, London.

Leather, P. (1983) Housing (dis?) investment programmes. *Policy and Politics* **11** (2), 215–229.

Lemessany, J. (1976) Estimates of the requirements for aggregates, *BRE Current Paper CP 17/76,* BRE, Garston, Herts.

Lemessany, J. and Clapp, M. (1980) Resource inputs in construction. *Proceedings CIB W55 Symposium, Quality and Cost in Building, Vol.V,* September, Institut de Recherche sur L'Environnement Construit, Lausanne.

Lewes, F.M.M., Parker, S.R. and Lickorish, L.J. (1975) *Leisure and Tourism,* Heinemann Educational Books, London, on behalf of the Royal Statistical Society and the Social Science Research Council.

Littlewood, Judith and Mason, Serena (1984) *Taking the Initiative, A Survey of Low Cost Home Owners,* HMSO, London.

Lund, P.J., Mellis, C.L. and Hamilton, V.J. (1976) *Investment Intentions, Authorisations and Expenditures,* H.M. Treasury, Government Economic Service Occasional Papers No.12, HMSO, London.

Lythe, Charlotte and Majmudar, Madhavi (1981) Scottish gross domestic product statistics for 1961–71. *Journal of the Royal Statistical Society,* Ser. A (General), **144** (3), 352–9.

Madge, Janet and Brown, Colin (1981) *First Homes. A Survey of the Housing Circumstances of Young Married Couples,* Policy Studies Institute, London.

Matthews, R. and Leather, P. (1982), Housing in England – the view from the HIPs, *Roof* **7** (3), 11–13.

Matthews, R. and Shaw, L. (1981), HIPs analysis – England, *Roof* **6** (4), 13–15.

Maurice, Rita (1968) *National Accounts Statistics – Sources and Methods,* HMSO, London.

Mayes, David G. (1984) *Statistics By or For Government? Recent Changes in Official Statistics,* NEDO, London.

Meeks, Geoffrey and Whittington, Geoffrey (1976) *The Financing of Quoted Companies in the United Kingdom,* Royal Commission on the Distribution of Income and Wealth, Background Paper No.1, HMSO, London.

Mellis, C.L. and Richardson, P.W. (1976) Value of investment incentives for manufacturing industry 1946 to 1974 in *The Economics of Industrial Subsidies,* (ed. Alan Whiting), Department of Industry, HMSO, London.

Mineral Resources Consultative Committee (1972) *Sand and Gravel as Aggregate,* Mineral Dossier No.4, by A.A. Archer, HMSO, London.

Mineral Resources Consultative Committee (1975) *Slate,* Mineral Dossier No.12, by R.N. Crockett, HMSO, London.

Mineral Resources Consultative Committee (1975) *Gypsum and Anhydrite,* Mineral Dossier No.13, by A.J.G. Notholt and D.E. Highley, HMSO, London.

Mineral Resources Consultative Committee (1977) *Sandstone,* Mineral Dossier No.17, by P.M. Harris, HMSO, London.

Mineral Resources Consultative Committee (1977) *Igneous and Metamorphic Rock,* Mineral Dossier No.19, by P.M. Harris, HMSO, London.

Mineral Resources Consultative Committee (1982) *Common Clay and Shale,* Mineral Dossier No.22, by J.M. Ridgway, HMSO, London.

Mineral Resources Consultative Committee (1982) *Limestone and Dolomite,* Mineral Dossier No.23, by P.M. Harris, HMSO, London.

Ministry of Labour (1967) *Accidents in the Construction Industry – report of a survey made during 1966,* HMSO, London.

Mitchell, Bernard (1978) Measuring value added from the census of production, *Statistical News,* **41,** 41.4–41.9.

Mitchell, Robert (1971) A tender-based building price index. *Chartered Surveyor,* **104,** 34–6.

Morrison, H. (1976) New system of statistics on homelessness. *Statistical News,* No. 35, 35.6–35.9.

Murie, Alan (1974) *Housing Tenure in Britain: A Review of Survey Evidence, 1958–71,* Research Memorandum No. 30, Centre for Urban and Regional Studies, University of Birmingham.

Neale, R.H. and Light, J.F. (1981) A comparison of the reimbursement provided by the Series 1 and Series 2 NEDO formulas for thirteen building projects. *Construction Papers,* **1**

(3), 21–5.

NEDO (1974) *Description of the Indices for Use with the NEDO Price Adjustment Formula for Building Works,* Economic Development Committee for Building, HMSO, London.

NEDO (1978) *How Flexible is Construction?* (EDC for Building), NEDO, London.

NEDO (1985) *Investment in the Public Sector Built Infrastructure* NEDO, London.

NFHA (1985) *Inquiry Into British Housing, Report,* National Federation of Housing Associations, London.

O'Connor, M. (1978) The Department of Industry's investment intentions survey. *Statistical News,* No.41, 41.15–41.19.

Osborn, W.T. (1973) The price index of local authority housebuilding. *Statistical News,* No.22, 22.23–22.25.

OPCS (occasional) *Census Monitors,* OPCS, London.

OPCS (occasional) *User Guides,* OPCS, Titchfield, Fareham, Hants.

OPCS (1970) *Classification of Occupations 1970,* HMSO, London.

OPCS (1978) *1971 Census, Income Follow-up Survey,* Studies on Medical and Population Subjects No.38, HMSO, London.

OPCS (1979) *Census 1971, England and Wales, General Report,* HMSO, London.

OPCS (1980) *Classification of Occupations 1980,* HMSO, London.

OPCS (1982) *Census 1981 Definitions, Great Britain,* HMSO, London.

OPCS (1983) *Census 1981, General Report, Part 3 (Statistical Assessment),* OPCS, London.

OPCS (1985) *Census 1981 User Guide Catalogue,* OPCS, London (available free from OPCS, Census Customer Services, Titchfield, Fareham, Hants).

OPCS and GRO(S) (1977) *Guide to Census Reports. Great Britain 1801–1966,* HMSO, London.

Pettigrew, C.W. (1980) National and sector balance sheets for the United Kingdom. *Economic Trends,* **325,** 82–100.

Polytechnic Careers Advisers Statistics Working Party (annually), *Polytechnic First Degree and Higher Diploma Students ...* [year], Central Services Unit for Careers and Appointments Services, Manchester.

Price, R.J. and Bain, G.S. (1980) The Industrial Distribution of Unions in Great Britain, 1892–1974. SSRC Industrial Relations Research Unit, University of Warwick, Coventry (unfinished

Discussion Paper).

PSA (1977a) *Price Adjustment Formulae for Building Contracts (Series 2), Description of the Indices,* HMSO, London.

PSA (1977b) *Price Adjustment Formulae for Building Contracts (Series 2), Guide to Application and Procedure,* HMSO, London (see also *Amendment No.1* dated May 1979).

PSA (1979a) *Price Adjustment Formulae for Building Contracts (Series 2 Revised), Description of the Indices,* 2nd ed, HMSO, London.

PSA (1979b) *Price Adjustment Formulae for Civil Engineering Contracts, Guide to Application and Procedure,* HMSO, London.

Revell, Jack and associates (1967) *The Wealth of the Nation – the National Balance Sheet of the United Kingdom 1957–61,* University Press, Cambridge.

Rhind, David (ed.), (1983) *A Census User's Handbook,* Methuen, London and New York.

RIBA (annually) *Annual Report of the Council,* RIBA, London.

RICS (annually) *RICS Yearbook,* Waterlow Publishers Ltd, London.

Roberts, D.L.H. (1980) Dwelling stock estimates from the 1981 Census of Population. *Statistical News,* **49,** 49.1–49.5.

Roe, A.R. (1971) *The Financial Interdependence of the Economy 1957–66,* Chapman and Hall, London.

Rogers, A.W. (1977) Second homes in England and Wales: a spatial view, in Coppock (1977).

Royal Commission on Trade Unions and Employers' Associations (1968) *Selected Written Evidence Submitted to the Royal Commission,* HMSO, London.

Sandles, A. (1973) *A Prospect for the Small Hotelier,* HMSO, London.

Sellwood, Roger and Griffin, Chris (1982) New developments in statistics at CIPFA. *Statistical News,* **59,** 59.12–59.17.

Singh, A. and Whittington, G. (1968) *Growth, Profitability and Valuation,* University Press, Cambridge.

Smith, C.T.B., Clifton, Richard; Makeham, Peter, *et al.* (1978) *Strikes in Britain,* HMSO, London.

South West Economic Planning Council (1975) *Survey of Second Homes in the South West,* HMSO, London.

Staton, Roger (1984) Analysis of 'Pay as You Earn' (PAYE) statistics. *Economic Trends,* **372,** 123–32.

Stock Exchange (annually) *The Stock Exchange Official Yearbook,* Thomas Skinner and Co. (Publishers) Ltd, Croydon.

Sykes, Stephen, G. (1983) The uncertainties in property valuation and performance measurement. *The Investment Analyst* **67**, 25–35.

Tew, Brian and Henderson, R.F. (eds) (1959) *Studies in Company Finance*, University Press, Cambridge.

Thompson, F.M.L. (1968) *Chartered Surveyors – The Growth of a Profession*, Routledge and Kegan Paul, London.

Tysoe, Brian A. (1981) *Construction Cost and Price Indices: Description and Use*, Spon, London and New York.

Wallis, K.F. (ed.), *et al.* (1984) *Models of the UK Economy*, Oxford University Press, Oxford.

Wanhill, Stephen (1980), *An Econometric Model of Wales*, University of Wales Press, Bangor.

Welsh Office (1976) *Index of Industrial Production for Wales*, Welsh Occasional Paper No.3, Welsh Office, Cardiff.

Wheatcroft, Anne (1981) A new output enquiry for the construction industry. *Economic Trends*, **333**, 99–104.

Whybrew, E.G. (1972) Qualified manpower: statistical sources. *Statistical News*, No.17, 17.11–17.18.

Wroe, D.C.L. and Bishop, H.E. (1971) Highly qualified manpower in the United Kingdom: relevant official statistics, in *Aspects of Manpower Planning* (eds D.J. Bartholomew and B.R. Morris), English Universities Press, London.

APPENDIX A
TOPICS COVERED BY THE GENERAL HOUSEHOLD SURVEYS, 1971–1985

	1971	1972	1973	1974	1975	1976	1977	1978	1979	1980	1981	1982	1983	1984	1985
Housing*															
Tenure and size	x	x	x	x	x	x	x	x	x	x	x	x	x	x	x
Amenities	x	x	x	x	x	x	x	x	x	x	x	x	x	x	x
Central heating	x	x	x	x	x	x	x	x	x	x	x	x	x	x	x
Heating fuel	–	–	–	–	–	x	x	x	x	x	x	x	x	x	x
Telephone and consumer durables	–	x	x	x	x	–	x	x	x	x	x	x	x	0	x
Housing costs	–	x	x	x	x	x	x	–	–	x	x	–	–	0	0
Household theft	–	x	x	–	x	–	–	–	x	x	–	–	–	–	x
High-rise accommodation	–	–	x	x	x	x	x	x	x	x	x	x	x	x	x
Satisfaction with housing	–	–	–	–	–	–	–	x	–	–	–	–	–	–	–
House mortgages and loans	–	x	x	x	x	x	x	–	x	x	x	x	x	x	x
House purchase intentions	–	–	–	–	–	–	–	–	–	x	x	–	–	–	–
Migration*															
Number of years at present address	x	x	x	x	x	x	x	x	x	x	x	x	x	x	x
Number of moves in last 5 years	x	x	x	x	x	x	x	–	x	x	x	x	x	x	x
Potential movers	x	x	x	x	x	x	–	x	–	x	x	–	–	–	–
Previous housing tenure	x	x	x	–	x	–	–	x	x	x	x	–	–	–	x
Housing tenure decisions	x	x	x	x	x	x	–	x	x	x	x	x	x	x	x
Country of birth	x	x	x	x	x	x	x	x	x	x	x	x	x	x	x
Parents' country of birth	x	x	x	x	x	x	x	x	x	x	x	x	x	x	x
Colour (white, other)	x	x	x	x	x	x	x	x	x	x	x	x	x	x	x
Education															
Type of school, college etc. attended	x	x	x	x	x	x	x	x	x	x	x	x	x	x	x
Terminal education age	x	x	x	x	x	x	x	x	x	x	x	x	x	x	x
Qualifications	x	x	x	x	x	x	x	x	x	x	x	x	x	x	x
Current education and apprenticeships	x	x	x	x	x	x	x	x	x	x	x	x	x	x	x
Father's occupation	x	x	x	x	x	x	x	x	x	x	x	x	x	x	x
Teacher training course experience	–	–	–	–	–	–	–	x	x	–	–	–	–	–	–
Use of nursery schools etc. for under-5s	–	–	–	–	–	–	–	–	x	–	–	–	–	–	–

		1971	1972	1973	1974	1975	1976	1977	1978	1979	1980	1981	1982	1983	1984	1985
Employment	Occupation (SEG and KOS)	x	x	x	x	x	x	x	x	x	x	x	x	x	x	x
	Industry	x	x	x	x	x	x	x	x	x	x	x	x	x	x	x
	Hours worked	x	x	x	x	x	x	x	x	x	x	x	x	x	x	x
	Job satisfaction	0	0	0	x	x	x	x	x	x	x	x	x	x	–	–
	Reasons for absence from work	x	x	x	x	x	x	x	x	x	x	x	x	x	x	–
	Job-finding methods	x	x	x	x	x	x	x	x	x	x	x	x	x	x	–
	Occupation pension and sick pay provision	x	x	x	x	x	0	0	0	x	–	x	x	x	–	0
	Unemployment (registered and unregistered)	x	x	x	x	x	x	x	x	x	x	x	x	x	x	x
	Unemployment experience (duration, cause)	0	0	0	x	x	x	x	x	x	x	x	x	0	.	x
	Attitudes to armed forces as a career	–	–	–	–	–	–	–	–	x	–	–	–	–	–	–
	Job mobility and change	x	x	x	x	x	x	x	x	x	x	x	x	x	x	x
	Second jobs	x	x	x	x	x	x	x	x	x	x	x	x	x	x	–
	Travel to work (and working at home)	x	x	x	x	x	x	–	x	x	x	x	–	–	–	–
	Government schemes (YOPS, TOPS, YTS etc.)	–	–	–	–	–	–	–	–	–	–	–	0	x	x	x
	Trade Union or Staff Association membership	–	–	–	–	–	–	–	–	–	–	–	–	x	–	–
Income	Earnings (main, second, occasional jobs)	0	0	0	0	0	x	x	x	x	x	x	x	x	x	x
	Unearned income (rents, interest etc.)	0	0	0	0	0	x	x	x	x	x	x	x	x	x	x
	Tax and NI deductions	–	–	–	–	–	–	–	x	x	x	x	x	x	x	x
	State benefits (pensions, FIS, UB etc.)	0	0	0	0	0	x	x	x	x	x	x	x	x	x	x
Health	Chronic and acute sickness	x	x	x	x	x	x	x	–	x	x	x	x	x	x	x
	Short-term and chronic health problems	–	–	–	–	–	–	–	x	–	–	–	–	–	–	–
	Sight and hearing problems	–	–	–	–	–	x	x	x	x	–	–	x	–	–	0
	GP consultations	x	x	x	x	x	x	x	x	x	x	x	x	x	x	x
	Hospital attendances and visits	x	x	x	x	x	x	x	x	x	x	x	x	x	x	x
	Use of health and welfare service	x	x	x	x	x	x	–	–	–	–	x	–	x	x	0
	Medicine-taking	–	0	x	–	–	–	–	–	–	–	–	–	–	–	–

Source: Hakim (1982) for the period 1971–81, amended and updated by the author.

		1971	1972	1973	1974	1975	1976	1977	1978	1979	1980	1981	1982	1983	1984	1985
	On hospital waiting lists	–	–	–	–	x	x	–	–	–	–	–	–	–	–	–
	Smoking habits	–	x	x	x	x	–	–	x	–	x	–	x	–	x	–
	Drinking habits	–	x	x	–	–	–	–	x	–	x	–	x	–	x	–
	Private medical insurance	–	–	–	–	–	–	–	–	–	–	–	x	–	–	–
	Dental health and treatment	–	–	0	0	0	0	–	x	–	–	–	–	–	–	0
Other topics	(S) Fertility and family formation	0	0	0	0	0	0	x	x	x	x	x	x	x	x	x
covered by	(S) Leisure activities	–	–	x	–	–	–	x	–	–	x	x	–	x	x	–
a section (S)	(S) Long-distance travel	x	x	–	–	–	–	–	–	–	x	–	–	–	–	–
	(S) Elderly persons	–	–	–	–	–	–	–	–	x	0	–	–	–	–	x
or questions (Q)	(Q) Proximity of relatives	–	–	–	–	–	–	–	–	0	0	–	–	–	–	–
	(Q) Possession or use of car or van	x	x	x	x	x	x	x	x	x	x	x	x	x	x	x
	(S) Driving licences and car usage	–	–	–	–	–	–	–	–	x	x	–	–	–	–	–
	(S) Bus travel	–	–	–	–	–	–	–	–	–	–	–	x	–	–	–
	(S) Activities on school premises	–	–	–	–	–	–	–	–	–	–	–	–	–	x	–
	(S) Careers	–	–	–	–	–	–	–	–	–	–	–	–	–	–	x
	(S) Household burglary	–	–	–	–	–	–	–	–	–	–	–	–	x	–	x

Notes: The table illustrates the range of information collected in the *GHS*, but does not list all topics or questions ever included. More detailed summaries are included as an Appendix to the *GHS* reports. The depth of interviewing on topics, the number and wording of questions, varies over time. Some data are collected from certain groups (identified, for example, by age, household tenure, or employment status). Variations in the amount of data on each topic listed are indicated as follows:

x most extensive information (more detailed questions, or data for most groups)
0 less detailed information (fewer questions, data for quarters or for some groups only)
– no information.
* More detailed summaries of these topics are given in Table 2.2

APPENDIX B
TOPICS COVERED BY THE LABOUR FORCE SURVEYS, 1973–1985

	1973	1975	1977	1979	1981	1983	1984	1985
Housing:* Household tenure	x	–	–	x	x	x	x	x
Type of accommodation (house, flat etc.)	x	x	x	x	x	x	x	x
Amenities	–	–	–	–	x	–	x	–
Rooms	–	–	–	–	x	–	x	–
Sharing	–	–	–	–	x	–	x	–
Owner-occupation	–	–	–	0	x	0	x	0
Tenancy	–	–	–	x	x	0	x	0
Waiting list (time on)	–	–	–	–	–	–	x	–
Household movement	–	–	–	–	–	–	x	–
Possession of second home	x	x	–	–	–	–	–	–
Household composition	x	x	x	x	x	x	x	x
Sex, age, marital status	x	x	x	x	x	x	x	x
Whether registered disabled	–	–	x	x	x	–	–	–
Country of birth	x	x	x	x	x	x	x	x
Nationality	x	x	x	x	x	x	x	x
Ethnic group	–	–	–	x	x	x	–	–
Age completed full-time education	–	x	x	x	x	x	x	x
Qualifications held (all)	–	–	x	x	x	x	x	x
Qualifications obtained in full-time education	–	–	–	x	–	–	–	–
Vocational training (location, type, duration, subject, when started, financial assistance obtained, special schemes – YOPS, YTS, TOPS etc.)	0	0	–	x	–	x	x	x
Migration: address one year previously	0	x	x	x	x	x	x	x
in relation to change of job/employer	–	x	–	–	–	–	x	x
Economic activity status: Last week	x	x	x	x	x	x	x	x
Usual	x	x	x	x	x	x	x	x
One year ago	x	x	x	x	x	x	x	x
Occupation and industry: Main or last job	x	x	x	x	x	x	x	x
Second job	x	x	x	x	x	x	x	x
Occasional work	–	–	–	–	x	x	x	x
One year ago	x	x	x	x	x	x	x	x
Hours worked last week in main and second job	x	x	x	x	x	x	x	x
Current unemployment: Duration	x	x	x	x	x	x	x	x
Whether registered	x	x	x	x	x	x	x	x
Whether receiving benefit	x	x	x	x	x	x	x	x
Reason for losing last job	x	x	x	x	x	x	x	x
Job-seeking activities	x	x	x	x	x	x	x	x
Discouraged workers	–	–	0	x	–	–	–	–
Unemployment after leaving full-time education	–	–	–	x	–	–	–	–
Job-seeking activities (people in employment):								
Different/additional job	x	x	x	x	x	x	x	x
Duration of search	x	x	x	x	x	–	–	–
Travel to work (time, distance, mode of transport)	–	x	–	–	–	–	–	–
Homeworking	–	–	–	–	x	–	–	–
Working conditions (shift work, night work, type of workplace, noise levels, hygiene, safety)	–	x	–	–	–	–	–	0
Receipt of pensions (type, number, when started etc.)	–	–	x	–	–	–	–	–
Health problems	–	–	–	–	–	–	x	x

Notes: The table does not identify each separate question asked; variations in the amount of data collected on each topic are indicated as follows:

x   most extensive information (more detailed questions)
0   more limited information (fewer questions, or for some groups only)
–   no information
*   A more detailed summary of the housing topics is given in Table 2.3

Source: Hakim (1982) for the period 1973–81 amended and updated by the author.

INDEX